FoxPro 2

A Developer's Guide

DBMS Magazine's Database Foundation Series

FoxPro 2

A Developer's Guide

Expert Guidance for
Industrial-Strength Programming

Edited by Jeff Winchell

M&T Books
A Division of M&T Publishing, Inc.
411 Borel Avenue
San Mateo, CA 94402-3522

Printed in the United States of America

Library of Congress Cataloging-in-Publication Data

FoxPro 2: a developer's guide: expert guidance for industrial strength programming/by Jeff Winchell...[et al.].
p. cm. -- (*DBMS* Magazine's database foundations series)
Includes index.
ISBN 1-55851-083-4 (book) -- ISBN 1-55851-084-2 (book/disk)
1. Database management. 2. FoxPro (Computer program)
I.Winchell, Jeff. II. Title: FoxPro 2. III. Series: *DBMS* Magazine's database foundations series.
QA76.9.D3F712 1992
005.75'65--dc20 92-6471
CIP

Cover Design: Lauren Smith Design
Project Editor: Sunny Pinneau

94 93 92 91 4 3 2 1

Foreword

The FoxPro 2.0 book you are holding represents the kind of practical, in-depth writing that I'm always looking for as Editor-in-Chief of *DBMS* Magazine. It will even read like a best-of collection of magazine articles, and for good reason. Rather than trying to be an all-inclusive treatment of FoxPro 2.0, the book covers only the most interesting and valuable topics, much as a magazine does. The book makes an assumption that the reader is already knowledgeable about dbase and/or FoxPro 1.x. And the authors of each chapter or group of chapters have been hand-picked for their expertise in the subject area, which is exactly how a high-quality magazine should be put together. To be honest, the biggest difference between the chapters in this book and very fine magazine articles is that the chapters always have the luxury of being as long as necessary in order to thoroughly cover their subject.

The result is a book that will move an experienced dbase programmer to the front of the FoxPro 2.0 pack. It doesn't waste time telling you what you already know or can find in the manual. For example, the opening chapter quickly explains why you'd be wise to ignore Fox Software's suggested approach to event-driven programming and graphic user interface design and details a better alternative. The performance-tuning chapters challenge some assumptions you may have long held about the impact of denormalization or the performance characteristics of *SET FILTER*. You even get code that can profile your program's performance on a line-by-line basis. And if you're like most of us, you'll welcome the coherent, in-depth treatment of relational database design by Dave McClanahan, a former Fox Software engineer who succinctly explains the practical value of a properly designed, properly relational database. If only the academicians could be so clear. I could go on, but an introduction should no more than whet your appetite for the goodies that lie ahead. I wish you good reading, and promise that your effort will make you a better FoxPro programmer.

—Kevin Strehlo
Editor-in-Chief, *DBMS* Magazine

Contents

PART II: OPTIMIZING AND TESTING

CHAPTER 4: USING FOXPRO'S KEYBOARD MACRO FACILITY FOR AUTOMATED TESTING

PART III: RELATIONAL PROGRAMMING

CHAPTER 7: THE RELATIONAL DATA MODEL

PART IV: DATABASE DESIGN

CHAPTER 9: CONCEPTUAL DATABASE DESIGN

CHAPTER 10: LOGICAL DATABASE DESIGN

CHAPTER 11: PHYSICAL DATABASE DESIGN

PART V: DEVELOPING MULTI-USER APPLICATIONS

CHAPTER 12: FOXPRO AND LOCAL AREA NETWORKS

CHAPER 13: THE CLIENT-SERVER ARCHITECTURE

CHAPTER 14: APPROACHING CLIENT-SERVER: EMERALD BAY, ORACLE, SQL SERVER, AND INTERBASE

PART VI: USING THE APPLICATION PROGRAM INTERFACE

CHAPTER 15: FOXPRO'S API

CHAPTER 16: THE FOXPRO API AND ASSEMBLER

CHAPTER 17: FOX'S MACINTOSH API

Why This Book Is For You

In producing FoxPro 2, Fox Software has added many new features that solidify FoxPro's stance as a mature development platform for corporate database applications. This book takes an in-depth look into the fundamentals of sound database programming and how they are addressed by FoxPro 2. This book serves three audiences:

Intermediate FoxPro programmers will learn to be more productive by writing more maintainable code, and at the same time, please users with intuitive interfaces. Programmers new to multiuser programming will avoid the subtle traps that await the unwary. Those who wish to make the move from programmer to systems analyst will benefit from the readings on database design.

Experienced FoxPro developers who are overwhelmed by the implications of SQL and event-driven programming will profit from the discussion of theoretical and practical considerations. Those who have reached the boundaries of multiuser programming with FoxPro will learn what lies on the other side in client-server computing. The chapters on automated testing and hardware optimization will help them make better use of their time and money.

Non-FoxPro programmers using C and Assembler will tap into the secrets of FoxPro's Application Program Interface and see how its approach compares favorably to the competition. Paradox, Oracle, and other relational database users will learn how Fox combines the world's most popular relational language (SQL) with the PC's most popular procedural language (dbase). Clipper, dBASE, and other dbase dialect programmers will learn much that they can apply to all their programs, including how to optimize for best performance.

FoxPro 2: A Developer's Guide is brought to you by top experts in the database industry:

• **Hamilton M. Ahlo Jr.** has programmed in a variety of languages while writing applications ranging from sewage flowing modeling to communications. His firm, Applied Logic, focuses on high performance multi-user database applications.

• **Randy Brown** is a senior consultant with Ernst & Young in the National Energy Group. He works extensively with Fox in both DOS and Macintosh platforms. He is the author of *FoxTools XCMD Library*.

• **Peter Colclough**, the developer of BITON, provides leading edge systems to clients worldwide. He is currently developing the FoxPro to Oracle client-server link for Fox.

• **Jeff Jochum** is President of SuccessWare 90 and creator of The Babelfish Database Drivers, API libraries that link FoxPro, Clipper, and dBase to Paradox, Emerald Bay, and 1-2-3.

• **David R. McClanahan** was a Senior Software Engineer at Fox Software where he implemented SQL and query optimization for FoxPro 2.0. He developed the DBMS for Bell & Howell's IDB-2000 Technical Reference System, a state-of-the-art network image database.

• **Ted Means** is president of SofTech Microsystems, a software consulting and development firm. He writes an assembly language column for *The Aquarium* and wrote DBFtrieve, a product that links FoxPro and Clipper to Novell's Btrieve.

• **Alan Schwartz** is a principal of MicroMega Systems, a consulting and training firm specializing in Fox databases. He has designed numerous custom Fox applications and products and is a columnist for *PC World*.

• **Ron Talmage** is a software developer for Infosystems International. He is responsible for the design and coding of TRAK-A-DIAL Telecommunications Facilities Management, a large vertical market application written in FoxPro and Foxbase Unix.

• **Jeff Winchell** is president of Practical Healthcare Innovations, a health care data analysis firm. He was a developer of CHAMP, a data analysis system used by employers of 10,000 to 500,000 life groups, for William M. Mercer. He also writes for *DBMS* Magazine.

Introduction

When the idea of writing an advanced FoxPro 2 book came up, I initially rejected it. It seemed like too big an undertaking; FoxPro 2 has so many new features. It might take me a year to fully explore the ramifications of improvements to the *READ* command alone. So how could I learn enough about this product to be able to inform others? Rather than sitting with my computer atop the Himalaya's waiting for enlightenment, I chose a more active plan: exchanging ideas with fellow travellers on the electronic forum for FoxPro 2 beta testers.

The amount of information one can learn and share via a BBS such as CompuServe (the home of Fox's Foxforum) can never be underestimated. The flow of ideas is swift, and the variety of approaches that fellow developers are willing to share is broad. The people I've "met" electronically have enriched my programming knowledge immeasurably. I met six of the eight co-authors this way. All eight were a part of the FoxPro 2 beta forum. So, it was natural decision for me to write a book that mirrors this experience — a collaborative effort of thoughtful explorers.

This doesn't mean that we are always in total agreement on the topics covered here. Within this book, you may occasionally encounter conflicting opinions. While this risks confusing the reader, I consider it a plus. I've found that the more you learn about a subject, the less black and white the answers are. Learning to appreciate and weigh these many factors and options adroitly is a crucial step on the path to programming craftsmanship.

This book is divided into six sections. The first, "Programming Paradigms," looks at the broad topic of how to program. While there is certainly a fair amount of FoxPro 2 code here, the concepts studied apply to programming almost any type of application in any language. The second section, "Optimizing and Testing," follows from the first. Once you have programmed an application, there is always a need to refine and debug it. Since performance is always on the minds of FoxPro programmers, considerable material is presented to keep you on the leading edge of high performance applications.

Whereas the first second of the book could be applied to any type of application, the third and fourth sections, "Relational Programming" and "Database Design" bring you back to your main line of business: developing database applications. Database design is an often neglected and critical part of database programming that is even more relevant now that FoxPro 2 has added valuable relational tools.

The last two sections, "Multiuser Programming" and "Using the Application Program Interface (API)," may not seem related until you realize that the potential for sophisticated multiuser programming via client-server databases that will be provided by FoxPro 2's new API. Client-server and APIs are new enough to FoxPro programmers, so that I believe a variety of approaches must be studied. To that end, the multiuser databases FoxPro 2, Emerald Bay, Oracle, SQL Server, and Interbase are studied and contrasted, along with the APIs of FoxPro 2 (both C and Assembler), Fox for the Macintosh, Clipper, Arago, Paradox, and Babblefish.

A crucial part of assembling a book written by nine authors with full-time consulting practices spanning 11 time zones was the work of our editor, Sunny Pinneau, at *DBMS* Magazine. She tolerated the delays caused by our crazy schedules (and those caused by Fox Software), without a complaint, focusing her energies on doing whatever was needed to make this book a success.

And lastly, acknowledgement is long overdue to the talented programmers at Fox Software who worked untold days, nights, and weekends so that we could experience the pristine view from atop the summit known as FoxPro 2. They are:

Eric Christensen
Brian Crites
Bill Ferguson
Amy Fulton
Dave Fulton
Dave Heindel
Dave McClanahan
Kerry Nietz
Marty Sedluk
Sally Stuckey
Brian Tallman
Chris Williams

PART I

Programming Paradigms

Précis of the Current State of Confusion

Event-driven, object-oriented, GUI, modeless, modular.... So many buzzwords; so little understanding. They're all attempts at developing techniques to create applications that are both easy to use and easy to write.

You've certainly been told that user-friendly applications aren't easy to write. After all, the human mind doesn't march lock-step through a finite set of *AND/OR* gates, saluting to Babbage all the while. As a programmer, you strive to use some common sense and plan for all contingencies. With over a million facts that fit the description of "Common Sense" (according to a research group that's busy cataloging these items), in addition to the facts that pertain to the particular business you are writing for, that makes a tall order indeed. Despite this, or perhaps because of it, you resolve to find a way to meet the challenge. With an army of programmers, or a year dedicated to endless nights filled with programs, pizza, and pop, The Application is finished—all 250,000 unmaintainable lines of it.

Then, one of the new users plucks out one of the other 750,000 aspects that you didn't quite get around to and says "I don't like the colors on this particular screen. Can you make it mauve when I forget to do this and chartreuse when the manager's bimonthly budget numbers don't agree? Also, right when I'm in the middle of doing A and B, sometimes a customer will call with a question. So, I need to be able jump immediately to G, R, and Z, and afterwards, I may need to reconcile G, R, and Z, with A and B, and sometimes Y. Would it be too hard to do this?" Wisely, you choose to consult the list of buzzwords, above, rather than George Carlin's "Seven Words" list to find an answer to your dilemma—only to encounter another. There are hundreds of programming languages and tools claiming to be object-oriented and event-driven, with graphical user interfaces (GUIs) that are designed to create rapid prototypes and ease the maintenance burden.

This first section of the book is titled, paradoxically, "Programming Paradigms." *Webster's Ninth New Collegiate Dictionary* defines paradigm as "an outstandingly clear or typical example or archetype." After reading this section, you still may not be able to determine which of the above applications is event-driven, but you will know how to make an application more event-driven. You won't reach nirvana, but the attempt to do so will strengthen you.

The first chapter in this section explores what event-driven programming is and how FoxPro 2's tools make it easier. (Please note the distinction between easier and easy.) These concepts and FoxPro's methodology are highly interwoven. This subject might best be explained by a hypercard book, more than any other chapter in this book. Since none exists, I did perhaps the next best thing and called on a veteran of event-driven programming, Randy Brown, to write about it. Event-driven programming isn't for the casual programmer, but the fruits of your labor can be highly rewarding and will not go unnoticed by your customers.

Most noticeable of all, to your customers, is the user interface of your application. Because of the highly subjective nature of this topic, the second chapter departs from the usual format of textbooks. Over a period of many weeks, opinions were bandied about by a host of experts, and all the messages were electronically captured courtesy of Tech III's forum on CompuServe. Whether you agree with the public opinion or not, user interfaces are critical to today's PC applications. You'll find plenty of ideas here to keep you competitive.

Why would I lump flashy, exciting topics like event-driven programming, GUIs, and user-friendly interfaces with a discourse in Chapter 3 on keeping your plumbing in order? Because if you don't spend some time keeping your code flexible and maintainable, you won't have any time to respond flexibly to the imprecise interface demands of your customers, not to mention keeping your event-driven programs from getting tied up in an event-driven knot. It's taken more than luck to keep a programming shop like Alan Schwartz's successful for many years. In the third chapter, Alan helps you "engineer for change."

—Editor

[2] By permission. From *Webster's Ninth New Collegiate Dictionary* ©1991 by Merriam-Webster Inc., publisher of the Merriam-Webster® dictionaries.

CHAPTER 1

Event-Driven Programming

by Randy Brown

If you've ever used a Macintosh or Microsoft Windows, you may already be familiar with event-driven programming. Both are designed to let the user choose the next course of action without regard for any previous action. Word-processing programs for the Macintosh are a good example. As I write this chapter, I can choose a menu option to underline this word. (I could also have underlined it using the keyboard shortcut Command+Shift+U.) Later in this chapter, you'll see a sample Macintosh software event loop written in Pascal. To bring the text for that code into my document from my word processor, I can open another window containing this routine, copy the code, and paste it into my document. Because the software is event-driven, each task was handled independently; I didn't have to close one window to open another or go into a special edit mode to add underline formatting.

Sounds simple, right? That's the goal of event-driven programming, or EDP: to offer the user both simplicity and flexibility. It allows a common task (like underlining) to be handled in several ways. It also lets users go forward from wherever they may be in an application; they should never be forced to backtrack through a program. And although you can create applications with just as much power using EDP as with any other approach, this advantage is often overlooked because an EDP application *looks* so simple.

Why isn't every program written this way? Complexity. The simpler the application appears on the outside, the more complex it is inside. Writing EDP code is a complex style of programming. The code must be able to handle any type of user event the computer will allow. Menu-driven (modal) programming, a common approach to database applications, forces the user to select a menu option. Such code is easier to write but makes for a more complex and confusing to use application.

It may seem odd that we're even considering EDP at this stage of the database evolution. But consider the impact of graphical user interfaces (GUIs) and mice, which created a need for new programming styles to handle the many possible courses of action available to the user. Fox Software incorporated many of the most common features of a GUI into FoxPro (primarily because the FoxPro interface was based on the Macintosh product, FoxBASE+/Mac). Although FoxPro's interface is character-based, it contains such GUI features as windows, menus, dialog boxes, alerts, and mouse control. This GUI emulation makes an event-driven approach one of the most efficient ways to handle the necessary user actions.

The Event Loop

Before we get into the specifics of FoxPro, let's take a closer look at an actual event loop. The event loop, the core of any event-driven application, is simply an endless loop similar to the common *DO WHILE .T.* used in many of our applications. The loop is in a constant state of waiting to process actions by the user. So when a user clicks on a window, that action is processed by the event loop and routed to the necessary event handler. In event-driven programs, the event loop usually terminates only when the application is terminated.

The following Pascal code is a typical example of an event loop associated with a commercial Macintosh application.

Listing 1-1. Macintosh Pascal event loop.

```
***Sample Macintosh Pascal Event Loop***

begin
   doneFlag := FALSE;
   repeat
      ApplLoop_Event;
      Handle_User_Event;
      if (theInput <> nil) then
```

```
   TEIdle(theInput);
if WNE then
   DoIt := WaitNextEvent(everyEvent,myEvent,
                         SleepValue,nil)
else
   begin
      SystemTask;
      DoIt := GetNextEvent(everyEvent, myEvent);
   end;
   ApplEvent_Event(DoIt,myEvent);
   if DoIt then
      begin
      case myEvent.what of
         MouseDown :
         begin
            code := FindWindow(myEvent.where,
                               whichWindow);
            case code of
               inMenuBar :
               begin
                  mResult : MenuSelect (myEvent.Where);
                  theMenu := HiWord(mResult);
                  theItem := LoWord(mResult);
                  Handle_My_Menu(theMenu, the Item);
            end;
            inDrag :
               DoDrag(whichWindow);
            inGrow :
               DoGrow(whichWindow);
            inZoomIn,inZoomOut :
               DoZoom(whichWindow,code);
            inGoAway :
               DoGoAway(whichWindow);
            inContent :
               DoInContent(whichWindow);
            inSysWindow :
               SystemClick(myEvent, whichWindow);
            otherwise
```

```
                        begin
                        end;
                    end;
                end;
            KeyDown,AutoKey:
                DoKeyEvent;
            UpDateEvt :
                DoUpdate;
            DiskEvt :
                DoDiskEvent;
            ActivateEvt :
                DoActivate;
            otherwise
                begin
                end;
        end;
    end;
    until doneFlag;
    ApplExit_Event;
end.
```

The program waits for the next event at either the *WaitNextEvent* or *GetNextEvent* call. *WaitNextEvent* is used for multitasking environments like Multifinder and System 7, while *GetNextEvent* is used for single-application environments. I won't go into all the details of the program; if you're interested, refer to Macintosh programming manuals such as *Inside Macintosh*, by Apple Computer (Addison-Wesley; Reading, Mass.).

Event Types

In this chapter, we'll be concerned with menu, window, and keystroke events. Notice in the listing that two of these categories are handled primarily by the *MouseDown* call. Windows are also handled in the *UpDateEvt* and *ActivateEvt* calls, and keystroke events are processed in the *KeyDown* and *AutoKey* calls. *AutoKey* controls actions in which the user holds down a key continuously for a specified period of time. This would be a good way to incrementally increase or decrease the level of some control.

The *MouseDown* call controls all window actions, including zooming, resizing, moving, and closing. Fortunately, FoxPro handles these actions automatically when you define a window to have such attributes. However, you need to control what happens when the window is closed. Are databases opened? Is another window activated? Should the state of the DBMS be saved before closing the window?

The menu handling in Listing 1-1 is similar to that implemented in FoxPro 2.0. Prior to FoxPro 2.0, EDP never really existed in the dBASE language. In fact, most of these so-called EDP programs included complex routines that only *emulated* event-driven characteristics.

To be truly event-driven, a FoxPro application must allow its objects—such as menus and windows—to exist and function independently. For example:

- It should allow menus to exist solely for a specific window.
- Menus should always be active unless a modal dialog box is displayed (we'll talk more about this later).
- Windows should appear on the screen independently of those already on the screen.
- Various types of windows (*READ*s, browses, and desk accessories, for instance) should be able to exist simultaneously. This includes the state in which only the menu bar is active and no windows appear on the screen.
- If the user clicks on a window, the environment associated with the window, which could be a separate application, should be restored. Figure 1-1 shows a typical multiple-windowed screen.

The program should also control any keyboard shortcuts that might be available. It's a good idea to have shortcuts for commonly used menu items (though you wouldn't want one for menu items that involve loss of data, such as *PACK* and *DELETE*). You can also have keyboard shortcuts for windows, but most users won't use them on *READ* windows for several reasons. First, shortcuts don't always work when a field is being edited. You can define menu shortcuts that will work during *@...GET*, but hot keys such as those on a set of pushbuttons won't work unless that button control is selected. Second, in editing mode, users may be more likely to use the mouse if one is available.

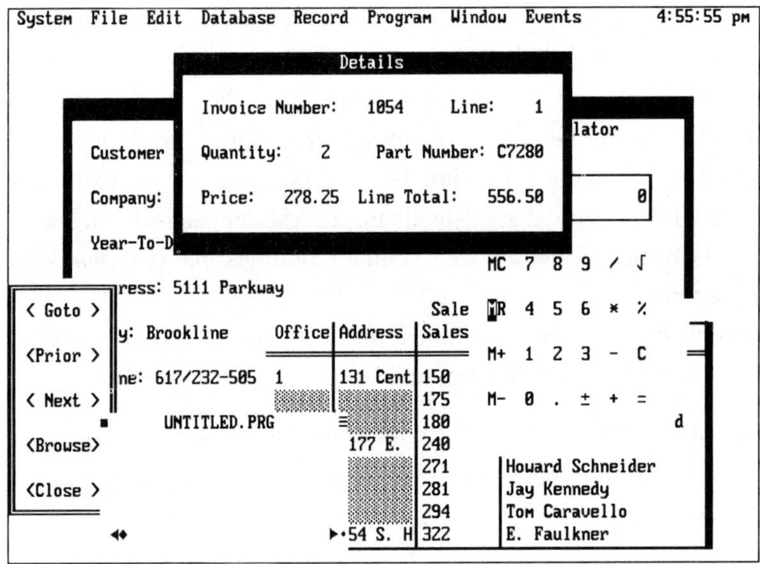

Figure 1-1. A FoxPro screen with multiple windows.

The Fox Approach

"Fox recommends not using a strict EDP approach, so why even consider it?" When people ask me this, I pull out my copy of *Apple Human Interface Guidelines*, by Apple Computer (Addison-Wesley; Reading, Mass.). The book details Apple Computer's extensive studies of how users believe software should function. It also offers guidance on writing software applications that are easy to learn and use. One of the lessons is that the user should always be in control of the program. If you force users into a corner, they'll be less productive. Event-driven programs give users the maximum number of options. As you'll see, Fox's approach often limits users in this regard.

Here's what Fox has to say on the subject of EDP:

> "In order to produce applications with event-driven interfaces like FoxPro's own interface, some sophisticated developers have resorted to event loop programming similar to that utilized inside FoxPro itself and in environ-

ments like the Macintosh and Windows.

"We feel that coding a real event loop in the FoxPro language has very limited practicality for three reasons. First, the speed of the resulting application will be sub-optimal. Second, such an application is always in hard execution and, therefore, a CPU hog and unfriendly in multiprogramming environments like DESQview, Windows, or the Mac Multifinder. Finally, such event loop programming is VERY complex conceptually, probably too complex for all but the most skilled developers and certainly inaccessible to beginners.

"Our general recommendation is that a single *READ* should correspond to a single interactive session, dedicated to a particular objective, regardless of the number of windows involved.

"The basic idea is to encompass in a single *READ* all the windows that you intend to interact with at a particular *READ* level."

Fox's philosophy is to simplify database programming while providing GUI features that make for a powerful, attractive, easy-to-use application. All the windows a specific application needs should be coordinated under a single *READ*.

In an event-driven program, the *READ* command becomes the equivalent of the *WaitNextEvent* call in the sample Macintosh event loop in Listing 1-1. Each independent screen object that users can act upon will have an associated *READ*. These objects are most commonly menus, windows, and window sets, but they can also be complete applications.

To see what a FoxPro application might look like under an event-driven and a nonevent-driven philosophy (modal), consider a client billing system that has four databases—for salespeople, customers, invoices, and checks—each with its own data-entry window.

Under Fox's recommended approach, all four data-entry screens could appear together under one *READ*. (FoxPro's *READ* command now allows browse windows to be incorporated into the window sets.) Each screen could also be called separately from a menu option; the idea is that all windows visible on the monitor should be controlled by a single *READ*, allowing the user to activate a window by clicking on it. This approach is simple and is handled entirely by FoxPro's screen painter and code generator. Now let's look at the EDP approach.

EDP implies that visible windows have separate *READ*s that are independent of one another. Activating a window that's partially hidden by another terminates the *READ* associated with the previously active window and calls a new *READ* for the just-activated one. The user can choose to have any combination of data-entry and browse screens visible at the same time.

Suppose you have four data-entry screens and one browse window. A user should be able to have any or all of the five windows visible at a given time. To provide this flexibility using Fox's recommended approach, you would need a separate *READ* for each potential scenario, or a total of 32 (31 separate screen sets for all the possible combinations and a special *READ* for no screens).

# of windows visible	# of possible combinations
0	1
1	5
2	10
3	10
4	5
5	1

An EDP approach would require only six *READ*s, one for each screen plus the foundation *READ*. So which method is really more complex?

Before jumping into the FoxPro methodology, we should briefly mention an important consideration of event-driven programs: memory overhead. If the system is on a conventional PC with no memory beyond the base 640K, the overhead (from extra windows, for example) could cause memory shortages. If the system can run using the extended version of FoxPro, however, it probably has enough memory to handle a properly coded event-driven program.

FoxPro Event Loop Code

The methodology described in the rest of this chapter is based entirely on the features and tools available in FoxPro 2.0. Because the remainder of the chapter digs fairly deep into the code and may become confusing, let's start with an overview.

- **Main event loop:** This is the mechanism that controls the event-driven program. All events should be processed through this *DO WHILE* loop.
- ***READ*s:** The *READ* command plays an important role in EDP. We'll also discuss the new foundation (or *GET*-less) *READ*.
- **Menu events:** These are easily handled with FoxPro's menu builder. We'll discuss ways to incorporate and improve menu handling in an event loop.
- **Keystroke events:** Keyboard events are usually handled by a specific object (such as a screen or menu). If you choose, however, these events can be run directly through the event loop.
- **Window events:** The most difficult event to handle is that associated with a window. Because FoxPro allows for a variety of different window types (including non-*READ* Windows, such as a browse), we'll discuss this subject at length and under various scenarios.
- **Environmental considerations:** Event processing often involves changing database views. We'll see which database environments to save between events.

Figure 1-2 illustrates the program flow of a typical event through the event loop and event handlers.

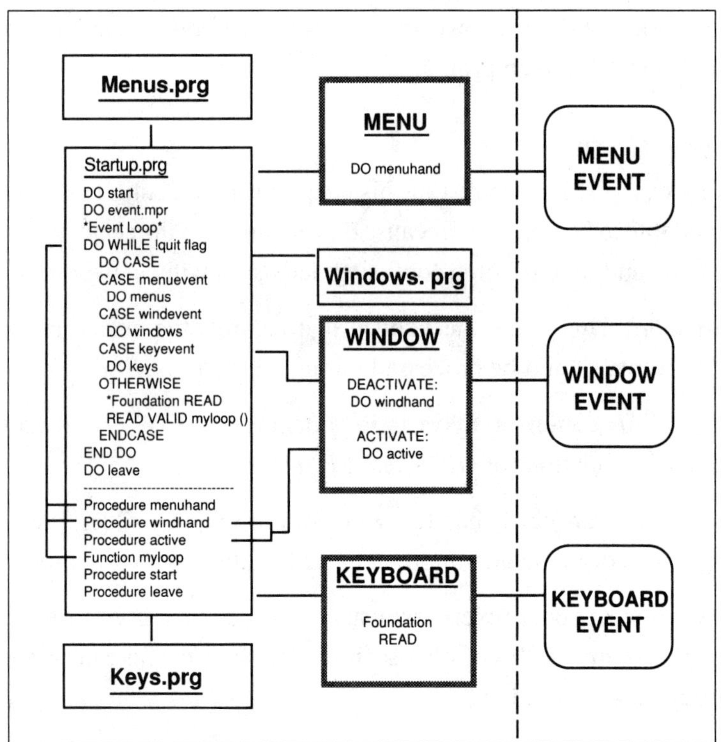

Figure 1-2. A roadmap of EDP.

Main Event Loop

The code in Listing 1-2 differs a bit from the sample programs distributed by Fox Software with FoxPro 2.0. The event loop in Fox's samples is simply a *GET*-less *READ* (one without a GET) with a valid clause, which always returns *.F.* unless an exit flag is triggered. While this method works, you may be better off using the more conventional *DO WHILE* loop shown in Listing 1-2. The primary advantage is that *READ* windows are at *RDLEVEL()*=1 because the *GET*-less *READ* is always terminated. Fox's *GET*-less *READ* always returns *.F.*, so any *READ* window must be at a minimum *RDLEVEL()*=2. This adds overhead to the program and uses up one of only five available *READ* levels. The *DO WHILE* loop is also easier to track during debugging.

Listing 1-2. The main loop in *STARTUP.PRG*.

```
***main event loop in STARTUP.PRG***

DO WHILE !quitflag
    DO CASE
        CASE menuevent                          && menu events
            DO menus with barname,barnum        && PROMPT(),BAR()
        CASE windevent                          && window events
            DO windows
        CASE keyevent                           && keyboard events
            DO keys
        OTHERWISE
            READ VALID myloop()                 && foundation READ
        ENDCASE
ENDDO

FUNCTION myloop
    windevent=.T.
RETURN
```

The main event loop is placed in the start-up/procedure program immediately after the initialization routines. Program control is centrally processed through this loop until the application is exited.

READs

Fox Software has made significant improvements to the *READ* statement, the mechanism that processes events and directs program control through the event loop. These improvements have made Fox's *READ* one of the most complex and powerful input-processing commands in any of the dBASE dialects. To understand the concepts of EDP, you must become intimately familiar with the *READ* statement. Considering the many new *READ* clauses as well as the *GET*-less *READ*, that may be harder than you think.

One of the nicer enhancements in FoxPro 2.0 is the ability to extend *GET*s across multiple windows under a single *READ*. The *GET*s are numbered as if the screens were transparent, so skipping through the *GET* fields activates the windows on which those *GET*s reside. If you add a mouse to your system, you can easily move back and forth between window fields and controls in a single *READ*.

I mentioned earlier that EDP requires a separate *READ* for each window. So why am I contradicting myself here by promoting the use of multiple windows under a single *READ*? You'll see why when we discuss *palettes*, multipurpose windows that can be used generically with another *READ* window.

The *READ CYCLE* clause prevents early termination of the *READ* statement. Instead of terminating the *READ* when the last *GET* is processed, program control returns to the first *GET*. Programming with *DO WHILE* loops to prevent early *READ* termination is no longer necessary. When you're working with multiple windows under a single *READ*, the *READ CYCLE* clause becomes an important part of event-driven applications.

You may be starting to see the path Fox has taken. Prior to FoxPro 2.0, the *GET VALID* clause was the only way to have programmatic interaction while under a *READ*. That clause worked, but it didn't address the needs of the *READ* statement itself. The new parameters add much-needed functionality to FoxPro. The *WHEN* and *VALID* clauses control when *READ*s are entered and terminated; the *SHOW*, *OBJECT*, and *CYCLE* clauses control the appearance of the *GET*s; and the *ACTIVATE* and *DEACTIVATE* clauses control actions underlying the windows associated with the *READ*. These clauses are part of a suite of powerful tools for handling the various courses of action users can take.

The key to handling window events is the *READ DEACTIVATE* clause. To understand it, let's briefly review what happens when one window is activated on top of another (not under the same *READ*):

1. Windows A and B are open, with Window A on top.
2. Window B is brought forward; it's now on top of Window A.
3. Window functions (*WONTOP()* and *WLAST()*, for example) are evaluated.
4. Window A's *READ DEACTIVATE* clause is evaluated.
5. If the *DEACTIVATE* clause evaluates to *.T.*, the *READ* is terminated.

In step 5, if the clause returns a *.T.*, the two windows are under separate *READ*s (assuming the current *GET VALID* and *READ VALID* also return a *.T.*). The concept of terminating the *READ* when an unrelated window is brought forward is a basic premise of window handling. On the other hand, related windows should not terminate prematurely when one is activated on top of the other (in this case, the *DEACTIVATE* clause should return an *.F.*).

Obviously, you need a routine to handle these critical functions. It should be able to distinguish between associated and nonassociated windows. A palette would be considered an associated window, so its activation should not cause the *READ* to terminate.

The *GET*-less *READ* is extremely important to the concept of EDP; through it we can begin to see how the *READ* really works. In FoxPro 1.0x, it was impractical to have a *READ* statement without an associated *GET*. This wasn't a problem because Fox didn't allow all types of windows to coordinate smoothly in an application. Now, with version 2.0, a variety of windows can interact almost seamlessly, like a true event-driven program. Browse-only applications that can display multiple windows can be created without the need for a *READ* window. The *GET*-less *READ* is now even more important because FoxPro 2.0 allows access to the system menus, which can be controlled interactively as well as programmatically.

Because no window is directly associated with the *GET*-less *READ*, many of the *READ* clauses we've discussed so far can't be used. The main *READ* clause that can be used is *VALID*. If a *VALID* returns an *.F.*, the *READ* is not terminated. This is similar to the standard *GET VALID*, which prevents the user from continuing with the next course of action if the current one doesn't meet the requirements for termination. In general, any mouse click or keystroke that isn't a menu selection or doesn't execute an *ON KEY LABEL* command will terminate a *GET*-less *READ*. (Note that a mouse click on a non-*READ* window—one without an @...*GET*, such as a browse, *MODIFY FILE*, *MODIFY MEMO*, or *MODIFY QUERY*—won't terminate the *GET*-less *READ*.)

The *GET*-less *READ* functions similarly to a standard *READ* but is more sensitive to mouse clicks and keystrokes. That's because there's no *GET* to *READ* these events, and hence no field or control to receive them. Think of a *GET*-less *READ* as a one-character field under a plain *READ* that can be terminated by a single keystroke. In essence, the *READ* metaphor hasn't changed with the new foundation *READ*; all user input events are still processed except those already handled internally or by such interrupt mechanisms as menus, *ON KEY LABEL*s, and non-*READ* windows. And now you can use the enhanced *READKEY(<expN>)* function to determine what caused the *READ* termination (the FoxPro manual discusses the return values).

As mentioned earlier, the event loop in Listing 1-2 differs from the samples distributed by Fox Software. Fox's event loop is simply a *GET*-less *READ* with a *VALID* statement that always returns an *.F.* unless the quit condition is met. The more conventional event loop in Listing 1-2 has several advantages:

- FoxPro 2.0 allows up to five *READ* levels. Under Fox's approach, you'll remember, any *READ* window will be at a minimum *RDLEVEL()*=2. Our approach gives the user an extra *READ* level.
- By keeping your modeless windows at *RDLEVEL()*=1, you can minimize much of the overhead and maintenance associated with each additional *READ* level. Most of the higher *READ* levels should be reserved for modal windows.
- It provides portability to the other platforms, such as FoxBASE+/Mac. The Macintosh program supports an event-driven style of programming along the lines of a *DO WHILE* loop, primarily because both menu and window events are detected through the interrupt *ON MENU* routine. (This may change with the release of FoxPro/Mac.)

The ability to incorporate system menus was a key influence on the evolution of the *GET*-less *READ*. FoxPro has opened up its own system menus so that users can modify any of the menu items.

With FoxPro 2.0, you can generate a menu program (.MPR) from the menu builder. When you run this program, the system will be changed to include the newly defined menu. At this point, FoxPro is in interactive mode because no program is running. (If the Command window is showing, it's in interactive mode.)

It's in program mode, however, that the foundation *READ* comes into play. The menu is always activated through the *ACTIVATE MENU* command; it can then be reactivated, without a pending *READ* window, only through the *GET*-less *READ*. Prior to the *GET*-less *READ*, interaction among non-*READ* windows such as browses, desk accessories, and text windows was impossible without a kludge.

Let's look at the events processed by the main event loop.

Menus

Menus are fairly easy to handle in an event-driven program. Using FoxPro's menu builder, you can create one in a matter of minutes or modify it on the fly without a great deal of recoding. (Note: The approach taken here for using the menu builder differs slightly from Fox's recommended method.)

The menu builder should be used only to create the menu system and not to handle the actions of individual menu items. Code for enabling and disabling menu items can be placed in the main-menu program (see MENUS.PRG), where all other menu actions are handled.

A generic menu handler that passes the item selected is the only code we need to add to the menu builder:

```
DO menuhand IN startup WITH PROMPT(), BAR()
```

This line is placed in the individual menu or menu-bar options procedure and is called if a menu item has no other command definition assigned. While performance may be degraded slightly, this approach has certain advantages. The primary benefit is known as *menu spoofing*, the act of simulating a menu hit. Let's say your menu system has a menu item, *View Updates*, that pops up a browse window showing all recently updated records. If you wanted to include this menu option as a button on one of your screens, you could spoof that item by calling the menu program from the text button:

```
DO menus WITH 'View Updates'
```

Another advantage to this approach is that it's portable to other platforms. FoxBASE+/Mac menu handlers are coded similarly to the examples shown here. The user selects a menu, triggering the *ON MENU* intercept routine. That routine calls a procedure similar to *menuhand* (shown below). In turn, *menuhand* is passed to the menu item handler, which is similar to the MENU.PRG program. By modifying only a few lines of code, you can convert FoxPro 2.0 menu routines to FoxBASE+/Mac-compatible routines. This menuing approach also reduces the excess code generated by FoxPro's menu code generator, GENMENU.

```
PROCEDURE menuhand      && menu handler routine in STARTUP.PRG
   PARAMETERS mymenu,mybar
   barname=mymenu
   barnum=mybar
   menuevent=.T.
   CLEAR READ
RETURN TO MASTER        && return to event loop
```

The *menuhand* routine notifies the event loop that a menu event was triggered and tells it which menu item was selected. Control is eventually passed to the main-menu program, where the associated action is performed.

Why didn't we include this routine with MENUS.PRG? MENUS.PRG handles both true menu hits and menu spoofs; if for some reason you wanted to capture only a true menu hit (in other words, only allow some action if a menu item was selected), you could do that in the *menuhand* routine.

If you've programmed in FoxPro or FoxBASE+/Mac, the code in Listing 1-3 should look familiar. The procedure is a *CASE* statement to handle choices made via the system menus. It's easy to modify if you change the items on your menu. The *OTHERWISE* clause is a nice way to handle menu items not yet implemented. The program ends with a *RETURN TO MASTER* command to ensure program control returns to the main event loop after the menu item is processed. Notice the *'Exit'* menu item. It also returns to the event loop, but first it triggers a flag. With the flag set (*quitflag==.T.*), control is returned to the event loop; the *DO WHILE !quitflag* command evaluates to true and exits the loop.

Listing 1-3. *MENUS.PRG.*

```
***Menus.prg***
PARAMETER barname,barnum
PRIVATE bname
bname=Barname
menuevent=.f.
DO CASE
   CASE Bname=='Exit'
      quitflag=.T.
   CASE Bname=='Customer'
      DO cust.spr
   CASE Bname=='Salesmen'
      DO sman.spr
   CASE Bname=='Offices'
      DO off2.spr
   CASE Bname=='Parts'
      DO part.spr
   CASE Bname=='Invoices'
      DO inv.spr
   CASE Bname=='Detail'
      DO detail.spr
   CASE Bname=='Sales Office'
      DO b1
   CASE Bname=='Customer Sales'
      DO b2
   CASE Bname=='Parts Detail'
      DO b3
   CASE Bname=='Salesman2'
      DO sman2.spr
   CASE Bname=='Customer2'
      DO cust2.spr
   CASE Bname=='Text File'
      MODIFY FILE 'Untitled.txt' NOWAIT
   OTHERWISE
      WAIT WINDOW 'Sorry, feature not implemented yet' NOWAIT
ENDCASE
RETURN TO MASTER
```

The double equal signs (==) ensure that menu hits are always processed. If *SET EXACT* were set to OFF, this program wouldn't process the *'Customer2'* option correctly because another *'Customer'* choice exists. Careful naming of menus and windows will prevent unexpected results in your event-driven applications. Leaving *SET EXACT ON* will assure that events are processed as expected but may have side effects that could impact database operations elsewhere in your application. The "==" operator can alleviate many of these conflicts and should be used whenever possible.

You may want to define special menus associated with specific windows or control the enabling and disabling of specific menu pads and items. Routines to handle these tasks can be placed inside your main-menu program or screen-painter code, as explained in the Fox manuals. If you do create special menus, it may be more appropriate to have a separate menu-handler program for each new menu. If you intend to have one menu system for the entire application, then only one menu handler in the menu-bar options procedure may be needed.

You can decide which items to include in your menus, though it's recommended that all systems maintain the standard System, File, Edit, and Window menus. Windows are so complex and can have so many events associated with them that the Window menu is necessary for users who rely on the keyboard to navigate and manipulate the user interface.

Keystrokes

In a normal event-driven application (non-FoxPro), all keyboard events are handled by the event loop. FoxPro, however, has several conventions for handling events directly at the interrupt level. Because of speed considerations, keyboard events generally shouldn't be processed by the event loop. In certain situations, however, you may want to capture the keyboard activity through the event loop.

Both the menu builder and the screen painter let you associate hot keys (keyboard shortcuts) with individual menu items and screen controls. Hot keys should be used whenever possible, but a common misconception is that keyboard shortcuts associated with system menu bars will always work in an application. This is only true if that menu item exists and contains the equivalent keystroke definition.

For example, the common *Cut*, *Copy*, and *Paste* keyboard commands (Ctrl+X, C, and V) will only work in an application if the Edit menu contains the three menu bars and their keyboard shortcuts.

FoxPro also has *ON KEY* and *ON KEY LABEL* interrupt commands, which are used to control the activity of a certain keystroke (including any modifier keys). The *ON KEY LABEL* command is preferable to the original *ON KEY* command because a number of keyboard routines can be assigned simultaneously. Another feature is the macro editor, used to define and record sets of keystrokes, which can then be played later, when the macro is activated.

As mentioned earlier, keystrokes can be processed through the event loop. Let's review some of the functional differences between standard and *GET*-less *READ*s as they relate to keystroke handling. Standard *READ*s always have an associated @...*GET*, so data is always being read into the item. Keystrokes normally won't terminate the *READ* unless the @...*GET* is the last field (assuming the *CYCLE* clause isn't used) or a control specifically designated to terminate, such as a text button. The *GET*-less *READ* has no associated @...*GET*. Unlike the standard *READ*, mouse clicks and keystrokes usually terminate the *GET*-less *READ* (assuming a *VALID* clause doesn't return an *.F.*). However, the *READ* isn't terminated if the keystroke is associated with a menu selection, non-*READ* window, or *ON KEY LABEL*.

Depending on the programming style used, a keystroke handler within the event loop may or may not be necessary. Users who go directly into edit mode once a *READ* window is activated may not need a handler because keystrokes will consist primarily of direct edits to the fields and memory variables. Those who activate a window but hold off editing until explicitly directed to do so may want a handler. For example, the user could go into edit mode by pressing *E*. The *GET*-less *READ* would terminate, process the *READKEY()* through the keystroke handler, and issue the @...*GET*s and *READ*.

The *ON KEY LABEL* command processes a key combination under any *READ* and may be preferable to a keyboard handler if the nature of the action is more universal to the overall application than a specific window. A keyboard handler can, however, offer a more efficient way of handling single-key shortcuts such as menu-pad and window selection.

Keystroke handlers should be limited to the *GET*-less *READ*. You can do this by triggering the *keyevent* flag only in the *GET*-less *READ VALID* routine. Incorporating a *keyevent* with a standard *READ* window may cause conflicts with hot keys and window events. As with any *READ*, the *READKEY()* function can be used to determine which key terminated the *READ*.

Windows

Window events are by far the most difficult to handle due to the variety of possible actions:

- **Open/close.** The actual window is created with the *DEFINE* command and closed with the *RELEASE* command, which destroys the window's definition and any components. Windows can be closed manually by the close box in their upper left corner; this action is similar to a *DEACTIVATE*.
- **Activate/deactivate.** Once a window is defined, it can be brought forward and made visible by the *ACTIVATE* command. When you use this command, the window brought forward becomes the current output window. When you *DEACTIVATE* a window, that window retains its identity but is no longer the current output window.
- **Show/hide.** A window can also be shown and hidden on the desktop without becoming the active output window. Unlike the *DEACTIVATE* command, *HIDE* won't affect the nature of any *@...GET*s active on that window.
- **Zoom.** The zoom box, located in the upper right corner of system windows, expands an open window to its maximum size.
- **Move.** You can move a window by dragging its title bar anywhere on the desktop (screen), or within its parent window if it's defined as a child window.
- **Grow.** The size of the window can be adjusted using the grow box in its lower right corner.
- **Minimize.** This feature is new to FoxPro 2.0 and allows you to collapse a window to the size of its title bar simply by double-clicking on it.

FoxPro handles the last four events internally in its event loop; the user simply needs to define the window with these attributes. Other events require some additional coding, as shown in the following sections.

Non-READ Windows

Non-READ windows are those that don't have @...*GET*s; they include browses, desk accessories, text files, query documents, and report definitions. The *GET*-less *READ* can handle these windows easily. In fact, the above event loop handles them automatically. Remember, the foundation *READ* isn't terminated when the user clicks on one of these windows.

The most interesting and complex of the non-*READ* windows is the browse. FoxPro 2.0 allows browses to interact with normal *READ* windows, as discussed later in this chapter. In many cases, a browse is suitable on its own. The guidelines for both situations are basically the same:

- Always check for the existence of a browse window so it isn't re-created.
- Open databases with the new *USE <dbf> AGAIN ALIAS <alias>* command. This will avoid any conflict with the database that might prematurely release the browse window. In an event-driven application, the database may or may not be open when the browse is issued. Because events are ordered at the user's discretion, it's best to take a conservative approach to database management.
- The actual browse window should be defined with the *NOWAIT* clause so it will immediately go into the *READ*.

The sample code in Listing 1-4, taken from the event-driven application on the disk available with this book, shows these techniques.

Listing 1-4. Segment from *MENUS.PRG*.

```
PROCEDURE B3
   IF WEXIST('Bits and Pieces')
```

```
        ACTIVATE WINDOW 'Bits and Pieces' TOP
        RETURN
    ENDIF
    =opendbf('Parts','Part')
    =opendbf('Detail','Det')
    SET ORDER TO pno
    SELE Part
    SET RELATION TO pno INTO Det
    SET SKIP TO Det
    DEFINE WINDOW detpart FROM 4,5 to 18,75 ;
        system float close grow shadow color scheme 8
    BROWSE NOMODIFY NODELETE NOMENU WINDOW detpart;
        NOWAIT COLOR SCHEME 10 TITLE 'Bits and Pieces';
        FIELDS pno:H='Part#', descript:H='Description',
                        Price:H='Price',;Det.qty:H='Quantity'
    RELEASE WINDOW detpart
RETURN

FUNCTION OPENDBF
    PARAMETER newdbf,malias
    IF USED(malias)
        SELE (malias)
    ELSE
        SELE 0
        USE (newdbf) AGAIN ALIAS (malias)
    ENDIF
RETURN
```

A Single READ Window

A single *READ* window implies that only one window is associated with the *READ*. Therefore, the *GET*s are contained in one window that includes any necessary controls, such as navigation buttons. See Figure 1-3.

FoxPro's screen painter and code generator provide all the necessary tools for creating windows in an event-driven application. The screen-code generator is the glue that binds many of the attributes and features created in the screen painter. Fox has done an outstanding job of providing a template that handles most of the events associated with windows. The code generator is extremely powerful; it handles not only the @..*GET*s but also the *READ*, database management, and windows. Effective incorporation of the screen painter and code generator in an event-driven application can reduce development time significantly.

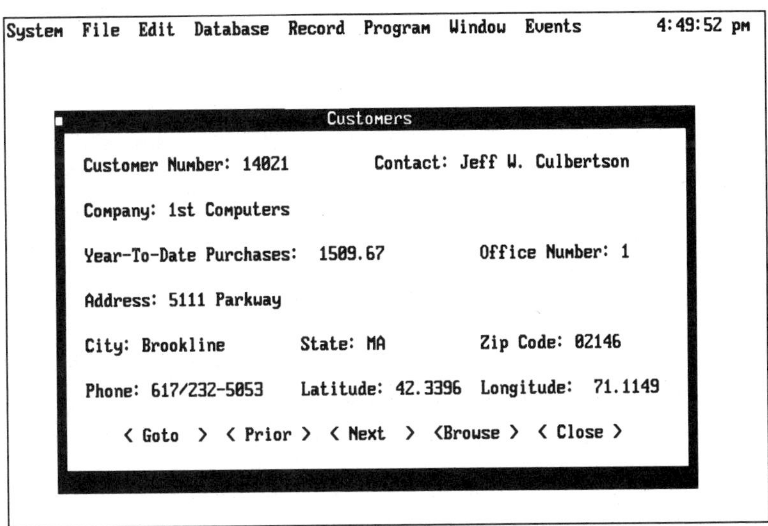

Figure 1-3. A single READ window.

Windows as defined under the screen builder should be entirely self-contained. This style of coding is similar to object-oriented programming in that a properly coded generic window can be inserted into any application. When using the screen painter, you need to do the following to make windows operational within an event-driven environment.

- Define everything in windows. Avoid using the desktop screen for @..*GET*s; that defeats the purpose of an event-driven program. Try to make your window definitions consistent (for example, all dialog boxes should have the same features).

- Call a generic window handler in the *READ DEACTIVATE* clause. Remember, the handler call is in the *DEACTIVATE* code because any window event caused by another *READ* window will trigger the current output window's *READ DEACTIVATE* clause. The handler can then take appropriate action based on the positions of the various windows on the desktop. The statement in each *DEACTIVATE* snippet is a simple call:

```
DO windhand
*** windhand() can be used if it's an expression

***window handler in STARTUP.PRG***
PROCEDURE windhand
     windevent=.t.
     CLEAR READ
RETURN TO MASTER
```

We'll return to the *READ DEACTIVATE* clause in a moment.

- Save the environment, including databases, indexes, and relations (this step is optional). When the code is later generated, these will be restored automatically. The screen-code generator is also smart enough to handle databases that are already open. You can always choose to generate code without the environment setup or cleanup.

- When you generate the code for certain attributes, mark the check boxes for the *Read Cycle* and *Define Windows* options. The *Release Windows* option on the menu should always be left unchecked. This is critical to EDP; if you check this item, code will be generated to release the window every time the *READ* is terminated.

  If you check the *Open Files* and *Close Files* options, code is generated to handle the necessary databases. You'll then need to make sure the screen-painter definition contains the saved environment of the databases that need to be opened. However, developers should provide their own database management routines in more serious applications, especially those for multiuser systems. In an event-driven application, you can't predict the order or combination of databases that will be used at a given time or the order in which they'll be used; your code should be flexible enough to handle rapid switching between databases. In addition, database environments can be saved and restored more efficiently.

The code created using the GENSCRN template will handle most of the events associated with windows, but one window event is left to consider: The close box in the upper left corner will trigger a *DEACTIVATE* event. The code in this clause (see the *windhand* code) will clear the *READ*, but control immediately passes to the event loop via a *RETURN TO MASTER*. Because program control isn't returned to the screen-generated program after the *CLEAR READ*, the code that released the window isn't processed and therefore the window is left defined. The window name will still appear in the Window menu, and you can activate it by selecting it; that triggers a window event that redefines the @...*GET*s and reactivates the window.

I mentioned earlier that the *READ DEACTIVATE* clause was the key to controlling window events. This clause is processed whenever the window is closed or another window is brought forward. The *DEACTIVATE* itself isn't actually handled until the new window is brought forward. When the clause is processed, the new window becomes the *WONTOP()* and the old one becomes the *WLAST()*. Later, we will show how the *WONTOP()* plays an important role in determining whether the *READ* is terminated.

As simple as it is, the *windhand* routine handles all single *READ* window events. When another window is brought forward, the current *READ* is cleared (terminated) and program control is returned to the event loop. (As we'll see, this isn't true for palettes.) A flag (*windevent*=.T.) is set to tell the event loop that a window event took place. All window events are processed in the event loop by WINDOWS.PRG:

```
***WINDOWS.PRG (partial)***
windevent=.F.
DO CASE
   CASE WONTOP()='CUST2'
      DO cust2.spr
   CASE WONTOP()='SMAN2'
      DO sman2.spr
ENDCASE
RETURN
```

The windows program must contain a list of all *READ* windows that have screen definitions. As you may have noticed, this program is similar to the menus program. Screens are called the same way, but the event is different; therefore, a new detection scheme is needed. In this case, the *WONTOP()* function can be used to determine the current *READ* window. If an active window isn't found on the *DO CASE* list, the program eventually returns to the foundation *READ*.

Palettes

Those of you who have used Macintosh software have seen the small floating windows that can be used universally among multiple working windows. For example, a drawing program may have several open documents, each with a different picture, and a common palette of drawing tools floating on top and accessible by all the working documents. This metaphor of a utility screen can also be brought into database software, since database operations on edit screens often include the same set of actions. These actions, often in the form of buttons, include *Next/Prev, View, Edit, Print, Add, Delete,* and any other function associated with database record operations. The sample windows shown in the preceding section had the same duplicate set of navigation buttons. By using a palette, you can avoid devoting screen space to redundant controls (Figure 1-4).

In our event-driven application, we want to keep the palette open whenever a *READ* window is open. But we must also detect when all the windows are closed so that we can close the palette. In addition, each time a *READ* window is closed, another *READ* window should be brought forward and attached to the palette.

Most of the rules described earlier for single-read windows also apply to palettes. We need to make a few enhancements to the overall scheme, but the palette window itself is almost identical to any other *READ* window. The palette should be included in all screen sets for each associated *READ* window when code is generated through GENSCRN.

One necessary enhancement involves terminating the *READ*. The *Close* button on the palette will release the associated *READ* window, but the palette is only released if this is the last *READ* window on the desktop. The code in Listing 1-5 shows how to handle this event.

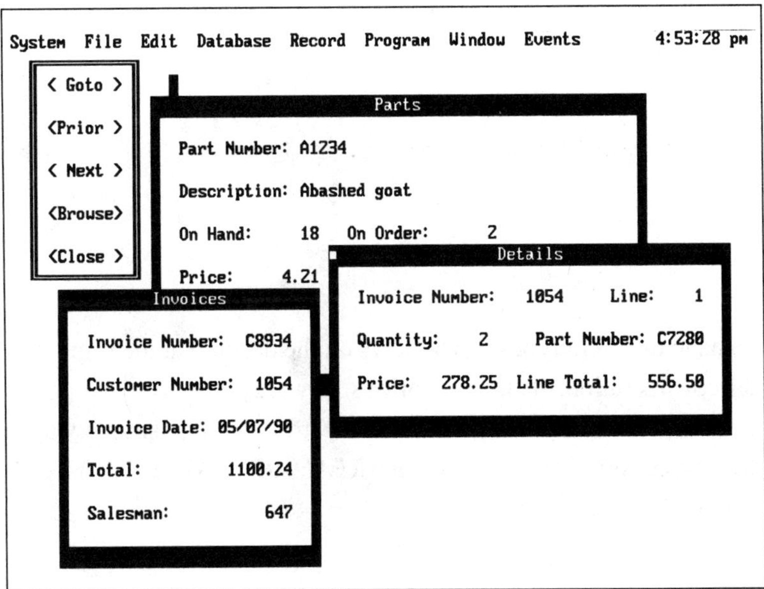

Figure 1-4. A single palette of window operations (<Goto>, <Prior>, <Next>, and so on) is available to all windows open on the screen.

Listing 1-5. Palette action code.

```
***palette button VALID code snippet statement***

DO CASE
   CASE act3 = 1
      DO goto.spr
   CASE act3 = 2
      SKIP -1
      IF BOF()
         GO TOP
      ENDIF
   CASE act3 = 3
      SKIP 1
      IF EOF()
         GO BOTTOM
      ENDIF
   CASE act3 = 4
      DO browser.spr
```

```
        CASE act3 = 5
            CLEAR READ
            STORE WLAST() TO lastwind
            IF lastwind<>'PALETTE' AND !EMPTY(lastwind)
                RELEASE WINDOW (lastwind)
            ENDIF
    ENDCASE
    SHOW GETS
    RETURN
```

The ability to have different types of windows on the desktop at the same time brings up another consideration. If the user brings forward a window that has an associated palette, the palette should be brought forward as well. A simple way to allow this is with an expression or procedure in the *READ ACTIVATE* code that calls the following routine:

```
***palette handler in STARTUP.PRG***
PROCEDURE active
    IF WEXIST('PALETTE') AND !WONTOP('PALETTE')
        ACTIVATE WINDOW 'PALETTE' TOP
    ENDIF
RETURN
```

The palette window is actually a *READ* window. Under the window handler described in the preceding section, clicking on the palette would terminate the *READ* because the *DEACTIVATE* clause always processes a *CLEAR READ* statement. The windows program doesn't activate the palette on its own, so the palette would be rendered useless. The best way to resolve this is to return an *.F.* from the *DEACTIVATE* clause to prevent premature termination of the *READ*.

You can also use the window handler to incorporate *READ* windows with palettes and those without palettes in the same event-driven system:

```
***window handler in STARTUP.PRG***
PROCEDURE windhand
    windevent=.t.
    IF WREAD(WONTOP())
        RETURN .F.
```

```
   ENDIF
   CLEAR READ
RETURN TO MASTER
```

The *WREAD(WONTOP())* function combination will return a *.T.* whenever an associated window, such as a palette, is activated. All windows defined under the same *READ* (including browses) will return a value of *.T.* to the *WREAD()* function.

During execution of an event-driven program, the user might open a window that doesn't have an associated palette (such as a text file). We need to handle the event in which the palette is brought forward on top of this unrelated window. We can do that using a routine that decides which associated *READ* window to activate along-side the palette:

Listing 1-6. Program to handle window events.

```
***WINDOWS.PRG***
windevent=.F.
IF WONTOP()='PALETTE'
   DO newwind
ENDIF
DO CASE
   CASE WONTOP()='CUST'
      DO cust.spr
   CASE INLIST(WONTOP(),'OFFICE','Associated Customers')
      DO off2.spr
   CASE WONTOP()='SMAN'
      DO sman.spr
   CASE WONTOP()='DETAIL'
      DO detail.spr
   CASE WONTOP()='PART'
      DO part.spr
   CASE WONTOP()='INV'
      DO inv.spr
ENDCASE
RETURN

PROCEDURE newwind
   PRIVATE hiwind,lastwind,wnum
```

```
      store 0 to wnum
      hiwind=''
      * Choose a window starting with topmost and continue
      * selecting until one is found which has associated
      * palette. WCHILD("",...) bases off of desktop
      * instead of a window.
      lastwind = WCHILD("",wnum)
      DO WHILE !EMPTY(lastwind)
         IF INLIST(lastwind, "CUST","PART","INV","SMAN",;
                        "OFFICE","DETAIL") and WVISIBLE(lastwind)
            hiwind=lastwind
         ENDIF
         wnum=wnum+1
         lastwind = WCHILD("",wnum)
      ENDDO
      IF !EMPTY(hiwind)
         ACTIVATE WINDOW (hiwind)
      ELSE
         RELEASE WINDOW 'PALETTE'
      ENDIF
   RETURN
```

The key to deciding which window to activate lies in *WCHILD()*. This function determines the order, from back to front, of the available *READ* windows and flags the topmost one. Include in the *INLIST()* function only those windows you want to be active with the palette; otherwise, a non-*READ* window such as a browse could be flagged and the palette would be stranded. Be careful when using the *INLIST()* function here if you have *SET EXACT OFF* since similar window names can cause conflicts.

Incorporating browses with READ Windows

In FoxPro 2.0, a browse can be incorporated directly into a *READ*. The techniques described in the section on non-*READ* windows create a stand-alone browse that's active under a foundation *READ*. If defined with a *READ* window instead, the browse becomes active under that window. A browse window under this *READ* will show screen refreshes when the database record pointer changes.

For example, you could have a one-to-many database in which database A (one) is related to database B (many). FoxPro 2.0 allows you to define a *READ* window for database A and a browse for database B. Because A is related to B, moving the record pointer in A will also move the pointer in B and update the browse. See Figure 1-5.

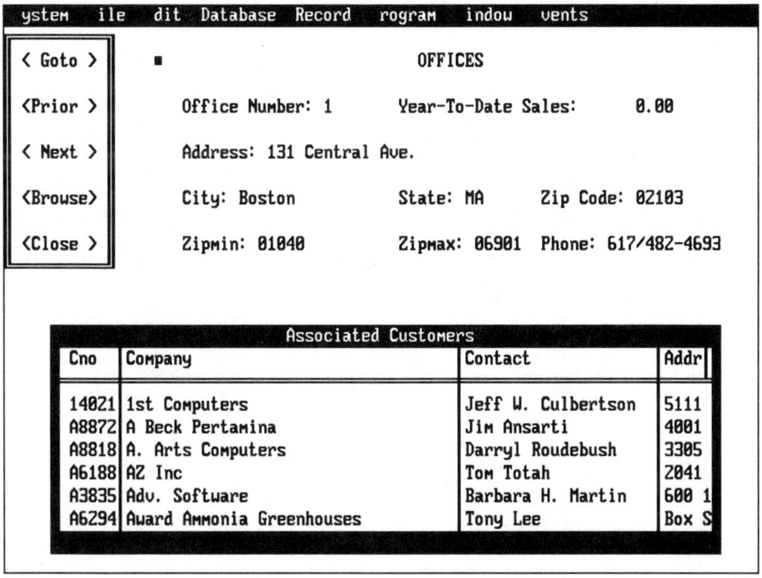

```
ystem  ile  dit  Database  Record  rogram  indow  vents

< Goto >                        OFFICES
<Prior >   Office Number: 1      Year-To-Date Sales:      0.00
< Next >   Address: 131 Central Ave.
<Browse>   City: Boston          State: MA    Zip Code: 02103
<Close >   Zipmin: 01040         Zipmax: 06901  Phone: 617/482-4693

                    Associated Customers
 Cno   | Company                    | Contact             | Addr
 14021 | 1st Computers              | Jeff W. Culbertson  | 5111
 A8872 | A Beck Pertamina           | Jim Ansarti         | 4001
 A8818 | A. Arts Computers          | Darryl Roudebush    | 3305
 A6188 | AZ Inc                     | Tom Totah           | 2041
 A3835 | Adv. Software              | Barbara H. Martin   | 600 1
 A6294 | Award Ammonia Greenhouses  | Tony Lee            | Box S
```

Figure 1-5. An example of a browse with *READ* Window.

The techniques used to create these active browses are similar to those used to design stand-alone browses. The few modifications needed are shown in Listing 1-7.

Listing 1-7. Screen code for browse.

```
***screen setup code snippet***
IF WEXIST('Associated Customers') AND;
   !WLAST('Associated Customers')
   ACTI WINDOW 'Associated Customers' TOP
ENDIF
IF !WEXIST('Associated Customers')
   DEFINE WINDOW offcust FROM 14,05 to 23,75;
      SYSTEM FLOAT NOCLOSE GROW SHADOW
```

```
    SELECT customer
    BROWSE NOMOD NODELETE NOMENU WINDOW offcust NOWAIT;
       COLOR SCHEME 10 TITLE 'Associated Customers'
    RELEASE WINDOW offcust
ENDIF
SELECT offices
```

This listing contains the code necessary to handle the browse. In this example, the offices database is related to the customer database. The *WEXIST()* function is needed to check for the existence of the browse window. This prevents the window from being re-created every time the main *READ* window is activated; because the *DEACTIVATE* clause calls Windows.Prg with the new window on top. The *NOWAIT* clause is also needed to force the browse into the *READ*.

The *ACTIVATE* code should be modified slightly to assure proper handling of the browse window when navigating among the other windows associated with the *READ*:

```
***READ ACTIVATE code snippet***
IF WLAST("Associated Customers")
   SELECT offices
ENDIF
DO active
```

This code is executed when the user goes from the browse window to the *READ* window. Because different databases are used depending on which window is active, they must be reselected when a new window is selected. The browse window does this automatically.

Saving Environments

Any event-driven application has the potential to create environmental problems. A database environment usually consists of the current open database(s), relations, *SET SKIP TO*, order, filters, and record numbers in addition to any other defined state. It's extremely important that a database environment be restored when its associated window is reactivated.

The screen template, GENSCRN, takes care of some of these activities for us, but you may want your own database management routines for opening, closing, saving, and restoring views, especially in a multiuser setting. Because GENSCRN doesn't generate code to save or restore the database environment, an outside routine is needed.

The code in this chapter doesn't contain specific details on managing database environments. There are several ways to store this data; arrays, memory variables, and databases will all work. If you want to restore a database environment from a previous session, it might be a good idea to have a database or memory file store the name of the window along with the record number, order, filter, and so on. A routine to save the environment could be put in the window-handler procedure called by the *READ DEACTIVATE* clause. A restore routine could be placed in a procedure called from the screen-setup code. Saving and restoring entire views can be a slow process; incremental view handling may be better under certain circumstances but would require special coding.

A Foundation for Database Development

This chapter has presented techniques many of you have read and heard about but may never have visualized how to incorporate into your FoxPro applications. Fox Software provided the interface objects in FoxPro 1.0x, but not until the release of FoxPro 2.0 could you create a truly event-driven program that allowed the transparent interaction of these objects. The techniques given here should give you a foundation for creating consistent applications that will benefit your users from both a learning curve and a productivity point of view. EDP also provides a common thread between other graphic platforms, such as Windows and the Macintosh. Future database development techniques will almost surely involve this style of programming.

CHAPTER 2

User Interface Design

by Jeff Winchell

When it comes to interface design, there are no absolute truths. Every designer has his or her own ideas about the most appropriate and attractive interface. Furthermore, each application has its own needs, and different users will need different kinds of information.

This chapter recounts a discussion between some people with strong opinions and considerable experience designing user interfaces. It's taken from a conversation that itself discards an old-fashioned interface (face to face) in favor of a modern one—a public forum of CompuServe.

The contributors are some of this book's authors—Ham Ahlo, Randy Brown, Peter Colclough, David McClanahan, Alan Schwartz, Ron Talmage, and myself—along with a few guests:

- Richard Grossman, the creator of a FoxPro accounting package called Wing It! He has also written and spoken on database topics for several publications and conferences.
- Paul Litwin, who wrote the R:Base column for *Data Based Advisor* and continues as contributing editor.
- Hal Pawluk, who has been head of marketing at Fox, Microrim, and Ashton-Tate in addition to having product design duties at those companies. He created the legendary "dBASE II vs. the Bilge Pump" ad.
- Mel Masuda and George Braly, longtime inhabitants of CompuServe's FoxForum. Mel founded a power engineering firm in Hawaii, and George is an attorney and pilot.

The following is an edited transcript of our message threads.

Jeff: User interfaces are all about making the program easier to use. What guidelines do we have to help us make those decisions? IBM's Common User Access (CUA)? Apple's Human Interface Guide (HIG)?

Randy: As someone with a strong Mac background, I want to give my impressions before we launch into the many HIG issues. People often misunderstand Apple's intentions in setting standards such as the HIG recommendations. Apple never intended to monopolize interface guidelines; that's why it uses the word *recommendations.*

Ever since Apple became involved with personal computers, the company has spent countless time and money researching ways of making personal computing easy for the layman. The HIG is the result of these studies. Apple paid particular attention to the five senses—in particular, sight, hearing, and touch. The intent was to come up with a uniform set of guidelines for developers.

Apple's HIG studies focused closely on software features that provided a fast learning curve and ease of use. User feedback was a very important consideration. Apple wanted software that removed any confusion on the part of the user.

So why do we examine this with FoxPro? Fox Software has given us many of the features of a GUI—menus, pop-ups, windows, dialogs, and so on.

Ham: Do you think adherence to the HIG increases productivity in the long term (apart from the initial ease of learning)? In my case, at least, I had to work at learning the GUI interface (Windows and the Mac) and found many elements of it less than intuitive. On the other hand, I'm a very fast typist and a confirmed command-line fan.

I'd also throw open for discussion the notion that perhaps what is touted as being intuitive on the Mac is a cultural artifact of its originators and promoters (in fact, these people were and are educated, upper middle-class

Americans who are interested in computers and who are predominantly white).

Jeff: I found several things in Windows nonintuitive. Someday I hope to master with 100% accuracy the decision on which upper right-hand corner button to push.

The cultural part of intuitiveness is an important one. When I read *The Design of Everyday Things* by Donald A. Norman (Doubleday Currency), I thought there was a universal "intuitive." As Lisa Slater (a regular on the FoxForum) pointed out to me, something might be intuitive for one culture and draw a blank with another.

Hal: I think a lot of people, some programmers among them, equate CUA and HIG with ease of use, but this is not an automatic connection.

Scroll bars and buttons are only the interface to the *machine* (the hardware and software combination), not thc functionality of the program. Sure, it's easy to move and resize windows, pull down menus, and click on buttons. But how easy is it for users to do their jobs? Check out some of the Windows and Mac software out there: The answer is often "not so easy." If it takes four clicks to perform a function that's hidden behind pull-downs, pop-ups, and dialog boxes, is this any easier than four hits on the return key in a character-based system?

Peter: Hallelujah! A like-minded soul.

While I'm not anti-GUI, I don't think it should replace text-based systems as a de facto standard. I believe there are places where a GUI is invaluable. There are also places where text-based systems work.

At a warehouse where I put in a system, the management insisted (against my suggestions) on a mouse-driven interface. They finally gave in after their fifth machine was accidentally hit by a forklift! It was a case of a mouse-driven system taking three times longer than the text-based version.

On the other hand, GUIs are *very* good at information retrieval and display, graphical information display, and most managerial tasks.

Jeff: Hal, I have to agree with you regarding the long series of mouse clicks many GUIs make you go through. But progress has been made on this front. Programs like Word for Windows put frequently used selections on a ribbon in the form of icons. The next step is for the buttons to be user-customizable. This would allow the user to get at the most common procedures quickly and without having to remember arcane keyboard shortcuts à la WordPerfect.

Randy: Although I admire WordPerfect for its power, I've always had reservations about all the keyboard shortcuts one must memorize, none of which appear onscreen unless you press F3 to show Help. One of the reasons I like the mouse so much is that I don't have to memorize a different set of keyboard shortcuts for each software product.

Peter: This is an area for CUA. Most keyboard shortcuts start with the first letter of the option or use a highlighted letter. You should *never* have to learn the shortcuts; they should be either on the screen or on a well-known F key.

Maybe we have room for a standard here.

Ron: CUA dictates that the keyboard shortcut be underlined, but that's not easy in text mode, so FoxPro highlights the letter. Unfortunately, this can cause problems for screen set colors on some laptops and white VGA screens. Not all shortcuts in CUA will be on the menu—cursor movement in data entry, for example.

Ham: It strikes me that while many of the programs have keyboard shortcuts, they seem like afterthoughts in some ways—in other words, "OK guys, we'll stick 'em in like the boss wanted, but we're *not* going to make it easy."

Jeff: The same can be said for some mouse implementations (like WordPerfect 5.1).

Randy: Peter, you mentioned implementing a mouseless system for your warehouse DBMS because the mouse took longer to use. My friend wrote a complete management system for his restaurant to record orders, handle seating, and even process credit-card payments. His system was entirely mouse-driven; he disconnected the keyboards and created buttons for each menu and drink item. Because his users were waiters, bartenders, cooks, and hostesses and may not have used computers before, he wanted to simplify everything as much as possible and alleviate any problems with keyboard integrity.

I think each situation presents itself differently. And it's nice to have the option of going either way.

Peter: I'm not anti-mouse, despite owning four cats. Seriously, though, a restaurant application will usually require less physical data entry, so a mouse is suited to that situation.

Another important factor is the user. If the user is proficient with—and likes—the mouse, then all well and good. If not, the keyboard ought to be around. I prefer the dead mouse, or trackball, when desk space is at a premium. There are areas where they're not useful but are still used. I *never* believed that a mouse on a text-based menu added anything for the user.

Paul: I think *real programmers* and *real writers* spend far too much time and energy trying to convince everyone that mice are useless. Any good user interface will allow both. If you don't like the darn mouse, don't use it already. Most decent GUIs offer plenty of keyboard shortcuts and customization (for example, Word for Windows and Excel). In fact, that was one of my complaints when I was reviewing Borland's ObjectVision—not enough keyboard shortcuts. Of course, the editor thought that was an unimportant complaint and cut it out of the review. I beg to differ.

Peter: Developers should have many types of interfaces at their disposal and should use the right one for the right job, not the one that sells the system.

Ham: I don't think a truly common interface to all applications will ever be possible or desirable (short of mind melds). I've seen applications designed for use with a mouse with very nifty dialog boxes and aesthetically pleasing screens that work consistently with other apps, but they simply didn't work for that particular situation.

A good example is a cash-register application, or a clerk whose only job is to enter receipts into a computer. Both require such standard, unvarying entries that the system ought to be optimized to accomplish the task with as few keystrokes as possible.

Some problems with mouse-driven approaches are that (1) fast data-entry operators never want to take their hands from the home position on the keyboard; (2) they can't type ahead of the machine with the mouse since you can't really stack mouse movements or clicks; and (3) they need to focus on their input, not the screen.

So is it possible to design a good GUI application that conforms to all the conventions of design in that environment yet is still efficiently and easily used via keyboard alone?

Paul: Yes, I think it is. It's funny how people think of data entry as a single entity that's easily generalized. Not so. Sometimes data entry needs to be head-down, full-speed-ahead. Sometimes it needs to have the user look at the screen but isn't terribly interactive. Sometimes it needs to be *very* interactive.

All these needs require a different program or paradigm. For example, I set up some data entry using a dedicated double-verification program (Rode/PC by DPX, Inc.). Other times, I'm using a standard DBMS that's mildly interactive. And other apps are GUI-like, with pop-up list boxes and value-driven branching.

Perhaps a well-designed data-entry application should allow a little of each—that is, allow optional on-demand pop-up list boxes and skipping ahead with a mouse click, but also allow data entry in the head-down fashion. I've created applications that can do both.

Hal: Data entry is a different case. I've found that unless the user is entering data from a preprinted form, the process is usually faster and more error-free if the entry fields are simply listed vertically, as in dBASE II. (No, I didn't slip a digit.) Heresy, huh?

For data entry (not viewing), if the source data is from a form with information sprinkled across as well as up and down, you probably should build a screen that corresponds closely to the form. The data-entry people can then check their work more easily because the item that's a third of the way down the page and two-thirds of the way across will be in approximately the same position on the screen.

Data to be entered, however, is often just listed. In that case, the vertical-field list makes it easier to check the entry on the screen. Even if the data to be entered is on the form, a vertical entry list doesn't cause as much difficulty for the operator as having the data on a list and the screen as a form.

A third possibility is to have the data to be entered on a form and make the screen look like a different form that will be used for output later. This is not the best of both worlds.

Ham: It depends on the source of the data. Even if data-input forms aren't used, in many instances it's helpful to structure the input screens to guide the data-entry person and to structure the solicitation of input values (such as when telephone order-takers are entering data directly into the computer). If you're popping up pick lists and additional information in various windows, you have to factor them into the screen design. In these cases there's no input form, but I would argue that the list-them-all-vertically approach might not be the best.

Hal: It was not a "thou shalt," but a "thou shouldst consider instead of saying no-way José." I deliberately avoided telephone order entry because this involves some elements of *scripting*, as you suggested, and that is both structure and, dare I say it, text.

Make it appropriate for the application. You might want to take the time to create different screens for each application, have the users use them, and watch what happens. That can be very instructive.

Jeff: Microsoft does this with its Usability Labs. Users of all flavors are invited to come and play with prototypes of Microsoft products and are interviewed afterward.

George: Ham, pilots file flight plans. The FAA has a form that has remained unchanged for decades. Pilots know from memory what's on the form but frequently can't remember the exact order of the 15 or so entries. It used to be that when you called (by telephone or, in flight, by radio) the Flight Service Station to file a flight plan, the FSS person would pull out the form, write in the information, and key it into the Teletype.

The FAA decided to computerize and consolidate all the Flight Service Stations. Now each FSS employee has a wonderful big-screen computer terminal. Pilots call on the radio and start dictating the entries for their flight plans. If they get the entries out of order, the terminal operator has to be quick on the up/down/left/right arrow keys or risk missing the entry. The result: When you file a flight plan verbally, the operators often revert to the old system, writing down the entry on paper and then keyboarding it into the fancy new computer. Progress!

David: This flight-plan example is a good one, but I think you're throwing the baby out with the bath water. You mentioned that pilots often dictate the items out of order. This should be carefully considered when the input screen is designed; either find a quicker way to get to each field (using keys assigned to jump directly to each) or pop up a memo field to begin with, during the dictation stage, to allow free-form entry. You then have it in the database and move it into the correct fields. The memo can be deleted or kept as a history (what happened to the piece of paper you wrote on if you mistyped it later?). Creative methods for cutting and pasting from the memo fields could speed up that part of the process. This is generally a problem in the design stage, when the user requirements are determined. The *user* should be designing the interface with the assistance of the developer!

Randy: Ham, I think your points about keyboards are good, but I want to note a few exceptions. I've worked with many software products and have found that word processors and databases tend to be the most keyboard-intensive. It takes time to go back and forth between mouse and keyboard. However, I still want to have the option of using both! I don't want to be limited to one particular input device.

For example, you may not want to leave the keyboard if you're entering data from forms. On the other hand, when you want to print out a specialized report, you may want to use a mouse to select options on the report screen.

Another example: If you're entering the results of a survey in which the respondent either checked a box or circled a number or letter, it would be easier to use a mouse to select the appropriate radio buttons or check boxes.

Hal: Not necessarily. I don't find it difficult at all to type "Y" or "N." Your example is *not* a case for GUI.

Ham: A man after my own heart. Randy and I went around on this on the beta forum a while ago. Everybody is using this OK/Cancel dialog when 90% of the time they could phrase it as a yes-or-no question. Yes/No is very intuitive and (as long as the question is understood) fairly clear even to those for whom English is a second language. I frequently have to explain OK/Cancel, and even have to ask myself what it means in many contexts.

Pressing "Y" for yes and "N" for no approaches the intuitive rather more cleanly than some of the alternate dialogs that are commonly presented.

Randy: I do recall that thread a while back. Hal, what Ham was referring to is the use of wording in dialog boxes according to Apple's new HIG, issued with the release of System 7. Take, for instance, a dialog that asks "Do you want to delete this record?" HIG would suggest two buttons, Delete and Cancel (use action verbs for the buttons, rather than Yes/No). The idea here is to leave no doubt in the user's mind what button to choose. Yes/No buttons can be misleading, especially if the dialog question contains a negative.

Ham, you're right in that Yes/No is very intuitive as long as the question is posed correctly, but not all of us do this. Using an action verb, I think, will alleviate any doubt one might have as to the interpretation of the dialog. In terms of a single keypress, hot keys work fine. Instead of "Y" and "N," use "D" and "C."

I just love this HIG stuff, although I don't always practice what I preach.

Jeff: CUA contradicts HIG on this one. They recommend either OK/Cancel and Yes/No as options.

Hal: One of the choices should also be a default that you can actuate by hitting the Enter key. Most programs I've seen on the Mac do that.

Randy: I use both a default and an escape hot key for the buttons, depending on which involves a greater loss of data.

Mel: In the example you cited earlier, I'd think Yes/No would be more intuitive to the user. It's a matter of deciding whether the user wants to delete or not delete. Delete is OK but Cancel can be confusing, especially for users who aren't native English speakers. To them, Cancel may sound more like deleting than aborting. As you said, it depends on how the question is worded. The intuitive response to "Do you want to do this?" is "yes" or "no," but some may also respond with "I'm not sure."

Randy: Cancel has always been one of those weird buttons. The way I now interpret it is that if I choose it, I'll be returned to where I was before the dialog was presented to me.

Paul: One thing I haven't seen discussed enough here is *consistency*. This is a major advantage of a standard like CUA. Interapplication consistency makes it much easier to switch between programs and learn new programs with a minimal learning curve. Moving data between programs (as with cut and paste) is another advantage of a standard user interface.

Jeff: And it's easier to remember when you haven't used the program in three months.

Randy: Apple's guidelines became the basis for a successful revolution of interface-consistent software. Developing software with consistent interfaces that use these GUI objects will only benefit the end user. And that's who we write software for.

Alan: Being against consistency is like being against motherhood and apple pie, but consistency may be in the eye of the beholder. To wit: We're building several applications in business environments where, believe it or not, the entire corporate culture understands the PC interface exclusively within the conceptual framework of the Lotus 1-2-3 interface. In this world, if it has a bounce-bar menu, it's consistent. If it doesn't, it's not.

The freedom to move about in the uncertain realms of a nonmodal system raises definite specters of complexity, vagueness, and mystery. A thought-provoking question: To what degree is our job to elevate users' sights or give them information-access tools that make use of the common conceptual metaphor they already hold?

I recently saw a critique of a system I wrote for a major corporate client about three years ago in FoxBASE+. The critic, a systems guy, excoriated my choice of highlighted bar menus over his preference, which was:

1. Enter new form
2. Revise existing form
   etc...
0. Leave this Program
__ Your choice

His point: Bounce bars require the user to hit the down-arrow key several times rather than pressing a single digit. (Of course, he didn't know the capital letters on the bounce bars were triggers.)

Jeff: This leads into event-driven programming. Randy?

Randy: This seems to be a confusing subject these days in the Fox camp. I get the feeling that some folks at Fox don't really understand all the issues involved.

First, let's consider the original dBASE programming style, which everyone has written and most still do. Suppose a data processor logs into his dbase app to input new orders. The first thing he encounters is a menu with five options. He chooses "A" for Add. This takes him to another menu, from which he chooses "S" for Special purchase order. After running through a series of screens, he finally arrives at the one in which he'll input data. When he's through, he must back out through all the original screens.

This application is menu-driven. If it were event-driven, the data processor could go to the input screen more directly; he wouldn't need to back through menus and could pull up a screen showing the client's history while editing the order. In fact, he might even be able to edit multiple orders at once.

Event-driven programming allows independent routines and tasks to interface with each other simultaneously. There shouldn't be a limit to how many screens exist on the desktop at a time or which screens are associated with each other.

Ham: Where did the term *event-driven* originate? Isn't there a more felicitous term for this type of behavior? How about *user-responsive*? And what happened to *modeless*?

Randy: I'm not sure where it came from, but Apple surely pushed it to the edge. It probably came from the origins of window environs at Xerox PARC.

Modeless is still around, but it's used more to refer to dialog boxes (modeless as opposed to modal) than to programming styles.

Ham: I don't think the term *event-driven* is meaningful in any way to a user. I can't think of any users who would want to know what it means.

I think of *event-driven* as a buzzword to indicate a particular style of programming, but in a literal sense pretty much everything in the world is event-driven ("for every action there is an equal and opposite reaction"). It doesn't have a lot of meaning for me.

Peter: You're right about users not knowing or needing to know about this term. Like you, I regard it as a methodology. FoxPro's API allows for event-driven applications, so FoxPro applications can and should be written as event-driven.

The concept of event-driven applications is that there is an *engine* that looks for something to occur (keystroke, mouse press, comm port activity) and, when it does, scans a list of routines that handle the event. If a routine isn't interested, it passes the event on.

What this means for the user is nonmenu-driven systems (remember them?). More specifically, the user can switch quickly and easily from one part of an application to another. This is one of the *real* benefits of the event-driven approach.

Jeff: One of the problems with some event-driven applications is that they present *too many* options without suggesting the best path. A user gets lost. Perhaps we need some sort of "angel program" to watch over us, maybe give us some advice along the way, and keep track of where we've been.

Peter: The beauty of event-driven applications is that you can show or hide parts of the application without any loss of speed. So you could have apps available for users who are at different levels of competence.

Theoretically, you could still have an event-driven, menu-driven application (must think up a name for that...*rushless?*). It's easy to keep track of where you've been; Brief has done that for years, as have others with Undo logs. It can be done with log files or with chains in memory.

Richard: One of the problems with event-driven programming is that the operating system FoxPro runs under doesn't virtualize memory (substituting disk for RAM when needed).

With an event-driven interface, in a hypothetical accounting application you could open invoices in independent windows, payables records, and other kinds of screens all at once.

How do you do this without crashing when the user has less memory than the developer/tester? An event-driven application must always be aware of the amount of memory remaining before popping open yet another window. This is a nasty housekeeping chore.

Jeff: Hardware limitations are a factor in the kinds of interfaces you can design. And it's not just memory; CPU speed is also a factor.

Randy: I think an event-driven application need not be confined by potential memory limitations. The memory taken up by objects, such as windows sitting dormant on a screen, is minimal. Once an object is brought forward and made active, you allocate lots of memory to that window, but that's essentially what you would do in a menu-driven application.

I could see your dilemma arising if you had unlimited *READ*s and each window had an active *READ*, but why bother? Limit your *READ* to the foremost screen, and event-driven apps will run like menu-driven apps. Window states can easily be stored in databases or mem files, and with Fox's speed the performance hit is minimal.

On the subject of memory checks, you can do this quite simply without making a mess of the app; just put a check in your event loop before any event is processed.

Richard: I guess you're right; you can write your own event handler, then write your own memory handler, then write your own memory-to-disk virtualizer when RAM seems to have run out.

If DBMSs are so easy to use, shouldn't they handle this stuff for us?

Randy: I've always been in favor of having Fox provide stronger error/memory management within the database engine itself. I guess it's the dBASE way of doing things, and many competitive products like to knock the dBASE products for insufficient internal error handling.

Richard: Event-driven programming means more choice for the user, but what about the developer? How much choice is there in interface design? Is GUI going to sweep the software world to the point where text becomes obsolete?

Hal: GUI will sweep the world as a platform, but it's amazing how, when you shift to the user's perspective and look at or for information, text somehow seems to have its place.

Richard: What I'm saying is that holding back on GUI is like spitting into the wind.

Several venture capitalists told us that if Wing It! were a Windows application, they could get us about 10 times what we were asking for. As a DOS app...ho-hum.

Meanwhile, if you tell them about voice user interfaces (VUI), their eyes glaze over. You need to be ready with the next technology but not try to sell it until everyone has decided it's the coming thing.

Peter: I think you have a point there. At the risk of getting slightly controversial, in my opinion GUI will sweep the software world for the following reason: Corporate requests proposals for their system, and various offers come in, text-based and GUI-based among them. The text system meets 85% of the system requirements (not bad these days); the GUI meets 85% but with a speed deficiency in the data-entry screens. The people who sign the contract aren't users. Which system wins?

I think we all know the answer, and I find that depressing.

Richard: I'd go so far as to say that even if the GUI delivered *less* functionality than the text-based system, many purchasers would still choose it. The initial impact of a GUI is intense, because most users aren't familiar with it.

Peter: Maybe when the GUI has been around a bit longer, users will realize where they're useful and where text-based systems are useful.

Hal: I've seen some really sloppy thinking (and programming), apparently based on the premise that GUI = Good User Interface. Probably the ugliest thing I've ever seen was a Smalltalk-based DBMS publishing program, but less-than-wonderful things are also being created and sold for the Mac, Windows, Motif, and so on.

In many applications or parts of applications, buttons and other objects don't really add anything. Mice are difficult for some people to use (the guys on the shipping dock, for example), and how much more difficult is it to press "6" and then Return than to mouse or tab over to the fourth button and click on it? With shorter lists of known items (and I think lists should be kept short), I don't think GUI implementation adds anything and can even get in the way.

David: What GUI adds in that case is an abstraction, objects that are *viewed* by nontechnical people (and some technical people). For me, a *cd \word\doc* is quick and direct, while using a mouse and a GUI to change directories seems less direct. Yet again and again I see Macintoshes in heavy use while a PC sits next to them unused. I just switched from WordPerfect to Word for Windows and was immediately able to cut and paste, open files, find the exit selection, search, replace, and format characters and paragraphs by selecting the object and applying the operation. The consistent interface allowed me to learn a great deal (including shortcut keys for those operations) without looking at a manual. I then spent an hour or two learning how to set up macros do to the more important, frequently used functions.

Hal: Abstraction of objects isn't just for GUIs; I actually did this in a character-based system with R:Base 3.0. I was senior VP of marketing at Microrim at the time and set up the main menu you see in 3.0. The information objects in a DBMS are tables, queries, forms, reports, labels, and applications, so I defined a menu system that has all of these listed at the top level. To run a specific report or see a table or other information, the user just pulls down the appropriate menu and selects the name of the desired object. Topologically (and if you squint), this is the same as double-clicking on a named report or table icon on the Mac.

David: Sometimes you need to have users test different methods. I implemented the DBMS for an image database system (Bell & Howell's Technical Reference System) that handled things like car-repair manuals, instruction manuals, and parts manuals. We used touch screens in plant work areas. By touching an onscreen image of a part, a mechanic could zoom in on that part. He could touch the carburetor in the picture, and that part would be blown up on the screen. The exploded view listed parts, so the mechanic need only touch a particular part to get instructions on how to remove it. This entire process would only take a second or two. Almost the same speed would have been possible with a mouse, but in this case desk space was a problem. The same navigation is possible with keystrokes, but it takes much longer because the user is then dealing with data (menus, shortcuts, etc.) rather than with objects. Objects are easier to understand. Images will soon be as common a data element as text, and productivity will be greatly improved when a picture is worth a thousand keystrokes!

Randy: I fully agree with you: Users do understand images and graphics much better than text. And they seem to enjoy using those systems more. Touch screens are a nice way to go if the client can afford it; many PC-installed bases may just want to limit hardware upgrades.

Your image system sounds similar to HyperCard. Users can click on any part of the object and go directly to another view. I've developed a few HyperCard applications that take full advantage of images (mostly paint and pict). HyperCard's free-form system does have some limitations and isn't as robust as a bonafide DBMS.

Hal: Actually, I'm *pro*-GUI to the extent that I do everything except database work on a Mac.

Jeff: IBM's CUA guide specifically mentions that CUA needs to evolve to include additional techniques for dealing with database applications. So, interface guidelines evolve. Where are we headed?

Peter: I know of a couple of programmers who are blind. To them, GUI is a waste of time. Voice user interfaces aren't.

In 1983 I saw a TI90 (Texas Instruments home computer) that had voice output. Last year, at a computer show in London, I was talking to someone who researches a natural-language query system (which he has on a Sun workstation). He believed that he was three or four years ahead of the rest of the world.... If you typed in something like "Give me the salesman in the southeast who sold less than average last month," the system would divide the sentence into parts of speech. If it didn't understand a word, it asked a series of questions about it and stored the answers in its database for future reference. It was heavily processor-bound (obviously), but it proved a point.

All we need now is a link from this system to voice input. OK, there's more to it than that, but we're a great deal closer than we were six years ago, when VUI was considered (outside of the research labs) to be impossible.

Paul: This sounds like Microrim's CLOUT, circa 1984-85. I believe other products have done the same—Lotus's HAL, for example, which hasn't become terribly popular because of one or more of the following:

(1) Poor implementation

(2) Poor marketing

(3) People don't want/trust it

(4) Too much time needed to train

(5) Too unreliable or too prone to error.

I think (2) can be ruled out, since Lotus is known for marketing. Perhaps a combination of (3), (4), and (5).

Ham: Q&A (even though it's more or less a flat-file system) has had something called the Intelligent Assistant for awhile. *If* you train it well (in other words, told it about your data and the synonyms you might use), it can answer questions quite well. It, too, is pretty slow at parsing sentences, but I know people who use it and love it. The new version of Q&A (4.0) is supposed to be much faster and better at this.

I'd like to see a query facility that combined free-form English-language queries with point-and-shoot stuff like Fox 2.0's RQBE. If the user could shift between query interfaces in the middle of a query in an attempt to get something across to the system, that user could probably do some very interesting things.

Peter: Paul, I tend to agree, but (3) stands out: People don't want/trust it.

It's like the voice user interface. Training is minimal because you speak your own language. Option (5)—too unreliable—may be true, but the system I saw (*not* CLOUT) was very reliable. Believe me, I spent three hours trying to junk it! Admittedly, that isn't a valid test, but it sure stood up to some strange words.

I still get the feeling that we have a situation where the techies want to preserve their domain and the users don't like new innovations. I realize that is a negative attitude, but in general (on this side of the pond) that's what we find.

Hal: The only voice user interface I've seen is the Voice Navigator on the Mac, and if you have two hands to type with it adds very little value. It basically replaces QuicKeys, a program that lets you define macros that you access with keyboard shortcuts. A real application might be taking in-store inventory, and I suppose it would be great for controlling the temperature and bubble level in the spa, but I don't think it will have much impact until artificial intelligence has advanced to the stage where I can ask for the sales results by territory since a week ago last Tuesday (in those words) and the computer will get them for me.

David: I did some natural-language research for data systems, and the real problem is that even when you've produced a correct answer you can't be 100% sure you have the *complete* correct answer. Determining accuracy is difficult if you're 90% sure that you're 100% correct. Is that usable? It depends on the effect of not being not 100% correct. For browsing, feeling your way around the program is fine—you're just using it as a tool to zero in on the solution—but for decision making, natural language interfaces are not mature enough. I think the next big step will be some graphical query mechanism that goes far beyond QBE in presentation (mouse-driven) and in the choice of operators. Now if it can be customized for an individual, with macros and perhaps user-definable operators, I could see a great increase in productivity and querying power. This is where I would put my development time; give natural language five more years.

Jeff: Perhaps we'll see that graphical query mechanism in FoxPro 3.0....

CHAPTER 3

Models of Maintainability

by Alan Schwartz

Applications development is changing. Organizations are demanding more from their custom database applications—more robust features, more flexibility, more adaptability, more durability, and more openness to user involvement and enhancement. The single-purpose, "black box" applications of the past are no longer sufficient.

FoxPro 2.0 delivers tremendous data-crunching power, as well as an agile suite of tools that invite rapid prototyping. Both features simplify the task of building easy-to-use applications, but harnessing FoxPro requires new skills.

Developers must abandon the traditional method of building applications: Design the entire system as a single monolithic unit, code it in a single pass, and walk away. New applications must be able to survive repeated rounds of modification and end-user torture testing. They need to be hardware-independent, easy to reengineer and test while in use, and user-extensible without programming. Most importantly, they must be designed and built to be effectively maintained by many different programmers. Building this kind of application requires new design and coding skills.

The design ideas and techniques in this chapter are components of a maintainable core for application development. Some are relevant to every new system, while others may be overkill for simple, one-user applications.

Though all of the following points are part of a maintainability strategy, this chapter attempts *not* to be:

- A tedious discourse on the value of embedding comments in your programs
- A lecture on why you should embrace *my* naming conventions

- A sermon in worship of relational theory
- Yet another repetition of the complaint that FoxPro doesn't have a data dictionary and the hopelessness of doing any *real* work until it does. (I'm certain that Fox Software fully appreciates the importance of a comprehensive data dictionary at the core of FoxPro applications. I'm equally confident that the company will add one, in time.)

This chapter *does* present:

- A group of proven techniques for making applications easier to maintain (see Table 3.1)
- A discussion of how these techniques fit into a comprehensive application-development strategy that can extend usability and reduce maintenance of complex applications without sacrificing efficient construction.

Table 3-1. Components of a maintainable model.

Model Components
Normalized data designs (that is, normalized within reason)
Centralized and organized application meta-data
A standardized environment
Naming standards
Organization, classification, and segregation of program code
Development and maintenance of library procedures
Plans for testing
Practical documentation
User-modifiable application components

The Problem

Good developers follow a basic two-step pattern in application development: Analyze patterns in the activity, then write the programs to fit.

But professional developers are the perfect example of the shoemaker's children going barefoot. Independent contractors are caught between the pressure to complete the current project and the fear of unemployment when it's done. Corporate developers have different problems: application backlogs, the unending stream of user requests, budgets, and the inevitable politics of information access. As a result, both groups are under intense pressure to complete projects as quickly as possible.

We have good reason to be concerned about development speed. First, by the time an application is commissioned, users need it badly. Second, the longer the application takes to build, the more likely that the requirements will change before it's complete, resulting in the budget-trashing, moving-target syndrome.

Few projects are free of budget and deadline pressures, but the pressure to go fast is often a false economy. What now appears to be a quick way of getting a job done can result in substantially more work in the future. It comes down to the question of whether to pay a small price now or a big one later.

For developers, that price is maintenance. On larger projects, up to 80% of the total cost of an application over its life cycle is spent on maintenance-related items: enhancements, fixes, redocumentation, retraining, and technical support. For long-lived applications like accounting and payroll, this number can exceed 90%.

Even if you halve development costs, you've still only reduced the overall cost by 10%. If you cut *maintenance* costs by half, you'd see some real savings.

Every application you write places a maintenance burden on your time. If you've done a careless job, that burden might be 10% of your time. If you build and test in a more disciplined way, each application might take only 5% of you time to maintain. Whether you're careless or careful, however, the result is the same: The maintenance burden reduces the time you have available for new development.

If you don't have a strategy for maintainability, each new application brings you one step closer to being overwhelmed by maintenance, giving rise to intense claustrophobia and the desire to be in a different line of work. To survive, you need a way to *conquer* maintenance, not just reduce it.

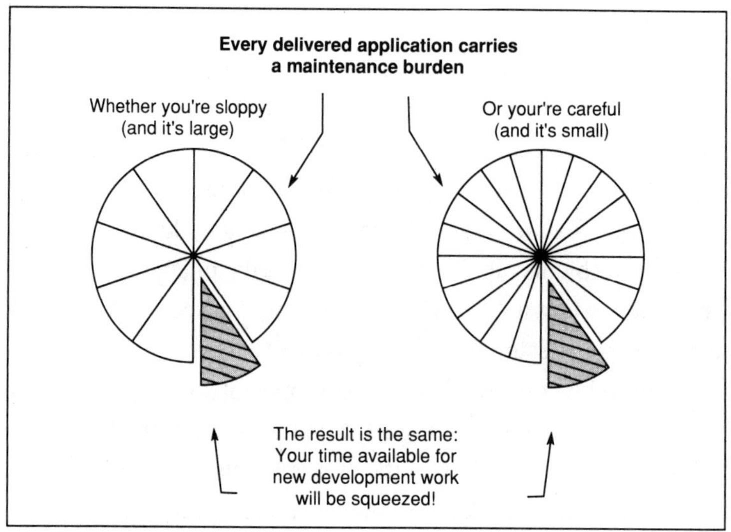

Figure 3-1. Whether you're a careful or careless developer, your availability for new work will ultimately be squeezed by the maintenance burden.

Doesn't FoxPro 2.0 solve the problem of maintainability? Yes and no. It extends the limits on PC application size and complexity by an order of magnitude and offers unprecedented power to users of all skill levels. But by extending the threshold of what can be done and making it look so easy, FoxPro invites ambitious development ideas that can quickly become large, unfocused, hard-to-understand (let alone maintain) applications full of work-arounds that increase the maintenance burden. This has been the pattern with every popular PC database.

Consider dBASE II. Ten years ago, it was a breakthrough product. Delivering the novel concept of data management via a "natural language" to the PC, dBASE opened database application development to a whole new class of self-trained programmers and users.

The result? Wave after wave of developers attempted increasingly ambitious applications with dBASE II that pushed it far beyond its internal data-handling capabilities. Because of the flexibility provided by its programming language, however, many creative work-arounds were engineered to overcome its limitations. Thousands of "impossible" applications were successfully developed, and dBASE gained the largest following of any major database product of its time. The penalty was added complexity that often confused even the applications' authors.

For example, you could circumvent dBASE II's limit of two open data files by swapping files in its two work areas and creating several temporary files. But such an application would exact a high price when modifications were needed, and an even higher price later when it was rewritten (by the same programmer, who had to rethink it, or by a different programmer, who first had to figure out how it worked).

dBASE III, with its 10 work areas, did away with the two-data-file limit. It also spawned a whole new generation of users hungry for more and more capabilities. The cycle was repeated when dBASE III+ users discovered the 15-file limit. The result was another round of costly maintenance and rewriting.

FoxPro is no exception to history. It will invite uses its authors never even dreamed of. But the challenges of maintainability remain—they simply move outward to a new boundary. FoxPro 2.0 has leapfrogged past the limits of competitors (for example, by allowing simultaneous access to 25 database files, each with unlimited indexing via CDXs). But within months of its release, FoxPro application builders will be demanding support for ever more complex data relationships and simultaneous, event-driven access to multiple screens. As these features are delivered, new maintenance "gotchas" will begin to appear.

While tools like FoxPro's screen designer greatly assist in maintaining screen designs, consider the application with screens sporting the look and feel of a video game, dozens of data files, hundreds of index tags, and a thousand variables. How is such an assemblage going to look when it's time for minor surgery?

Maintenance Failures

The Dead Application

It's the classic postmortem, a scene repeated thousands of times over the last 25 years in businesses of all sizes. Consultant and clients are gathered around a PC like guests at a funeral, eyes cast down. The consultant's face reflects genuine sympathy while delivering the judgment: "I'm sorry, but it's a mess. It'll have to be rewritten."

Or, in a variation on the theme: "Well...I could fix it, but I must warn you that it would probably be cheaper to rewrite it."

I've witnessed this scenario, and even played a role in it, more times than I'd care to admit. Every experienced developer has maintenance war stories. In most cases, our crime was not incompetence but in responding to changes over time. As Gerald Weinberg says in his book *The Secrets of Consulting*, "Things are the way they are because they got that way." But if you're serious about learning how to prevent maintenance failures, take the first lesson to heart: Good intentions alone never prevent them.

Just One More Minor Change...

Applications that have to be scrapped and rewritten are the most dramatic examples of maintenance failure, but they aren't the only ones. Have you ever set out to make "one little change," only to see bugs appear in a previously stable application? Or perhaps you've had one of those "this can't be happening to me" nightmares—watching yourself waste enough time to write an entire new program when your goal was to fix one minor problem. Often the reason for this mini-drama is a deeper structural design flaw. If the code logic had only been organized into a library, the data had been normalized, or a tool had been controlling the process, the problem could have been avoided.

The following are some of the traps to avoid when building applications engineered for maintainability.

Private Knowledge

Private knowledge is a serious problem in an application. The more creative the wizard, the more archeology will be needed to piece together how the application was created after he or she's gone. And if you can't figure out how an application does what it does, it's guaranteed you'll be rewriting it.

The need for a standardized approach to application architecture is intensified in FoxPro because it gives you so many ways to accomplish a task. Many of the techniques presented here will help prevent the "departed-expert" scenario from hobbling your applications.

Nonnormalized Data Designs

Nonnormalized data designs are a maintenance liability because they often depend on a stash of private knowledge. One of my first applications was for a quality-control group that needed a way to tally up to six defects on each job. I designed the application around a single data file structured to hold basic job-ID information and six defect-ID fields. This simple design made it especially easy to build the data-entry screen. To report the frequency of defects, a procedure scanned the data file six times for defect IDs, copied them into a temporary file, and counted them from there. And it worked.

As any student of relational design will tell you, however, this is an incorrect database design. If the users later needed eight slots for fault IDs, a programmer might reasonably assume that he or she could simply add fault-ID fields to the entry file and place *GET*s for them on the entry screen (*GET mErr7*, *GET mErr8*,...). Report forms would also need new fields. But the procedural logic to tally the defects, needed in most of the system's reports, would be sabotaged by such an alteration. The programmer would likely be unaware of the need to modify the program that prepares the temp file until a user detected missing data in the reports. The nonnormalized data design forced the *knowledge* of how to tally the defects *out* of the data itself and *into* the programs, where it's easily overlooked and, therefore, at perpetual risk of being unwittingly broken (a "dormant bug").

Metadata: The Application's Roadmap

Many bugs and maintenance problems are caused not by coding errors, but by conceptual errors in the application's overall design. It's at the design level that the operational specifications, the "DNA" that comprises the core characteristics that make a payroll program different from a portfolio analyzer, is stored. In relational jargon, this is known as *metadata* (information about information), and much of it can be assembled into tables (see Table 3-2). It has several components: data structures, index definitions, and relationships, of course, but also screen layouts, formatting requirements, data validation rules, user preferences, and so on.

Table 3-2. Metadata is information about the application and how it's put together.

Type of Metadata	Used For	Where to Store
List of Data Files	Opening files Reindexing files Diagnostics Ad-hoc query/report routines Technical documentation	Stored in DOS directory or A single .PRG that opens everything or A data file you define (see example)
List of Fields	Ad-hoc query/report routines Ad-hoc sort selection Change file structures programmatically Technical documentation Entity-relationship modeling work	Read from .DBF header or A data file you define
List of Index Keys	Ad-hoc query/report routines (sort orders) Ad-hoc sort selection Rebuild indexes programmatically Technical documentation	Read from the .CDX or .IDX files, or a data file you define
Data Validation Rules	Data validation checks in data entry or data import	.PRG files (UDFs) or One or more data files (if the rules can be table-ized)
Menus	Generating menu programs On-the-fly modifications Security activated menus	Menu design objects or Data file

Table 3-2. Metadata is information about the application and how it's put together. *cont.*

Type of Metadata	Used For	Where to Store
Screens	Generating screen programs Screens requiring on-the-fly modification or user-specified degrees of flexibility	Screen design objects or Data file
List of Workstations	User preferences, hardware variations security implications	Data file
List of Users	Security Preferences	Data file

Scattered Metadata

In FoxPro, the metadata can be embedded in data-file headers, index-tag expressions, procedural logic, memory-variable files, and so on. In addition, FoxPro stores metadata in the screen-, menu-, and report-design objects. This open-architecture approach (in FoxPro 2.0, these design objects are all tables) offers great advantages in compatibility and access but tends to spread the metadata all over the application.

One example of scattered metadata concerns field sizes. In FoxPro 2.0's screen designer, a field's width on the screen and its width in the data structure are unrelated. Yet a width is hard-coded into every screen program (unless you modify FoxPro's screen generation program GENSCRN.PRG). Thus, if you need to expand a field size, you'll have to hunt around for every reference to it in screen-design objects.

Buried Metadata

Metadata you can't find is a huge obstacle to maintainability. Metadata that exists only in the program code was probably known only to the person who wrote the application and was probably so obvious to him that he was unlikely to document it except as program comments. Even if he was conscientious enough to leave clear comments, you're likely to find them the hard way—after you've encountered the problem. It's like writing down the combination of your safe so you won't forget it, then tucking it away inside the safe so it won't get lost.

Redundant Metadata

Another problem is redundant metadata. For example, an application might presume a basic "view": Certain data files are always open, and some relationships are always asserted. When you wish to introduce a modification that adds a new file to the system, in how many places must you adjust the program? There's no sure way to find out. Compounding the problem, FoxPro 2.0 now allows environments to be embedded in every screen and report. While this feature greatly simplifies life for casual users and novice developers, it makes subsequent modification risky unless you find and modify every instance where the view is embedded.

Inaccessible Constructs

There are many ways of programming FoxPro. Besides writing procedural code, you can draw screens with the screen designer, set up data views in the View window and embed them in screens and reports, store browse preferences for reuse in the resource file, and even play back keystroke sequences with the keyboard macro facility.

If you can't return to the source of the instruction, however—whether it's a screen-design object or a keyboard macro file—you'll lose the hours you saved (and more) when it's time to maintain what you built. For example, if you change the system menu, you're liable to break any keyboard macros that automate menu selections. At least macros can be edited in FoxPro 2; a nastier problem is buried in a browse preference, as we shall see.

If you change a field name, the preference breaks and you'll have no direct way to repair it. An application that relies on inaccessible constructs like browse preferences or view files is inherently unmaintainable. If you're still skeptical, ask any developer who used browse preferences extensively in FoxPro 1.02 how his or her 2.0 upgrade went. And be sure to duck. (Note: Chapter 4 shows how you can turn your keyboard macro file into a readable document that can be edited and "recompiled" back into a keyboard macro file.)

Clone-and-Modify

Once you have a particularly nice feature working just the way you want it to, you may be tempted to clone and modify that routine the next time you need something similar. If you're being paid by the line of code produced, it's hard to blame you, but this shortcut is the kiss of death for maintainability. The problem is, as soon as you copy a routine and make even a single change, you've got two distinct maintenance objects to support. If you later discover a bug in one module, you'll never know if the bug exists in the clones you made from that routine (you'll most likely not remember how many siblings you spawned from that module). If the bug has been propagated, you probably can't easily retrofit a fix without risking the creation of new bugs because each clone is different.

When attempting to modify a program in which the clone-and-modify technique was used, you enter a minefield of problems. If you change a piece of user-interface code, you risk making it visually inconsistent with other parts of the application. To remedy this, you'll have to make similar modifications to several (perhaps dozens) of programs. The work increases geometrically, as does the likelihood of introducing new bugs along with the new features.

Death by Temp File

Applications that rely on an abundance of temporary files, passing data from file to file, are easy to build but hard to maintain. I've seen many examples where a developer, perhaps backed into a corner by one or more of the problems mentioned earlier, "solved" an enhancement-request problem by creating a duplicate set of data. This approach is usually self-defeating, creating even more maintenance problems downstream.

Just When You Thought You Understood the Rules...

There's a wild West story about a greenhorn who takes on some locals in a high-stakes poker match. Things heat up when the greenhorn is dealt a full house and is taken to the limit by an old-timer, who lays down a 2, 3, 4, 5, and 7. As the greenhorn reaches for the pot, the old-timer stops him. "Not so fast, son; this here hand's an Old Cat." Pointing to a sign on the wall reading "An Old Cat Beats Anything," he chuckles and rakes in the pot.

The greenhorn is furious, but the onlookers verify the old-timer's claim, so he plays on. Toward dawn, he is dealt a 2, 3, 4, 5, and 7 and bets the limit until his money is exhausted. Proudly laying down his hand, he reaches for the pot, but the old-timer—who has called him with a pair of queens—stops him again and points to another sign across the room: "Only One Old Cat Good Per Night."

dBASE's *SET <you name it>* commands are the Old Cat of programming. Although the effects of these environment-modifying directives (nearly 100 of them) vary widely, the dBASE language offers them in a single alphabetical list with no distinction as to impact. They run the gamut of:

- Useful specialty commands suited to developers' diverse requirements. (For example, *SET DEFAULT* performs a useful DOS *CHDIR* as well as choosing a new default path for FoxPro. *SET BLOCKSIZE* is handy when you're using memo fields extensively.)

- Vestiges of prehistoric times. Commands like *SET SCOREBOARD* and *SET INTENSITY* are essentially brain dead but are offered for dBASE product/language compatibility. You'll rarely, if ever, use them.

- The Old Cats—the ones that wreak havoc on an otherwise stable application by making global changes to core processing rules. Some of the remaining *SET* commands have profound, often devastating effects on the behavior of the dBASE data engine (*SET DELETED*, *SET EXACT*, and *SET DECIMALS*, for example). Flipping just one of these *SET* states can blow holes in application segments that appeared to be running smoothly. Applications that use *SET* states "creatively" to modify the database environment will drive you crazy.

Programmed-in Job Insurance

Many applications show signs of permanently embedded dependence on programmer intervention. Some programmers have, unconsciously or otherwise, locked users into highly constrained black-box applications. This "feature," when added to some of the problems already described, practically guarantees that the maintenance time bomb will detonate. And when it does, the postmortem scenario is imminent.

Maintainable applications need much more independence from the programmer who built them than did the PC database applications of the '80s. The requirement that a programmer be called to tweak a report, produce a different sort order, or support a new printer will no longer be acceptable.

Components of a Maintainability Strategy

To avoid these problems altogether, start by establishing a clear structure for the application's metadata and gaining programmable control of the most important parts. By building utility programs whose behavior is directly controlled by the metadata, you'll gain geometrically increased functionality and control. And as you'll see, applications that work directly from the metadata can often be modified later without additional programming.

Taken as a whole, this chapter does not present a group of unrelated tips and techniques, but rather the components of a single strategy: to apply the principles of data normalization to the metadata in your applications. The benefit is that you'll never have to rewrite any of my FoxPro applications, and I'll never have to rewrite any of yours.

Normalizing Metadata

Having read this far, you're probably convinced of the virtues of a normalized database architecture: All redundancy within the data is eliminated (greatly simplifying maintenance), and you're assured of a single, predictable path (table, field, and unique key) guaranteeing access to each piece of information in the system.

The benefits are just as great if you collect and control the metadata, the repository of information about the application and the nerve center of its maintainability. A critical element of design, therefore, is deciding exactly where the metadata is best stored and how to maintain it in a comprehensive, controllable form.

Consider the following simple commands, written a million times in dBASE to initialize a memvar prior to *GET/READ*:

```
STORE SPACE(20) to m.Name
```

or

```
STORE SPACE(LEN(Name)) to m.Name
```

What's the difference? None, as long as the Name field has a length of 20. But what happens when the users decide that field needs to be 24 or 16 characters long? The second line is adaptable—it will work regardless of length—while the first line will become a bug if Name's length changes.

The principle is important here, not the details of coding technique. In dBASE, the application draws its behavior in regard to field sizes from the data file header. Line 2 in the example references the header, but line 1 makes a copy of a piece of it. It's an instance of redundancy and as big a threat to maintainability as the data redundancy we try to eliminate by normalizing our data design.

To normalize our application's metadata, we need to take a second look at where it resides. When FoxPro provides a logical place to hold metadata, we'll gladly use it. In other cases, we'll build our own if we have to. In many instances, several good alternatives offer trade-offs between simplicity and functionality. Our goal is to have a single point of reference for each type of metadata.

This construct supports a rational maintenance strategy that reduces the risk of bugs during modifications. It also creates a foundation for generic utilities that don't just work whenever they're called from the current application; they'll *always* work. They're a bit more demanding to write, but the payoff is in having to write them only once, while reusing them at will. Building applications is then like assembling Lego toys—at the end of each component is a hook for the next one.

Field Names and Attributes

Since data file structures are stored in the file header, *COPY STRUCTURE* and *AFIELDS()* can provide field names and attributes on demand. This is handy if you're giving users the ability to pick fields, as in an ad hoc quick-report feature. And it's self-maintainable—you don't have to change the program that builds the list if you add fields to the files or change a field name.

In big systems, however, dBASE's 10-character field names can become quite cryptic. If you require longer, clearer descriptors for fields, or if an application needs a bulletproof way for users to define new fields on the fly, you might build a utility that maintains a data file containing file-structure information, including longer descriptors. If you do, always refer to *that* file as the source of your field-name pop-ups or to rebuild data structures when necessary.

Our "field dictionary" file-maintenance screen supports structure changes in both directions. It lets you add or change fields in your file list, then rebuilds the data files automatically. It also imports new and changed file headers into the file list, where all you add are the descriptions.

Inventory or Data Files

FoxPro provides no storage slot for an inventory of data files, but we can easily build one ourselves. Besides providing a source from which to print an application data dictionary, it can control a generic file-opening utility that replaces the embedded "views" described above.

Index Tags

The *TAG()* function lets you read index tags. If you're building a pop-up that sets a new order for a file being browsed, what options do you offer? Just loop through some calls to *TAG()*, store the return values to an array, and pop it up.

But how did you construct that .CDX file? If you've just built it from the View Window Setup dialog box, how will a user reconstruct it if the .CDX file is trashed? There's an advantage to making the tag definitions explicit in a reindexing utility program with lines like:

```
INDEX on YEAR tag YEAR
INDEX on MAKE + MODEL tag MAKE_MODEL
INDEX on LICENSE tag LICENSE        &&...
```

If you moved these specs to a data file, however, you could easily create a generic program that would work in all your applications, regardless of the number of files or tags. Whether you choose the data-file or program-file method, be aware that's where you're placing the metadata. When you need a new tag, you'll define it in that one place.

General Components

FoxPro's project manager does a fine job storing the miscellaneous components of an application—screens, memory variable files (.mem) reports, keyboard macro definitions, and so on. I recommend you allow the project manager to catalog all your miscellaneous read-only components in the project file. Since it's just a standard .DBF with a different extension (.PJX), you can easily open it and read its contents when necessary.

Data-validation Logic

What about highly customized, case-specific data-entry validation, such as "Reject freight charge as a cost type if the amount is over $50 and the shipping location is within the 940xx zip-code area"? To enforce this, you would build some *IF...ELSE* logic.

In this case, the program lines themselves contain the validation metadata. The screen designer invites you to store the validation metadata in the VALID code for the entry field. But what if you want to execute the same validity check on multiple screens? Resist the temptation to clone the code. Instead, write a free-standing user-defined function (UDF) and invoke it from the *GET* fields by entering its name as an expression in the VALID code. This way, you'll only have to make one adjustment in the application if the rule changes.

On the other hand, don't go to extremes. Defining a data file to hold file names is the beginning of a data dictionary. I don't recommend trying to build a complete data-driven data dictionary unless you're writing an extremely complex application. Fox Software will undoubtedly define a data-dictionary standard in upcoming releases. There's no point inventing elaborate, self-styled systems that will become obsolete as soon as an industry standard arrives. So use common sense and apply the 80-20 rule: Select the 20% of the work that will yield 80% of the benefits.

Normalized Data Design

Sidestepping a discussion of relational theory, we know that maintainability is vastly enhanced when database designs conform to third normal form. The primary benefit of normalized data is the creation of an unambiguous path to every element of stored data in the system. Because the combination of table name, field name, and key to access each data element is unique, you don't need to embed access logic (in other words, directions) in your programs as you would in the quality-control application described earlier. If you build tables to hold your application's metadata (elements of a data dictionary), these should be normalized as well.

Performance considerations occasionally dictate compromises in relational rules. The best way to do this is to know the rules and normalize the database before implementing compromises. FoxPro 2.0's data engine is strong enough that fewer compromises are needed. When you must compromise a normalized design, however, you should understand the implications up front and provide the necessary program logic to compensate for the redundancy you're introducing into the data. Build in the diagnostic and maintenance routines from the beginning; you'll need them eventually, in any case. Document these routines carefully—and not just in the code itself—or they'll become instances of buried metadata.

An example: We built a large budgeting application that needed to hold nearly 100,000 detail records. A series of subdepartment screens showed budgeted and actual amounts for the year to date. Flashing through these screens quickly while summing the detail records for each account was impossible, so we chose to store balances in a second summary file and update them in real time as details were added.

The code to compensate for this redundant data consisted of:

- A program that locked and updated summary records with adjusted balances whenever a detail record was entered
- A batch utility to check each balance against its associated detail records and report any discrepancies in an error log
- A batch utility to rebuild all balances from detail records.

These programs compensated for the redundancy in the system by detecting inconsistencies in the data, then reporting and reconciling them.

Naming Standards

Many developers, while grudgingly acknowledging that naming files and fields systematically is a good practice, fail to exploit the power of naming standards. I've been shocked to find that many commercial source-code libraries for dBASE products fail to implement even basic naming standards. Among other problems, the names don't indicate which routines depend on each other, making it hard to extract a small group of functions from the library into an application.

When a good naming standard for procedures is used, a glance at the file name can tell you the type of activity—such as report, batch, or screen process, validator, calculating function, or dialog box—as well as the general applicability and "ownership" (fully generic, generic within an application, or specific to one screen or context, plus the ID of the application or subapplication to which it belongs).

When naming variables, don't pepper your code with instances of *X*, *I*, *jawbone*, or other meaningless names. If the variable belongs to a single procedure or family, incorporate that information into the name somehow (for example, *RptPageCtr* is better than *P*). You'll appreciate the difference when you run global cross-references or need to do a text search through the entire application.

When a project is too big for one developer to complete, naming standards are the glue that binds the work of individual programmers into a seamless unit. The bigger and more complex the project, the greater the benefit of deciding on a clear set of standards at the start.

Built-in Testability

Everyone agrees that systems should be tested. The trouble is, it's hard to get anyone to do it. You must budget for test time during development, then build the system with support for a test mode. A properly scaled test plan will increase users' confidence, yield a more stable and maintainable result, and pay for itself many times over.

Programmer self-testing stops the first time an application works correctly. After that, the programmer tests to see that the program works, not to find where it doesn't. Don't count on the person who wrote the code to test it.

End users are also less-than-ideal testers. This is a time-consuming and frustrating task, and they're usually impatient to start using the system for real work. Besides, their workload actually *increases* during the testing/cutover period before it gets better. It's no wonder users often do a poor job of reporting exactly what they were doing when the system crashed ("I wasn't doing anything!").

The need for testing doesn't end with installation. In industrial-strength applications, it's just the beginning. You'll need to revisit test mode whenever you deliver enhancements. If a system administrator or primary user can switch a workstation into test mode easily, a good test suite will be a terrific asset in training new users on the system.

To benefit from testing, your plan must include:

- A testing budget
- A realistic staffing plan
- A generous schedule
- A plan for building a suite of test data (this might have to be updated as the application is modified)
- Enough disk space for two copies of the test suite: one for testing and a second that can be used to reset the system if the test data is damaged
- A menu-selectable program that toggles the application between test and production modes (and data sets).

Casually built FoxPro 2.0 systems aren't easy to switch into test mode. Because of built-in default assumptions about the paths to data files, swapping a new set of data into a large application will be awkward. You'll be tempted to create a second copy of the application's .APP file instead, creating yet another maintenance liability. For more ambitious systems, therefore, you should engineer a pathing strategy into the application that lets users toggle between test and production modes directly.

Managing the Directory Path

To maintain compatibility, FoxPro inherited dBASE's somewhat bizarre method of directory path management. The permissiveness of the *SET PATH* command creates opportunities for ambiguity, exposing you to the risk of reading and writing files in places you never intended. This can cause trouble in larger systems.

You might think the *SET PATH TO* command gives FoxPro the information it needs to find your files because you can specify a whole series of paths to be searched. The problem is that the command is so permissive, you'll create unanticipated results. Even the simple commands

```
USE XXFILE
```

and

```
COPY TO TEMP FOR <any condition>
```

may give you a temp file in a directory other than the one in which XXFILE is located. The problem worsens if you have two or more subsystems in different directories and have to open files from both.

In more complex systems, use an explicit pathing convention within the application code to access your data files. Our applications rely on a group of global variables (we initialize them from a one-record control file) to hold paths to data files, report forms and other utility files, screen objects, application source code, and library source code. FoxPro supports indirect referencing in every command that names a file, so your programs can read like the code in Listing 3-1.

Listing 3-1. FoxPro lets you use indirect referencing to store a path that you can later join to a file name.

```
STORE "C:\APPATH\" to DR
**  or
**  STORE "C:\TESTPATH\" to DR
*...to initialize a path variable...
*...then, when it's time to open the file...
USE (DR + "INVOICES")  && any FP command that names a file

REPORT FORM (DRRPT + "INVBATCH" ) ;
   TO FILE (DROUTPUT + "INVBATCH.TXT")
```

This way, it's easy to direct file access to either production or test directories. Just run your file opener with the new path, and it's in test mode.

Some of FoxPro 2.0's new features can cause some problems for this approach, however. First, you won't want to generate file-opening commands in screen programs unless you modify GENSCRN.PRG to include your path references. (File opening can be switched off entirely in the Generate dialog box). If the system is large, you're probably better off with your own centralized file-opening procedure anyway, rather than FoxPro's method, which establishes a different view for each screen or report, as described earlier in the section on redundant metadata.

Second, pathing by indirect reference will cause a small glitch when you use FoxPro's SQL *SELECT* statement. SQL *SELECT* can automatically open data files and structural indexes. This is a great convenience, particularly for users, but its *FROM* clause doesn't accept path references (either explicit or indirect). It can only find data files in the current *SET DEFAULT* or *SET PATH* directories. Therefore, when pathing by indirect reference, you have to open any files from other paths first, then reference them by alias when using an SQL *SELECT* command.

Standardizing the Application Environment

The best way to cure the "Old Cat" syndrome and an entire class of infuriating bugs in FoxPro applications is to develop a set of baseline environment rules to be followed throughout your application. Establish the internal rule that every program deviating from the standard must return the environment to its original settings before exiting.

As mentioned earlier, the dBASE *SET <you_name_it>* commands can radically modify the behavior of the data engine. The side effect of just one command may be major run-time computing errors. You may have built an entire application with *SET EXACT OFF*, for example. But if a newly added module to the application turns it ON, you'll have a hard time figuring out why your relations are suddenly broken. These bugs are particularly nasty because the symptoms appear far from the source of the problem.

You can banish this type of bug from your projects by applying the principles of scoping to environment-modifying commands. At the top of every application, call a standard initialization module to establish *SET* positions for every relevant command. From then on, if you need to change one or more of these in a program, code it as shown in Listing 3-2.

Listing 3-2. Using a variable to handle resetting any changed environment settings.

```
PRIVATE WAS_EXACT
STORE SET("EXACT") to WAS_EXACT
SET EXACT ON

**... Your code goes here.

**... Switch SETs back again if there are
**... any internal callouts.

IF WAS_EXACT = "OFF"
   SET EXACT OFF
ENDIF

RETURN
```

Don't call out to external functions or procedures without resetting any "altered states" to their standard values. The same technique can be applied to *ON* commands, colors, active windows, and work areas. Get in the habit of declaring private variables to hold information about existing states of the environment, then resetting from these at the end of the module.

This technique is easier to apply if you also uphold the coding standard of a single entry and exit point for each module. Use *EXIT* to break out of loops when you need to drive processing out through the *RETURN*. This will greatly reduce the number of side effects in your programs.

Developing Library Procedures

Library procedures are probably the single most important part of a maintainability strategy. This isn't a new discovery; in the 1970s it was known in MIS departments as *reusable code*. It has recently reappeared under the banner *object-oriented programming*.

Whatever you call it, a strong procedure library is a substantial investment but returns equally substantial benefits:

- Application development is streamlined because time isn't spent reinventing the wheel.
- Bug fixes can be retroactively applied to all applications sharing the library, without reengineering.
- Enhancements to the library become transparently available to all applications built on them.
- When members of the development team have the same architectural perspective, they can support each other's code even if a project or component is new to them.
- Weaker team members can accomplish more, and their productivity is improved, rather than their being shunted off to low-priority tasks.

Library development also requires the biggest ongoing investment, discouraging many developers from trying at all. A wiser approach is to build the library incrementally, adding modules driven by the needs of current projects. Need a letter writer, for example? Do the job properly once, and it will be available for all your applications, past and future.

If you don't need a letter writer just yet, set this task aside for now. Maybe you'll see one published on CompuServe, in a Fox newsletter, or in FoxPro's sample applications and won't need to invent it. Deciding when to implement and when to procrastinate is important in library development.

Defining a Library Program

A generic procedure (or function) is one that always accomplishes a given task, independent of the details of the application in which it is used.

When is a procedure or function *not* generic?

- When it names any files or fields of a specific application explicitly.

- When it enforces a rule (as in the validation example discussed earlier) that is highly specific to a single application.
- When it directs a batch process that is highly customized to a specific application.

You perform a task *generically*, on the other hand, by reading specifications about which objects to act upon from data files rather than from hard-coded identifiers in programs, or by using native FoxPro functions to "read" information about specific objects being managed. For example, *SYS(2000)* tells you about files on disk; *DBF()* and *ALIAS()* tell you about open files; and *WOUTPUT()* tells you which window is active for output.

Once you become accustomed to thinking about code this way, this type of program can produce amazing results. And it's not confined to procedural mechanics; look at the utility screens that come with FoxPro 2.0 and you'll see very powerful user-interface screen objects that are also entirely generic.

Suppose we're building an eight-file relational system and want a high level of maintainability. Rather than relying on FoxPro to reset the environment for each screen and report, we've decided to centralize management of the data environment.

We build a file—DBFLIST.DBF, in this case—that has one record for each data file in the system. Typical fields include file name, description, and perhaps a flag (*ALWAYSOPEN*) to indicate whether this file will always be open or opened on demand.

```
Structure for database:    DBFLIST.DBF
Number of data records:      5
Date of last update:       07/07/91
Field   Field Name      Type        Width    Dec    Index
    1   DBFNAME         Character   8
    2   DESCRIP         Character   20
    3   ALWAYSOPEN      Logical     1
                        ** Total ** 30
```

Sample contents of DBFLIST.DBF:

Record#	DBFNAME	DESCRIP	ALWAYSOPEN
1	CUST	Customer file	.T.
2	INVOICE	Invoice file	.F.
3	EMPLOY	Employee file	.T.
4	VEND	Vendor file	.T.
5	TRANS	Transaction file	.T.

At its core will be a loop that reads the file to determine which files are specified for opening, as in Listing 3-3.

Listing 3-3. A loop to centralize management of the environment by opening files from an array of file names.

```
******************
PROCEDURE FILEOPEN    && bare bones
******************
** For now, assume no files are open.
USE DBFLIST
COPY TO ARRAY OPENDBF FIELDS DBFNAME ;
   FOR ALWAYSOPEN    && requesting flag in the file

** or, for those preferring the SQL SELECT version...

SELECT Dbfname FROM Dbflist WHERE Alwaysopen INTO ARRAY opendbf

FOR OPENCTR = 1 to ALEN(OPENDBF)
   USE (DR + OPENDBF(OPENCTR)) IN (OPENCTR)
   ** Note indirect reference for path, file name, and work
   ** area.
ENDFOR
RETURN
```

This procedure can be run once during application start-up. To switch the application into test mode easily, issue a *CLOSE DATABASES*, store the test directory path to *DR*, and call it again.

This procedure will work in any application that has a DBFLIST.DBF. As we add files to the system, we build the metadata by adding records to DBFLIST.DBF. We get new functionality and a second benefit: The technical documentation has been assembled for easy reporting.

FoxPro supports easy transfer of file data to a memory object with the *COPY TO ARRAY* and SQL *SELECT* commands. Once the array is open, the *ALEN()* function lets us know how many times we'll have to loop.

Couldn't we do all this without DBFLIST? Maybe. FoxPro has functions to read the file names from the disk directory, but we'd have nowhere to store descriptions or other attributes (such as when a file should be opened). If we could do without those items, the metadata could be the DOS directory (the existance of the file on disk). If a file is accidentally erased, however, the program has no way of knowing that something is missing until it tries to access the data. From a maintenance perspective, there's no audit trail.

The Modifiable Library Environment

Passing parameters into a generic program allows you to tailor its behavior to a specific purpose. Suppose we wished to open different data files to support two views—AR and AP, in this case. We would select a view by passing a parameter and control which files would open from a field in DBFLIST. Now the metadata looks like this:

```
Structure for database:    C:\ACS\DBFLIST.DBF
Number of data records:    5
Date of last update :      07/07/91
 Field  Field Name          Type          Width    Dec    Index
     1  DBFNAME              Character    8
     2  DESCRIP              Character    20
     3  ALWAYSOPEN          Logical       1
     4  INVIEW               Character    12
                            ** Total **   42
```

DBFLIST contains the following records:

Record#	DBFNAME	DESCRIP	ALWAYSOPEN	INVIEW
1	CUST	Customer file	.T.	AR
2	INVOICE	Invoice file	.F.	AR
3	EMPLOY	Employee file	.T.	AR
4	VEND	Vendor file	.T.	AP
5	TRANS	Transaction file	.T.	AR,AP

The code in Listing 3-4 uses the *PARAMETERS()* function to detect whether or not a view parameter has been passed, and the control logic will work in either case. The default behavior, in this example, is to open every file flagged *ALWAYSOPEN* regardless of view.

Listing 3-4. Using the PARAMETERS() function.

```
******************
PROCEDURE FILEOPEN&& enhanced for optional views
******************
** For now, assume no files are open.
PARAMETER VIEWSPEC
IF PARAMETERS() = 0
   COPY TO ARRAY OPENDBF FIELDS DBFNAME ;
      FOR ALWAYSOPEN
ELSE
   COPY TO ARRAY OPENDBF FIELDS DBFNAME ;
      FOR ALWAYSOPEN and VIEWSPEC $ INVIEW
ENDIF

USE DBFLIST
FOR OPENCTR = 1 to ALEN(OPENDBF)
   USE (DR + OPENDBF(OPENCTR)) IN (OPENCTR)
   ** Note indirect reference for path, file name, and work
   ** area.
ENDFOR
RETURN
```

It's a critical characteristic of FoxPro that parameters are always optional unless your program logic fails in the absence of one or more of them. Exploiting this feature is an essential technique when building library routines. By using the *PARAMETERS()* function and assigning carefully chosen default values whenever no parameter is passed, you can add optional features to your library routines with *no effect whatsoever* on applications that already use those routines. The benefit: You can add enhancements to generic programs *after* they're in widespread use.

FoxPro Language Support for Library Routines

FoxPro's extensions to the dBASE language provide strong support for generic procedures. Its major benefits are discussed in the following paragraphs.

Arsenal of Functions

Perhaps it's compensation for the lack of a data dictionary, or maybe it's just that Fox listens to its loyal developers; whatever the reason, FoxPro has an incredible collection of functions that let you "read" from the environment nearly anything you can imagine about data files, records, indexes, relationships, windows, states, and status information. Any status that can be controlled with Fox's 100 *SET <state>* commands or six *ON <event>* commands can be retrieved from the environment on demand with the *SET()* and *ON()* functions. And a number of *SYS()* functions return all kinds of techno-trivia, from the number of files in the user's CONFIG.SYS to the available work-space memory inside FoxPro.

Say you've written a library error routine that needs to post a screen message. It can "ask" the system if output is currently directed to the screen (a report may be in progress). If not, it can capture the current output device with *STORE SET("DEVICE")* to *WAS_DEVICE*, set the device to *SCREEN*, display its message, get the user's keystroke, and reset the device with a *SET DEVICE* command.

Strong Support for Arrays

FoxPro's support for two-dimensional arrays is strong, featuring a full suite of array functions (many of which will be familiar to Clipper programmers) and allowing arrays of up to 3,600 elements (65,000 in FoxProX). In addition:

- You can mix data types freely.
- You can initialize every element in the array with a single command.
- You can reinitialize arrays dynamically without losing existing contents.
- Commands such as *COPY TO ARRAY*, *APPEND FROM ARRAY*, *SCATTER*, *GATHER*, and the SQL *SELECT*'s *TO ARRAY* extension support fast, easy transfer of file data from disk to memory.
- Perhaps most importantly, arrays can be passed as parameters by reference. This feature allows blocks of application-specific information to be passed easily into generic programs. For example, you may pass a list of customers into a generic multitagging dialog box.

Incremental Compiling and Automatic "Make" Facility

By relying on FoxPro's project manager, you'll be relieved of two time-consuming tasks: rebinding and recompiling the entire library every time you change a single program, and checking version dates and times to ensure you're running the latest version in your application.

One warning: If several programmers are working on an application, only one person at a time can use the project-manager tool to open the project file and rebuild the application. Since the project manager doesn't restrict access to source code, screen-design files, and so on, other members of the team may modify them freely. The project-manager tool can keep versions current only if it is aware of the existence of all modules.

Building a Library Program

Building a library from scratch follows a predictable pattern of steps.

1. Recognize the pattern and abstract the problem. You're in the midst of writing a procedure and you recognize something you've needed before or expect you'll need again. Can the task be done generically?
2. Play with the code to get the functionality you want. Don't create extra work for yourself by trying to formalize the routine too early. First capture the

ideas that offer the most functionality. Then build the logical flow. Finally, identify exceptions but don't worry about them yet.

3. Look for application-specific content—field names, file names, hard-coded character strings, and so on. Determine whether any of these are really required in the routine. If so, the routine is not a candidate for a library. If possible, replace them all with function calls, parameters, or other indirect reference.

4. Define a parameter list. Think about the dimensions of control you'd like to have over the routine when it's done. Define parameters to enable this control, even if you don't finish coding all the bells and whistles just yet.

5. Prioritize the parameter list. Based on the program's objective, some parameters may be required for the module to execute; all others are optional. Arrange the required parameters at the front of the *PARAMETERS* list so that calls to the routine need not contain references to every optional parameter.

6. Write a programmatic test for the contents of each optional passed parameter and assign default values for parameters not passed.

7. Try to build in application-independent intelligence. For example, can a lookup utility figure out where best to display itself onscreen? Or can a pick-your-printer dialog be smart enough not to bother you when only one printer is available?

8. Determine a name for the procedure or function. To what class or family does it belong? Choose variable names to identify the program they belong to.

9. Polish any rough edges in the code. Eliminate unnecessary macro expansions (very few are needed in FoxPro 2.0). Reduce code to its most concise form. Add comments. Declare as private any memory variables that aren't passed parameters or globals.

10. Identify any changes to *SET* states within the module. Carefully reset any states that you had to change. To do so, you'll need to store the state you found it in as follows:

```
Private was_device
STORE SET("DEVICE") to was_device
   SET DEVICE TO SCREEN
      ***balance of program
   IF was_device <> "SCREEN"
      SET DEVICE TO &was_device
   endif
```

11. Write a clear, descriptive header block. At a minimum, include:

    - A description of the routine's intended use
    - A definition of the use, limitations, and data type of each parameter (stating which optional parameters are stubbed out for now, if any)
    - A sample call to the routine (which you can cut and paste right into your programs)
    - A list of known side effects
    - A place for maintenance notes.

    Hint: Don't bother requiring programmers to write header information that can be generated by FoxDoc or other documentation utilities. Concentrate on describing the private knowledge publicly.

12. Thoroughly consider the side effects. Most can be eliminated by storing a preexisting state or status to a variable and restoring it before returning from the program. Always make these variables private. It is far easier in the long run to eliminate side effects than to document them.

13. Compile the program to check for syntax errors.

14. Subject the routine to a round of torture-testing. If it supports a screen-based process, mock up a short driver program that lets you test its optional

features and boundaries. Or write a test loop that sends randomly generated parameters to the module. Take a second, critical look at side effects.

15. Write an error-trapping section (this step is optional). If the library is to be used by more than just yourself, consider an error-trapping section at the top of the routine. You can establish a global variable like *G_ERRORCHK* that would be false in production but true during development; there's no need to increase execution time once the application is in daily use. Inside your *IF G_ERRORCHK* branch, run sufficient tests on the parameters to ensure the routine will work correctly. Some useful tests are:

    - The *TYPE("")* function. While a bit slow, it returns the data type of the named element or *U* if undefined.
    - The *EVAL("")* function. Also slower than average but very powerful; it returns the evaluated value of a dBASE expression stored to a character string memory variable (memvar).
    - *BETWEEN()*, *MIN()*, and *MAX()* for testing values within bounds. *EMPTY()* works with all data types.

    If a test fails, a clear, explanatory message in a *WAIT WINDOW* command is sufficient. Don't bother with recovery logic for bad calls; the developer will find out soon enough.

Ongoing Library-Development Strategies

As mentioned earlier, you will not develop a useful library within a single project. It grows over time and in the direction defined by your own development goals. A synergy is created when routines begin to call one another. For example, you'll probably develop a group of alerts, error messages, and modal dialog routines early on. More complex programs can then call these services whenever necessary.

In projects too large for one programmer, coordinating library development among the entire development team yields huge productivity benefits. Here are some tips for coordinating shared use of a core development library.

- Funnel enhancement requests to a list and confers on priorities and schedules.
- Let everyone know when updates are available and test new features as soon as possible. You can maintain a log of even the most obvious changes to the library and keep production applications up to date, fixing bugs before users find them.
- Build an on-line reference tool for programmers using the library. If the documentation is laid out consistently, this task is manageable; simply adopt a format that includes predefined characters to flag each section. One I worked on was built, not surprisingly, around a data file containing one record for each library procedure or function. Fields hold description, status, change date, family, and type information; memo fields hold sample calls, parameter specs, tips, and maintenance notes. This tool includes utilities to:
  - Refresh the file automatically from the contents of the library program headers (which are formatted with characters to flag the different sections)
  - Turn the file into a pop-up programmer's reference (programmers can cut and paste any sample calls into their code)
  - Strip out all headers into a single text file (for updating the documentation in a word processor)
  - Place all program headers back into the programs when the documentation updates are completed.

Gaining a Maintainability Edge with Libraries

The goal is to support updates to every application you build with a single library, just by inserting the new library code—like plugging a new cartridge in a Nintendo machine. If you follow the above development guidelines closely, it's very achievable.

FoxPro's project manager makes it unnecessary to bind programs into a procedure file, which makes FoxPro 1.02's FOXBIND.EXE obsolete—good riddance to the long bind and compile times! If your development and production environments are all located on a single network, just establish one or more subdirectories exclusively for tested, ready-to-run versions of library modules (and utility screens, as well). When the project manager rebuilds an application, the latest and greatest versions of the library routines will be melded into one new application file.

When maintaining many applications supported by the same library, or a single large application at many sites, life is much easier if the library procedures can be kept as a free-standing .APP, rather than merged into a single .APP with the application-specific code. Then you can truly plug an entire generic cartridge into any project—repairing, upgrading, or enhancing its core without rebuilding anything—just by copying in a new object file.

Unfortunately, the project manager makes this a little tougher. As it resolves references during rebuilds, it requires access to all source code, even if the library modules are all marked "Exclude," or if you make a library into an "APP" and bring that into the project. Rebuilding the project generates a "NOT FOUND" error message for each call to the library. Ironically, this assemblage executes just fine, but the error messages are disconcerting, and tend to obscure the *real* errors you *do* want to know about during builds.

Therefore, this final step of partitioning the library into a completely separate, maintainable object requires a workaround. Usually I stay away from "kludges," since they often create maintenance liabilities later, and there's occasionally a risk of their being clobbered by a future version of the DBMS. But for large or multi-site projects, in the inimitable TV words of the Mercedes safety engineer, "Some tings are just too imPAWtant not to shay-ahr."

Here are the steps to create a freestanding library object:

1. Place all your generic procedures into their own project (we'll call it PRCLIB here).

   Here's a shortcut: It's time consuming to point-and-click on these one-by-one. Instead, build a "dummy" program that names each program in the library. It looks like this:

```
** FOR LOADING THE PROCEDURE PROJECT FILE
** DUMMY.PRG **
   DO LIBPROG1
   DO LIBPROG2
   DO LIBSCRN1
   DO LIBSCRN2
      ...etc.
```

When you "build" this project, all the modules in dummy.prg are added to the project automatically. You may then click to remove the "dummy," or click to exclude it from future rebuilds.

2. In the mainline of your production application, place the line

```
SET PROCEDURE TO ("PRCLIB.APP")
```

No, it's not a typo. When you place the library application inside the parentheses and quotes it will execute fine, but dissuades the project manager from automatically including a copy of all its object code in the application project. In this case, it would be of no benefit, and would merely slow down rebuilds.

3. Create one more dummy program (sorry). It should look like this:

```
** ONE CALL FOR EACH PROGRAM IN THE LIBRARY PRCLIB
PROCEDURE LIBPROG1
PROCEDURE LIBPROG2
PROCEDURE LIBSCRN1
PROCEDURE LIBSCRN2
**END OF DUMMY.PRG
```

Add this into the production project, and mark it "Exclude." When you build, the product manager won't report errors on the library programs it can't find.

The benefits of this construct are twofold. First, you may now make updates and enhancements to the library, and have these appear in production applications, *without* rebuilding the production application. Just copy the new PROCLIB.APP over the old one.

Second, specific project rebuilds go much faster—you avoid time-consuming checks of version dates against a voluminous number of generic procedures, which don't change that often, anyway.

There's a downside to FoxPro's SET PROCEDURE command—you are limited to just one active procedure file. If your generic libraries are very large, or contain specialized components, there's a decent workaround for this limitation, which fulfills the original goal of a separate maintainable object for each library.

The trick is to create a "call-back" loop at the top of your program. Your mainline calls one procedure library with a DO..., which in turn calls the second, etc. When all your libraries are open, the last one to open "calls-back" to the mainline, instead RETURNing. Thus all the libraries are available for procedure calls as if they were all opened with SET PROCEDURE TO.

Listing 3-5. Opening multiple library .APP files without SET PROCEDURE TO

```
** ANYAPP.prg
dimension procstak(4)
** size to the number of procedure libraries to open
store "PRCLIBA.APP" to procstak(1)
store "PRCLIBB.APP" to procstak(2)
store "RESTOFAP" to procstak(3)
** This is the rest of the mainline below
store 1 to stakptr
do (procstak(stakptr)) with procstak, stakptr
** Open everything up
return

procedure restofap  && the "procedure file" has been hooked !
parameters procstak, stakptr

** After this point, the rest of the mainline follows
** any procedures in PRCLIBA.APP or PRCLIBB.APP may be called

** End of ANYAPP.app
```

Evaluating the array PROCSTAK will cause DO PRCLIBA.APP command to execute. That library's main segment looks like Listing 3-6.

Listing 3-6. Main segment of PRCLIBA.APP

```
** The Procedure Calling list manager for procedure files
** This code must be designated the 'Main' program
**in a procedure library

parameters proclist, listptr
external array proclist
store listptr + 1 to listptr

** The next procedure named in the array list will be called.
** The last call in the array list chains to the main program.

do (proclist(listptr)) with proclist, listptr
return
```

See ANYAPP.PRG and the module PRCLIB_M on the disk that accompanies this book.

Naming Strategies for Library Procedures

There are many reasons to adopt a naming strategy that recognizes the domain of program files. It's a great way to manage and catalog files without having to remember what those programs do and which ones work together.

Your naming strategy should clearly reflect whether each module is:

- Totally generic (will always work in any application)
- Generic within an application (can be called from anywhere within a specific application)
- Application-specific (works only when and where called and is only called once).

Completely generic modules may be further classified by "family," such as modal interface or event-loop interface, and further by service, such as print, message, menu, metadata, or entry validation. Properly selected, these classifications will allow you to subset a production library and tell at a glance which programs are interdependent.

Finally, application programs should be classified by what they do: validation, utility, batch process, calculation, report, and so on.

Given DOS's file-name length limitation of eight characters, this is a bit of a challenge, but it can be done. The cryptic names may bother you at first, but you'll get used to them quickly enough by typing them over and over, if nothing else.

Be sure to draft your naming standards and distribute them to the developers on your team. Get feedback and extend the standards when necessary. When someone contributes a suggestion that is later incorporated, that person will be far more likely to buy in to the concept.

Templates vs. Engines

The term *template* has been used to describe a pattern of program logic that, when fed into a code generator, automatically produces a working application. First seen in the dBASE family with UI and ViewGen, this approach found its way into dBASE IV and FoxBase Plus. In my opinion, it is one of the worst maintenance horror stories of the 1980s.

Perhaps it was the thrill of seeing thousands of neatly typed, beautifully formatted lines of code streaming across the screen that hypnotized programmers. I found the template approach to be a disappointment for two reasons. The first is the learning curve. If you were committed to building applications using a template, you weren't supposed to make changes to the output code directly. When you encountered bugs or needed to make an enhancement, you modified the template. That way, you could always (theoretically) regenerate your application designs. For some sadistic reason, the architects of these products insisted on inventing a second language for the template, creating a hideous learning curve for the average dBASE programmer and adding a long intermediate step to the code-compile-execute-crash-debug cycle.

The second problem was the maintenance liability (as described earlier in the "Clone-and-modify" section). When you think about it, the template approach is nothing more than an automated clone-and-modify machine. If you build 15 applications before finding a bug in the template, you have to fix the template, then regenerate each of those applications. You're unlikely to have the time or the patience for this, even if you were sure you could do it without creating any new bugs.

Fox Software deserves a humanitarian award for awakening from the template-language nightmare. FoxPro does a capable job of generating code using regular FoxPro programs, with a few simple language enhancements to support text merge.

But if you look at the code FoxPro generates, you'll notice there's no template as such. FoxPro has chosen not to generate any procedural logic, but only the declarative code sufficient to execute the menu and screen designs built in its power tools. In my opinion, there's wisdom in that restraint.

If you're accustomed to the template approach, you'll be tempted to beef up GENSCRN.PRG to include "Save, Escape, Change" branches, record locks, file I/O commands such as scatter and gather, various bells and whistles, and even a whole application into your screen programs. After all, it's far easier in FoxPro than it has been ever before. But resist that impulse. If these components are truly generic, there's no need to merge them into the screen-specific code. You're far better off keeping them separate, for the reasons stated earlier. In fact, when you think about it, a template-driven code generator is simply a blender mixing together the application-specific design specifications with repetitive procedural logic, two components that are much more maintainable if you keep a fence between them.

Any complex process like a screen program will have generic parts and application-specific parts. These can be mated quite closely without being in the same file. Your code could be structured like the examples in Figure 3-2.

In fact, FoxPro works just like that. A good example is the *READ* clauses (*ACTIVATE*, *DEACTIVATE*, *SHOW*, *WHEN*, and *VALID*), where control is passed out to customization code up to five times at the point where one window is clicked on top of another.

Whether you prefer to have the screen program or your library code in control, the results are the same: You can branch back and forth wherever you need to keep the generated screen separate from the procedural logic. That same procedural logic can drive all your screens, with only one module to maintain.

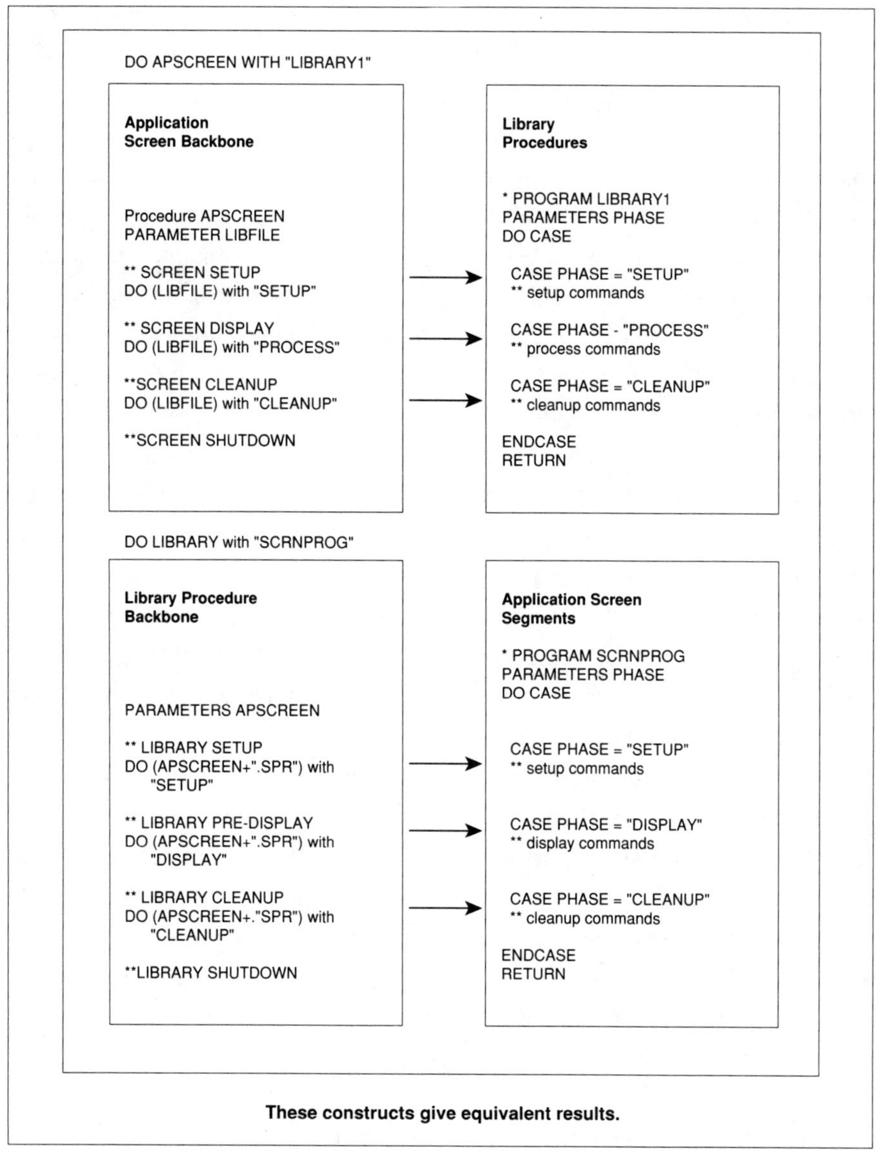

Figure 3-2. A sample application structure.

The goals, then, are:

- to add generic features to screen processes, without embedding the logic in the screen code itself
- to be sure you can always regenerate a screen design without placing hand-sewn modifications in the generated screen program. Anyone unwittingly regenerating the screen would overwrite your changes, breaking the application.

Screen Object or Generic Procedure

Generally, it's a safe bet that a program that displays things on the screen is best maintained as a screen object. However, depending on the overall size and objectives of your application, you might think about the benefits of building some of your screen functions as generic procedures. Consider the case of a modal dialog box, for example, the one in Figure 3-3.

```
+==============================================================+
|                                                              |
|                    Your Report is Ready.                     |
|                                                              |
|     <Print>   <View>   <Save as>   <Modi form>   <Done>      |
|                                                              |
+==============================================================+
```

Figure 3-3. A modal dialog box.

FoxPro makes this easy to build as a screen object. In average applications, it's no doubt in its most convenient and maintainable form as a screen object.

But what of the large application that may have dozens of these? Perhaps there are some additional twists, such as user-definable colors for different contexts or contents, or perhaps there's a multi-lingual requirement.

In this example, consider the benefits of a single data-driven procedure that would allow you to control the dialog box parametrically.

Could you build this procedure to support the following features?

- One or more lines of text
- One or more button prompts
- Color string or scheme

Based on the button prompts and messages, the procedure could calculate the best dimensions of the box. Called as a function, the program could return either the prompt of the selected button, or its number. If the number were returned, the program logic would be independent of the actual contents of the button. This would support displaying the dialog box in different languages, for example.

You could pass arrays to the procedure to hold the text and prompts. For/Endfor loops within the library procedure would display these, as follows:

```
** This type of logic displays the message lines
FOR dlog_i = 1 to alen(msg_arr)
   @ dlog_i, 0 say PADC(msg_arr(dlog_i), wcols())
ENDFOR
** A similar loop could build up a list of text button prompts
** which would be displayed in an @ GET pushbutton command
```

If the application has a very large number of these dialog boxes, you might consider storing all the prompts, text, and optional parameters in a data file. That way, the text (and even the prompts) might be easily modified by the user.

User-Modifiable Application Components

There are still a few programmers who maintain Neanderthal attitudes about users, building each application as though the users' I.Q.s are in the teens. More often than not, users are regular people who happen to need software to get their jobs done. Their only "crime" is not being programmers.

But one byte-head's obstacle is another's opportunity. By building software that empowers users to do more for themselves, users WILL do more for themselves, allowing a good developer to off-load many of the most time-consuming and trivial tasks in a project, and drastically reducing the number of call-backs. (Of course, we're not ignoring the need to limit this functionality to a system administrator or other responsible and properly-trained person.)

The data-driven interface design described in the previous section is an example of a technique that lends itself well to user involvement. If a user can modify the prompts and buttons without harming the application, you can concentrate on the real problems.

I've seen programmers react in total shock upon learning that we build applications that offer a button allowing users to modify simple report forms. "The users will break it, then they'll call me in a panic," they object. But how tough is it to programmatically protect the user from breaking a report by only allowing them to change a *copy* of it, trapping run time errors, and offering to reset a broken report back to its former version?

Here are some areas where user-modifiability reduces the maintenance burden:

- On-line help system
- Assignment of security levels and levels of system access
- Printer assignments
- Color selections
- Report form adjustments and ad-hoc report creation
- Ad-hoc query building

Each of these areas lends itself to an engine-based, generic library solution. And every time you construct a module that delivers one of these features generically, you gain at least three major benefits:

- You'll be able to carry the feature forwards (and sometimes even backwards) into all your applications
- Your customers will benefit from increased functionality
- Even though the module may be more complex than a "quick and dirty" solution, your maintenance liability will be reduced on balance.

FoxPro 2.0's Impact on Application Development

The Promise

The essence of a fourth-generation language is that you should be able to tell a computer *what* you want rather than *how* to do the job. FoxPro delivers much of this power in SQL *SELECT*, Screen and Menu Tools, Report Designer, Quick Report, Create Report, and the RQBE Query Screen while retaining a command language that's understandable to the legions of dBASE programmers.

FoxPro has become a far more *declarative* environment than any PC database language preceding it. In so doing, it has greatly reduced the need for you to churn out procedural logic.

The Price

We will, however, pay a price for this cutting-edge technology. While FoxPro's language enhancements open a whole new world of user-interface design, quite a few subtleties lurk just beneath the surface.

Before you launch all those windows, for example, be aware that two or more vastly different coding techniques support *READ* from multiple windows. You can close a window in at least five different ways, possibly bringing an unintentional end to that *READ*. In your first event-driven application, you may find it takes 20 minutes to lay out the basic design for a complex dialog box and the rest of the week (or month) to debug it.

Browse isn't as simple as it looks, either. Building interfaces with multiple browse windows or incorporating more than one browse into a multiwindow *READ* can be hazardous. For example, closing a browse window doesn't trigger the *DEACTIVATE* clause of the *READ*; you lose programmatic control at a point where you may need it to protect data integrity.

Even *SQL SELECT* has a few surprises. It "borrows" some of your work areas to open temporary files, but it doesn't tell you how many it will need or what will happen if all the work areas happen to be occupied (it stops).

The Rewards

Using FoxPro 2.0, users will be able to do more for themselves than ever before. This will be perceived as threatening by those database programmers clinging to a narrow view of the service they provide.

On more complex applications, the ratio of programming hours per analysis/design hour will fall rapidly. As high as 10 to one in mainframe environments, that number has been about three to one in FoxPro 1.02. A one-to-one ratio is likely as developers become more productive in automated approaches to development.

On the other hand, analytical and design skills will be in terrific demand. The requirements of more ambitious applications, more complex user interfaces, and wider distribution of applications will demand a higher level of engineering and design. Challenges will abound for those whose professional skills can grow with the rate of change in FoxPro. And one of the worthiest of those challenges is that of building for maintainability.

PART II

Optimizing and Testing

Is Something Worth Doing, Worth Doing Well?

This question was posed to an associate of mine during the oral examination for his Ph.D. in Economics. His answer was No. The point where something is worth doing, is the point where a profit is made. Spending more resources to improve it further will yield no payback and, therefore, be unprofitable. In concept, I agree with this assessment, as long as you are able to determine the scope of the project. Taking a loss in the short term may result in a long-term gain. However, in practice it can be difficult to predict what will yield a long-term gain.

Ron Talmage's chapter in this section concerns software testing. Everyone loves it, a few people do it, and almost no one automates it. Many software developers say you should release a new product when it's 80 to 90 percent finished. Waiting until it's 100 percent finished to sell it will bankrupt you. Perhaps consumers are starting to accept buggy products as the standard. If this is so, then the economic logic above, simply applied, cautions you not to spend too much time improving your product. On the other hand, if you can distinguish yourself in a crowded market by being the most bug-free product, perhaps it is worthwhile to spend the extra resources to do extensive testing.

Performance optimization is an area where many developers spend both too many resources and too few. For example, you can spend an enormous amount of time analyzing whether the standard version of FoxPro is better than the protected mode version for a particular application, hoping you can extend what you've learned to *all* applications. But if you spend too little time uncovering all the relevant factors, your predictions may be meaningless.

For some developers, the decision to switch to FoxPro 2 from another, much slower, platform is the only one they need to make about performance optimization.

These are the kinds of results that Fox Software makes its reputation on. Fox doesn't encourage optimization because it does so much of it itself. The lack of published material on the topic from Fox and other writers reflects this. However, there are some developers who constantly push the performance envelope. They provide the impetus for Fox to keep moving. This type of developer will profit greatly from a careful study of the chapters on optimization.

For me, performance optimization provides the challenge of doing what everyone said couldn't be done. Going that far can be risky, but if you find a solution that costs far less than what was considered possible, the payback can be great.

Finally, there is the non-economic matter of pride in your craftsmanship. There is no way to put a dollar figure on that. It may take many days of trial-and-error testing of different optimization strategies. Even running an automated test on a complicated application could tie up your computers for quite a while.

For some people, the time is not an impediment, it's part of the dues you pay to achieve excellence. These are the people I prefer to work with and whose products I will pay top dollar for. If your product is an important one, it's worth doing well, or it's not worth doing at all.

—Editor

CHAPTER 4

Using FoxPro's Keyboard Macro Facility for Automated Testing

by Ron Talmage

For developers, software testing can be more than drudgery—it can be a conflict of interest. They aim for software that performs as designed under expected conditions, while testers examine its performance under unexpected conditions. The developer can't focus on building a new product according to the design *and* on finding weak spots in the finished product.

Large organizations solve this dilemma by assigning development and testing to separate teams that may not even communicate with each other. But smaller companies and consultants may not have access to someone who can give the application a thorough workout. So why not automate the process?

Automated testing involves putting as much of the process as possible under computer control, which means programming the tests. This chapter looks at FoxPro 2.0's keyboard macro facility as an automation tool and examines the extent to which keyboard macros can give us programmatic control over testing.

Don't confuse keyboard macros with macro substitution in variable names. Keyboard macros are accessed primarily through the *Macros...* bar of the System menu, whereas macro substitution occurs when you place a "&" before the variable name in a program or in the command window. A keyboard macro replays a set of keystrokes when triggered by a keystroke combination or invoked by the *PLAY MACRO* command; macro substitution replaces a variable name with a character string when the name is referenced by the FoxPro execution engine.

In this chapter, we'll examine keyboard macros, not mouse macros. For reasons we'll explore later, FoxPro 2.0's keyboard macro engine can generate nearly any keystroke combination, but no usable mouse presses. We'll be talking about some ways to get around this, so hang on!

FoxPro 2.0's Keyboard Macro Implementation

The original intention of FoxPro 1.0's keyboard macros was probably to allow redefinition of the function keys, if the .FKY file extension for saved keyboard macros is any indication. Nevertheless, the earlier FoxPro keyboard macros go beyond function keys to include most combinations of the Ctrl, Alt, and Shift keys. The FoxPro 2.0 keyboard macro facility is significantly enhanced.

The purpose of a keyboard macro is to take a nonalphanumeric keystroke, made up of some relatively rare but memorable combination of alphanumeric keys prefixed with Ctrl, Alt, Shift, or a function key, and redefine it as a sequence of often-repeated keystrokes. The recorded keystrokes are then sent automatically to FoxPro when the defined key is invoked. The sequences are usually fairly short; a macro is most useful when it replaces tedious or easily mistyped keystroke sequences. (FoxPro 1.0's keyboard macro facility did the job nicely as long as the sequences were short and didn't need editing.)

FoxPro implements keyboard macros differently from most of its other facilities. The keyboard macro facility seems to be modeled on the idea of recording tape. As with a VCR or cassette deck, we can *PLAY*, *SAVE*, and *CLEAR* a macro; however, unlike the commands that affect databases, menus, screens, and reports, we cannot *CREATE*, *EDIT*, or *MODIFY* a macro (see Table 4-1 for a comparison).

Table 4-1. Comparison of FoxPro and keyboard macro commands.

FoxPro Command	Keyboard Macro Facility
CREATE	Keyboard Macros dialog box <Record>
DO	PLAY MACRO or keystroke
EDIT/MODIFY	Keyboard Macros dialog box <Edit>
Ctrl+End	SAVE MACROS
CLEAR	CLEAR MACROS

FoxPro 2.0's implementation of keyboard macros is just different enough from the other facilities to steepen the developer's learning curve. Once you're past these differences, however, the macro facility is quite easy to use.

The Keyboard Macros Dialog Box

Beginning a keyboard macro's recording session is as simple as invoking the Keyboard Macros dialog box (Figure 4-1) either from the menu or by pressing Shift+F10. You can do this at the start of an application's execution or at any keyboard-input point during its execution. You can end the recording session, or insert pauses or literals into the sequence, by pressing Shift+F10. Once you've finished recording, you can invoke the keyboard macro by pressing the defined keystroke combination or by issuing a *PLAY MACRO* command with the keyboard macro name. For other aspects of the keyboard dialog box, see FoxPro 2.0's developer's guide.

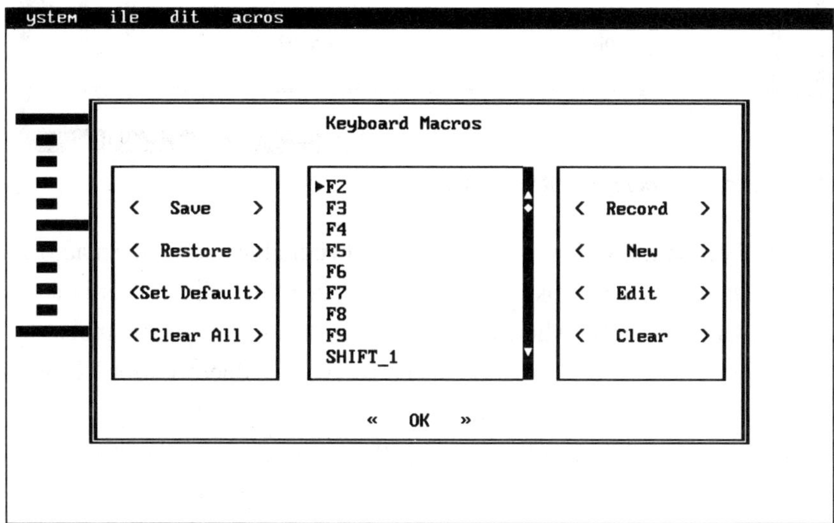

Figure 4-1. FoxPro 2.0's Keyboard Macros dialog box.

FoxPro 2.0 improves on earlier versions by adding an editing feature (notice the <Edit> button in Figure 4-1). For example, if you click on the default F5 keyboard macro name in the dialog box and then click <Edit>, you see the new Macro Edit window shown in Figure 4-2.

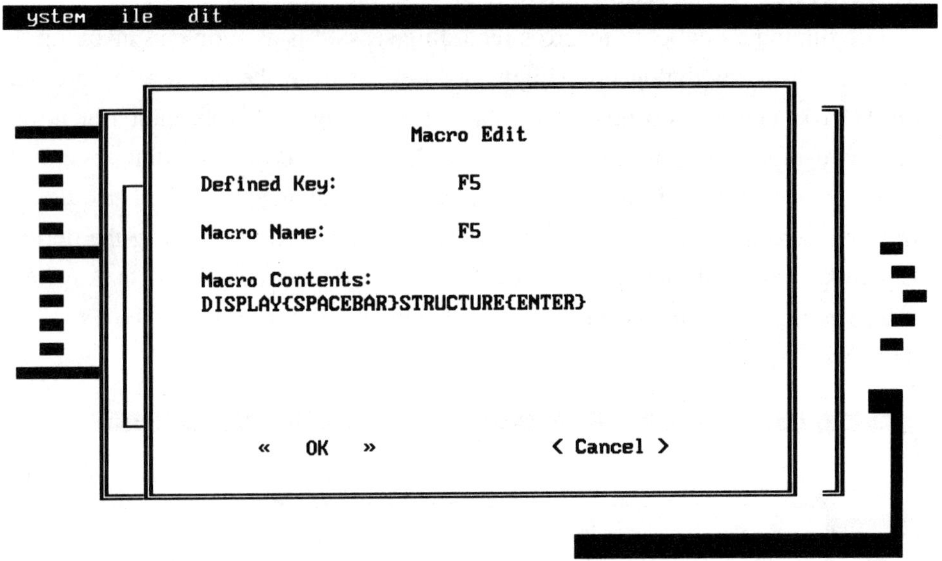

Figure 4-2. FoxPro 2.0's Macro Edit window.

The Macro Edit window gives us visual access to editable text for the macro and the ability to change its keystroke sequence without rerecording. This is a vast improvement over FoxPro 1.0, where the only way to change a keyboard macro was to record it again. The following section, "The Keyboard Macro Editor," looks at editing in greater detail.

A FoxPro 2.0 keyboard macro consists of three components: the "trigger," or defined keystroke combination that replays the recorded keystrokes; the keyboard macro name, referenced by the *PLAY MACRO* command; and the keystroke sequence that defines the macro. A macro normally has the same name as the keystroke combination that triggers it. For example, if F5 is the keystroke being defined as the trigger, then F5 is the most logical name for it. In FoxPro 2.0, the keyboard macro facility will offer this name as a default.

This facility distinguishes a keyboard macro's name from the keystrokes that trigger it using the labels defined in the *ON KEY LABEL* documentation (found in the FoxPro 2.0 Help file and the FoxPro *Commands and Functions* manual). In addition to those labels, the keyboard macro facility uses the following:

^	CARET
-	HYPHEN
\	BACKSLASH
[	LBRACKET
]	RBRACKET
;	SEMICOLON
space	SPACEBAR
{	LBRACE
}	RBRACE

The keyboard macro facility detects the trigger keystroke for a new keyboard macro when you type it with the *Defined Key* field highlighted. It labels the keystroke combination using key labels and the plus sign and offers a default keyboard macro name, usually the same keystroke labels with an underscore in place of the "+." When a label combination is very long, however, it is abbreviated.

For example, defining a new keyboard macro by holding down Ctrl and tapping the X key results in the keystroke trigger label *CTRL+X* and the default macro name *CTRL_X*. The macro name can then be edited. Although the macro-name field has room for 23 characters, only 19 are recorded. Also note that the label name must begin with a character.

The Keyboard Macro Editor

After choosing the macro's trigger and name, you can enter and edit the keystroke sequence in the Macro Edit window. Ordinary keystroke sequences can be typed in normally. For example, you can enter either:

```
DISPLAY MEMORY
```

or

```
DISPLAY{SPACEBAR}MEMORY
```

You'll see key labels again in this window, but notice that they now need to be surrounded by left and right curly braces ({ and }). However, a slightly different superset of the *ON KEY LABEL* list is used. This time, the key labels that can be referenced by themselves in the editor and don't appear in the *ON KEY LABEL* list are {SEMICOLON} and {SPACEBAR}. If the syntax of the labels in curly braces is legal, the keyboard macro editor's <OK> button will let us store it.

Now you can see why the *DISPLAY STRUCTURE* command is rendered in the editor as *DISPLAY{SPACEBAR}STRUCTURE{ENTER}*. The keyboard macro editor requires that you convert nontextual keystrokes to their textual equivalent by enclosing the appropriate key labels in curly braces. This allows you to enter something like Ctrl+X into a keyboard macro as {CTRL+X} and edit it. Without the curly braces, you wouldn't even see the sequence as text.

The keyboard macro editor is not a recorder, however. Many keystrokes aren't detected by the macro editor, and their labels must be entered character by character. These include the screen-control keys ({PGUP}, {PGDN}, {HOME}, and {END}); the arrow keys ({DNARROW}, {UPARROW}, {RIGHTARROW}, and {LEFTARROW}); and the function keys. To make a PgUp keypress part of a macro using the macro editor, for example, you must enter the string {PGUP}. The macro *recorder*, on the other hand, will detect and record such keystrokes; the macro editor will then display their names in braces.

The fact that the macro editor doesn't recognize certain keystrokes is not necessarily a disadvantage because it allows us to reference defined keystrokes without invoking them. The Esc key, for example, causes you to exit the editor. When you place the Esc key in a sequence of macro keystrokes, therefore, you simply type the key's textual equivalent, {ESC}, rather than the key itself. Now it's editable. Or suppose *Ctrl+X* has already been defined as a keyboard macro, but you want to enter it as part of a keystroke sequence. The keyboard macro editor forces you to key it in as a label, {CTRL+X}, avoiding the problem of triggering the macro itself.

By the way, curly braces cannot appear in the contents of a keystroke sequence other than to enclose a label. To the macro editor, they signal the beginning and end of a special name; to get a macro to type the braces themselves, you must use {LBRACE} and {RBRACE}.

Literals in Keyboard Macros

You can force the editor to ignore another defined keyboard macro in a keystroke sequence by putting the keyword *LITERAL* into the textual equivalent. For example, you can cause the sequence to type Ctrl+X and not trigger the *CTRL_X* keyboard macro by entering {LITERAL+CTRL+X} rather than {CTRL+X} in the macro editing window.

Not all keystrokes that can be defined as macros can be referenced as literals in a keystroke sequence. Such keystrokes probably shouldn't be defined as keyboard macros so they will never be invoked accidentally. (A database containing a table of the English equivalents, binary codes, hex codes, and decimal codes of these keystrokes appears in the database FKYCODES.DBF that's provided on the disk that accompanies this book.)

Macros That Call Other Macros

Incidentally, keyboard macros can trigger other keyboard macros; in other words, F3 can be programmed to do F2 plus something else, F4 to cause an enhanced F3 action, and so on. Now if you put these in a circle (F2 calls F3, F3 calls F4, F4 calls F2), an error message appears telling you you're out of stack space. The keyboard macro facility doesn't automatically detect circularity, it seems, except when the macro is played.

Does the macro facility allow recursion? If you make the value of F2 simply {F2}, then press that key, nothing happens. Macro keys don't appear to execute themselves. No error message results; it's just as if they weren't there.

Definable Keyboard Macro Keys

The keyboard macro facility can reference most keystroke events as triggers or as part of the macro's contents. Some keystroke combinations would be inappropriate as keyboard macro triggers. These include Ctrl+Alt+Delete, the keystrokes that access a PC's CMOS setup, and those that cause certain actions in Windows, DESQview, the DOS 5 shell, or other TSRs. These reserved keystrokes are not recordable, and playing them in a macro may well invoke the original program. These keystrokes are:

- Ctrl+Alt+Delete
- PrintScreen
- Pause/Break
- Caps Lock
- Scroll Lock
- Num Lock

These exceptions may seem insignificant, but they do limit control of the keyboard.

How many definable keystrokes are possible? To find out, we can classify the available keys into five groups:

- Alphabetic (A through Z, upper and lowercase)
- Numeric (0 through 9, with and without Shift)
- Function (F1 through F12)
- Editing (Ins, Del)
- Direction (Home, End, PgUp, PgDn, arrows)
- Punctuation (^, -, \, [,], spacebar, and tab; the other punctuation keys are never defined).

Table 4-2 summarizes the combination keystrokes you can use in macros.

Table 4-2. Definable keystrokes for keyboard macros.

	Alpha	Num	Fn	Dir	Total
(alone)	no	no	12[1]	10	22
Shift+	no	no	11[2]	10	21
Ctrl+	25[3]	no	12	10	47
Alt+	26	10	11[4]	10	57
Shift+Ctrl	26	no	12	10	48
Shift+Alt	26	10	12	10	58
Ctrl+Alt	26	10	12	9[5]	57
Shift+Ctrl+Alt	26	10	12	9[5]	57
Alt+F10	26	no	no	no	26

Punctuation	Legal Combinations	Quantity
^	Ctrl+^, Ctrl+Shift+^	2
-	Ctrl+-, Ctrl+Shift+-	2
\	Ctrl+\, Ctrl+Shift+\	2
[	Shift+[[6]	1
]	Shift+[, Ctrl+Shift+]	2
spacebar	Ctrl+sb, Shift+sb, Ctrl+Shift+sb	3
tab	Ctrl+tab, Ctrl+Shift+Tab	2
	Total	407

1 F1 is usually reserved as the Help key.

2 Shift+F10 is reserved as the default key for invoking and ending the macro recorder.

3 Ctrl+J is equivalent to the Enter key; neither is an acceptable keyboard macro trigger.

4 Alt+F10 can be combined with alphabetic keys only.

5 Ctrl+Alt+Del and Shift+Ctrl+Alt+Del reboot the computer.

6 Ctrl+Shift+[and Ctrl+[are equivalent to the Esc key and will not trigger a keyboard macro.

Oddly, Shift+backspace produces Shift+Ctrl+H.

The Internal Structure of Keyboard Macro Files

We can see why the keyboard macro editor gives us only an interpreted view of a macro's contents when we look at the internal structure of an .FKY file. This file format is crucial to understanding the limits and working conditions of FoxPro keyboard macros.

Keyboard macros are stored in a mixed text and binary .FKY file format, the structure of which is rather confusingly (and erroneously) documented in Appendix B of FoxPro 2.0's developer's guide. Figure 4-3 represents the structure more accurately.

I. The .FKY file header (fixed size of 18 bytes).

Bytes 1 and 2:	File signature, FFh followed by 79h
Bytes 3 through 15:	Space-filled (20h)
Bytes 16:	One null byte
Bytes 17 and 18:	Integer count of number of macros

II. The keyboard macros (variable length). For each macro:

A. The keyboard macro header (fixed size of 24 bytes):

Bytes 1 through 20:	Keyboard macro name followed by nulls
Bytes 21 and 22:	Integer count of keystrokes
Bytes 23 and 24:	Keystroke being defined (the trigger)

B. The keystroke sequence itself:

Bytes 25 through 25+ (the integer count * 2).

III. The end-of-file marker, value 1Ah.

Figure 4-3. The structure FoxPro 2.0 uses to store keyboard macros.

One-relative numbering is used here because we're really just counting, not addressing. Briefly, bytes 1 through 18 contain header information, while variable-sized blocks contain the keyboard macros themselves. Each block has its own fixed-size header, with a maximum name length of 20 characters (actually 19, since the name is a null-terminated string) and a count of up to 1,024 recorded keystrokes. The integers are stored as two bytes and, as in all Intel-based CPUs, in reverse order: 01h followed by 02h becomes 0201h when combined in the CPU. (Though the keystroke count is officially limited to 1,024 keystrokes, it could in principle go as high as 65,535 because it's stored as a 16-bit integer.)

At this point it might help to look at an example. Figure 4-4 shows the hexadecimal values of the default macros built into FoxPro as viewed in the MS-DOS debugger (DEBUG).

```
-d
5E0C:0100  FF 79 20 20 20 20 20 20-20 20 20 20 20 20 20 00   .y             .
5E0C:0110  10 00 46 32 00 00 00 00-00 00 00 00 00 00 00 00   ..F2............
5E0C:0120  00 00 00 00 00 00 04 00-3C 01 53 00 45 00 54 00   ........<.S.E.T.
5E0C:0130  0D 00 46 33 00 00 00 00-00 00 00 00 00 00 00 00   ..F3............
5E0C:0140  00 00 00 00 00 00 05 00-3D 01 4C 00 49 00 53 00   ........=.L.I.S.
5E0C:0150  54 00 0D 00 46 34 00 00-00 00 00 00 00 00 00 00   T...F4..........
5E0C:0160  00 00 00 00 00 00 00 00-04 00 3E 01 44 00 49 00   ..........>.D.I.
5E0C:0170  52 00 0D 00 46 35 00 00-00 00 00 00 00 00 00 00   R...F5..........
-d
5E0C:0180  00 00 00 00 00 00 00 00-12 00 3F 01 44 00 49 00   ..........?.D.I.
5E0C:0190  53 00 50 00 4C 00 41 00-59 00 20 00 53 00 54 00   S.P.L.A.Y. .S.T.
5E0C:01A0  52 00 55 00 43 00 54 00-55 00 52 00 45 00 0D 00   R.U.C.T.U.R.E...
5E0C:01B0  46 36 00 00 00 00 00 00-00 00 00 00 00 00 00 00   F6..............
5E0C:01C0  00 00 00 00 0F 00 40 01-44 00 49 00 53 00 50 00   ......@.D.I.S.P.
5E0C:01D0  4C 00 41 00 59 00 20 00-53 00 54 00 41 00 54 00   L.A.Y. .S.T.A.T.
5E0C:01E0  55 00 53 00 0D 00 46 37-00 00 00 00 00 00 00 00   U.S...F7........
5E0C:01F0  00 00 00 00 00 00 00 00-00 00 0F 00 41 01 44 00   ............A.D.
-
```

Figure 4-4. The hex values of FoxPro's default macros.

The 18-byte file header, from 0100h to 0111h, consists of a starting byte (FFh) and a signature byte (79h), followed by spaces and a count of 10h (or 16) macros in the default .FKY file. Past the header, byte 112h contains the ASCII characters that form the textual name of the first macro in the file, F2. Let's take a closer look at its keyboard definition.

Nulls fill the remaining 18 bytes of the 20 reserved for F2's name. At byte 126h, we convert the two-byte integer, low byte first, giving us 0004h, for a count of four keystrokes. Next, starting at byte 128h, we see bytes 3Ch and 01h. These produce 013Ch, the keystroke value for F2. This is the defined key that invokes the keyboard macro. What follows, starting at 12Ah, is a string of three two-byte integers for each keystroke of the string "SET." The last two bytes add 000Dh, a carriage return.

The use of a second byte to specify the keystroke combination is actually quite complex. In spite of the complexity, we can draw some conclusions about how keystrokes are stored. The keyboard macro itself is stored as a raw sequence of keystrokes, two bytes each, with the exception of pauses. For ordinary keystrokes, the first byte appears to be a code indicating whether the Ctrl, Shift, or Alt key, or a combination of these keys, has been pressed. If the first byte is 00h, then the following byte is the ASCII code for the character; if it's something other than 00, the two bytes indicate the combination of keystrokes involved. A complete list of keyboard scan codes appears in the FKYCODES.DBF file on the disk that accompanies this book. (Scan codes are the codes that are stored in the computer's memory when keys are pressed.)

Table 4-3 shows the combination of keystrokes involving the letter *A* (taken from FKYCODES.DBF).

Table 4-3. .FKY combinations of the letter *A*.

Stored Bytes	Keystroke	Interpretation
00h 41h	A	null+ASCII
00h 61h	a	null+ASCII
20h 01h	CTRL+A	Ctrl+scan code
41h 1Eh	ALT+A	Alt+scan code
30h 01h	SHIFT+CTRL+A	Shift+Ctrl+scan code
51h 1Eh	SHIFT+ALT+A	Shift+Alt+scan code
61h 1Eh	CTRL+ALT+A	Ctrl+Alt+scan code
71h 1Eh	SHIFT+CTRL+ALT+A	Shift+Ctrl+Alt+scan code
80h 41h	LITERAL+A	literal+ASCII
A0h 01h	LITERAL+CTRL+A	literal+Ctrl+scan code
C1h 1Eh	LITERAL+ALT+A	literal+Alt+scan code
B0h 01h	SHIFT+LITERAL+CTRL+A	Shift+literal+Ctrl+scan code
D1h 1Eh	SHIFT+LITERAL+ALT+A	Shift+literal+Alt+scan code
E1h 1Eh	CTRL+LITERAL+ALT+A	Ctrl+literal+Alt+scan code

In Fox's scheme for coding the various possible keystroke combinations, not all combinations are possible, and the keyboard macro editor will automatically perform the following translations:

CTRL+LITERAL+key	=>	LITERAL+CTRL+key
LITERAL+SHIFT+CTRL+key	=>	SHIFT+LITERAL+CTRL+key
LITERAL+SHIFT+CTRL+ALT+key	=>	ALT/F10+key

So a keyboard macro definition is stored as a series of two-byte keystroke sequences, a null byte with an ASCII code for regular characters, and an initial byte plus perhaps a modified keyboard scan code for special keystrokes and keystroke combinations. The exception to this rule is the pause, which is stored in four bytes (see Table 4-4).

Table 4-4. Pause codes.

Stored Bytes	Interpretation
FEh FFh FFh FFh	Pause until keypress
FEh FFh FEh FFh	Pause 655.34 seconds
...	
FEh FFh 01h 00h	Pause .01 seconds
FEh FFh 00h 00h	Pause .00 seconds

Revenge of the Nulls

An .FKY file is composed of many data types: 16-bit integers, two-byte key-code and scan-code combinations, four-byte pauses, nulls, and ASCII codes. Unlike a text file, it doesn't comprise one-byte ASCII characters. No wonder it's not an easy file to edit! The FoxPro 2.0 editor will read an .FKY file, but it will read it as a string of characters, showing as characters many bytes not intended to be characters and not showing many others. The Brief editor (Solution Systems, Wellesley, Mass.) will also read an .FKY file, but it will return the message "Nulls in file fixed" and replace the nulls with spaces; the result is a file that FoxPro 2.0 no longer recognizes as a keyboard macro file.

The Keyboard Macro Editor as Translator

It should be clear at this point what the keyboard macro editor is doing with both character and noncharacter keystrokes and keystroke combinations: translating the curly-braced names into the corresponding two- or four-byte values for storage in the .FKY format. In other words, what we see in the keyboard macro editor is the editable, textual equivalent of the keystrokes; what is stored in the .FKY file (and therefore internally, in the RAM areas where keyboard macros are loaded) is the binary translation.

Far from being a mere text editor, the keyboard macro editor is also a macro translator. Somewhat like the FoxPro 2.0 compiler, it translates straight text into intermediate tokens that the FoxPro engine can execute. The translation must take place immediately after the <OK> button in the Macro Edit window is pressed, because that's when any error messages will appear.

Limitations of the Keyboard Macro Edit Window

A major limitation of FoxPro 2.0's Macro Edit window is its size. Only five lines by 43 characters, it's reminiscent of early laptops' LCD screens. If the keyboard macro is at all large and exceeds the size of the window, a scroll bar appears. Still, the window is just too small and is not sizable. Fortunately, FoxPro gives us a couple of tools to overcome this limitation.

The first tool is the clipboard. You simply mark the Macro Edit window text with the mouse or select it with Ctrl+A, cut it to the clipboard, exit the Keyboard Macros dialog box, and paste the result into a text file using the FoxPro editor. This way, you can edit keyboard macros in the movable, sizable window of the FoxPro text editor and store them as text files. After editing the text, you select it, copy the keyboard macro portion back into the clipboard, reenter the Keyboard Macros dialog box, open the edit window of the chosen key, and paste the modified text into a blank keyboard macro edit box. This method is simple and effective, but it has some limitations:

- All keystrokes requiring key labels must be typed as character text enclosed in curly braces. For labels like {SPACEBAR} and {ENTER}, this can become quite tiresome.
- No more than 1,024 keystrokes can be stored for each keyboard definition.

- The keyboard macro editor checks syntax during the paste. If the curly braces have been misused, you must either fix the problem in the edit window or cancel the paste and return to the FoxPro editor to fix the errors.
- Because comments cannot be pasted into the edit window, it's difficult to keep them in the text file.

The first two items are limits built into the keyboard macro facility, and there's not much we can do about them.

The second tool is to use keyboard macros to automate the entry of tedious key labels such as {ENTER} and {SPACEBAR}. For example, we could use a mnemonic key combination such as Ctrl+Spacebar to automatically type the string {SPACEBAR}.

Table 4-2 showed that although both Ctrl and Alt work with the alphanumeric keys, only the Ctrl key works with the spacebar and braces. If we want a keyboard macro to type the string {SPACEBAR} for us in the FoxPro editor, we can enter the Keyboard Macros dialog box and define the key CTRL+SPACEBAR. We can't type the character string {SPACEBAR} in the Macro Edit window because the keyboard macro would, when invoked, simply type a space rather than the character string {SPACEBAR}. One way to get what we want is to enter Shift+[, then the character string SPACEBAR, then Shift+]. If you press the <OK> button and look at the result in the Macro Edit window, you'll see

```
{SHIFT+LBRACE}SPACEBAR{SHIFT+RBRACE}
```

You can edit out the *SHIFT*s, giving

```
{LBRACE}SPACEBAR{RBRACE}
```

Of course, you could simply type the entire character string, with the label {LBRACE}, letter by letter. If this keyboard macro is active while you're editing a keystroke sequence that has been cut from the Macro Edit window, we can trigger the *Ctrl_Spacebar* keyboard macro by typing the Ctrl and spacebar keys together, and the string {SPACEBAR} will be played.

All this effort to edit keyboard macros using the FoxPro 2.0 editor seems quixotic when you realize that the edit window of the keyboard macro facility won't ignore comments and will remove carriage returns and line feeds. Any formatting to make the keyboard macro text more readable will be lost.

To solve this problem, we'll write a filter to remove comments from a keyboard macro text file so the result will be acceptable to the Macro Edit window. We'll then enhance the filter by adding some compiler logic, bypassing the keyboard macro translator entirely.

Creating a Keyboard Macro Filter

First, we need to decide what sort of comments we'll allow. Let's follow the commenting techniques in FoxPro itself and ignore comment lines that begin with an asterisk and those that have in-line comments beginning with a double ampersand. We won't allow a semicolon as a continuation character; because keyboard macro text is just a sequence of keystrokes, continuing a line makes no sense.

We should also establish a convention for naming keyboard macro text files, something more meaningful than .TXT and less misleading than .PRG or .FKY. Let's follow the style of the FoxPro 2.0 generator programs and use the extension .KPR for macro "source-code" text files, much like FoxPro 2.0 uses .SPR and .MPR to indicate screen and menu source-code files.

The short program FKY_FILT.PRG (see Listing 4-2 at the end of the chapter) uses the low-level file format (LLFF) commands of FoxPro 2.0 to get the file name from the user and read the .KPR file. As each line is stripped of comments, it's added to the variable *mClipText*. When the end of the file is reached, *mClipText* is loaded into the FoxPro 2.0 internal variable *_CLIPTEXT*, which puts the results in the FoxPro clipboard.

After running this program, we can paste the results back into the Macro Edit window, where they will be translated into a keyboard macro for saving or playing. The macro translator will check the program for correctness. What FKY_FILT.PRG gives us is the ability to store comments in the keyboard macro text file and strip them out when we want to create a real keyboard macro. Thus, we can clone a portion of keyboard macro text over and over simply by copying the text files and modifying the keystroke sequences to take a different path.

A Keyboard Macro Mini-Compiler

A more thorough method than using a filter is writing directly to an .FKY file. Not only is this technique more powerful, it's also a good test of how much programmable control we can have over keyboard macros. The approach we'll take is to expand the filter program into a keyboard macro mini-compiler. Fortunately, we have FKYCODES.DBF to help us translate key labels into keyboard scan codes. First, we have a decision to make: How do we let the source text tell us the name of the keyboard macro? Just as FoxPro 2.0 uses a "#" to send directives to its compiler, we can use the pound sign as a directive for a keyboard macro name. If the source text has a "#Name" in the first nonblank column of a line, we'll take the remaining text (minus in-line comments) as the name of the macro and its keystroke trigger.

FKY_COMP.PRG, a functioning mini-compiler, appears at the end of this chapter as Listing 4-3. It uses the FKYCODES.DBF table as a cross-reference to write the correct bytes to the .FKY file. The compiler writes them using the LLFF, as before, processing the input file line by line. After removing the comments, the program examines each line to see if it begins with a directive (as in *#Name {some-label}*) giving the name of the macro. If so, the program stores the label with braces in a variable, seeks the variable, and gets the trigger key, storing it as well.

The compiler examines each line byte by byte, then writes each character to the new .FKY file. The exception is key labels like {CTRL+SPACEBAR}, whose trigger keystrokes are found in FKYCODES.DBF. The program also features an error message identifying the part of the line that caused the error and logic to handle the {PAUSE x} key label.

The output of the mini-compiler is an .FKY file that needs to be restored into the keyboard macro facility before the macros can be played. One of the limits of this program is that the input file can have only one keyboard macro directive, so it can't read a series of macros. Also, if the keyboard macro text must send keystrokes that begin with a "#," it must be positioned so that it won't be mistaken for a directive.

Using Keyboard Macros to Test FoxPro 2.0's CONVERT.APP

To see how the minicompiler and the filter can be used to test an application, let's look at the conversion application that comes with FoxPro 2.0 in the SAMPLE subdirectory. CONVERT.APP is a program that converts between metric and nonmetric measurements and is part of the ORGANIZE project, though it can be compiled separately. To activate the ORGANIZE application, enter the File menu and choose *Open*, then *Project file type*. Open ORGANIZE.PJX in the SAMPLE subdirectory, choose *Rebuild All*, and click the <OK> button. Then pull down the Program menu, choose *DO*, and select ORGANIZE.APP. When the System menu bar returns, pull it down; toward the bottom you'll see *Conversions*, one of two new options installed by ORGANIZE.APP.

A keyboard macro recorded to exercise this application appears in FKY_ORG1.KPR (provided on diskette and, with comments, as Listing 4-1). Assuming the ORGANIZE application has been installed into the System menu, this macro chooses the *Conversions* option, changes the type to *Volume*, changes the input side to cubic feet, and enters *60* into the input window. As the application shows the result, the keystrokes move over to the <OK> button and pause for four seconds; the Esc key is sent, and the macro ends.

Listing 4-1. A commented keyboard macro for the Convert application.

```
*.........................................................*
* FoxPro 2.0 keyboard macro for exercising the Convert application*
*.........................................................*

#Name {CTRL+X}
{ALT+S}n                             && Do Convert
** core part
{BACKTAB}{ENTER}                     && Choose volume (backtab =
                                     && shift+tab)
{TAB}{ENTER}&& Pull up list
{DNARROW}{DNARROW}{ENTER}            && Choose cubic feet
60{ENTER}                            && Enter 60
{TAB}{TAB}{TAB}{TAB}{PAUSE 4.00}     && Tab over to button and pause
                                     && the end
{ESCAPE}                             && Leave the application
```

I recommend that you try both FKY_FILT and FKY_COMP with FKY_ORG1.KPR as the input file, then pressing Alt+S to exercise the Convert application. However, this keyboard macro is not an extensive test. To enhance it, we can use FoxPro's editor to copy the core part of the application several times and choose other paths through the application. When we're close to exceeding the 1,024-keystroke limit, we can copy the resulting file into another .KPR file and vary the number of paths being exercised.

Strategies for Automated Testing

To fully test an application, we need to test a wide variety of execution paths. The advantage of copying keyboard macro text from the Macro Edit window into a text file is that you can use your favorite editor to modify the keystroke sequence to take different paths through an application. The ability to document the paths is crucial, and hand-recording each one would be tedious. For a real application, however, we'll need much larger and more complex macros. What we need are modifications to both the filter program and the mini-compiler to make the automated testing more realistic.

The filter program could be modified slightly to process the clipboard text rather than a file. We could then build a library of keyboard macros in a text file and simply copy the relevant macro into the clipboard, process it using the filter, and paste the result into the Macro Edit window. The result would be a large library of test sequences that we could exercise selectively.

This text library would not be very well organized, but we could improve it by making it a database in which each portion of the macro text is in a memo field, something like the FoxPro 2.0 Help file. We could then define fields for the keyboard macro name, a title, and possibly a description of each macro. We could index on the name, the description, or some kind of ordering code that reflects the macro's role in the application we're testing. FKY_COMP.PRG could then be modified to read the memo fields and write a single .FKY file with a selected set of tests. This would allow us to group the tests, picking and choosing from our database to fit our needs. A driver program could then execute the keyboard macros in sequence or according to some other data, such as a menu presented to the tester.

To make sure the test is realistic, we need to examine the results. A testing program would need to store the results in a database or message file or compare the results in the data files with a correct set in another directory.

Limitations of FoxPro 2 Keyboard Macros

Some of the limitations of the FoxPro 2 keyboard macro facility interfere with the automation of software testing.

Mouse Events

In the *ON KEY LABEL* documentation, mouse events have names, which stem from the fact that the values that mouse events return to *INKEY("M")* can be detected by *ON KEY LABEL*. Investigating further, we see that we can key in the names {MOUSE}, {LEFTMOUSE}, and {RIGHTMOUSE} in the keyboard macro edit window. Then, the keyboard macro is triggered, "playing" the mouse clicks. This seems to suggest that mouse events can be recorded and played back.

Close, but no cigar. First of all, the macro recorder will not detect a mouse click, though the macro editor will allow {MOUSE} and its siblings to be entered in a macro, and the macro engine will play them. Even more important, a keyboard macro can't move the mouse to a given screen location (the Microsoft Windows 3 Recorder, on the other hand, does record mouse events into the macro.) Programs usually access the relative screen location (window) of the mouse after a click and act accordingly. For example, see the sample procedure for detecting a double click that Fox includes in the Help system under *INKEY()*. In order for the macro editor to record and play back mouse movements, it would need some kind of *MOUSE_GOTO x,y* command that would send the mouse cursor to a position on the 25-, 43-, or 50-line screen. However, there is hope: If you want to do more with the mouse than just send a squeak, try the API function *SetMPos* that's included on the disk that accompanies this book.

FoxPro 2 applications have become increasingly mouse intensive, and the necessity for simulating mouse events is obvious. Software testing by means of keyboard macros will be incomplete until we can include the mouse.

One further drawback: Not all keystrokes can be macro'd. As noted before, we can't access the lock state keys, even though they have keyboard scan codes. That means that we can't record or play the NumLock, CapsLock, or ScrollLock keystrokes.

Control Structures

Another area I'd like to see Fox improve is the way keyboard macro sequences are stored in an .FKY file, namely as a pure sequence of keystrokes. There does not seem to be any method for adding control structures to this raw sequence. Compare Lotus macros in this regard: like Lotus, the FoxPro 2 keyboard macro edit window recognizes special keys as keynames surrounded by the curly braces, "{" and "}." Unlike Lotus macros, though, FoxPro 2 keyboard macros do not contain control structures for repetitions, variables, and the ability to call subroutines.

This problem probably stems from the fact that FoxPro 2's programming language is separate from the keyboard macro facility. We can use a program command to *PLAY MACRO*, but the resulting macro is a literal sequence. We cannot pass parameters to keyboard macros, vary the keystroke sequence based on the values of variables, or even record macros through procedures. Therefore, keyboard macros are extremely static entities.

FoxPro 2 encourages us to incorporate menu bars in our applications, bars which may be enabled or disabled. Yet no method is provided that will change the keystroke sequence of a keyboard macro, based on whether a given bar is enabled or not.

Further, keyboard macro labels force us to invoke iteration by repetition. We have to write {TAB}{TAB}{TAB}, rather than using a shortcut such as {TAB 3}, which is Lotus's method. So it would be helpful to have the DO WHILE and FOR/NEXT control structures available to make writing iteration more efficient. We also need an IF/ELSE/ENDIF structure to vary keystroke sequences on the fly, in response to the value of certain variables, counters, or internal status values, and so on.

Closer Integration

My last enhancement request (for now!) is for a closer integration of the keyboard macro facility with FoxPro 2's screen and menu building facilities, as well as the FoxPro 2 programming language. The keyboard macro facility has its own commands, a unique interface with the System menu, even its own editor. It would be nice to see keyboard macros created in much the same way that screens and menus are built from a combination of database files and generator programs.

The keyboard macro facility should also be more closely integrated with the *KEYBOARD* and *ON KEY LABEL* commands. It would be nice to be able to DO a keyboard macro, for example. If the keyboard macro could make use of FoxPro 2's control structures, it could access built-in functions to determine which paths of a menu are enabled and can be traversed.

On the Positive Side...

Nevertheless, the ability to turn keyboard macros into text, clone and modify them, add comments to them, and store them in libraries makes automated testing of keyboard events for a FoxPro 2 application a realistic undertaking, in my opinion. In one of the applications I am currently working on, a baseline test consists of one keyboard macro, taking a circuitous path through a particularly complex set of data entry screens.

My current plans are to assemble a set of cloned macros into a library, varying each macro just enough to test a complete variety of paths. The end result will be a test suite to exercise one fork of an application.

Just ponder the implications from the developer's standpoint: We spend considerable effort with an editor to produce a working application, then we turn the software over to the user. Editable macros take this process one step beyond: Using keyboard macros, we can program the use of the software.

Could we automate all testing? Probably not. Highly dynamic applications would require new test cases for each customization. It could easily take more effort to design automated test cases for an installation than to carry out the customization, and the resulting test cases would apply only to that installation. That hardly seems practical, especially when hand-testing would probably work better.

However, a stable application undergoing only minor customization and enhancement could be tested against a standard set of metrics. The more standard the tests across all installations, the more advantageous automation would be. The principle is that the more stable and less customized the application, the more practical it is to automate testing. Based on this reasoning, the primary benefit of automated testing is to keep the application stable and ensure a certain level of correctness.

Another way automated testing can help preserve the working core of an application is by ensuring that the bug fixes and patches that protect an application's weak spots aren't lost. We can use automated testing to reproduce the conditions leading to the worst bugs and anomalies and incorporate those conditions into the testing process.

Automated testing might also improve the user interface, with its abundance of selection combinations and complex data-entry screens. Here users are likely to try more things than the developer anticipated or intended. When we learn of new and unusual combinations, we can embody them in the testing algorithm.

Could we ever automate the testing process enough to anticipate crafty users who never use our software as it's intended? This is the same as asking whether or not all possible combinations of user input can be tested. For even moderately complex applications, the number of permutations and combinations of user input is simply too large. Maybe those users who have an instinct for trouble spots and can bring an application to its knees just can't be duplicated by automated testing!

Listing 4-2. A keyboard macro text filter.

```
*.......................................................*
* FKY_FILT.PRG                                    *
* Ron Talmage, August 10, 1991                         *
* A program to strip a keyboard macro text file of comments. *
* Assumes the text file has an extension of .KPR and puts   *
* the result in the clipboard.                              *
*.......................................................*

CLOSE ALL
SET TALK OFF
SET SAFETY OFF
CLEAR
*.......... Get the source file name in .KPR format
fInFile=GETFILE('KPR','Pick a source kb macro file for compiling:')
IF fInFile==''
   RETURN
ENDIF
hInHandle=FOPEN(fInFile,0)
```

```
IF hInHandle < 0
   RETURN
ENDIF

*........... Write the header
mClipText=''
cDblAmp='&'+'&'
DO WHILE NOT FEOF(hInHandle)
   * Strip tabs and trim
   mLine=STRTRAN(ALLTRIM(FGETS(hInHandle)),CHR(9),'')
   IF LEFT(mLine,1) = '*'
      LOOP
   ELSE
      IF AT(cDblAmp,mLine)<>0
         mLine = LEFT(mLine,AT(cDblAmp,mLine)-1)
      ENDIF
      mLine=ALLTRIM(mLine)
   ENDIF
   IF LEN(mLine)=0
      LOOP
   ENDIF
   mClipText=mClipText + mLine
ENDDO
_CLIPTEXT = mClipText
=FCLOSE(hInHandle)
CLOSE ALL
RETURN
*................*
* End of Program *
*................*
```

Listing 4-3. A keyboard macro mini-compiler.

```
*.............................................................*
* FKY_COMP.PRG                                                *
* Ron Talmage 8/10/91                                         *
* A program to compile a text keyboard macro file.            *
* Assumes the input text file has an extension of .KPR.       *
* Produces a FoxPro 2.0 readable .FKY file.                   *
* Defaults to putting the kb macro in F2 if no #Name directive.*
*.............................................................*
```

```
CLOSE ALL
SET TALK OFF
SET SAFETY OFF
CLEAR

*.......... Get the source file name in .KPR format
fInFile=GETFILE('KPR','Pick a source kb macro file for compiling:')
IF fInFile==''
   RETURN
ENDIF
hInHandle=FOPEN(fInFile,0)
IF hInHandle < 0
   RETURN
ENDIF

*........... Get the target file name in .FKY format
fInFile=SUBSTR(fInFile,1,ATC('.',fInFile)-1)+'.FKY'
fOutFile=PUTFILE('Name of the .FKY file?',fInFile,'FKY')
IF fOutFile==''
   RETURN
ENDIF
hOutHandle=fcreate(fOutFile)
USE FKYCODES
INDEX ON keyname TAG keyname

*........... Write the header
mLabel=''
DO WriteHdr
nKeyCount=0
kbmTrigger=''
kbmName=''
cDblAmp='&'+'&'                    && Work-around for Fox bug
DO WHILE NOT FEOF(hInHandle)
   * Strip spaces, tabs, cr, and lf and convert to uppercase
   mLine=STRTRAN(ALLTRIM(FGETS(hInHandle)),CHR(9),'')
   IF LEFT(mLine,1) = '*'
      LOOP
   ELSE
      IF AT(cDblAmp,mLine)<>0
         mLine = LEFT(mLine,AT(cDblAmp,mLine)-1)
```

```
      ELSE
         mLine=ALLTRIM(mLine)
      ENDIF
   ENDIF
   IF LEN(mLine)=0
      LOOP
   ENDIF
   IF UPPER(SUBSTR(mLine,1,5))='#NAME'
      z=5
      mLabel = ALLTRIM(SUBSTR(mLine,6,LEN(mLine)))
      SEEK mLabel
      IF FOUND()
         kbmTrigger = CHR(Dec1)+CHR(Dec2)
         kbmName = SUBSTR(mLabel,2,LEN(mLabel)-2)
         kbmName = STRTRAN(kbmName,'+','_')
         LOOP
      ELSE
         ? '<< ERROR >> Key Name not found '
         * In this version, every error is fatal!
         RETURN
      ENDIF
   ENDIF
   z = 1
   DO WHILE z<=LEN(mLine)
      char=SUBSTR(mLine,z,1)
      DO CASE
         CASE char = chr(32)
            LOOP
         CASE char = '{'
            mLabel = char
            DO GetLabel WITH mLabel
            mLabel=UPPER(mLabel)
            IF 'PAUSE'$mLabel
               DO WritePause WITH mLabel
               LOOP
            ELSE
               SEEK mLabel
            ENDIF
         OTHERWISE
            SEEK char
            z=z+1
```

```
      ENDCASE
      IF FOUND()
         =FWRITE(hOutHandle,CHR(Dec1)+CHR(Dec2))
         nKeyCount=nKeyCount+1
      ELSE
         IF AT('PAUSE',mLine)>0
            DO WritePause
         ELSE
            ? 'ERROR >> '+ mLine
            ? SPACE(9+z-1)+'^'
            * In this version, every error is fatal!
            RETURN
         ENDIF
      ENDIF
   ENDDO
ENDDO
=FWRITE(hOutHandle,CHR(26))   && Write the eof marker
IF LEN(kbmName) > 0
   DO WriteKey WITH kbmTrigger,kbmName
ENDIF
DO WriteLngth WITH nKeyCount  && then write the length
length
=FCLOSE(hInHandle)
=FCLOSE(hOutHandle)
CLOSE ALL
RETURN

*.........................................................*
* Procedures for FKY_COMP.PRG                             *
*.........................................................*
PROC GetLabel                 && Parse the label out
PARAMETERS mLabel
PRIVATE q
q=z+1
DO WHILE SUBSTR(mLine,q,1) <> '}'
   mLabel=mLabel+SUBSTR(mLine,q,1)
   q=q+1
   IF q-z>23
      EXIT
   ENDIF
ENDDO
```

```
z=q
mLabel=mLabel+SUBSTR(mLine,z,1)
z=z+1
RETURN

PROC WriteHdr                         && Write header bytes
* for one kb macro,
Hdr=CHR(255)+CHR(121)+REPLICATE(CHR(32),13)+CHR(0)+CHR(01) ;
   +CHR(0)
Hdr=Hdr+CHR(70)+CHR(50)+REPLICATE(CHR(0),18) && Default to F2
Hdr=Hdr+CHR(0)+CHR(0)                 && Zero length for now
Hdr=Hdr+CHR(60)+CHR(01)               && And now the trigger
=FWRITE(hOutHandle,Hdr)
RETURN

PROC WriteKey
PARAMETERS kbmTrigger, kbmName
=FSEEK(hOutHandle,18,0)
=FWRITE(hOutHandle,kbmName)
=FSEEK(hOutHandle,40,0)
=FWRITE(hOutHandle,kbmTrigger)
RETURN
PROC WriteLngth                       && Writes the length
PARAMETERS nKeyCount
IF nKeyCount > 256
   chCount = CHR(MOD(nKeyCount,256))+CHR(INT(nKeyCount/256))
ELSE
   chCount = CHR(nKeyCount)+CHR(0)
ENDIF
=FSEEK(hOutHandle,38,0)
=FWRITE(hOutHandle,chCount)
RETURN

PROC WritePause                       && Converts Pause
PARAMETERS mLabel
pLabel=''
w=1
DO WHILE SUBSTR(mLabel,w,1)<>' ' && Skip past 'Pause'
   w=w+1
   pchar=SUBSTR(mLabel,w,1)
```

```
ENDDO
w=w+1
DO WHILE SUBSTR(mLabel,w,1)<>'}'     && Collect numeric digits
   pLabel=pLabel+SUBSTR(mLabel,w,1)
   w=w+1
ENDDO
=FWRITE(hOutHandle,CHR(254)+CHR(255)) && Write id bytes
IF pLabel = 'KEY'                    && Wait for a key
   =FWRITE(hOutHandle,CHR(255)+CHR(255))
ELSE
   pSecs = VAL(pLabel)               && Convert to a number
   pSecs = pSecs * 100               && Multiply by 100
   pSecs = MOD(pSecs,65535)          && but not over 64K
   chNum = CHR(mod(pSecs,256))+CHR(INT(pSecs/256)) ;
                                     && Set up two bytes
   =FWRITE(hOutHandle, chNum)        && Write them out
ENDIF
nKeyCount=nKeyCount+2                && two bytes' worth
RETURN
*.....................*
* End of Program
*.....................*
```

REFERENCES

Myers, Glenford J. *The Art of Software Testing*. New York, N.Y.: John Wiley and Sons, 1979. The classic on software testing.

Sanchez, Julio, and Maria P. Canton. *IBM Microcomputers: A Programmer's Handbook.* New York, N.Y.: McGraw-Hill, 1990. A good preliminary explanation of the IBM keyboard scan codes.

ACKNOWLEDGMENTS

This chapter and the keyboard macro compiler would not have been possible without the aid of Jeff Winchell, who produced the FKYCODES.DBF table of keyboard macro scan codes and unearthed some of the more obscure aspects of the .FKY file structure.

CHAPTER 5

Optimizing FoxPro 2.0

by Jeff Winchell

Webster's *Ninth New Collegiate Dictionary* defines scientific method as "principles and procedures for the systematic pursuit of knowledge, involving the recognition and formulation of a problem, the collection of data through observation and experiment, and the formulation and testing of hypotheses."[1] You probably know a performance problem when you see one in your FoxPro applications, so this chapter will address the issues of collecting data and formulating hypotheses.

Data collection is fairly straightforward in most cases. You can usually run a few specific tests to pinpoint the problem, so the volume of data you'll need to collect isn't overwhelming. When you aren't sure where to look, however, the volume of data increases; in that case, you'll need an execution profiler teamed with a good query tool (like FoxPro's RQBE).

Another problem with data collection is published benchmarks. We all seem to be cynical about their value, but still we read them. Later, we'll talk about how to get the most out of benchmarks.

Formulating and testing hypotheses requires that you understand how FoxPro works on your computer. The FoxPro documentation focuses on the syntax and general effects of using various commands and functions rather than the details of what goes on inside the computer and how those commands and functions interact. Because many database programmers haven't been exposed to these complexities, this book covers them in three chapters: Hardware is covered in Chapter 6, multiuser considerations in Chapter 12, and the rest in this chapter.

[1] By permission. From Webster's Ninth New Collegiate Dictionary ©1991 by Merriam–Webster Inc., publisher of the Merriam–Webster ® dictionaries.

The scientific method also assumes strong analytical skills. Many would respond, "I'm a programmer. Of course I know how to analyze a problem." The reality is that we're often too pressured to find a solution *now* to bother with rigorous investigation. Since you've made the time to read this chapter, let's begin with a little math, logic, and common sense.

Developing Your Analytical Skills

To understand a process, you need to build a conceptual model of it for testing. Models are simplifications of reality created for convenience. As such, they will always leave out variables. The question is, are those other variables ever important?

As an example, one publication, attempting to describe how FoxPro 2 works, concluded that performance doesn't deteriorate as the number of index tags in a structural compound index increases. This model has two flaws.

First, the obvious problem: After you load a new table with data and index it, reading from the table based on indexed access won't slow down when you add more indexes. *Writing* will, however, because additional indexes need to be updated. This seems obvious, but not everyone thinks of it when designing a database.

A second, less obvious problem is a result of the first. After the table and indexes have been updated, reading from the table may slow down, sometimes dramatically. That's because the index nodes fragment during the update process. When the indexes were created, the Rushmore process[2] could sequentially scan the nodes, almost all of which are filled. As records are added or updated, the index nodes become scattered randomly throughout the compound index file and are often only partially full or almost empty. Scanning the compound index to create a Rushmore bitmap is no longer so efficient.

The moral of the story is that you can never have complete information in a model, even if you could dedicate your life to understanding it. You shouldn't be paralyzed by the prospect of unexpected results, but overconfidence isn't warranted either.

Keeping these caveats in mind, we need to limit the scope of our inquiry. By setting up hypothetical best-and-worst performance tests, we can quickly determine whether further investigation is necessary.

2 Winchell, Jeff. "FoxPro 2's Rushmore" *DBMS*, 4(10) : 54 (Sept.1991).

Take the following example. When a record is appended to a shared table that's indexed on many fields, several steps are required to lock relevant sections of the table's file and any associated index files. If many records need to be added at once, the large number of *APPEND* statements, required locking, and reading and writing to files will take time. We can speed up FoxPro's buffering techniques most efficiently by *SET*ting *EXCLUSIVE ON*. If that doesn't solve the problem, we have a larger problem that might require a completely different solution (such as hardware or network operating system changes).

Another example of applying a best-and-worst performance test involves macro substitution. Conventional wisdom says macro substitution is slow and should be replaced by indirect referencing whenever possible, but is it worthwhile to change existing programs? A common application of this change is to open a table:

```
tablename = 'Yourdbf'
USE &tablename
```

The indirect referencing syntax is

```
tablename = 'Yourdbf'
USE (tablename)
```

When a macro is encountered, FoxPro must evaluate this expression at run time and compile it. If using macro substitution here is a worst case, the best case would be to reference the table directly:

```
USE Yourdbf
```

If the time to execute *USE &tablename* is .216 seconds and the time to execute *USE Yourdbf* is .209 seconds, you probably won't want to bother changing all your macro substitutions to indirect referencing. This won't be true in all cases (we're using a simple model); depending on the command, the PC, and the application, the time to call the macro compiler could be significant compared to the execution time of the command itself. If the macro compiler is called repeatedly in a small loop, it could significantly slow the application.

Repeating a procedure in a loop is a common test in published benchmarks. Ostensibly, it's designed to minimize random fluctuations to get more accurate average timings. The tester will mention things like "the law of large numbers guarantees a statistically reliable result" or something similar.

One problem with this design is caching. If a routine is executed repeatedly, various caches (CPU caches, operating-system buffers, disk caches, hard-disk controller caches, FoxPro's internal cache, and so on) can speed up the process. The average execution time will be less than that of the first iteration. This is fine if the real-world event is executed repeatedly in a loop; otherwise, it may be a problem. Perhaps a better measure would be multiple timings: first iteration, maximum, and steady state (including the number of iterations needed to achieve the steady state). The method you choose will be greatly influenced by your understanding of the process being measured.

A variation is to create multiple copies of the same data, ensuring a sufficiently large table to measure small times. In one publication, a benchmark table was created by appending the same 1,000 records five times. This redundancy resulted in index seek times for two products that were vastly different from those results for a table with nonredundant records. Of course, this index redundancy sometimes models the real world accurately (such as when an index on an invoice-number field in a line-item table has five line-item records for each invoice number).

These examples point up the difficulties in measuring results. Processing the same data repeatedly can't always be avoided. In a test to determine a math coprocessor's effect on FoxPro, several of these issues came to bear.

Consider the time it takes FoxPro to evaluate the expression

```
total = subtotal * 1.081
```

The execution time without a coprocessor is less than the .001-second resolution of the *SECONDS()* function (*TIME()* is limited to a resolution of .01 seconds). If you include the expression in a *FOR/NEXT* loop, the total time will be more than .001 seconds.

```
start = SECONDS()
FOR i = 1 TO 100
   total = subtotal * 1.081
NEXT
? SECONDS()-start
```

Besides the effects of caching (in this case, there should be none), this example adds the time required to go through any loop 100 times. I considered writing 100 lines of code instead of the loop, but the time needed to interpret the extra code made the problem worse. The following code times the execution of an empty *FOR/NEXT* loop and subtracts that from the time needed to execute the loop in the last example.

```
emploop = SECONDS()
FOR i = 1 TO 100
   NEXT
emploop = SECONDS()-emploop

start = SECONDS()
FOR i = 1 TO 100
   total = subtotal * 1.081
NEXT
? SECONDS()-start-emploop
```

The next most significant problem is the time spent assigning the result to a variable. This isn't related to the effects of a math coprocessor on multiplication, so I removed that step.

```
FOR i = 1 TO 100
   =subtotal * 1.081
NEXT
```

Because operations on a memory variable invoke several internal FoxPro subroutines, I substituted a constant.

```
FOR i = 1 TO 100
   =99.95 * 1.081
NEXT
```

This caused a major problem. Suddenly, the time taken to run the loop dropped to nothing. By increasing the iterations to 50,000, I was able to get a .001-second total execution time. However, quick calculations led me to conclude that I had exceeded the MIPS (millions of instructions per second) rating on my PC. Something was wrong.

The culprit turned out to be FoxPro's ability to do *constant folding*. Because FoxPro evaluates and simplifies expressions involving multiple constants at compile time rather than at run time, my test to measure multiplication became a test to measure empty loops. I had to return to using variables in my tests.

Another factor to be considered was the time to run the *SECONDS()* function. Through further tests, I concluded that this wouldn't change the total times by more than .001 seconds, so I made sure my iterations were large enough to make the total run time much greater than .001 seconds. Finally, I rounded the final results to two significant digits to emphasize the lack of precision in these very short operations.

The preceding example demonstrates the need to try to disprove a test. The MIPS test provided a separate strand of evidence to validate test results. If you rely on a single chain of evidence (A implies B, which implies C, which implies D), an error early in the chain will be propagated. In fact, it's usually valuable to run tests designed to *disprove* your hypothesis.

Automating Data Collection

The level of measurement you use can vary greatly. Sometimes a simple, subjective observation—such as timing a routine externally using the second hand of your watch—is all that's called for. Other times, you need more. That's where automated tools come in.

A simple, automated method is to insert the following code into your programs manually:

```
begtime = SECONDS()
   do some routines
endtime = SECONDS()
WAIT WINDOW STR(m.endtime-m.begtime,9,3)
```

This method works if you can isolate the problem quickly. You may have problems with memory-variable overlap or variable scoping, in addition to remembering to take the code out when you're done, but in simple cases these aren't too troublesome.

A more irksome problem is the need to have someone monitor these timings and manually log them. If the system is multiuser, it's virtually impossible for one person to monitor the entire system manually. In addition, some performance problems occur sporadically. If these issues are relevant to your program, consider writing a small function to automate the logging of information for later study.

Unless you can afford to cut program performance in half, you'll want to take timings only at certain points. That means hard-coding these checkpoints into your program. You'll probably change the checkpoints' location as your knowledge of performance problem areas increases.

The following code describes a simple usage recorder:

```
CREATE TABLE Usagelog (Userid C(3),Routine C(30), ;
   Startdate D(8), Starttime N(9,3), Finishdate D(8), ;
   Finishtime N(9,3))
```

In your program's start-up code, you define a public array to store the timing information between function calls. You then create two functions to start the timing and end it, as in Listing 5-1.

Listing 5-1. Functions to collect usage data.

```
PUBLIC usagelog[6]
usagelog[1] = userid    && assumes you ask for the user's ID
FUNCTION Begtime
PARAMETER routinenm
usagelog[2] = routinenm
usagelog[3] = DATE()
usagelog[4] = SECONDS()
RETURN
```

```
FUNCTION Endtime
usagelog[5] = DATE()
usagelog[6] = SECONDS()
INSERT INTO Usagelog FROM ARRAY usagelog
RETURN
```

Then, wherever you want to measure performance, you add the following:

```
=Begtime("My slowest routine")
DO slowprg
=Endtime()
```

When you want to analyze this data, SQL and RQBE make it easy to look at the data from a variety of angles.

The problem with this method is that you still have to know beforehand what to measure. Inserting these function calls around every statement is a lot of work; what you need is a mechanism external to the program.

This mechanism is the debug window. The following idea for a debug window came from Dave Heindel and Janet Walker at Fox Software: Replace all your calls to *Begtime* and *Endtime* with a single call to both at the start and end of your application. (You won't need the public array to store information.) Then you simply change those functions to:

```
FUNCTION Begtime
RELEASE WINDOW DEBUG
__loghand = FCREATE('D:\PROFILER.LOG')
KEYBOARD
FPUTS(__loghand,PADR(SUBSTR(SYS(16),RAT('\',SYS(16))+1),12)+;
   "+;

PADR(PROGRAM(),10)+STR(LINENO(),5)+STR(SECONDS(),9,3)"+CHR(13)
ACTIVATE WINDOW DEBUG
RETURN

FUNCTION Endtime
=FCLOSE(__loghand)
RELEASE WINDOW DEBUG
RETURN
```

(Note: As of this writing, a bug in the *ACTIVATE WINDOW DEBUG* command causes the *KEYBOARD*ed string to skip the debug window and spill into the next *READ* object. To prevent this, call the *Begtime* function from outside your application at the command window and then start your application.)

The *FPUTS()* statement *KEYBOARD*ed into the debug window is evaluated for every statement executed. It places a line in the PROFILER.LOG file with data about the program file, procedure/function name, line number, and time of execution for each program statement. By creating this file on a RAM disk, you minimize the measurement process's effect on execution time. If you don't want to see the debug window on your screen, use the statement *HIDE WINDOW DEBUG*.

Some caveats:

Using the profiler on a FoxPro application running under Windows will probably give spurious results. That's because the timing algorithm Fox uses is overly sensitive to certain interrupts in Windows (and some TSRs), causing it to miss clock ticks. As a result, the *SECONDS()* time isn't quite accurate to three decimal places. You'll have to clean up this data (perhaps by assigning those records an elapsed time of .001 seconds). The easiest way to recognize this problem is to look for elapsed times close to one day (86,400 seconds).

You can't have a *CLOSE ALL* or similar statement in the program being run; that would close the log file prematurely. *CLEAR MEMORY* and other statements that release or overwrite the memory variable *_loghand* are also a problem. If this happens, you will need to *QUIT* or *CLOSE ALL* to close the PROFILER.LOG file.

You can use this technique to measure a single program or an entire application. If you want to hard-code references to these functions in your program, make sure the *_loghand* variable is public to all called procedures.

To collect this information into a useful table, use the following code:

```
CREATE TABLE Profiler (Procfile C(12),Procname C(10),;
   Linenum N(5),Elaptime N(9,3))
APPEND FROM D:\Profiler.log SDF
endtime = Elaptime
DO WHILE NOT BOF()
```

```
      begtime = Elaptime
      REPLACE Elaptime WITH m.endtime - m.begtime + ;
         IIF(m.endtime<m.begtime,86400,0)
      endtime = m.begtime
      SKIP -1
   ENDDO
```

You still need to match the source code to this information. By reading the source-code file name, stored in the *procfile* field, you can build a related table with unique source-code lines (see Listing 5-2).

Listing 5-2. Program to associate source code with profiler log.

```
SELECT Procfile,Procname,Linenum DISTINCT FROM Profiler ;
   ORDER BY Procfile,Linenum INTO TABLE Temp
CREATE TABLE Source  (Procfile C(12),Procname C(10), ;
   Linenum N(5),Sourcecode M(10))
APPEND FROM Temp
USE IN Temp
DELETE FILE Temp.dbf

GO TOP
DO WHILE NOT EOF()
   procfile = Procfile
   extension = TRIM(SUBSTR(Procfile,RAT('.',Procfile)+1))
   DO CASE
      CASE m.extension = 'FXP'
         extension = 'PRG'
      CASE m.extension = 'MPX'
         extension = 'MPR'
      CASE m.extension = 'SPX'
         extension = 'SPR'
      CASE m.extension = 'QPX'
         extension = 'QPR'
      CASE m.extension = 'EXE' OR m.extension = 'APP'
         extension = 'PRG'
   ENDCASE
   sourcefile = LEFT(Procfile,RAT('.',Procfile))+m.extension
```

```
    handle = FOPEN(m.sourcefile)
    currline = 1
    SCAN WHILE Procfile = m.procfile
       DO WHILE Linenum <> m.currline
          =FGETS(m.handle)  && skip this program statement
          currline = m.currline + 1
       ENDDO
       REPLACE Sourcecode WITH FGETS(m.handle)
       currline = m.currline + 1
    ENDSCAN
    =FCLOSE(m.handle)
ENDDO
```

At this point, you can use SQL and/or RQBE to search the execution profile data for trouble spots. A possible query might be something like the following:

```
SELECT Procfile,Procname,SUM(Elaptime) ;
   FROM Profiler GROUP BY Procfile,Procname ;
   ORDER BY 3 DESCENDING INTO CURSOR Temp

m.slowproc = Temp.Procname

SELECT A.Linenum,A.Sourcecode,SUM(B.Elaptime),AVG(B.Elaptime) ;
   FROM Source A, Profiler B GROUP BY A.Linenum ORDER BY 1 ;
   WHERE A.Procname = m.slowproc
```

Understanding FoxPro

By taking the time to learn how database programs work, you can explore FoxPro's nuances to optimize your applications effectively.

Normalization

Incorporating normalization techniques (described in Chapter 7) can either degrade or improve performance. Many database programmers are familiar with the former, but few know about the latter.

It's obvious that normalization frequently decreases performance. If you need to retrieve many rows of data in two related tables, you need a join. Joins are among the most resource intensive operations in database programming. If all the fields are in one table, the expensive join operation isn't necessary. The tables are then denormalized, as described in Chapter 11.

The problem with non-normalized tables is described thoroughly in Chapter 7. Updating these tables is more difficult. However, some systems are used exclusively for decision support via read-only databases. In this case, one of the chief benefits of normalization isn't relevant.

You might think all read-only query systems should denormalize their tables, but consider the following tables:

Billline (SSN C(9),Billdate D(8),Billamt N(8,2), Billcode C(4))
500,000 records

Patient (SSN C(9),Zipcode C(5),other fields - 200 bytes total)
100 records

A one-to-many relationship exists between Patient's SSN and Billline's SSN. The report collects most of its data from the Billline table, as described in the following code:

```
SELECT Patient
SET ORDER TO SSN
SCAN
   LIST NEXT 1 Ssn,Zipcode
   SELECT Billline
   LIST Billdate,Billamt,Billcode FOR Ssn = Patient.Ssn
ENDSCAN
```

The data in the master table is smaller because the tables have been normalized, so retrieval time from the master table is faster. If the tables are combined and the same information is retrieved, the report may run slower on a denormalized database. Other queries on that single, larger table may then be slowed down. If the query doesn't involve any of the new fields, the entire larger record will have to be read in anyway.

For read-only query systems, denormalization often makes sense. You'll still want to determine what the common queries are and keep rarely used fields in their normalized tables.

In update-intensive systems, normalization can enhance performance. Denormalized tables mean redundant data, and updating multiple copies of the data means locking multiple rows and/or tables and performing more write operations than a normalized structure would require. Writes are generally twice as slow as reads, so the penalty for denormalization may be even more noticeable than in the retrieval operations mentioned earlier.

However, if the data doesn't change frequently (as in a patient file that only contains fields like sex and birthdate), normalizing probably won't improve update performance because there aren't many updates. In this case, the usual retrieval penalty may outweigh potential performance gains for updates.

Optimizing for Contrasting Problem Domains

Every optimization is a compromise; it may solve one type of problem but make another worse. This is typically the case with the contrasting domains of transaction processing and decision support systems (DSSs). Transaction processing spends most of its time writing to files and perhaps reading some very small subsets, while DSSs spend their time reading very large subsets and only sometimes write to files.

To enhance DSSs, add more indexes. Indexed access makes SQL joins faster and improves Rushmore's optimization. Since DSSs usually retrieve larger result sets, Rushmore's optimization is generally superior to manual optimization using a combination of *SEEK* and *DO WHILE* statements. DSSs also tend to be more ad hoc, so you can't plan ahead to optimize every possible query. This is another reason to add more indexes. If your routines create temporary tables, are those tables used frequently? If so, consider adding indexes to them.

To enhance transaction processing, you want to limit the number of indexes. Each additional index means more data to write when you add or change records. Remember, writing data is generally twice as slow as reading it, so you'll want to try writing it in big blocks rather than having many statements write small chunks of data. Typical read operations are lookup functions to find a single record. *SEEK*s and

*LOOKUP()*s are more valuable than Rushmore searches; the transactions are usually more predictable, so you spend more time optimizing them than you would in the ad hoc, Rushmore/SQL realm of DSSs.

Another important set of contrasting domains is the single-user-versus-multiuser optimization. Multiuser optimization is covered in Chapter 12.

While balancing the opposing objectives can be difficult, one bit of advice is valid for all these scenarios: If you have multiple hard drives, consider placing indexes and tables on separate drives. Since you normally access the table and its index together, keeping them on separate drives minimizes disk-head movement. The only downside is in some DSS applications. Users who want the interactive version of FoxPro may be shielded from the need to open indexes if structural .CDX files are used. When you put the indexes on separate drives, they have to be opened manually.

Code Size: More Lines = Less Performance?

In most cases, combining multiple lines of code into one line increases performance because you're interpreting once and allowing FoxPro's internal routines to optimize the many steps a single line of code implies. In the case of data retrieval, the SQL *SELECT* statement may show this effect even more (although in certain cases the reverse is true).

A common example is a small body of code running in a loop:

```
GO TOP
DO WHILE NOT EOF()
   fld1 = Master.Fld1
   fld2 = Master.Fld2
   SELECT Other
   SEEK m.fld1
   IF FOUND()
      REPLACE Other.Somefield WITH m.fld2
   ENDIF
   SELECT Master
   SKIP
ENDDO
```

The first thing to do is change the *DO WHILE/SKIP/ENDDO* construct to *SCAN/ENDSCAN*. *SCAN* implicitly does a *GO TOP* and *SELECT*s the master table before *SKIP*ping the record in the master table at the end of the loop. This results in a loop like the following:

```
SCAN
   fldl = Master.Fldl
   fld2 = Master.Fld2
   SELECT Other
   SEEK m.fldl
   IF FOUND()
      REPLACE Other.Somefield WITH m.fld2
   ENDIF
ENDSCAN
```

Also, a *SEEK()* function can replace the *SEEK* command and *FOUND()* function:

```
SCAN
   fldl = Master.Fldl
   fld2 = Master.Fld2
   SELECT Other
   IF SEEK(m.fldl)
      REPLACE Other.Somefield WITH m.fld2
   ENDIF
ENDSCAN
```

You can replace fields in a table that aren't in the current work area (provided you aren't at the end-of-file in the current work area). Therefore, you can take out the change of work area (*SELECT*) and use the alias reference in the *SEEK* function to *SEEK* in another work area:

```
SCAN
   fldl = Master.Fldl
   fld2 = Master.Fld2
   IF SEEK(m.fldl,'Other')
      REPLACE Other.Somefield WITH m.fld2
   ENDIF
ENDSCAN
```

We don't really need to store those fields in memory variables; they can be addressed directly:

```
SCAN
   IF SEEK(Master.Fld1,'Other')
      REPLACE Other.Somefield WITH Master.Fld2
   ENDIF
ENDSCAN
```

Using the *SET RELATION* command reduces this program to two lines of code, with the second line taking almost the entire execution time:

```
SET RELATION TO Fld1 INTO Other
REPLACE Other.Somefield WITH Master.Fld2 ALL
```

Much of this may seem obvious to you, but it outlines the basic strategy. The difficulty lies in choosing the best commands or functions out of the 1,000 pages of commands and functions in the manual. Try to spend a few minutes each day trying new ones.

Sometimes you have code in your program that reflects your early programming days. Both you and the product may have changed, resulting in the need for less code (another reason to keep current with the commands and functions manual).

The opposite situation is when you combine multiple lines of code into one line that provides additional—and unwanted—functionality, added baggage that can slow down your program. You may be able to write your own *BROWSE* procedure that does less than FoxPro's native *BROWSE* command but that, because the added functionality isn't needed, performs more crisply.

At some point, you'll want to reduce the total lines of code in your application by writing generic functions and procedures. This technique mimics the process of software development that shrinks large bodies of code into a single command.

The positive side of function modularity is that you have more maintainable code. Besides winning praise from the programmers who inherit the code, you'll make the code easier to optimize. If one function is called in many sections of the program, you only have to optimize it once. You're likely to see benefits throughout the application, encouraging you to spend more time optimizing that function. Taking optimization a step further, consider rewriting the function in assembler or C using the FoxPro API, especially if that function is called thousands of times in a loop or in a large data-processing command.

You might think using the API is only worthwhile for complex routines and functions, but even very simple ones benefit noticeably. This is due in large part to the speed of the API compared to function handling with FoxPro code.

Try timing the following loop:

```
FOR i = 1 TO 1000
   ? Benchmark2(0)
NEXT

FUNCTION Benchmark2
PARAMETER para1
RETURN para1
```

With the disk that accompanies this book, try using SAMPLE.PLB to time this alternative:

```
SET LIBRARY TO Sample
FOR i = 1 TO 1000
   ? Benchmark(0)
NEXT
```

The code for the *Benchmark* function is also included in listing 16-2.

The assembler function, *Benchmark*, does the same thing as the FoxPro function, *Benchmark2*. In this case, using FoxPro's standard version, the performance gain in assembler will be about 100%. If you try passing a date or string rather than the number zero, the difference increases to as much as five to one.

As of this writing, this assembler function proves to be slower than FoxPro under FoxPro's Extended version. This is probably due to inefficiencies in switching from protected mode to real mode and back (the assembler routine runs in real mode, while FoxPro Extended programs run in protected mode).

The downside to modular programming with functions is that, in some cases, in-line code (code that doesn't call a function) performs significantly better because the function-calling overhead is eliminated. FoxPro isn't optimized to handle many repeated function calls as is a more compiler-oriented language like Clipper. Here is an optimal method, using in-line code:

```
x = 7
? x*3
```

and a suboptimal method, with a function call:

```
x = 7
? Udf1(7,3)
```

The following is a ludicrous example of suboptimal function-heavy code.

```
FUNCTION Udf1
PARAMETERS para1,para2
RETURN Udf2(para1,para2)

FUNCTION Udf2
PARAMETERS para1,para2
RETURN Udf3(para1,para2)
...

FUNCTION udf100
PARAMETERS para1,para2
RETURN para1 * para2
```

By stretching the definition of *function* to mean compacting many lines of code into very few lines, one can make a case against slower in-line code. The optimal method becomes:

```
y = 3
z = 4
FOR i = 1 TO 1000
   x = y * z
NEXT
```

and the suboptimal method becomes:

```
x = y * z
x = y * z
x = y * z
* ... 996 more lines of the same
x = y * z
```

These examples are extreme, but they demonstrate the point that blind faith in the religions of modular or in-line code may result in poor performance. Both examples have more lines of code and execute slower. In the function-heavy example, the difference is extreme because the function-calling burden is greater than the extra line-interpretation burden. In general, functions are preferable to in-line coding, but if you take them too far you pay the price.

Memory Management

While the topic of memory management is usually confusing given its vast nomenclature, its primary purpose is to keep information in fast RAM rather than on slow hard disks. The problem is that few people can afford to buy enough memory to avoid using their hard disks. (I'm temporarily ignoring the practicality of managing shared, updateable files with FoxPro LAN and the problem of data that's lost when you turn off the power.) How do you efficiently use the memory you have with minimal manual intervention?

Before FoxPro was introduced, most databases required you to optimize your memory use manually. This usually meant creating arrays of data that copied your databases in RAM or loading the database on RAM disks when they weren't being updated in a shared environment. Managing the large amounts of code often entailed tweaking the overlay management to fit everything into the 640-KB world of real-mode programming.

Many products have advanced their memory management to partially address these needs. FoxPro 2.0 has gone well beyond them. With its dynamic buffering techniques, FoxPro efficiently decides which *parts* of the tables and indexes should reside in memory. The 386 version removes the artificial boundary between working memory (usually no more than 400 KB for variables, arrays, and windows) and buffer memory (typically many megabytes of expanded memory for buffering files) so that all of your memory can be used for any purpose.

The segment loader, combined with bound applications from the project manager, makes overlay management invisible. Because these overlays/programs are also managed by FoxPro's buffering techniques, in many cases, these files need not be kept on RAM disks. This isn't to say these techniques are never necessary; the performance of FoxPro's buffering system won't always match your needs.

Arrays may be useful in data structures that don't map well to a relational model. Also, the standard version of FoxPro 2.0 could benefit from the memory-conservation techniques in FoxPro 1.0.

Chapter 6 and the article on FoxPro memory usage[3] provide more information about FoxPro's use of memory.

Testing Your Hypothesis: Benchmarking

Most people don't associate benchmarking with optimizing their applications. The type most people know about is more appropriately called "benchmarketing."

A much more productive use of benchmarking is to see how specific code works in your own applications. This is important in FoxPro because of its dynamic run-time optimization, its rapidly evolving enhancement by Fox Software, and the fact that Fox isn't in the business of teaching detailed FoxPro optimization techniques to its customers. Occasionally, the company will legitimize a performance finding in its documentation, but it's rare. Instead, Fox focuses its resources on making the product self-optimizing.

After optimizing your application, you may want to extend your research by varying the parameters—in other words, going beyond what you're currently using to what you might use later on (for example, trying other PCs with different hardware configurations or using smaller and larger tables). As the scope widens, others may dignify your work, calling it a benchmark and suggesting that you publicize your findings. This can be beneficial to people who know how to interpret those findings. For others, it can be a source of confusion and may support the "benchmarks are worthless" theory. A discussion on interpreting other benchmarks later in this

[3] Winchell, Jeff. "Memory Hog" *Data Based Advisor*. 9(4): 106 (April 1991).

section will lessen the chances that this will happen.

If you do decide to broaden your scope, creating a scalable data set will make the task easier. The normal way to do that—with a program to generate random data—can be enhanced if you know the distributions of your fields. If most of the values of a given field are between one and three but extend all the way to 1,000, a better randomizer would avoid uniform distributions. Correlations between fields may also exist; at some point, you'll find it too difficult to take into account all significant correlations and distribution parameters.

Before deciding whether to upgrade a Fox product, many customers like to see a benchmark comparing the new and the old. Unfortunately, most benchmarks from Fox emphasize file I/O, the area Fox spends the most resources improving. (Most public benchmarks are also of this variety.) In your application, other factors may be more important.

For example, you may find that FoxPro 2.0 running a FoxBASE+ application is slower than FoxBASE+. This is particularly true if you have 640 KB of memory or less. You might not even be able to run the application in FoxPro 2.0 if your memory restrictions are tight. FoxBASE+ was designed when most PCs had only 640 KB of memory; if your application needs haven't changed since then, you might not want to switch. In this case, the best benchmark is your application running on your PC. However, a little investigating may tell you the source of the slowdown in FoxPro 2.0.

Comparing different platforms (386 versus Macintosh II or a SPARCstation) is interesting to some, but finding the same database on multiple platforms makes such a benchmark difficult. Fox does support several platforms, but the products are at different versions. Nevertheless, the architectural differences may be important enough, as verified by the benchmarks, to convince you to choose one product over another. Although released later than FoxBASE+/Mac, FoxPro 1.0 runs in real mode, making the 640-KB memory barrier a real limit. The architecture of the Mac is different, so the memory barrier is much higher (many megabytes). For some applications, the result could be an earlier version on the Mac performing better than a later version on a PC.

The most common use of benchmarks is to compare different vendors' products. In my view, this is the least compelling reason to use them.

Understanding how a product works is much simpler than trying to understand how several products work and devising a fair comparison. Generally, you'll already have decided which product to use by the time you want to do a benchmark test on it. You probably used many other criteria when choosing that product. Further benchmarks are best aimed at making the most of that decision by learning how to use the product more efficiently.

The best reason for using multiple-product benchmarks is to get a feel for how different products perform in different problem domains. SQL Server is tuned for on-line transaction processing, while FoxPro is superior at ad hoc querying for DSSs.

Network model databases like db_Vista III are good at retrieving data for parts-explosion-type problems (for example, traversing a "tree" to find, in order, the bones connected to the neck bone). Magellan makes a far more efficient free-form text searcher than FoxPro.

Various benchmarks are published in magazines and journals. Often, the methods used to create those benchmarks are not. The hardware is usually chosen based on convenience. But differences in equipment usually make big performance differences in databases optimized to take advantage of hardware like FoxPro 2.0. Why are certain avenues investigated and others ignored? What contradictory evidence isn't investigated or reported?

The "War of the Wizards"[4] has gained appeal, but perhaps it answers one question while obscuring another. In this war, vendors or their appointed experts tweak their code to make it the best possible implementation of a specific task. This is useful for those of us who intend to learn our chosen product well, and seeing the source code may give us guidance as to good techniques. For the rest of us, however, it doesn't answer the question "How does this product perform in the hands of the average programmer, or even the above-average programmer?" The more complex the product (and the more undocumented its performance secrets), the worse this tendency is. It does, however, provide a source of revenue for database vendors who have their own consulting groups.

Of course, vendor-provided benchmarks that are unaudited and for which few or no details are available are essentially worthless.

[4] Sawyer, Tom. "Doing Your Own Benchmark," in *The Benchmark Handbook,* edited by Jim Gray. San Mateo, CA: Morgan Kaufmann, 1991.

On the other hand, not all published benchmarks are worthless. Some groups work very hard at creating objective benchmarks; some even publish their benchmarks along with the source code and complete details on their methods. If you dig for details, these benchmarks may be useful. A casual reading of the bottom line will only be worth your billing rate for the 15 seconds you spend on it.

Some Final Questions

Are you optimizing assuming the best case, the worst case, or somewhere in between? The answers to this question can be astounding. In an event-driven application, especially one that encourages ad hoc querying, do you assume the application will always have enough work areas available? If you don't, perhaps you're closing databases as soon as they aren't being used. This flushes the index cache, which may affect later retrievals from that table.

The best way to speed up a program is to take out the slow parts. As obvious as this solution is, it's often overlooked in the pursuit of warp-speed routines.

Have you stopped to consider whether you really need that slow routine? Have you thought about whether you really need to optimize a routine any further? Optimizing code can be a fascinating exercise in understanding how FoxPro works. It can also be a tremendous waste of time. Spending a few hundred dollars on hardware upgrades may be the best business decision in the short term and sometimes in the long term. Too many factors enter into the decision on when to stop optimizing for me to make any recommendations; you'll have to let experience be your guide.

It's also important to note that by saving execution time now you may be adding to maintenance time later. Tricky tuning solutions can swallow up your company's resources when someone tries to modify your programs. Fully document any tricks you've employed. Going so far as to write several paragraphs in the code is worthwhile if it prevents mishaps later.

Maintenance issues touch on one other area of optimizing: maintaining your performance tricks. You can't rely on a trick you learned four years ago to work with today's programming tools. Rushmore's use of *SET FILTER* is a good example.

Prior to FoxPro 2.0, how many dBASE programmers would have thought *SET FILTER* would *improve* performance? The current preference of .DBFs cached in memory over arrays is a less dramatic example (though *trick* might be a better description since it isn't publicized by Fox as the *SET FILTER* command is).

When all else fails, here are some "virtual" performance techniques to get you out of a jam.

Interactive speeds are often more important to a user's impression of system speed than a long batch procedure. If the batch procedure isn't too slow, it's the right amount of time for the user to get a cup of coffee or take a break from pounding the keys. However, slow data-entry response and screen refreshes that visibly paint the screen are annoying. The wasted time can't be used for anything but thinking about how slow the system is. If your users don't have VGA screens, consider acquiring them to enhance their perception of system performance.

Sometimes you just can't enhance performance any further, or you have to take a performance hit in one place to keep performance high in the others. In these cases, you can improve the situation using psychological tricks. If an interesting screen (other than the ubiquitous "Please Wait") is displayed, the user might not notice how long it takes to run a routine. Pete Olympia has gone so far as to provide a procedure to display random jokes on the screen while the process is running.[5] Be creative. You never know when an imaginative solution like this in your application might lead to additional assignments, rather than causing the management to pull the plug because it's too slow.

[5] Olympia, P.O. "Graphic Dbase" *DBMS,* 4(1): 99 (Jan. 1991).

CHAPTER 6

Optimizing Hardware

by Hamilton M. Ahlo, Jr.

While the ratio of computing power to computing cost has increased dramatically over the last decade, the ability of general-purpose application software to harness that power has not kept pace. As evidenced by its performance in database operations, FoxPro has proved to be an exception to that rule. But FoxPro demands adequate hardware. Indeed, if you expect it to jump through the hoops of user benchmarks with the agility it displays at trade shows, you must pay close attention to the hardware on which you run it.

FoxPro makes good use of system memory and 32-bit processors and can, when running on the appropriate hardware, manipulate large files with greater ease than any other DOS-based DBMS. Still, many FoxPro 2.0 applications will have to run on platforms ranging from the original IBM XTs (or members of its generic class) on up. Cost constraints and the need to use existing systems conspire to make life a little more difficult for the developer who must tell clients how they can optimize their hardware for use with FoxPro while preserving their current base of computing hardware. This chapter is addressed to that developer and suggests some general approaches to optimizing hardware for use with FoxPro 2.0 for both new and existing systems. For the developer who isn't subject to constraints of time and money, optimization is not an issue; such developers may proceed smugly to the next chapter.

Asking the Right Questions

It's surprising how few discussions of "appropriate" hardware for FoxPro begin with the fundamental question "What are we trying to do?" An excellent example is a question posted on CompuServe by a consultant who sought advice on hardware for a LAN that was to run FoxPro as the main task. The person asking the question was deluged with replies. The respondents all had very definite opinions as to the optimal hardware, and in the end the consultant appeared to be satisfied with the quality and quantity of replies he had received.

Interestingly, during the exchange of messages only one person asked this fellow what the end user (his client) was trying to accomplish with FoxPro. Was he doing free-form queries of large or small databases? Was this a transaction-entry application? Were all workstations likely to be equally busy at once? Would file- and record-locking contention be a major issue in program design? Was reporting to be handled in batch mode or constantly throughout a workday by multiple stations? Were other applications likely to be added to the system in the foreseeable future? What cost constraints applied? What level of reliability was required?

These and other critical questions have (or, in this instance, should have had) a significant bearing on the nature of the hardware this person recommended to his client. Without anyone asking these questions and without the originator of the request volunteering this information, respondents saw fit to recommend complete server and workstation configurations, disk drives, cabling types, network topologies, and so forth.

The consultant got what he paid for—free advice. Whether his client got any value from this approach is unknown. The point is that hardware recommendations, be they for configuring existing computers or purchasing new ones, must be made with specific goals in mind and with an awareness of the various constraints (the most common of which is cost) that accompany the decision. Without a clear notion of where we're going, we'll never know when we arrive.

The following are some prerequisites to understanding what the client requires and recommending a system.

First, you must understand the purpose of the application. Make sure you have identified those portions of your application that are speed-critical, then ask yourself: Can hardware improvements help? Many speed-related issues can be resolved by throwing additional hardware at them. Others cannot, and for those, other solutions (software modifications, user training programs) may be more appropriate.

Second, you need to understand the constraints involved. Monetary constraints are usually the most important, but others may also apply (for example, a system may need to be designed for handicapped users, or a policy may dictate that the most senior individual gets the newest system rather than the user who would most benefit from it). It's important to identify those constraints early in your evaluation.

Third, you must identify functional areas in your programs that may benefit differentially from optimization. Workstations used for intensive data entry by people taking telephone orders and working with real-time shipping and inventory databases may benefit from certain optimizations that a workstation devoted to printing batch reports might not. If cost is an issue, it may be useful to optimize only the data-entry workstation hardware and leave printing and reporting workstations for later.

Finally, an understanding of the computing environment is essential. Your program lives in an environment in which many other applications may exist on the same computer. You must ensure that the recommendations you make won't harm these other programs. Too often, a software vendor requires certain hardware configurations that preclude the use of other software. FoxPro should be able to coexist with most other software on the market today; however, you should be aware that certain configurations of hardware that may be optimal for FoxPro may unnecessarily restrict other software. For example, what if the client wants to use Windows in enhanced mode and you feel the extended version of FoxPro—which is currently incompatible with enhanced-mode Windows—is required?

Evaluation Criteria

The pure and simple truth is rarely pure and never simple—Oscar Wilde

Benchmarks for database systems abound. Almost every week someone is demonstrating in a journal or magazine that this function is faster than that function or this hardware configuration is faster than another. It's fairly easy to devise simple benchmarks to time the execution of simple programs in static environments and to arrive at the desired conclusions. Can these reports help you? Maybe.

Benchmarks are commonly atomistic in approach. That is, they make generalizations based on repetitive speed tests of specific functions or commands. Real-world applications, however, are usually a good deal more complex. Additionally,

FoxPro is a complex environment. Both standard and protected-mode versions of every FoxPro product are available in either a single-user or multiuser (LAN) configuration. Each operates in a completely different memory environment and requires separate evaluation. Differences in these environments may warrant different programming strategies to maximize performance. In addition, the hardware at end-user sites is usually heterogeneous; different CPUs, various memory configurations, and disk drives of varying speeds complicate generic approaches based on benchmark-derived rules. Benchmarks performed under controlled conditions on one computer or on a host of identical computers may not apply to another computer with a different memory configuration.

Most importantly, while benchmarks are interesting and can yield insights into design issues for programs under construction, they are not typically useful for evaluating installed hardware and may be only minimally useful for recommending new hardware.

The emphasis here is on optimizing hardware for programs written in FoxPro. Hardware adequacy on interactive systems (and this usually includes developers' systems) is entirely dependent on the task being performed and calls for specific recommendations on a case-by-case basis. For example, a member of a development team assigned to designing screens day in and day out in the screen builder won't need a powerful machine to keep up with his or her mouse movements or typing. Conversely, an actuary doing interactive data analysis with large data sets should have the most powerful machine possible given financial and other constraints.

Other than optimizing your program code, four areas of hardware optimization can help FoxPro deliver its promised speed: memory, disk-drive speed, video, and the CPU.

Memory

FoxPro is unusual among database programs in that it will use almost as much memory as you can offer it. It also uses this memory efficiently and intelligently. FoxPro will use up to 32 megabytes (MB) of expanded memory in the standard version and up to four gigabytes (GB) of extended memory in the protected-mode version, though current practical considerations limit this to 64 MB. Adding memory is perhaps the most cost-effective hardware upgrade you can offer FoxPro.

Memory can be used two ways to enhance FoxPro's performance. You can let FoxPro manage all conventional, expanded, and/or extended memory for its own use, or you can manually configure all or a portion of that memory for other uses, such as a virtual disk or a disk cache. The standard and extended versions of FoxPro use memory differently.

Standard Version

The standard version of FoxPro will use all available expanded memory and any free upper memory blocks (those portions of system RAM between 640 and 1,024 kilobytes, or KB) made available via a memory manager like QEMM or 386 To The Max. The way it uses that memory is contingent on the type of expanded memory, the memory manager, and the processor type. Two versions of the expanded-memory specification originally promulgated by Lotus, Intel, and Microsoft are in common use. LIM 4.0, the current version, has significant functionality beyond that in version 3.2. FoxPro's use of each is described below.

LIM 4.0

The first 64 KB of expanded memory is used the same way as conventional memory; all other expanded memory is used for I/O buffers. FoxPro requires strict compliance with the 4.0 specification. Memory managers presenting themselves as 4.0 implementations but that are, in fact, incompletely or incorrectly implemented will result in problems for FoxPro.

LIM 4.0 memory is implemented on 80386 and 80486 systems via device drivers. These drivers take advantage of the chips' ability to provide the hardware functionality specified in LIM 4.0. LIM 4.0 expanded memory on other platforms is provided by specific hardware on either the memory cards or the system boards in addition to a device driver.

LIM 3.2

FoxPro will use LIM 3.2 expanded memory but, due to the limitations of this version, less efficiently than at the 4.0 level. It will use all expanded memory for buffering I/O. LIM 3.2 expanded memory will increase file-processing speed, but it won't ease the RAM crunch on an otherwise memory-starved application.

Extended memory on 80286 systems is not used directly by either the standard or extended version of FoxPro.

On 80386 systems that provide expanded memory via a device driver, FoxPro can also use free upper memory blocks.

FoxProX—The Extended Version

The extended version of FoxPro doesn't use expanded memory at all. It uses both conventional memory (below 640 KB) and extended memory on 80386 and 80486 processors (DX and SX versions). It uses a DOS extender licensed from Ergo Computing to run in protected mode as a 32-bit application. With enough available memory, all FoxPro code and user code, as well as system and user objects, can reside in memory while still providing ample buffer space for disk I/O. The extended version also raises the limit on items such as string length and array size.

If FoxProX has less than 2 MB of extended memory when it's loaded, it enables a feature called *demand paging* that swaps Fox's code in and out of memory as needed. However, the extended version with demand paging enabled offers almost a negligible performance advantage over the standard version. Indeed, in tests it appears to be slower than the standard version when executing several complex SQL *SELECT*s in an environment of only 1.5 MB of memory.

FoxProX executes in protected mode out of extended memory; it no longer requires conventional memory except to execute its loader program, which puts the code into extended memory and sets up the protected-mode environment. It doesn't use upper memory blocks at all in protected mode.

You can tell FoxProX to minimize its use of conventional memory by including the line *DOSMEM=OFF* in your CONFIG.FP file or by specifying how much of it to preserve with the line *DOSMEM=nnn* (where *nnn* represents, in kilobytes, the amount of memory to exclude from the general memory pool). With *DOSMEM=OFF*, Fox will consume only about 130 KB of conventional memory (the resident portion of the loader and certain buffers). With *DOSMEM=ON*, FoxProX will use all conventional memory as well as all extended memory. Use *DOSMEM=OFF* if you need to reserve all conventional memory for executing external programs (via the *RUN* command) from within FoxProX. Otherwise, *DOSMEM=ON* or *DOSMEM=nnn* will provide additional memory and should probably be a default.

Memory Speed

When estimating application performance on a computer, people tend to give much weight to the processor's clock speed. This is a valid strategy for computational operations that are CPU-bound. For programs like FoxPro that depend on rapid disk I/O and intensive use of memory, such emphases need to be tempered.

Though the cost of memory has decreased significantly in recent years, the speed of that memory has not increased. Typical dynamic RAM chips in 80486 systems today aren't much faster than the chips in the 12-MHz 80286 systems that were the state of the art several years ago. This has posed a problem for computer architects because the CPU can now process data much faster than 70- or 80-nanosecond dynamic RAM can provide it. To take advantage of a faster CPU, we need ready and unimpeded access to data stored in RAM. If the system RAM can't supply that data fast enough, the CPU will spend some portion of its time waiting for it to catch up. Until 80386 systems appeared, this wasn't a problem; earlier processors made fewer demands on memory, and it was easy to provide RAM that operated at or near CPU speeds. Today it is a problem, one that will be exacerbated as processor clock speed increases.

For a program like FoxProX that uses memory intensively, the efficiency of memory architectures is a major concern. If a 25-MHz CPU spends half its clock cycles waiting for RAM chips to read or write, the processor will be operating (with regard to many memory operations) at an effective CPU speed of 12.5 MHz. A Fox Software utility, MEM2.EXE, will estimate the effective speed (in megahertz) at which your system is running with regard to the types of memory operations FoxPro performs. If you have an 80386 or 80486 system with extended memory, try running this program. (MEM2.EXE is provided on the disk that accompanies this book.) The results may surprise you. If you receive a rating that is less than the nominal clock speed of your CPU, your system memory is having trouble keeping up with your processor. If the rating is roughly equal to the nominal clock speed of your processor, congratulations—your system should run FoxPro efficiently.

Budget-conscious purchasers commonly choose computers based on the 80386SX. While this processor offers distinct advantages over the 80286 (primarily due to features other than speed), it still communicates with memory via a 16-bit bus.

Virtually all 80386 and 80486 systems communicate with memory via a dedicated (and proprietary) memory bus that permits 32-bit access to memory even on ISA (Industry Standard Architecture) bus architectures. In data-intensive operations that use system memory extensively, an 80386SX processor can't be expected to perform as well as its 80386DX cousin due to this limitation in addressing memory. If you're contemplating new hardware for a FoxPro application and are considering purchasing an 80386SX-based system, explore your options with the full 32-bit processors. The price differences are generally small.

Configuring Memory for FoxPro

Unfortunately, there are no hard-and-fast memory-configuration rules for FoxPro; its internal memory management is both efficient and dynamically self-tuning at run time. Each application is different, and only actual testing of your target applications will provide accurate information on performance in a given situation. Several common hardware configurations are discussed in the following paragraphs, along with suggestions for configuring RAM in each situation. Remember, these are general suggestions and can no doubt be fine-tuned for specific applications.

Machines based on the 8088 are evolutionary dead ends. Use them if you must, but don't expect FoxPro or other state-of-the-art software to run happily on them. Typically you can only do two things to augment memory in these systems. First, you can add expanded memory; this will boost speed significantly. Second, on certain machines, add-in memory cards let you expand conventional memory from the 640-KB boundary up to 768 KB, depending on the graphics card, disk controller, network cards, and other hardware installed in the machine. However, use of this part of memory is nonstandard and should be approached cautiously. If one card in your system doesn't coexist peacefully with the other, opt for expanded memory.

An 80286-class machine is slightly more useful than an 8088-class machine if expanded memory is available. If you have a fast local hard disk, allocate all expanded memory to FoxPro. If you have a slow local hard disk and are using files that reside on your local drive (in other words, they would benefit most from FoxPro's I/O buffering), allocate all expanded memory to FoxPro. If you're doing interface-intensive tasks with little data manipulation, are using very small files, or share data files resident on a network drive, allocate at least 512 KB of expanded memory for FoxPro to manage. Up to 2 MB of expanded (or extended) memory can then be used as a RAM disk to cache FoxPro's program cache and the FoxPro standard-version overlay file. Any additional memory should be configured as expanded memory. In most cases, using DOS 5.0 and loading it into the high memory area using the command *DOS=HIGH* in the CONFIG.SYS file will provide significant extra conventional memory for FoxPro.

If you're working with 80386-class machines, add enough memory to your system that you can use the extended-mode version. Four MB of total system RAM (3 MB of which is extended) is the minimum. Though the extended-mode version will run with less, 4 MB will preclude unnecessary disk thrashing at minimal cost.

Whether or not to use the extended version in minimal memory environments is a difficult question. In environments with less than about 2.5 MB free memory available (depending on the setting of DOSMEM, as discussed earlier), FoxPro can't load the entire program into memory. Instead, it reserves part of memory for use as I/O buffers, storage of executing user code, and object and variable storage. It also switches to what Fox refers to as *demand paging operation*. Similar to the overlays used by the standard version, it swaps its code to disk so that it has adequate memory to perform the requested tasks. It tunes this swapping based on usage patterns during a session. If you're running a program that uses a wide variety of FoxPro commands and interface features, this swapping may *never* tune itself optimally and may degrade speed somewhat. In the typical interface-intensive application, however, the extended version should be faster than the standard version.

In data-intensive operations, the story is a bit different. With only 2 MB of free memory, Fox allocates about .5 MB to user programs, I/O buffers, user objects, variable storage, and so forth. The remaining memory is used to store FoxPro's executable code. If you're working with large data files and performing data-intensive tasks, .5 MB may not be sufficient to buffer data effectively. If you were to use the standard version, which uses the conventional memory below 640 KB as well as expanded memory and upper memory blocks, you would have about 1 MB of memory for I/O buffers. While that memory is not available as quickly through expanded as it would be through extended, it far outpaces disk I/O speeds and thus should provide performance gains over the extended version in certain situations.

As a general rule, we can offer the following: Always use the extended version of FoxPro on machines with 3 MB or more of free memory. Try to use the extended version of FoxPro on machines with less than 3 MB of free memory unless you're doing very intensive data operations on machines with less than 2.5 MB of free memory, in which case you should probably experiment with your application to determine which version is more appropriate.

Disk Speed

A database program typically performs both sequential- and random-access operations off a local hard disk or a hard disk on a network file server. FoxPro is unlike other database software for the DOS environment in two ways.

First, FoxPro makes much more sophisticated and intelligent use of computer memory to speed disk I/O than does any other product on the market. To some extent, this mitigates the disadvantages of computers with slower hard disks. FoxPro also caches indexes and, to a lesser extent, databases on single-user systems (and sometimes multiuser systems; see Chapter 12). This buffering is responsible for much of FoxPro's speed in database benchmarks. Compared to the competition, it makes extremely good use of both conventional and expanded or extended memory (depending on the version of FoxPro you're using).

Second, Fox's Rushmore technology relies rather more heavily than average on rapid, sequential access to index files. (The *COUNT()* function, for example, uses *only* the index files read in sequential fashion.) Generally, any command that takes advantage of this technology will use sequential access somewhat more than commands that use the traditional seek algorithms. SQL enhancements to the FoxPro language rely heavily on Rushmore technology, which in turn relies heavily on scans of index files and the use of temporary files.

While FoxPro is extremely adept at optimizing disk I/O, it never hurts to have a fast hard disk. What constitutes a fast hard disk, however, is a subject of some confusion. A common measure of hard-disk speed is *seek time* (expressed in milliseconds), the average time required to move the read head to a randomly selected track on the disk. The time taken to perform many random seeks is averaged to produce this figure. While useful, this criterion is frequently used to the exclusion of other relevant measures.

Another measure of disk speed (a critical one for our purposes) is the rate at which data is transferred from the disk to the system RAM and from RAM to disk. Disk transfer rates are usually measured in kilobytes per second. Because this speed tends to be directly proportional to disk read speed, in this discussion write speed is considered to be dependent on read speed. (Norton Utilities' SYSINFO is a well-known program that presents both figures.)

Average disk access speeds today range from about 12 to 30 milliseconds for drives that normally accompany 386-class hardware. The original IBM/AT hard disk averaged about 40 milliseconds, while the original XT hard disk averaged 80 milliseconds. The average seek time depends on the drive-head positioning mechanism.

Disk transfer rates depend on three factors: the speed of the computer (system RAM, CPU, and bus), the efficiency of the drive controller, and the transfer rate of the hard disk, which in turn depends on the data density of the drive platters as well as circuitry on the drive itself. In the case of IDE (integrated drive electronics) and SCSI (small computer system interface) drives, the controller mechanism is incorporated into the drive; a circuit board installed in the computer or built into the motherboard is typically an interface device rather than an actual drive controller.

Typical disk transfer rates on 386-class systems range from 350, at the low end, to 800 KB per second as measured by Norton's SYSINFO and Core Technologies' CoreTest. Very fast 386 and 486 systems can achieve transfer rates in excess of 1 MB per second, depending on the drive/controller combination.

The reason these figures are useful is simple: although vendors supply the numbers for average access speed, users should consider data transfer rates as well. Operations that require very intensive random access with few or no sequential reads will benefit from systems with high average access speeds, but in fact, this type of file access is relatively rare. Sequential processing of a database and its associated indexes occurs far more frequently than does truly (and sustained) random access.

The greater the proportion of sequential access to random access in your application, the greater the benefit from a hard disk with a larger sustained transfer rate. If you do little or no sequential access, consider investing in a drive with the fastest possible seek times (about 10 milliseconds).

These discussions don't consider caching controllers that buffer disk I/O in on-board RAM. These controllers vary widely in performance and should be evaluated on an application-specific basis. If your application is disk-bound rather than processor- or memory-bound, a caching controller may help. However, FoxPro buffers disk I/O so effectively that the benefits of these controllers may be marginal given their cost. To test the efficacy of a caching controller for your application, try using a cache in expanded or extended memory of equivalent size and timing the items of interest.

Usually, you will find that disk access speed is so closely correlated with transfer rates and drive size as to make selection of a drive based on one or the other criteria pointless. Still, many advertisers and vendors present drive statistics as a simple "average access speed" figure. You should be skeptical when purchasing from such firms.

Disk Maintenance and FoxPro Performance

Database files that reside on local disk drives and grow with some regularity present a management problem in that they tend to become highly fragmented over time. This fragmentation will severely affect both sequential and random processing of all files in your system. Defragmenting your disk regularly with a utility like PC Tools' Compress or Norton Utilities' Speed Disk can enhance application speed substantially.

Disk Caches

Many FoxPro users claim significant performance improvements when using a disk cache. Though these claims are difficult to substantiate, a good disk cache will help in situations where very large numbers of files are in directories and files are optimized (all clusters are contiguous) on disk. In other cases, they have minimal value and require memory to which FoxPro would otherwise have had access. Generally speaking, you'll gain little from a disk cache unless you're already providing FoxPro with a great deal of RAM.

Fastopen

Fastopen is a utility that is shipped with DOS. Like a disk cache, it is memory-resident and speeds access to commonly used files but provides no benefit if you only use a file once. Unlike a disk cache, it maintains only directory- and file-location information to speed access for programs that are opening and closing the same files repeatedly in heavily populated directories. Fastopen uses less memory than a disk cache but is much more limited in scope. If you have memory to spare, a good disk cache (like Super PC Kwik) configured for 256 or 512 KB of extended memory should provide much faster access than Fastopen. If you're short of memory but are experiencing delays in opening files due to heavily populated directories, give Fastopen a try.

General Disk-Drive Recommendations

Short of purchasing new drive/controller combinations, you can do very little to improve older and slower drives. On older 80x86 systems that have MFM (modified frequency modulation encoding) drives with interleaves of less than one, a new controller that can support a 1:1 interleave may help somewhat.

For 8088 systems, there is also little you can do to speed up disk I/O. While faster drives can be installed in an XT, they usually aren't available for this class of machine. In many cases, controllers for these drives aren't available in eight-bit cards. Don't use disk-caching software on an XT; insufficient RAM is available to FoxPro in this configuration to justify using it for other purposes.

For 80x86 systems, select your drive based on the capacity you'll need. You won't see much increase in speed until the drive reaches 300 MB and above. ESDI (Enhanced Small Device Interface) and SCSI drives' performance correlates directly with data densities on the disk platters. A 1.8-GB drive is almost certain to have a higher average transfer rate than a 330-MB drive of similar physical construction using the same controller. We won't get into a debate over whether SCSI or ESDI is better. Either will do, and neither is inherently faster or slower than the other. Don't use MFM or RLL (run length limited encoding) drives; they're obsolete and offer a very poor price/performance ratio.

Unless you're using an IDE drive (in which case the interface card is probably built into the motherboard), think about buying a 16-bit controller. If you can afford it, a 32-bit EISA (Enhanced Industry Standard Architecture) controller will further improve performance. Don't buy a caching controller just for FoxPro; the price doesn't justify the performance since FoxPro buffers file I/O so effectively on its own. If you need one for other applications, however, FoxPro won't be negatively affected.

If you must use disk-caching software with FoxPro, set it up to use extended memory and, if conventional memory needs to be conserved, load its executable code into the upper memory blocks.

Video

For a text-based application, FoxPro can present a visually rich interface to the user. It makes very good use of colors and makes multiple output windows easy to program and manipulate. As a result, most programmers take advantage of these features in their designs.

While the overhead to manage these features is almost negligible on higher-end systems, on marginal hardware the speed of the video system and the amount of memory needed to manage multiple screen objects can affect the user's perception of application speed. Screens don't snap into place quite as quickly on an XT as on a 386 system; nor do menus pan along the menu bar as quickly. While little can be done to improve the native speed of the XT, a graphics card can be upgraded to give the machine a snappier feel. The IBM VGA (Video Graphics Adapter) graphics display standard typically accesses and manipulates video RAM much faster than earlier standards (MGA [monochrome], CGA [color], and EGA [enhanced]).

Installing a VGA card in these systems may cause some users to swear the application has been speeded up significantly. Someone who looks at the screen frequently, such as a data-entry operator, is more likely to perceive an increase in speed than, for example, an interactive data analyst who spends much of her time waiting for the results of real-time queries.

On 80x86 systems, the 16-bit graphic card will be significantly faster than its eight-bit rivals.

CPU Type

Generally, the faster the computer, the happier you'll be with FoxPro's performance. But how fast is fast enough? I'll venture a guess: For both multiuser and stand-alone configurations—assuming that a local hard disk with a data transfer rate of at least 500 KB is installed and the machine has 4 MB or more of RAM and a VGA display—a 20-MHz 386 with a 32-KB processor cache should be sufficient for most data entry and simple reporting. For some reason, 20-MHz 386s seem to be in short supply nowadays; the SX version, though slower than the equivalent DX version, makes a satisfactory substitute. For interactive data analysis with large files, use a 33-MHz 386 with at least 4 MB (and preferably more) of RAM.

Pay close attention to how effectively the machine you select uses memory by running MEM2 or an equivalent utility. Machines vary widely in their use of memory, and this can be a good indicator of quality design and probable performance under a real FoxPro application.

Unless you do repetitive calculations using the native FoxPro trigonometric functions, forget math coprocessors; they won't enhance performance.

Scrolling through windows and browses can be accelerated by a keyboard speed-up utility (available only on 80x86-class machines). Users generally appreciate the increased responsiveness. Many shareware versions of this utility are available.

A General Approach to Hardware Optimization

With the obligatory disclaimer that the following suggestions may not apply in every instance, here are some general suggestions to use for optimizing hardware for use with FoxPro.

- **The Application.** Know your system, and particularly, understand what situations create a bottleneck. Evaluate their importance to your application as they relate to user productivity. Consider whether problems may be more readily solved by hardware or software solutions. Problems caused by poor programming can extract a severe performance penalty that even unlimited hardware budgets cannot remedy. On the other hand, software bottlenecks that may bother a programmer for months may not really be important to the actual users.

- **System Memory.** FoxPro's performance is usually improved by additional memory. (In fact, I'm not aware of any program that is adversely affected by additional memory.) Memory is cheap these days. If you can add an additional 4 MB of memory for $200, it may provide the most dramatic performance gain you will achieve. Try this first.

- **Disk Speed.** If your data files are on local hard disks, defragment your disks regularly. If you have a lot of files, use Fastopen or a small cache. If you are working on very large databases, FoxPro will not be able to buffer all disk input/output in system memory. As a result, the speed of your hard disk (in a single-user situation) will have a significant impact on FoxPro's performance. Today, a hard disk with a transfer rate near 1 MB per second and with average access times in the 15 millisecond range are common. Unfortunately, you cannot buy very fast disk drives in smaller sizes (less than 300 MB) These are not inexpensive solutions, but they frequently yield dramatic impacts in speed. Be aware, however, that the capability of your CPU to process data at these speeds should also be considered. Installing a one-gigabyte drive with a 1.4 MB transfer rate into a 6 Mhz. PC-AT is not going to yield very large performance gains.

- **CPU Speed.** At some point, the incremental gains occasioned by memory additions, new hard disks, and program modifications vanish. At this point only a new system will suffice. If you are purchasing a new system for use predominantly with FoxPro, you may want to run the MEM2 utility on it prior to purchase to ensure that the speed of memory access in this system is consistent with the clock rate of the processor.

- **Multiuser Considerations.** Assuming that the server drive and memory are already optimized, common limiting factors in network situations (apart from the workstations on which FoxPro runs) tend to be the speed of the network interface cards, in both servers and workstations, and wire traffic. Assuming that your server's utilization is not currently at its maximum, adding additional network interface cards in the server and segmenting the network into separate wire runs will usually reduce wire traffic on any individual wire segment. It will not reduce the load on the server and may actually increase it somewhat, because it will require extra server overhead to manage the multiple cards. Usually this still translates into increased throughput for the end user.

Obviously, keeping abreast of the state of the art in hardware is a difficult task when software development is your full-time job. Nevertheless, it's necessary if your clients are to derive the maximum benefit from your FoxPro applications. Someday, when IBM compatibles run the 32-bit operating system that will replace DOS, the problems of extended versus expanded memory will be a thing of the past. By then, the marginal systems that strain to accommodate FoxPro will be rare, and virtually all hardware will run your applications without requiring attention to hardware configurations. Until then, the suggestions presented here may help.

PART III

Relational Programming

Theory *Can* be Practical

My initial reaction to SQL and the relational model was negative, a common response amongst dbase language programmers. I had three main criticisms of it:

- It was too theoretical. There were too many foreign terms and I could see no practical benefit to my programming efforts.
- Who cares if I could write my program in one huge SQL statement as opposed to 20 lines of FoxPro code?
- The theorists are constantly blaming the implementers at database companies for poorly performing products that only partially adhere to the 12 Commandments of Codd. Besides the shades of religious fervor in these diatribes, it seemed to me that there was quite a bit of back-peddling going on to explain why their "perfect" view of the world didn't match reality.

In spite of these objections, with the introduction of FoxPro 2 I have embraced SQL wholeheartedly as a solution to many of my problems. What changed?

In the summer of 1990, I spent considerable time exploring the inner workings of FoxPro 1.0's performance as I attempted to stretch the known boundaries of database management on the PC. I was creating a system to allow ad hoc queries that might include summarizing millions of records of data, with a performance goal of under five minutes: It proved to be a daunting task. I began with an overly complex scheme of database design that incorporated a large amount of redundant data. I really wasn't sure how I was going to handle the programming complexities of this scheme in under 5 MB of programs.

Sometimes, you have to be drowning before you will accept a life preserver.

When I finally read about relational theory and SQL, I took the life preserver. The first SQL book I read was Fabian Pascal's *SQL and Relational Basics* (M&T Books, Redwood City, Calif.). It presents the theory in simple terms. As I read on, my math background reemerged, and with it, an affinity for the theoretical cleanness of relational databases. As I write this, I'm also finishing an application for a substitute teacher dispatch with an elaborate set of conditional searches that I wouldn't have even considered attempting without FoxPro's SQL and an understanding of relational databases. Frankly, I wouldn't have known where to begin.

Part of the clean simplicity of SQL is due to the reduction in code that relational languages afford. Once you understand the model, it is simple to read SQL. For those who don't like the long statements typical of complex SQL *SELECT*s, I recommend breaking it up with continuation characters. It will then look like the many statements of your old FoxPro code, except that it will be 50 to 95 percent less code. You will also appreciate the maintenance benefits that come from such a simplification process.

So what's the cost of all these wonders? Well, for too many database programmers it has been performance. While it is easier for application programmers to write SQL programs than to do their own optimization, this makes it harder for the database engine implementers to handle all possible cases. Many programmers have given up trying to create their own generic optimizer and consequently fault the relational model for even encouraging this.

The author of this section of the book, David McClanahan, brings a different perspective to the arguments over SQL's usefulness. Having designed and implemented the SQL engine in FoxPro 2, one that outperforms the large majority of manual FoxPro coding, he is well-suited to argue the merits of SQL, both from a theoretical view and a practical one.

This first chapter in this section provides the conceptual framework of the relational model so that you can better understand its usefulness in FoxPro 2. The second chapter takes an in-depth look at the SQL implementation in FoxPro 2. After you read them both, as an exercise, I recommend you recode some particularly tricky routines in one of your existing applications. Don't be surprised if you find yourself standing in awe of the resulting simplicity and speed. Such is the power of one of FoxPro 2's greatest achievements.

—Editor

CHAPTER 7

The Relational Data Model

by David McClanahan

The relational model, introduced by E. F. Codd in 1970,[1] has evolved considerably over the years into a second version, which Codd covers in his text *The Relational Model for Database Management: Version 2*.[2] It has the virtues of being conceptually simple and formally based on sound mathematical principles, including set theory, the theory of relations, and the first-order predicate logic, modified as necessary for use in database theory. The view of the system provided by the data model describes the structure of the data in a natural form that users can understand without extensive training.

Two of the goals of the relational model are to supply *data independence*, by separating the physical format of the data from the view the user has of that data, and *data integrity*, by avoiding inconsistencies and anomalies when processing that data. Codd realized that if the data model was based on set theory, the standard set operations could be applied to the data with predictable results and that these operations could be modified and extended to meet the requirements of a data model.

The relational data model defines the following:

- **System architecture:** The structure of the data system, and the way data objects are represented.

1 Codd, E.F. *A Relational Model of Data for Large Shared Data Bands*, Communications of the ACM. 13:6, June 1970.

2 Codd, E.F. *The Relational Medel for Database Management: Version 2*. Reading, MA: Addison-Wesley, 1990.

- **Data operations:** With operators who provide methods for manipulating those data objects.
- **System constraints:** Rules that govern the operations so that the result of each operation will be predictable and will ensure data integrity.

Relational Architecture

The relational model defines the user's conceptual view of the data objects in the system. The data and the relationships between that data are represented as a collection of related tables. In fact, in the relational model, all data is viewed as existing *only* in tables, giving a consistent, uniform view of the database.

The fundamental structure in a relational system is the *relation*, a two-dimensional matrix consisting of columns and rows of data elements. A *table* is an *instance* (or *occurrence*) of a relation in the database system. (The terms *table* and *relation* are often used interchangeably, but as you'll see they are slightly different.)

Figure 7-1 is an example of a relational table with 12 elements of data. Terms for both the database view and the mathematical view of the relation are given in the example. The database terms are underlined, and the mathematical terms are capitalized.

A field in a database represents one data fact. Each field of data is drawn from a set of possible values. *Set* is a mathematical term for a collection of distinct elements and is one of the fundamental concepts on which the relational model is based. The *cardinality* of a set is the number of objects in that set. We can define the elements of a set by listing them all or by describing them. For example, the set of all invoice numbers might be described as the set of numbers from 100,000 through 999,999, or the set of sales representative numbers might be the numbers 1 through 999.

A table must consist only of atomic fields of data; in other words, each field must be a simple, indivisible type of data such as a number or a character string.

The table in Figure 7-1 has three columns and four rows. Each column has a label, called its *attribute* or *attribute name*, describing the information in the column. The label allows references to values in a specific column. Each column entry is drawn from a set of possible values called the *domain* of the attribute. This domain has a data type, such as numeric or character, as well as a specific format. Generally, we'll refer to the domain of each column as its data type, but this is a simplification used for convenience. The relational model requires that all data items in a domain consist only of atomic values. Every attribute value in a column is drawn from the domain of the defining attribute and, therefore, has the same data type as every other attribute value in its column.

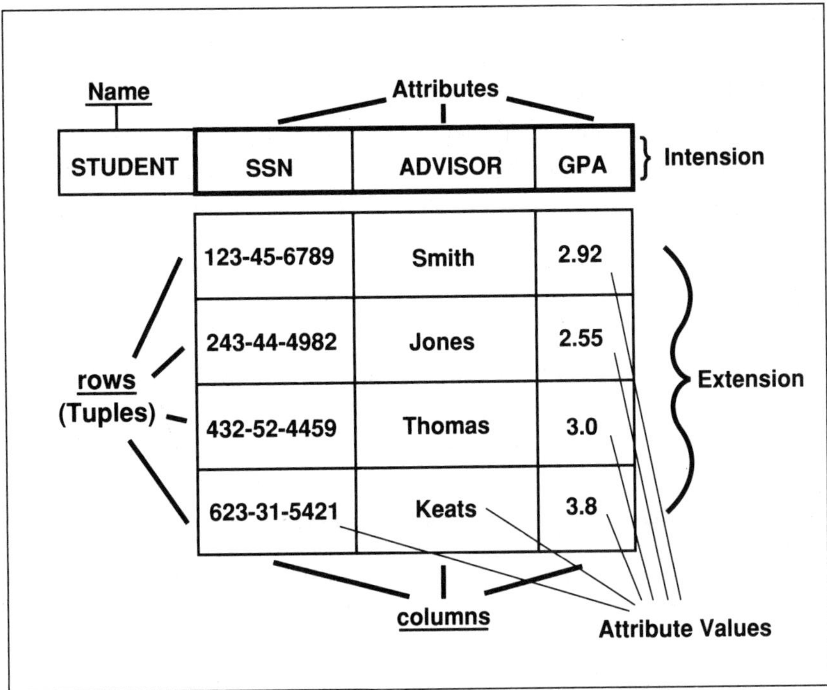

Figure 7-1. A relational table with 12 data elements.

SSN is an attribute used to identify a particular student by his or her social security number. *123-45-6789* is an attribute value, drawn from the domain of possible values ranging from 000-00-0000 through 999-99-9999, used to identify each student currently enrolled in the college (and entered into the database). The domain of the GPA (grade point average) is the rational numbers between 0.0 and 4.0, inclusive. For each column, there is exactly one attribute and zero or more attribute values.

The structure, or *schema*, of a relation for this example is a name and the set of attributes for the relation, in the form R(X,Y,Z). The schema of this relation would be:

```
STUDENT(SSN, ADVISOR, GPA)
```

Since the table has three attributes, it is said to have a *degree* of three. The schema is called the *intension* of the relation, and the attribute values making up the current body (or *instance*) of the relation are called the *extension.*

Each row consists of one value drawn from each attribute's domain and is called a *tuple*. A tuple for the student relation could be 123-45-6789, Smith, 2.92. The tuples in a relation are all of the same type; that is, they are based on the same relation schema. Tuples often are classified by the number of attribute values they contain. In this case, the tuples of the STUDENT table are 3-tuples and are said to have an *arity* of three.

The purpose of a table is to capture and store the characteristics of some entity or relationship between entities. Each row represents a unique entity or relationship in the real world, as each row in the student table represents a distinct student entity in the college.

Another example of a table is INVOICE (Table 7-1).

Table 7-1. INVOICE, a table of six columns and three rows.

INVOICE	INVOICE#	CUST#	DATE	REP#	AMOUNT	SHIPPED
	112233	1024	05/05/91	123	1345.50	.T.
	112234	4319	05/05/91	451	985.44	.F.
	112235	2055	05/07/91	451	2440.75	.T.

This table has six columns and three rows. *INVOICE#* is an attribute consisting of a numeric value that identifies a particular order. *112233* is an attribute value, drawn from the domain of invoice numbers (perhaps limited to a range from 100000 to 999999), that identifies one distinct invoice for the business. The schema of this table is:

```
INVOICE(INVOICE#, CUST#, DATE, REP#, AMOUNT, SHIPPED)
```

INVOICE is a *base* relation; in other words, it's a table that actually exists and is stored in the database system. Another type of relation is derived from other relations and is called a *view*. This is a virtual table defined as a view of other tables in the system. For example, the following schema is for a view (*SHIP-INV*) based on the INVOICE table but is designed to allow the shipping department to see which invoices have been shipped.

```
SHIP-INV(INVOICE#, CUST#, DATE, SHIPPED)
```

The collection of table schemas defines the overall relational database schema for a system. If table schemas must be distinguished from the database schema, the table schemas may be called *subschemas*. A *relational database*, then, is the current instance of all the relations in the database system. FoxPro programmers often refer to a table as a database, but this is not consistent with the relational use of the term, where a database is the collection of interrelated tables. We'll use the term *table* to refer to a single relation and *database* to refer to the collection.

Relations

Now that we have some background, we can define relations and tables more precisely. *Relation* is a mathematical term for a special kind of set: a set of tuples for which each attribute value is drawn from the domain of its corresponding attribute. A relation can also be defined as a set of tuples that form a subset of the set of all possible combinations of all possible values for each attribute (this is called the *Cartesian product* of the domains and is explained in detail later in this chapter).

In our sample INVOICE table, the values for the column *INVOICE#* are drawn from the set of possible invoice numbers, *CUST#* values from the customer-number domain, and so on. So the INVOICE relation contains tuples (rows) with each component drawn from a set of values defined in its domain. A table is actually an instance of a relation and, therefore, slightly different in meaning, but we'll use the terms interchangeably.

The corresponding (though not exactly equivalent) terminology for relational database theory, file systems, and mathematics is shown in Table 7-2.

Table 7-2. The terminology of relational databases as it translates into file systems and mathematics.

Relational Database	File System	Mathematics
Table	File	Relation
Column	Field label	Attribute
Column value	Field	Attribute value
Row	Record	Tuple
Extended data type	Data type	Domain

Each column in the database system can be referred to by a unique pairing of the table name with the attribute (column label). An example is *customer.id*, which refers to the ID column in the customer table. Each data element in the database can be located by the combination of the column and the primary key (discussed later in this chapter) of that table. Referring to each attribute value this way frees the user and the data from ordering dependencies, such as having to know the order of the attributes or the tuple's position within a table. While the display of the table may list the columns in a certain order, that order is insignificant and can be changed without changing the meaning of a tuple.

Each row represents a data object that is an entity or a relationship in the real world. The information in a tuple must be detailed enough to distinguish one object from another. The position or the order of the rows within the table is not significant and record number may not be used to access a tuple. This conflicts with dBASE programming, in which the record number is always used as part of the row's identity. In relational theory, a row's identity is determined by its unique *content*, not by its location. This doesn't mean you can't produce a list of rows sorted on one or more columns; it simply means the ordering within the table is not to be taken as a significant aspect of the tuple's definition.

Another important feature of the relational model is that tables contain no duplicate rows. Again, this conflicts with the dBASE world, but there are excellent reasons to enforce this rule. If a row's identify is defined by its information content, what meaning can a duplicate row have? If duplicate rows refer to the same object, they are redundant. If they actually refer to different objects, they don't contain sufficient information to be distinguishable from one another and should be corrected by the addition of one or more attributes. Remember that a table is an instance of a relation, and relations are sets of data. By definition, no duplication exists within a set. Relations that contain duplicate rows are called *improper*.

If the value for a particular field is unknown or does not apply, the relational model gives that field a *null value*. This entry indicates that no attribute value exists for a column in this row. It is not the same as zero. There are two types of null values. The first uses a system called *three-valued logic*, where the null value means MAYBE because its value is unknown (the other two values are TRUE and FALSE).

In the other system, called *four-valued logic*, the relative importance of the missing value is also noted. In this system, the null can be one of two types: MAYBE BUT APPLICABLE or MAYBE BUT INAPPLICABLE. FoxPro 2.0 doesn't support null values, but future versions almost certainly will if they continue to add relational functionality.

No multivalued attributes are permitted in a table. This means that no attribute in the relation's schema can consist of repeating groups of values used to capture multiple occurrences of one type of item. For example, in a table called CUSTOMER we might reserve a series of attributes to hold invoice numbers for each customer:

```
CUSTOMER(CUSTOMER#, ADDRESS, PHONE, INVOICE1, INVOICE2, INVOICE3)
```

or

```
CUSTOMER(CUSTOMER#, ADDRESS, PHONE, {INVOICES})
```

This schema contains a group of repeating attributes for successive invoice numbers. In addition to violating a fundamental rule of the relational model, it would be a poor design for two reasons. First, tuples would have empty fields if customers placed fewer than three orders. Second, where would we store a fourth invoice number? We can solve this simple problem by using a variable-length tuple, with attributes extended as necessary. But the need for a variable-length tuple is a signal that the schema contains repeating groups. To correct this, we can move the repeating group of attributes into its own table. The restructured tables look like this:

```
CUSTOMER(CUSTOMER#, ADDRESS, PHONE)
INVOICE(CUSTOMER#, INVOICE#)
```

Each tuple in the new INVOICE table will have an attribute value to link it back to the CUSTOMER table.

Normalization

The process of identifying the correct location of each attribute and the correct structure of the relations in the system is called *normalization.* We normalized the CUSTOMER table when we restructured it into the INVOICE and CUSTOMER tables. This syntactic normalization resulted in tables that are in *first normal form.* The relational model requires that all tables be normalized to this degree. For now we'll look at the most important types of normalization; the others are optional and will be covered later in this chapter.

The technique of dynamically relating tuples in two tables via attribute values (the *CUSTOMER#*, in this case) is another fundamental feature of the relational model and will be discussed in great detail when we cover joins between tables. For now, information content is what's important. In Table 7-3, it's used to create the link (or relationship) between CUSTOMER and INVOICE.

Table 7-3. Two tables with a common attribute: Customer#.

CUSTOMER	CUSTOMER#	ADDRESS	PHONE
	1022	123 Main	421-4543
	1023	32 Second	424-2343
INVOICE	CUSTOMER#	INVOICE#	
	1022	101	
	1023	102	
	1022	103	

Remember that a table is a data abstraction, a conceptual tool. The underlying physical file format may or may not be similar to the table. Several tables may be combined into one physical file, or one table may be split into several files (as is often the case with tables that contain an attribute that's a variable-length text field). The relational database management system, or RDBMS, handles the details of translation from the conceptual to the physical through some relational language. This isolation of the physical storage format from the conceptual view is one of the great strengths of the relational model: You can change the physical representation or access methods without changing the logical design of the data system. Even extreme changes can be implemented without requiring changes to the program code.

In summary:

- A relation is a two-dimensional matrix consisting of columns and rows of data elements. A table is an instance of a relation.
- Each table has a unique name by which we refer to it.
- Each table consists of zero or more tuples (rows of attribute values), and each value is a data fact.
- Each column has a label that should describe some aspect of the object being represented.
- Each column contains atomic values of the same data type. Each of these attribute values is drawn from the set of possible values (that column's domain).
- While the display of the table may list the columns in a certain order, that order is insignificant and can be changed without changing the meaning of a tuple.
- Each column in the database system can be referred to by a unique pairing of the table name with the column label. Referring to each field this way frees the user from any ordering dependencies.

- Each row represents an entity or a relationship. The order of the rows is not significant. A row's identity is determined by its (unique) content, not by its location.
- No duplicate rows or duplication within a set is allowed.
- If the value for a particular field is unknown or does not apply, the relational model marks that attribute value with a null.
- The domain for every attribute must consist of atomic values with no repeating groups. All tables must be in first normal form.

Keys

Tables contain information about entities or the relationships between entities. Each tuple refers to a different object, and each attribute value in that tuple supplies information about one characteristic of that object. Each table must have a column or group of columns that uniquely identifies the tuple. Each set of attributes that ensures the uniqueness of each tuple is called a *superkey*. An example of a superkey is the set of all the attributes in a relation, since each tuple is distinct.

Primary Keys

There may be multiple superkeys in a relation, but one of them must be designated as the *primary key*. The possible choices for a primary key are sometimes referred to as *candidate keys*. A candidate key must consist of the minimum number of columns that will ensure uniqueness. The other keys are *secondary*. If a single column is used to create a key, it is a *simple* key; if it consists of two or more columns, it is a *composite* key. Each table must have exactly one primary key. Any attribute that is part of a primary key is a *prime* attribute; the other attributes are *nonprime*.

What would be a good primary key in the REP (sales representative) table shown in Table 7-4?

Table 7-4. The REP table.

REP	LAST-NAME	FIRST-NAME	ADDRESS	CITY	STATE
	McKay	Kristen	123 Main	Lakewood	Ohio
	Smith	John	44 Apple	Cleveland	Ohio
	Russell	Kyle	9 Surrey Rd.	Middletown	Ohio

At first, you might think *REP(LAST-NAME+FIRST-NAME)* would make a good composite primary key. But what if a large company has two employees with the name John Smith? Another column, such as a sequence field that counts the number of duplicate names, would have to be added to ensure uniqueness. Another possibility would be to add the address column to the composite key.

A better solution is to create a new column with an ID for each salesperson (Table 7-5). Uniqueness is assured because we assign a number to each person.

Table 7-5. The REP table with primary key *REP#*.

REP	REP#	LAST-NAME	FIRST-NAME	ADDRESS	CITY	STATE
	101	McKay	Kristen	123 Main	Lakewood	Ohio
	102	Smith	John	44 Apple	Cleveland	Ohio
	103	Russell	Kyle	9 Surrey Rd.	Middletown	Ohio

The importance of the primary key can't be overemphasized. This key tells us what differentiates one tuple from another. And because the identity of a tuple is determined by its value and not by its position in the table, the primary key is the only way each tuple can be accessed. No column in the primary key can be null; if you don't have the information for that column, you don't have the minimum data required to enter the tuple into the table.

Foreign Keys

Suppose we need to know which salesperson made a sale so we can give that person credit (and a commission). The best approach is to include the *REP#*, which was defined in the REP table Table 7-5, in the INVOICE table (Table 7-6). The primary key of this table is *INVOICE#*. The *REP#* column is called a *foreign key*—that is, a key taken from another table to create a link between the two tables. A table can contain as may foreign keys as necessary to enable navigation between related tables.

Table 7-6. INVOICE table.

INVOICE	INVOICE#	CUST#	DATE	REP#	AMOUNT	SHIPPED
	112233	1024	05/05/91	123	1345.5	.T.
	112234	4319	05/05/91	451	985.44	.F.
	112235	2055	05/07/91	451	2440.75	.T.

Data Dictionary

An essential feature of a relational database system is a *data dictionary*, a repository of information concerning the system's data, architecture, and constraints. It stores the details of the system's structure, such as:

- Base relation names, attribute names, and data types
- View definition (how a view maps to source tables)
- Authorization privileges for users of the system
- Integrity constraints and assertions
- Triggers
- Statistical information used to optimize queries or analyze usage.

The data dictionary is a set of tables just like any other in the system and can be accessed using the same methods, but you may encounter security constraints when using these tables.

The Relational Operations

Relational languages, used to express operations on the data in relational tables, are generally based on relational calculus or relational algebra. *Relational calculus* is a nonprocedural language in which a logical notation represents the formula that satisfies a query against the database. *Relational algebra* is a simpler procedural notation of the operations that must be executed to create the relation. Codd has shown them to be equivalent, but we'll use the simpler one—relational algebra—in our discussion of relational operators.

Relational Operators

Selection

The result of any operation on one or more relations is always a new relation containing zero or more tuples. The select, or theta-select, operator lets us restrict the tuples that are added to the resulting table. We can formulate an expression to specify the conditions that one or more attribute values in each tuple must meet. In other words, a subset of the named relation is chosen for the resulting table.

Any of the comparison operators can be used in the selection operation. A theta symbol (θ) is often used to represent those operators and the operation is then called a theta-selection. The format of the theta-select operation is

```
σ <attribute> θ <constant or attribute> (RELATION)
```

where

- the symbol σ (sigma) is the selection operation
- the symbol θ (theta) is the theta-operator (one of the six comparison operators: {=, <, <=, >, >=, and ≠)
- *RELATION* is the name of the relation from which the selection takes place.

To name the output table, we use the following notation:

```
OUTPUT_NAME ←
```

For example, the expression to select the invoices from May 7, 1991, in Table 7-7 would be:

```
RESULT ← σ date = 05/07/91 (INVOICE)
```

Table 7-7. INVOICE table.

INVOICE	INVOICE#	CUST#	DATE	REP#	AMOUNT	SHIPPED
	112233	1024	05/05/91	123	1345.5	.T.
	112234	4319	05/05/91	451	985.44	.F.
	112235	2055	05/07/91	451	2440.75	.T.

This expression would result in Table 7-8.

Table 7-8. The RESULT table containing the invoice for May 7.

RESULT	INVOICE#	CUST#	DATE	REP#	AMOUNT	SHIPPED
	112235	2055	05/07/91	451	2440.75	.T.

Multiple conditions can be combined to create more complex conditions using the *not* operator or the connectives *and* and *or*. The following symbols may be used for these new operators:

¬ not

∧ and

∨ or

For example, to select the invoices dated May 7, 1991, or those credited to sales representative 123, we would use the expression

```
RESULT ← σ date = 05/07/91 ∨ rep# = 123 (INVOICE)
```

which would result in Table 7-9.

Table 7-9. The RESULT table containing invoices for May 7 or REP# 123.

RESULT	INVOICE#	CUST#	DATE	REP#	AMOUNT	SHIPPED
	112233	1024	05/05/91	123	1345.50	.T.
	112235	2055	05/07/91	451	2440.75	.T.

To select the invoices that are dated May 5, 1991, and credited to sales representative 451, we use the expression

```
RESULT ← σ date = 05/05/91 ∧ rep# = 451 (INVOICE)
```

or combine two selections

```
RESULT ← σ date = 05/05/91 (σ rep# = 451 (INVOICE))
```

Either expression would result in Table 7-10.

Table 7-10. The RESULT table containing invoices for May 5 and REP# 451.

RESULT	INVOICE#	CUST#	DATE	REP#	AMOUNT	SHIPPED
	112234	4319	05/05/91	451	985.44	.F.

Projection

The project operator allows certain columns to be selected from a table to create a new relation. The format of the project operation is

```
π <attribute>[,<attribute>] (RELATION)
```

where

- the symbol π (pi) stands for the projection operation
- <attribute> is the attribute to be projected
- *RELATION* is the name of the relation from which the projection takes place.

For example, to select from Table 7-7 the *CUST#* of customers who have placed orders, we formulate the expression

```
RESULT ← π CUST# (INVOICE)
```

The result is Table 7-11:

Table 7-11. The RESULT table containing *CUST#*.

RESULT	CUST#
	1024
	4319
	2055

Operators can be combined to perform selection and projection. To select the CUST# of every customer whose order has not yet been shipped, we use the following formula:

```
RESULT ← π CUST# (σ SHIPPED = .F. (INVOICE))
```

The results are shown in Table 7-12.

Table 7-12. The RESULT table.

RESULT	CUST#
	4319

Renaming

The rename operator allows us to rename attributes in a relation. The format of the rename operation is

```
δ <attribute1> ← <attribute2> (RELATION)
```

where

- the symbol δ stands for the rename operation
- *attribute1* is the new name of the attribute
- *attribute2* is the original name of the attribute
- *RELATION* is the name of the relation in which the renaming takes place.

Binary Operators

Binary operators are those that require two relations as operands. They include union, intersection, difference, division, and product.

Union

A union produces a new relation containing all the tuples from both source relations. Codd now stipulates that duplicate tuples be removed from the resulting table, but this is only done in the current SQL implementations of the union operator if it's explicitly specified.

A union operation is only permitted if the two source relations are *union compatible*; that is, the relations must have the same degree (the same number of columns), and each corresponding column in the two relations must be drawn from the same domain (must have the same data type). The format of the union operation is

```
RELATION1 ∪ RELATION2
```

where

- the symbol "∪" stands for the union operation
- *RELATION1* is the name of one relation
- *RELATION2* is the name of another relation.

For example, the CUSTOMER and SALES LEADS tables of Table 7-13 have the same number of columns with the same data types for each column.

Table 7-13. Two union-compatible tables.

CUSTOMER	COMPANY	ADDRESS	CITY	STATE	PHONE	CONTACT
	Apple Toys	42 Short	Littleton	MA	523-4523	Kristen
	Peach Printing	1 Last St	Davison	NY	354-3423	Mark

SALES LEADS	COMPANY	ADDRESS	CITY	STATE	PHONE	CONTACT
	Beach Gadgets	12 Shore	Boston	MA	426-7521	Jane
	Maple Furniture	4 Beatle	James	NM	526-6334	Mary

The result of *RESULT* ← *CUSTOMER* ∪ *SALES-LEADS* would be as shown in Table 7-14.

Table 7-14. The union result.

RESULT	COMPANY	ADDRESS	CITY	STATE	PHONE	CONTACT
	Apple Toys	42 Short	Littleton	MA	523-4523	Kristen
	Peach Printing	1 Last St	Davison	NY	354-3423	Mark
	Beach Gadgets	12 Shore	Boston	MA	426-7521	Jane
	Maple Furniture	4 Beatle	James	NM	526-6334	Mary

Intersection

The intersection of two relations produces a new relation with only the tuples common to both source relations. An intersection operation is only permitted if the two source relations are union compatible.

The format of the intersection operation is

```
RELATION1 ∩ RELATION2
```

where

- the symbol "∩" stands for the intersection operation

- *RELATION1* is the name of one relation
- *RELATION2* is the name of another relation.

So the result of *RESULT* ← *COMPANY* ∩ *CUSTOMER*, based on Table 7-15, would be Table 7-16.

Table 7-15. COMPANY and CUSTOMER tables.

COMPANY	COMPANY	ADDRESS	CITY	STATE	PHONE	CONTACT
	Apple Toys	42 Short	Littleton	MA	523-4523	Kristen
	Peach Printing	1 Last St	Davison	NY	354-3423	Mark
	Beach Gadgets	12 Shore	Boston	MA	426-7521	Jane
	Maple Furniture	4 Beatle	James	NM	526-6334	Mary
CUSTOMER	COMPANY	ADDRESS	CITY	STATE	PHONE	CONTACT
	Apple Toys	42 Short	Littleton	MA	523-4523	Kristen
	Peach Printing	1 Last St	Davison	NY	354-3423	Mark
	New News	14 First	Wayne	OH	424-1234	Nicole

Table 7-16. The intersection result.

RESULT	COMPANY	ADDRESS	CITY	STATE	PHONE	CONTACT
	Apple Toys	42 Short	Littleton	MA	523-4523	Joe
	Peach Printing	1 Last St	Davison	NY	354-3423	Mark

Difference

The difference of two relations produces a new relation containing only those tuples that were in the first relation and not in the second. A difference operation is only permitted if the two source relations are union compatible. The format of the intersection operation is:

```
RELATION1 - RELATION2
```

where

- the symbol "–" stands for the difference operation
- *RELATION1* is the name of one relation
- *RELATION2* is the name of another relation.

So the result of RESULT ← COMPANY– CUSTOMER based on the tables in Table 7-15 would be Table 7-17.

Table 7-17. The difference result.

RESULT	COMPANY	ADDRESS	CITY	STATE	PHONE	CONTACT
	Beach Gadgets	12 Shore	Boston	MA	426-7521	Jane
	Maple Furniture	4 Beatle	James	NM	526-6334	Mary

Division

Division produces the quotient of two relations. The relations need not be union compatible, but the divisor relation's schema must be a subset of the dividend relation's schema. While the division operation is more difficult to understand than the other operations, it's useful for expressing a type of query that occurs frequently in database systems. The division operation is the equivalent of the universal quantifier in the first-order predicate logic (found in relational calculus); it formulates a query that looks for a set of tuples with attribute values that match all those in another set's tuples. The following are examples of such queries:

- "List the employees who have visited all the following cities..."
- "List the manager who oversees all the following employees..."
- "List the tools that contain all the following parts..."
- "List the employees who work on all the following projects...."

The format of the division product operation is

```
RELATION1 ÷ RELATION2
```

where

- the symbol "÷" stands for the division operation
- *RELATION1* is the name of one relation
- *RELATION2* is the name of another relation.

The new relation will contain a projection of only those attributes in *RELATION1* that aren't in *RELATION2*. The schema of the resulting relation will be *schema(RELATION1) – schema(RELATION2)*. For example, for the following schemas:

```
SUBSTITUTE_TEACHERS(NAME, COURSE)

COURSES_TO_COVER(COURSE)
```

the resulting table's schema would be

```
RESULT(NAME)
```

Suppose *Y* is the attribute(s) in *RESULT*. The attribute(s) to be examined for the comparison are in *Z*, the intersection of the schemas of the two tables. In this case, *Z* would be *COURSE*. Now consider a number of sets derived from the SUBSTITUTE_TEACHERS table that have the same attribute values for all attributes in *Y* (in this example, three sets are grouped by JONES, SMITH, and WILLIAMS). If, for any of these sets, all the attribute values in COURSES_TO_COVER have an equivalent value, then the *Y* attributes in that set are entered into the resulting table.

Let's look at another example. Suppose we have a table of substitute teachers with the names of the courses each is qualified to teach. A second table lists the courses that need to be covered, perhaps as a result of one teacher's absence (see

Table 7-18). By dividing the SUBSTITUTE_TEACHERS table by the COURSES_TO_COVER table, we obtain a table (Table 7-19) that has only the names of substitute teachers who can cover all the required courses.

Table 7-18. Two tables showing the available substitute teachers and the courses to be covered.

SUBSTITUTE_TEACHERS	NAME	COURSE
	Jones	American History
	Jones	World History
	Smith	Algebra 1
	Smith	American History
	Smith	Geometry
	Smith	World History
	Williams	Algebra 1
	Williams	Algebra 2
	Williams	Calculus
	Williams	Geometry

COURSES_TO_COVER	COURSE
	Algebra 1
	Geometry
	World History

Table 7-19. The result of SUBSTITUTE_TEACHERS Π COURSES_TO_COVER.

RESULT	NAME
	Smith

Smith is the only substitute teacher qualified to teach all three of the courses to be covered: Algebra 1, Geometry, and World History.

Let's step through the division process. First, each attribute value in the COURSES_TO_COVER table is compared to a set of tuples from SUBSTITUTE_TEACHERS, defined as a set by a common value for the attribute *NAME*. If all the COURSES_TO_COVER values for *COURSE* are in that set, the *NAME* is selected for the RESULT table. If the COURSES_TO_COVER table is changed to comprise only American History and World History, the result will be Table 7-20.

Table 7-20. New COURSES_TO_COVER and the resulting table.

COURSES_TO_COVER	COURSE
	American History
	World History
RESULT	**NAME**
	Jones
	Smith

Cartesian Product

The Cartesian product of two relations is a relation in which each tuple in one relation is joined with every tuple in the other relation. The relations need not be union compatible. The format of the Cartesian-product operation is

```
RELATION1 × RELATION2
```

where

- the symbol "×" stands for the product operation
- *RELATION1* is the name of one relation
- *RELATION2* is the name of another relation.

Table 7-21. Two tables: CUSTOMER and INVOICE.

CUSTOMER	CUSTOMER#	ADDRESS	PHONE
	1022	123 Main	421-4543
	1023	32 Second	424-2343
INVOICE	CUSTOMER_ID	INVOICE#	
	1022	101	
	1023	102	
	1022	103	

The result of *PRODUCT1* ← *CUSTOMER* × *INVOICE* is shown in Table 7-22.

Table 7-22. The Cartesion result.

PRODUCT1	CUSTOMER#	ADDRESS	PHONE	CUSTOMER_ID	INVOICE#
	1022	123 Main	421-4543	1022	101
	1022	123 Main	421-4543	1023	102
	1022	123 Main	421-4543	1022	103
	1023	32 Second	424-2343	1022	101
	1023	32 Second	424-2343	1023	102
	1023	32 Second	424-2343	1022	103

The table resulting from a Cartesian product is of limited use in itself because it contains some random associations between attribute values. When combined with selection, however, it can produce a meaningful result. Consider the following selection for the PRODUCT1 table and its results in Table 7-23.

```
RESULT ← σ CUSTOMER# = CUSTOMER_ID (PRODUCT1)
```

Table 7-23. Result of CUSTOMER# = CUSTOMER_ID.

RESULT	CUSTOMER#	ADDRESS	PHONE	CUSTOMER_ID	INVOICE#
	1022	123 Main	421-4543	1022	101
	1022	123 Main	421-4543	1022	103
	1023	32 Second	424-2343	1023	102

The RESULT table lists all the customers and their invoices, so it does present more meaningful information than does PRODUCT1. We could get the same results using the following formula:

```
RESULT ← σ CUSTOMER# = CUSTOMER_ID (CUSTOMER X INVOICE)
```

However, a number of tuples are joined and then not used in the Cartesian-product operation. Relational algebra has another way to produce the same result: using the join operator.

Joins: The Essence of Relational Systems

Perhaps the most interesting feature of the relational model, and the one that gives it a great deal of its power, is the way relationships between tables are established. A logical interrelation between tables is expressed by the join mechanism in relational systems. Tables are linked dynamically through comparison of the values of columns in two tables. The joining columns are related in some way, as are the tuples in the two tables. For example, we saw a relationship between the CUSTOMER and INVOICE tables created by a column in each table that referred to a customer ID. The format of the theta-join operation is

```
RELATION1 [ATTRIBUTE1 θ ATTRIBUTE2] RELATION2
```

where

- the symbol θ (theta) is the theta-operator, one of the six comparison operators
- *RELATION1* is the name of one relation

- *RELATION2* is the name of another relation
- *ATTRIBUTE1* is an attribute from *RELATION1*
- *ATTRIBUTE2* is an attribute from *RELATION2*.

ATTRIBUTE1 and *ATTRIBUTE2* must have the same domains (or at least the same data types, for many implementations). Any tuples that satisfy the theta expression are placed in the resulting table.

Table 7-24. CUSTOMER and INVOICE tables.

CUSTOMER	CUSTOMER#	ADDRESS	PHONE
	1022	123 Main	421-4543
	1023	32 Second	424-2343
INVOICE	CUSTOMER_ID	INVOICE#	
	1022	101	
	1023	102	
	1022	103	

The result of

```
RESULT ← CUSTOMER [CUSTOMER# = CUSTOMER_ID] INVOICE
```

would be Table 7-25.

Table 7-25. The result of the join of CUSTOMER and INVOICE.

RESULT	CUSTOMER#	ADDRESS	PHONE	CUSTOMER_ID	INVOICE#
	1022	123 Main	421-4543	1022	101
	1022	123 Main	421-4543	1022	103
	1023	32 Second	424-2343	1023	102

The RESULT table holds one entry for each order a customer places. Instead of entering information about the customer—such as company, address, contact, and so on—and thereby creating redundant data, we simply enter the *CUSTOMER_ID* to link each invoice back to the corresponding customer tuple. Then, to find all the invoices placed by a specific customer, we need only look up the *CUSTOMER#* in the CUSTOMER table and list all the rows from the INVOICE table that have matching *CUSTOMER_ID*s.

This technique is called a *join* because tuples from the two tables are joined by the matching column values to create a new tuple in the resulting table. To be comparable, the columns must have similar data types. The join is *the* relational operator.

The join result is most meaningful when the two joining attributes have the same domain. It makes sense to join *CUSTOMER#* to *CUSTOMER_ID* because, although they're attributes of different relations, they have the same meaning. Current RDBMSs only require that the types of the joining attributes be compatible; they don't enforce domain constraints. Therefore, the following join is permissible:

```
RESULT ← CUSTOMER [CUSTOMER# = INVOICE#] INVOICE
```

but the relationship between *CUSTOMER#* and *INVOICE#* has no meaning in our sample tables and would produce a useless table.

There are several types of joins. The join condition in the preceding example compared two columns for equality. Known as an *equijoin*, it is by far the most common and useful join. In Table 7-25, notice the redundancy caused by the inclusion of two columns, *CUSTOMER#* and *CUSTOMER_ID*, that will always have the same value after an equijoin. To avoid this duplication, we can eliminate one of the columns through projection. This is called a *natural join* and is denoted by the symbol ⋈

Table 7-26. Two tables with a common attribute (*CUSTOMER*).

CUSTOMER	CUSTOMER	ADDRESS	PHONE
	1022	123 Main	421-4543
	1023	32 Second	424-2343

INVOICE	CUSTOMER	INVOICE#
	1022	101
	1023	102
	1022	103

The natural join of the CUSTOMER and INVOICE tables in Figure 7-26 would be expressed as

```
RESULT ← CUSTOMER ⋈ INVOICE
```

The natural join will join on columns with identical attributes and project one column for each matching pair, as in Table 7-27.

Table 7-27. The result of the natural join of CUSTOMER and INVOICE.

RESULT	CUSTOMER	ADDRESS	PHONE	INVOICE#
	1022	123 Main	421-4543	101
	1022	123 Main	421-4543	103
	1023	32 Second	424-2343	102

Any other comparison operator can also be used for the join condition. For example, the result of

```
RESULT ← CUSTOMER [CUSTOMER# < CUSTOMER_ID] INVOICE
```

is shown in Table 7-28.

Table 7-28. Two tables and a less-than join.

CUSTOMER	CUSTOMER#	ADDRESS	PHONE
	1022	123 Main	421-4543
	1023	32 Second	424-2343

INVOICE	CUSTOMER_ID	INVOICE#
	1022	101
	1023	102
	1022	103

RESULT	CUSTOMER	ADDRESS	PHONE	CUSTOMER_ID	INVOICE#
	1022	123 Main	421-4543	1022	102

Each *CUSTOMER#* in CUSTOMER is compared to each value of *CUSTOMER_ID* in INVOICE. If the value of *CUSTOMER#* is lower, that tuple is placed in the RESULT table. Non-equijoins, while not as useful as equijoins, are sometimes required.

If we wish to join CUSTOMER to INVOICE so that the RESULT table contains all the customers in CUSTOMER, whether or not they have generated an invoice, a special type of join is required. An *outer join* can include all the tuples from the left table in the expression, the right table in the expression, or both. When a tuple is found that doesn't join to the other table, the attribute values from that tuple are entered in the resulting table; the attributes from the second table are then given null values to mark the tuple as an outer one (generated outside the join). The format of the outer-join operation is

```
RELATION1 ⟕ ATTRIBUTE1 = ATTRIBUTE2 RELATION2
```

where

- the symbol "⟕" is the left outer-join operator
- "⟖" is the right outer-join operator
- "⟗" is the full outer-join operator
- *RELATION1* is the name of one relation
- *RELATION2* is the name of another relation

- *ATTRIBUTE1* is an attribute from *RELATION1*
- *ATTRIBUTE2* is an attribute from *RELATION2*

Table 7-29. Two tables with a common attribute (*CUSTOMER#*).

CUSTOMER	CUSTOMER#	ADDRESS	PHONE
	1022	123 Main	421-4543
	1023	32 Second	424-2343
	1024	55 Trail	462-2366
	1025	901 Ridge	422-2535

INVOICE	CUSTOMER#	INVOICE#
	1022	101
	1023	102
	1022	103

The left outer join of CUSTOMER and INVOICE would be expressed as

```
RESULT ← CUSTOMER ⟕ INVOICE
```

and result in Table 7-30.

Table 7-30. The result of the left outer join of CUSTOMER and INVOICE.

RESULT	CUSTOMER#	ADDRESS	PHONE	INVOICE#
	1022	123 Main	421-4543	101
	1022	123 Main	421-4543	103
	1023	32 Second	424-2343	102
	1024	55 Trail	462-2366	Null
	1025	901 Ridge	422-2535	Null

The Relational Rules

Integrity constraints that restrict the data values allowed in a column, limit relationships, constrain operations, or require existence dependencies are just some of the rules of relational database systems. The ANSI standard for SQL now supports relational integrity, and mechanisms to implement it are required in relational database systems. This is an area in which dBASE dialects' relational support is particularly weak. In FoxPro, the DBMS doesn't support integrity constraints; however, the developer can add support for these features using the FoxPro language.

Integrity

There are two types of relational integrity. *Entity integrity* means that primary-key attribute values may not be null. The column values in the primary key must be enough to identify the subject to which the tuple refers to ensure key integrity. *Referential integrity* means every foreign key in a table must refer to an existing key in the related table or must be null, meaning it doesn't refer to any key in any table.

An RDBMS should support the declaration of primary keys in its relational language and the enforcement of uniqueness for designated attributes. If a new tuple is added, its primary key should be checked for uniqueness and an error generated if it's not distinct or contains a null value. Any other attribute may be declared as unique within a table.

The RDBMS should also support the referential-integrity rule, which requires that the system administrator define what is allowable and what effect operations have. Consider the tables in Table 7-31.

Table 7-31. EMPLOYEE and DEPENDENT tables.

EMPLOYEE	EMPLOYEE#	L-NAME	F-NAME	DEPT#
	1021	Smith	Dave	101
	1022	McKay	Kristen	103
	1023	Russell	Kyle	102

DEPENDENT	EMPLOYEE#	F-NAME	BIRTHDATE
	1022	Keith	03-24-81
	1022	Shawn	11-29-89
	1023	Caitlin	10-29-88
	1021	Christine	05-14-80

If an employee tuple is deleted from EMPLOYEE, what should happen to the child tuple(s) in DEPENDENT? There are several possibilities:

- Delete the child tuples automatically upon deletion of the parent tuple
- Insert a null value into the foreign key (*EMPLOYEE#*) of the child tuples
- Prohibit the deletion of any parent tuple until all dependent tuples have been deleted.

If an employee number needs to be changed, a similar set of problems will arise.

When a new tuple is entered into the child table, it should be checked against the parent table for integrity. Again, the action taken if a parent tuple isn't located is determined by the database administrator.

Functional Dependencies

A *functional dependency* is the reliance of an attribute or group of attributes on another attribute or group of attributes for its value. (Pay close attention here—you'll need to understand this concept before we get to the discussion of normalization in the next section.) For any given instance of a relation, the dependent attribute(s) can have one and only one value for a certain value of the attribute(s) on which it is dependent (the determinant set). In other words, for each value of the determinant attribute(s), there is only one value for the dependent attribute(s). This requirement constrains the possible values in a tuple. A table, then, may not consist of all the possible combinations of the attribute values from each attribute's domain because a functional dependency will limit the dependent attribute's value. A dependency is said to be *fully functional* if you can't remove attributes from the determinant set without removing the functional dependency.

For example, in a relation with the following schema:

```
EMPLOYEE(EMP#, SSN, LAST-NAME, FIRST-NAME, POSITION, SALARY)
```

the value of the *LAST-NAME* attribute depends on *EMP#*. Thus, we can say that the *LAST-NAME* attribute is functionally dependent on *EMP#* and that *EMP#* functionally determines *LAST-NAME*. If you know an employee's *EMP#*, you can determine that employee's *LAST-NAME*. The notation for this functional dependency is

```
EMP# → LAST-NAME
```

or

```
LAST-NAME = f(EMP#)
```

In this example, is *EMP#* functionally dependent on *LAST-NAME*? No, because multiple *EMP#* values may exist for a particular *LAST-NAME* value. There may be many employees with the last name *Smith* and therefore multiple *EMP#* values in the database associated with *Smith*. A functional dependency implies a one-to-one association between the determining attribute(s) and the dependent attribute; in this example, each employee has one *EMP#* and one *LAST-NAME*.

Consider the functional dependencies in the following relational schema:

```
PART(SUPPLIER#, PART#, COST)
```

Is *COST* functionally dependent on *SUPPLIER#*? No. There may be as many values for *COST* as there are for *PART#*, so no one-to-one association exists between the attribute values of *SUPPLIER#* and *COST*. Then is *COST* functionally dependent on *PART#*? Again, the answer is no; the same part might be supplied by more than one supplier at a different cost. *COST* does have a functional dependency upon *SUPPLIER#* and +*PART#*. If you know the supplier and the part number, only one *COST* value is possible:

```
SUPPLIER#, PART# → COST
```

A relation's intension includes a set of functional dependencies. These dependencies are necessary to capture the meaning (or *semantics*) of the relation's attributes.

A *multivalued dependency* (Table 7-32) deals with many-to-many associations between attributes. Such dependencies have the following property:

> For any set of attribute values for schema *R(X,Y,Z)*, *X* multidetermines *Y* if there is a tuple *x1,y1,z1*; a tuple *x1,y2,z2*; a tuple *x1,y2,z1*; and a tuple *x1,y1,z2* (where *X*, *Y*, and *Z* are attributes and *x1*, *y1*, *z1*, and so on are attribute values).

Table 7-32. A multivalued dependency.

M-VALUED	X	Y	Z
	a	d	g
	a	d	h
	a	e	g
	a	e	h

Notice the multiple values of *Y* (*d* and *e*) and *Z* (*g* and *h*) for each value of *X*. Each value of *Z* also occurs with each value of *Y* for each value of *X*. Notice that Z = R – (X, Y) and that multivalued dependencies occur in pairs.

Suppose each project in a company requires two leaders and that these leaders are required to meet twice a week to review the status of their project. A relation to show the meetings, the employees, and the project they're leading is shown in Table 7-33.

Table 7-33. Another multivalued dependency.

MEETING	PROJECT#	DAY	HOUR	LAST-NAME
	81	MON	10:00	Jones
	81	WED	8:00	Jones
	81	MON	10:00	Smith
	81	WED	8:00	Smith

Notice that for each project number there is a set of multivalued attributes in *{DAY, HOUR}* that repeats (*MON 10:00* and *WED 8:00*). Note also that there is a similar set of values for *LAST-NAME* (*JONES* and *SMITH*). To show all the meeting times and all the meeting participants, the table must repeat each time *{DAY + HOUR}* for each employee name (*MON 10:00* for Jones and Smith, *WED 8:00* for Jones and Smith). This multivalued dependency is noted as

```
PROJECT# ->> {DAY, HOUR)
```

and

```
PROJECT# ->> LAST-NAME
```

or combined as

```
PROJECT# ->> {DAY, HOUR}/LAST-NAME
```

To see the multivalued dependency more clearly, look at Table 7-34 (where *X* is *PROJECT#*, *Y* is *{DAY, HOUR}*, and *Z* is *LAST-NAME*).

Table 7-34. Multivalued dependency.

	MEETING	PROJECT#	DAY	HOUR	LAST-NAME
x1,y1,z1		81	MON	10:00	Jones
x1,y2,z2		81	WED	8:00	Smith
x1,y2,z1		81	WED	8:00	Jones
x1,y1,z2		81	MON	10:00	Smith

Look at Table 7-35. Is this a multivalued dependency?

Table 7-35. The MEETING relational table.

MEETING	PROJECT#	DAY	HOUR	LAST-NAME
	81	MON	10:00	Jones
	81	WED	8:00	Jones
	81	FRI	2:00	Jones
	81	MON	10:00	Smith
	81	WED	8:00	Smith
	81	FRI	2:00	Smith
	81	MON	10:00	Thomas
	81	WED	8:00	Thomas
	81	FRI	2:00	Thomas
	81	MON	10:00	Verdi
	81	WED	8:00	Verdi
	81	FRI	2:00	Verdi

Each value of *PROJECT#* creates three distinct values of the {*DAY, HOUR*} attributes and also generates four unique values of *EMPLOYEE*. Notice that for each unique combination of *PROJECT#*, *DAY*, and *HOUR* there are four values of *LAST-NAME* and that those four values occur with all combinations of *PROJECT#*, *DAY*, and *HOUR*. This is another example of a multifunctional dependency.

Normalization

We'll be discussing the five most important classes of normalization, the process by which incorrectly constructed relations are decomposed into multiple correctly constructed relations. The other types of normalization are concerned with avoiding anomalies when tuples are updated. (Anomalies are unexpected effects on the system resulting from a database operation.)

As mentioned earlier, the concept of functional dependencies is central to the normalization of relations. For example, consider a relation with the following schema:

```
INVOICE(CUSTOMER#, ADDRESS, CITY, STATE, ZIP, REP#, AMOUNT)
```

A customer may place a number of orders to your company, resulting in multiple invoice tuples. If the customer mentions while placing an order that his or her address has changed, enter the correct address in the new invoice tuple. But now all the previously generated tuples for this customer have an old address. If you had simply stored the customer's address in one location, you would only have to update it once rather than finding all those tuples and then updating the address information. The normalization process would have detected this problem and led to a better schema design, as we'll discuss shortly.

First Normal Form

As mentioned earlier, the relational model requires that all tables be in at least first normal form; in other words, a relation's domains must consist only of atomic values for each attribute. No repeating sets of attributes or multivalued attributes are allowed. For example, if we have a CLASS relation with the schema

```
CLASS(CLASS#, TITLE, INSTRUCTOR)
```

we might also have a STUDENT relation with the schema

```
STUDENT(STUDENT#, MAJOR, ADVISOR, ADVS-ROOM, {CLASSES})
```

where the attribute *CLASSES* is a multivalued field containing the class numbers for each student. This relation is not in first normal form.

You can look at this problem as containing a series of repeating fields of the same type:

```
STUDENT(STUDENT#, MAJOR, ADVISOR, ADVS-ROOM, CLASS1, CLASS2,CLASS3)
```

The STUDENT relation would then be as shown in Table 7-36.

Table 7-36. An un-normalized table.

STUDENT	STUDENT#	MAJOR	ADVISOR	ADVS-ROOM	CLASS1	CLASS2	CLASS3
	1022	81	Jones	412	101-07	143-01	159-02
	4123	84	Smith	216	201-01	211-02	214-01

Again, this table is not in first normal form. An attribute type is repeated (*CLASS1*, *CLASS2*, *CLASS3*) in an attempt to store a data element that has multiple occurrences for each student. If a student has more than three classes, we'll have a problem; if the student has fewer than three classes, some default value must be assigned. Putting the table in first normal form results in the following schema:

```
STUDENT(STUDENT#, MAJOR, ADVISOR, ADVS-ROOM, CLASS)
```

and could result in the relation in Table 7-37.

Table 7-37. First normal form.

STUDENT	STUDENT#	MAJOR	ADVISOR	ADVS-ROOM	CLASS#
	1022	81	Jones	412	101-07
	1022	81	Jones	412	143-01
	1022	81	Jones	412	159-02
	4123	84	Smith	216	201-01
	4123	84	Smith	216	211-02
	4123	84	Smith	216	214-01

Here the student information is repeated for each class that student is enrolled in. But if a student's advisor changes, we have to find and update all the student tuples. And if a student drops all his classes, the student information will be lost. To solve these problems, we need higher classes of normalization.

Second Normal Form

To be in second normal form, a relation must already be in first normal form and its nonkey attributes must be fully functionally dependent on the primary key. This means all the functional dependencies should be noted and each nonkey attribute must be functionally dependent on *all* (not a subset) of the attributes that make up the primary key. Any attributes that don't meet this restriction must be moved into another relation.

Consider the previous example, where we left the new schema in first normal form and where *STUDENT#* is the primary key. Notice the multiple *CLASS#* values for each *STUDENT#* value. This means *CLASS#* is not functionally dependent on the primary key, so this relation is not in second normal form. We need to decompose the student schema into two tables with the following schemas:

```
STUDENT(STUDENT#, MAJOR, ADVISOR, ADVS-ROOM)

ENROLLMENT(CLASS#, STUDENT#, GRADE)
```

The relations are shown in Table 7-38.

Table 7-38. Second normal form.

STUDENT	STUDENT#	MAJOR	ADVISOR	ADVS-ROOM
	1022	81	Jones	412
	4123	84	Smith	216
ENROLLMENT	**STUDENT#**	**CLASS#**		
	1022	101-07		
	1022	143-01		
	1022	159-02		
	4123	201-01		
	4123	211-02		
	4123	214-01		

Third Normal Form

To be in third normal form, a relation must be in second normal form and have all nonprime attributes that are nontransitively dependent on the primary key. In other words, each nonkey attribute must depend only on the primary key and on the entire primary key. In the last example, *ADVS-ROOM* (the advisor's office number) is functionally dependent on the *ADVISOR* attribute. Since *ADVISOR* is nonprime, this example violates third normal form. The solution is to move the attribute out of the student relation (see Table 7-39).

Table 7-39. Third normal form.

STUDENT	STUDENT#	MAJOR	ADVISOR	CLASS#
	1022	81	Jones	101-07
	1022	81	Jones	143-01
	1022	81	Jones	159-02
	4123	84	Smith	201-01
	4123	84	Smith	211-02
	4123	84	Smith	214-01
FACULTY	NAME	ROOM	DEPT	
	Jones	412	42	
	Smith	216	42	

Normalization to third normal form is generally considered to be sufficient, but higher forms can be useful. Each higher form will also ensure that the relation is in third normal form.

Boyce-Codd Normal Form

Boyce-Codd normal form is a stronger constraint than third normal form. To be in BCNF, the table must be in first normal form and every functional dependent attribute must be dependent on a superkey attribute.

In Table 7-40, {*STUDENT#+SEMINAR*} is the primary key. The students may sign up for one or more seminars. Each seminar is taught by two instructors, and each student is advised on his or her seminar research by one of the instructors. Each instructor may take part in only one seminar. In this example, {*STUDENT#, SEMINAR*} $\rightarrow$ *INSTRUCTOR*.

Table 7-40. SEMINAR table in third normal form.

SEMINAR	STUDENT#	SEMINAR	ADVISOR
	1022	281	Smith
	3088	281	Jones
	1432	291	McKay
	3088	291	Huston
	4343	291	Huston

Notice that the *SEMINAR* number is functionally dependent on *ADVISOR*, since each instructor can teach only one seminar. *SEMINAR*'s functional dependency on a nonsuperkey attribute violates BCNF. We can put the SEMINAR table in BCNF by creating a separate relation, shown in Table 7-41.

Table 7-41. TEACHES and SEMINAR-ADVISOR tables in Boyce-Codd normal form.

TEACHES	INSTRUCTOR	SEMINAR
	Smith	281
	Jones	281
	McKay	291
	Huston	291

SEMINAR-ADVISOR	STUDENT#	ADVISOR
	281	Smith
	281	Jones
	291	McKay
	291	Huston
	291	Huston

Fourth Normal Form

Fourth normal form is concerned with multivalued dependencies. To be in fourth normal form, a table must be in BCNF and the determinant set of attributes in a multivalued dependency must be a superkey.

In Table 7-42, all the attributes make up the primary key. {*DAY, HOUR*} and *LAST-NAME* are multivalued dependencies on *PROJECT#*. Because *PROJECT#* isn't a superkey, this is a violation of fourth normal form. Table 7-43 shows the normalized tables.

Table 7-42. Multivalued dependency.

MEETING	PROJECT#	DAY	HOUR	LAST-NAME
	81	MON	10:00	Jones
	81	WED	8:00	Jones
	81	FRI	9:00	Jones
	81	MON	10:00	Smith
	81	WED	8:00	Smith
	81	FRI	9:00	Smith

Table 7-43. Fourth normal form.

MEETING	PROJECT#	DAY	HOUR
	81	MON	10:00
	81	WED	8:00
	81	FRI	9:00
PROJ-LEAD	PROJECT#	LAST-NAME	
	81	Jones	
	81	Smith	

The process of normalization rarely progresses through each of the normal forms as our example has. Data analysts will recognize an unnormalized relation and put it directly into third normal form (or higher). With a little experience, you'll begin to design relations intuitively in normalized forms. Normalization is extremely important to relational database design and is covered in more detail in Chapter 10, "Logical Database Design."

CHAPTER 8

Relational Programming

by David McClanahan

This chapter explores programming in an RDBMS environment and is concerned with the features of the relational data model. In FoxPro 2.0, that means implementing relationships between tables and implementing features of the relational model that FoxPro doesn't support (such as integrity constraints). This chapter focuses on the relational statements that have been added to the latest version of FoxPro and how to use them to increase the power of your applications.

On the subject of terminology, *database* will be used to refer to a collection of related tables. FoxPro programmers often refer to a .DBF file as a database; we'll use the term *table* instead. For consistency with Chapter 7, we'll also use the definitions given earlier in Table 7-2.

FoxPro and Relationality

While the dBASE language is only minimally relational when judged against Codd's criteria,[1] PC DBMS's relationality is expanding with the incorporation of SQL. In the near future, we should see the introduction of data dictionaries, null values, and integrity mechanisms to increase the relational aspects of the dBASE languages.

There are those who maintain that no derivative of dBASE can ever be fully relational. That's certainly true theoretically—the relational model doesn't permit record-level access to bypass the relational constraints—but it doesn't mean the relational aspects can't be expanded enough to give FoxPro developers more relational programming power. In fact, for these developers the classification is

1 Codd, E.F. *The Relational Model for Database Management: Version 2*. Reading, Mass.: Addison-Wesley, 1990.

irrelevant; what matters is that they know enough about relational theory to use the relational functionality that's available to them. Use of relational theory begins on the conceptual design level and filters through the entire development process, right down to defining the physical aspects of the database system and writing the code.

Other features of the relational data model that FoxPro doesn't currently support can be added or enhanced programmatically, as discussed later in this chapter.

Programming Relationships in FoxPro

A relationship between two tables is established by correlating attribute values in one table to attribute values in the other table. The technique of dynamically relating tuples in two tables via attribute values is a fundamental feature of the relational model and is called a *join*. A join is almost always used when data from more than one table is being referenced. Consider the relationship between the tables in Table 8-1.

Table 8-1. Two tables with joining columns *CUST_NO* and *CUST_ID*.

CUSTOMER	CUST_NO	COMPANY	ADDRESS	ZIP
	1021	K.K's Gym	1428 Lake	34214
	1022	Joy's Toys	123 Main	44543
	1023	Kyle's Cars	32 Second	42343
	1024	Rola's Pets	19 Harbor	55252
INVOICE	**CUST_ID**	**INVOICE**	**DATE**	
	1022	101	03/24/91	
	1023	102	03/24/91	
	1022	103	03/25/91	

That relationship is expressed by a joining value that represents the customer's ID in each table. The *CUSTOMER.CUST_NO* and *INVOICE.CUST_ID* columns have the same type and the same meaning. It's easy to see that they're referring to the same entity when they list 1022 as a customer's ID. To find the invoices placed by Joy's Toys, we look for matching values of the *CUST_NO* (1022) in the *INVOICE.CUST_ID* column and find two invoices, 101 and 103.

Joins are fundamental to relational systems and will be covered in more detail throughout this chapter. For now, let's look at the different ways of handling joins between tables. This can be managed programmatically in several ways.

In the next series of examples, we'll be seeking the same result set from the CUSTOMER and INVOICE tables. We want to select a range of customers with a *CUSTOMER.CUST_NO* of 1022 or 1023 and list information about those customers and the invoices they've generated. This requires a join between CUSTOMER and INVOICE on the customer-ID columns. The resulting table should look like this Table 8-2.

Table 8-2. The result of the join of CUSTOMER and INVOICE tables.

RESULT	CUST_NO	COMPANY	INVOICE	DATE
	1022	Joy's Toys	101	03/24/91
	1022	Joy's Toys	103	03/25/91
	1023	Kyle's Cars	102	03/24/91

The first method is to program the join without using relational statements. We need to open each file, locate the customer record, and use the *CUST_NO* value to find any matching records in the INVOICE table (Listing 8-1).

Listing 8-1. Programming the join condition.

```
CLEAR ALL                        && get ready
SELECT B                         && in work area 2
USE invoice                      && open the invoice table
INDEX ON cust_id TAG cust_id && index on the JOIN column
SELECT A                         && then in work area 1
USE customer                     && open the customer table
```

```
INDEX ON cust_no TAG cust_no && index on cust_no so we can
                             && find a series of customer id values
SET HEADING OFF

SEEK '1022'                  && find the first value in customer
STORE cust_no TO joinValue   && and store it in a memory variable
DO WHILE cust_no <= '1023' .AND. .NOT. EOF()
SELECT invoice               && activate work area 2
IF SEEK (joinValue)          && find the first matching record
SCAN WHILE cust_id = joinValue && while there are matching values
DISPLAY NEXT 1 OFF FIELDS A.cust_no, ;
SUBSTR(A.company,1,20), invoice, date
ENDSCAN
ENDIF
SELECT customer              && activate work area 1
SKIP                         && find the next customer record
STORE cust_no TO joinValue   && store its value in joinValue
                             && continue if <= 1023
ENDDO
```

In this case, the programmer handles the details of establishing a relationship and retrieving values from the tables.

In the next example (Listing 8-2), the same records are selected using the relational FoxPro statements *SET RELATION* and *SET SKIP*. *SET RELATION* defines a relationship between two tables, a parent and a child. It requires that the column being joined (in the child table) be indexed and that the child table's order be set to that column.

Listing 8-2. Using *SET RELATION* and *SET SKIP*.

```
CLEAR ALL
SELECT B
USE invoice
INDEX ON cust_id TAG cust_id
SELECT A
USE customer
INDEX ON cust_no TAG cust_no
```

```
SET RELATION TO cust_no INTO invoice     && customer.cust_no to
                                         && invoice.cust_id
SET SKIP TO invoice                      && set up SKIP

SEEK '1022'
LIST NEXT 3 OFF FIELDS cust_no, SUBSTR(company,1,20),;
    invoice.invoice, invoice.date
```

In this example, the statement

```
SET RELATION TO cust_no INTO invoice
```

followed activation of the index on the joining column in the INVOICE table, *CUST_ID*. The correct index for the INVOICE table could also be selected with a *SET ORDER TO cust_id* statement if the index already existed. The relationship is set from *CUSTOMER.CUST_NO* to *INVOICE.CUST_ID*. In this relationship, CUSTOMER is the parent (or driving) table and INVOICE is the child table. Each time a record is accessed in the CUSTOMER table, a pointer in INVOICE is set to the first matching record, or to end-of-file if *INVOICE.CUST_ID* contains no matching value.

SET SKIP determines what the *SKIP* command does with the joined tables. It causes the next *SKIP* in the program to move a record pointer in the child table to the next record with a matching join condition (if one exists) before going to the next record in the parent table.

In this example, the statement

```
SET SKIP TO invoice
```

causes the following SKIP statement to increment the record pointer in INVOICE to the next record with a matching *CUST_ID* value if one exists. If no matching value is found, *SKIP* increments the pointer in the CUSTOMER table to the next record, and *SET RELATION TO* defines the relationship between the tables.

SET RELATION and *SET SKIP* are useful when browse windows are set up for the tables (Listing 8-3).

Listing 8-3. Using *BROWSE* with *SET RELATION* and *SET SKIP*.

```
CLEAR ALL
SELECT B
USE invoice
INDEX ON cust_id TAG cust_id
SELECT A
USE customer
INDEX ON cust_no TAG cust_no
SET RELATION TO cust_no INTO invoice
SET SKIP TO invoice

SEEK '1022'
SELECT B
BROWSE NOWAIT
SELECT A
BROWSE NOWAIT
```

Now, as you select rows in the CUSTOMER table, the browse window for the INVOICE table will be updated based on the join condition (cust_no = cust_id).

The two tables can also appear in a single browse window, as shown in Listing 8-4.

Listing 8-4. Using a single browse window with *SET RELATION* and *SET SKIP*.

```
CLEAR ALL
SELECT B
USE invoice
INDEX ON cust_id TAG cust_id
SELECT A
USE customer
INDEX ON cust_no TAG cust_no
SET RELATION TO cust_no INTO invoice
SET SKIP TO invoice
SET FILTER TO cust_no >= '1022' and cust_no <= '1023'
BROWSE FIELDS cust_no, company, invoice->invoice, invoice->date
```

The following example (Listing 8-5) shows the equivalent join using FoxPro 2.0's new SQL *SELECT* statement. Notice that the tables need not have been opened in advance, no *SET RELATION* or *SET SKIP* is necessary, indexes aren't required, and *SET ORDER* isn't used. The *SELECT* does all the work for you; it even creates temporary indexes if necessary.

Listing 8-5. Using the SQL *SELECT* statement in FoxPro 2.0.

```
CLEAR ALL
SELECT cust.cust_no, (cust.company,1,20), ;
    inv.invoice, inv. date:
FROM customer cust, invoice inv ;
WHERE cust.cust_no BETWEEN '1022' AND '1023' ;
AND cust.cust_no = inv.cust_id
```

The SQL *SELECT* statement has access to internal information about the database system and can therefore make the best decision on how to execute a query. A single *SELECT* statement is generally equivalent to several FoxPro 1.0 statements (or even a small program) and can outperform the hand-coded equivalent. The next section explains this statement in greater detail.

Programming with FoxPro and SQL

One of the fundamental requirements of the relational data model is a high-level language to express relational operations on the table data in the database system. The most popular relational language is SQL, which stands for Structured Query Language. SQL is based on relational algebra and has been standardized by several organizations, including the ANSI committee. ANSI is about to finalize a second version of SQL, which will greatly extend the current standard and add integrity constraints.

FoxPro 2.0 has expanded its relationality by incorporating four SQL statements:

- SELECT queries the database tables
- CREATE TABLE defines a new table
- INSERT appends new rows to the end of a table
- UPDATE modifies values in a table.

The last three SQL statements are considerably simpler than *SELECT*. *CREATE TABLE* defines a new table. The field names are followed by the data type and format for each field. This statement doesn't support the *ANSI* clauses that allow specification of a non-null value, generate default values, and define key constraints. An example of the *CREATE* statement is:

```
CREATE TABLE customer (cust_no N(6, 0), ;
    company C(20), ;
    street C(20), ;
    zip C(10), ;
    phone C( 12), ;
    crdlimit F(10, 2))
```

INSERT appends new rows to the end of a table:

```
INSERT INTO customer (cust_no, company) ;
    VALUES (2001, 'New Software Inc.')
```

If you're inserting a value for all the fields, the field list may be omitted:

```
INSERT INTO customer VALUES (2001, ;
    'New Software Inc.', ;
    '123 Main', ;
    '45242', ;
    '(593)999-1111', ;
    150250.50)
```

FoxPro 2.0 doesn't have an *UPDATE* function, though Fox had mentioned one in early advertisements. When *UPDATE* is included, it will modify values in a table and will probably look like this:

```
UPDATE customer SET crdlimit = 0.0 WHERE cust_no = 2005
```

Other SQL statements, such as *DELETE*, will likely be implemented if Fox continues to expand FoxPro's relationality.

The SQL implemented in FoxPro 2.0 generally follows the ANSI standard for the language, with three kinds of modifications. First, the SQL may need to be changed to match the existing FoxPro environment; such changes include the choice of data types, naming conventions, and punctuation. Second, features of the relational data model that aren't supported by FoxPro 2.0, such as null values and primary keys, aren't implemented in the SQL statements.

Third, deviations resulted from the fact that Fox was adding SQL to an already powerful database language. Crippling the SQL implementation just to follow a standard intended for nondatabase languages was neither desirable nor acceptable. SQL is a sublanguage designed to be placed in a programming language (such as C, COBOL, or PL/1) that has no direct method of expressing relational database operations. The SQL statements are embedded in the host language and precompiled into database library calls (see Listing 13-1 in Chapter 13). Some effort is required to set up and move host variable values to and from the SQL statements being executed. A cursor, which is a special type of record pointer, is used for accessing sets of records in a record-oriented host language.

FoxPro 2.0 works quite differently from SQL in this respect. The integration of set-oriented SQL into record-oriented FoxPro is unique. Because FoxPro is a database language with some relational functionality, the SQL statements could be added at the same level as any other statement. The result is far more powerful than with the embedded approach because the language can directly manipulate the resulting records. The point is to use SQL's relational power to enhance FoxPro's relationality.

SQL is not a perfect relational language; many of its problems are well-known and have been written up by Codd and Date, among others. Some SQL experts may have been surprised at the language's implementation in FoxPro 2.0, but the goal is really to expand FoxPro's relational capabilities. SQL (or any relational language, for that matter) gives us a way to perform operations from the logical view of the database rather than the file level. Access is set-oriented and is implemented through the content and structure (schema) of the database system, not by record number or the address of a record.

An example of the shift in view is in the implementation of the cursor in FoxPro 2.0. In standard SQL, a cursor is a special kind of record pointer that allows access to the individual records in a set resulting from a previous SQL statement. In FoxPro 2.0, the cursor is a temporary table created with an alias and is usually referenced by that name.

The *SELECT* Statement

The SQL *SELECT* statement performs the relational-algebra operations of selection, projection, and theta-join. It finds the set of tuples from one or more tables that meet the query's restrictions on the values of the resulting attributes. The result of the *SELECT* is a set of tuples that creates a new table of some type. The columns that appear in the resulting set may also be a subset of the attributes of the selected tables. If the result is listed only to the screen, the resulting table isn't stored.

The following is an example of a *SELECT* statement:

```
SELECT * FROM customer WHERE cust_no = '1021'
```

When formulating a *SELECT* statement, you normally start with the *FROM* clause. This clause lists the tables, such as CUSTOMER and INVOICE, that are involved in the query and determines your options for the remaining clauses. Therefore, your first consideration is generally which tables you wish to query.

Next, consider which columns, functions, or constants you want to project from the tables in the *FROM* clause. These will be listed in the *SELECT* clause. If you wish to project all the columns, you can use an asterisk as a shorthand notation rather than explicitly listing the columns.

The *WHERE* clause lists any restrictions you require for the resulting set. If the *FROM* clause lists more than one table, the *WHERE* clause will almost always contain a join expression for each table. The *SELECT* statement does the work required to set up internal relationships; because it can open the tables mentioned in the *FROM* clause, tables need not be open when the *SELECT* is executed. Joins between tables are set up automatically when you list their conditions in the *WHERE* clause. The *SET RELATION* and *SET SKIP* commands are not required.

The tables being joined need not have their order set (with *SET ORDER*) and don't require the joining columns to be indexed, though joins on indexed columns are much faster. Indexes are automatically accessed, and multiple tags in the existing structural indexes are used for optimal performance. As the query is executed, temporary indexes may be created and used as required.

SELECT statements are optimized; that is, they may be translated into more efficient statements that execute more quickly but produce the same results. As mentioned earlier, although one *SELECT* can equal many FoxPro statements, in most cases the optimizer can outperform the hand-coded equivalent FoxPro code. In general, you should use the *SELECT* statement and let it figure out the best way to get the results you require.

The simplest example of selection is a single table reference with no restrictions (no *WHERE* clause) and projecting all the columns in the table (represented by *SELECT* *). The query

```
SELECT * FROM customer
```

lists the entire CUSTOMER table to the screen.

The *SELECT* clause of the *SELECT* statement contains the select list, which consists of the columns, constants, or expressions that need to be attributes of the output relation. Each column reference must be to a column in one of the tables in the *FROM* clause. If we wanted to see only the customer companies and customer numbers in the CUSTOMER table, the following *SELECT* clause would stipulate that projection:

```
SELECT company, cust_no FROM customer
```

This statement would list on the screen every company and every customer number from the entire CUSTOMER table.

The following statements list all the states found in the zip-code file but list a state once for each zip code in that state:

```
SELECT state FROM zip
SELECT ALL state FROM zip
```

ALL tells the *SELECT* statement to list every occurrence of every state and is the default. The *SELECT* won't remove duplicate tuples from the result unless you explicitly ask it to. To eliminate the duplicate listings, place *DISTINCT* at the beginning of the select list:

```
SELECT DISTINCT state FROM zip
```

Each state is then listed only once.

The *WHERE* clause of the *SELECT* statement lists the restrictions to be applied in the selection of output tuples. Each criterion in the restriction list is of the form

```
[NOT] <ATTRIBUTE> <comparison operator> <ATTRIBUTE or value>
```

as in

```
SELECT * FROM customer WHERE cust_no = '123'
```

This statement selects only the tuples that have a *cust_no* value of 123.

The following statements select only the tuples that *don't* have a *cust_no* value of 123:

```
SELECT * FROM customer WHERE NOT cust_no = '123'
SELECT * FROM customer WHERE cust_no <> '123'
```

In the case of Boolean expressions, the format of the restrictions is

```
[NOT] <expression>
```

as in

```
SET DELETED OFF
SELECT * FROM customer WHERE deleted()
```

These statements list all the customer tuples that have been deleted since the last time the database was packed.

The *LIKE* predicate is useful for selection based on a character-string pattern to be matched in a particular column. It allows the use of wildcards in the pattern being selected and takes the form

```
<ATTRIBUTE> [NOT] LIKE <string-pattern-to-be-matched>
```

In the TEST table (Table 8-3), we have assigned a number to each name for reference in the following examples. We'll reference the table only through the name column, which is a character-string field, and refer to the tuples selected by the *NUMBER* value.

Table 8-3. The TEST table.

TEST	NAME	NUMBER
	Kristen McKay	1
	Kyle Russell	2
	Nicole Russell	3
	Christine McKay	4
	Chris Russell	5
	Kris McKey	6

To select the tuple for *number = 1*, we could use

```
SELECT * FROM test WHERE name = 'Kristen McKay'
```

or

```
SELECT * FROM test WHERE ALLTRIM(name) LIKE 'Kristen McKay'
```

The *LIKE* predicate is most useful when used with the wildcard character "%" (to match any set of characters) or "_" (to match any single character). If we wished to select all the tuples with the last name *McKay*, for example, we would use the following query:

```
SELECT * FROM test WHERE TRIM(name) LIKE '%McKay'
```

This would select all tuples that end with *McKay* and return tuples 1 and 4.

To select all the tuples that have a first name beginning with *K*, we would use the following query:

```
SELECT * FROM test WHERE name LIKE 'K%'
```

This would return tuples 1, 2, and 6.

To select all tuples that have *Mc* in them, we could use the following query:

```
SELECT * FROM test WHERE name LIKE '%Mc%'
```

This would return tuples 1, 4, and 6.

Suppose we want to find the tuple for someone whose last name is McKey, but we're not sure of the first name—it could be Chris, Christine, or Kris. How can we find the correct tuple (assuming there are many tuples with that last name)? The statement

```
SELECT * FROM test WHERE TRIM(name) LIKE '%ris%McKey'
```

will find the correct last name and then find the first names that contain the set of letters *ris*. Therefore, this query will find *Kris* or *Chris* or *Christine*.

If you want to find all the tuples with a last name that begins with *McK* and ends in *y*, with a single intervening letter, use the following:

```
SELECT * FROM test WHERE TRIM(name) LIKE '%McK_y'
```

This selects tuples 1, 4, and 6.

To select all the tuples that don't have the last name *McKey*, use the *NOT LIKE* predicate:

```
SELECT * FROM test WHERE TRIM(name) NOT LIKE '%McKey'
```

This selects tuples 1 through 5.

If you're unsure of the name's case, use the *UPPER* function:

```
SELECT * FROM test WHERE UPPER(name) LIKE 'KRIS%'
```

This selects tuples 1 and 6.

If you want to search for a string that contains a percent sign or underscore, you must use the *ESCAPE* clause of the *LIKE* predicate to specify a special character that will precede the symbol you're looking for. For example,

```
SELECT * from TEST2 WHERE title LIKE '%he \% %' ESCAPE '\'
```

will find the title "The % method of investment." Only the "%" that is immediately preceded by the escape character (\) is taken literally; the other occurrences are treated as wildcards.

FoxPro 2.0 includes a new system variable, *ANSI*, that controls string matching. With *ANSI* set to OFF, the comparisons are for the number of characters of the shorter string; the string's placement in relation to the equal sign is irrelevant:

```
SET ANSI OFF
SELECT * FROM test WHERE name = 'Kris'
```

or

```
SET ANSI OFF
SELECT * FROM test WHERE 'Kris' = name
```

With *ANSI* off, the query returns tuples 1 and 6. With *ANSI* on, the shorter string is padded with spaces (*chr(32)*) to equal the longer string. In this case, the previous example would return no tuples.

The double-equal (==) comparison operator is always the same as a single equal sign with *ANSI* set ON. The double-equal compare means the statements

```
SET ANSI OFF
SELECT * FROM test WHERE name == 'Kris'
```

will return no records because the comparison is made against "Kris." Since "Kris" is shorter than the *name* column, it's padded with spaces.

The following query selects tuples 3, 4, and 5 (see Table 8-4) because only the first five letters (the length of the shorter string, "Steve") are compared:

Table 8-4. Another TEST table.

TEST3	FNAME	NUMBER
	Kristen	1
	Kyle	2
	Steve	3
	Steve T.	4
	Steven	5
	Kris	6

```
SET ANSI OFF
SELECT * FROM TEST3 WHERE Fname = 'Steve'
```

With *ANSI* set ON, these statements would return only 3 because the string "Steve" is padded with spaces before the comparison is made.

The statement

```
SELECT * FROM TEST3 WHERE Fname == 'Steve'
```

returns only tuple 3 whether or not *ANSI* is set ON or OFF.

Multiple conditions can be combined using the *and* and *or* connectives. To list the companies that are in Ohio and also in the first half of the alphabet, you would need the following statement to formulate the correct query:

```
SELECT * FROM customer WHERE state = 'OH' AND company < 'N'
```

To list the companies that are in Ohio, Michigan, or Indiana, you would use the following statement:

```
SELECT * FROM customer WHERE state = 'OH' OR state = 'MI' OR state = 'IN'
```

The *IN* operator offers a shorter way to express the same query:

```
SELECT * FROM customer WHERE state IN ('OH', 'MI', 'IN')
```

The connectives can be combined as follows:

```
SELECT * FROM customer ;
WHERE (state = 'OH' AND company < 'N') ;
OR (state = 'NY' AND company >= 'N')
```

The parentheses are for clarity only and are not required; that's because the *and* connective has a higher precedence than the *or*. In other words, the *and* binds the state and company restrictions on both sides before the *or* is applied. The order of precedence (from highest to lowest) within the *SELECT* statement is *NOT*, *AND*, and *OR*.

A number of column functions are available; *COUNT*, *SUM*, *AVG*, *MIN*, and *MAX* are the standard ANSI functions. The statement:

```
SELECT COUNT(emp_no) FROM invoice
```

counts the number of *emp_no*s (and the number of tuples) in the INVOICE table. This could also be stated as:

```
SELECT COUNT(*) FROM invoice
```

To count the number of unique employee numbers in the INVOICE table for 1991, you would use the following:

```
SELECT COUNT(DISTINCT emp_no) FROM invoice ;
WHERE date >= {01/01/91} AND date <= {12/31/91}
```

The following would list the largest sale, the smallest sale, the total sales, and the average sale for 1991:

```
SELECT MAX(amount), MIN(amount), SUM(amount), AVG(amount) ;
FROM invoice WHERE date >= {01/01/91} AND date <= {12/31/91}
```

When the results are listed to the screen, the display will pause after each screen of data is presented. If you want to omit the pause, add the *NOWAIT* parameter:

```
SELECT * FROM customer NOWAIT
```

The forms of the *SELECT* statement shown so far have displayed the results on the screen. You do have other output options; for example, the following statements are similar in that the resulting set of records is placed in a new table:

```
INTO DBF (TABLE) tablename
INTO CURSOR cursorname
```

INTO CURSOR creates a temporary table that is deleted when it's closed.

The statement:

```
SELECT * FROM customer INTO DBF cust2
```

creates a copy of the CUSTOMER table and calls it *cust2.dbf.*

The following also creates a copy of the CUSTOMER table called *cust2.dbf* but renames the columns to create the schema *CUST2(NUMBER, STREET, PH)*:

```
SELECT cust_no AS number, address AS street, phone AS ph ;

FROM customer INTO DBF cust2
```

The statement:

```
SELECT * FROM customer INTO CURSOR tmpcust
```

also creates a copy of the CUSTOMER table, but *tmpcust* is deleted when closed.

The following statements are similar, but *TO FILE* creates an ASCII version of the result and stores it in a file, while *TO PRINTER* sends it directly to a printer.

```
TO FILE filename
TO PRINTER
```

To omit the header, use the keyword *PLAIN*:

```
SELECT * FROM customer where cust_no = '123' TO FILE out1
SELECT * FROM customer where cust_no = '124' TO FILE out1 ;
ADDITIVE PLAIN
```

The first statement writes the header and the tuples for *cust_no = '123'* to an ASCII file named *out1.txt*. The second statement appends to that file without duplicating the header information.

You can assign each table a correlation name in the *FROM* clause by adding that name after the table name. The correlation name, an alias by which a table is referenced in the remainder of the *SELECT* statement, is most useful for assigning shorter names to tables and establishing correlated references in subqueries. The term *alias* is used here not as a reference to a work area, which is how FoxPro programmers normally use the term, but as a synonym for a table name.

In the following statements, the alias *C* is established in the *FROM* clause for CUSTOMER and the alias *In* is created for INVOICE:

```
SELECT C.cust_no, C.address, In.invoice ;
FROM customer C, invoice In ;
WHERE C.cust_no = In.cust_id
```

Remember, the *C* doesn't refer to work area 3. The column references are qualified in the *SELECT* and *WHERE* clauses using the correlation names.

If you want to specify the order of the result, use *ORDER BY*. This clause allows output to be sorted on an expression involving columns of the tables in the *FROM* clause. The ordering can be in ascending (*ASC*, the default) or descending (*DESC*) order.

```
SELECT * FROM customer ORDER BY state, city, company DESC INTO out1
```

The output is sorted first by state (in ascending order), then by city (in ascending order), and finally by company within each city but in descending order, resulting in the output in Table 8-5.

Table 8-5. Output of the query, sorted by STATE in ascending order.

OUT1	COMPANY	CITY	STATE	CONTACT
	Kristen's Toys	Calif. City	CA	Caitlin
	Zebra Systems	Boston	MA	Joe
	Peach Printing	Boston	MA	Mark
	Beach Gadgets	Boston	MA	Jane
	Apple Stereo	Littleton	MA	Joe
	A.A. Furniture	James	NM	Mary

Cartesian Product

The Cartesian product of two tables produces a new table; each tuple in the first table is joined with every tuple in the second table. You can express this operation in the SQL *SELECT* statement by listing two or more tables in the *FROM* clause with no joining condition between them in the *WHERE* clause.

Consider the tables in Table 8-6.

Table 8-6. CUSTOMER and INVOICE tables.

CUSTOMER	CUST_NO	ADDRESS	PHONE
	1022	123 Main	421-4543
	1023	32 Second	424-2343
INVOICE	CUST_ID	INVOICE	
	1022	101	
	1023	102	
	1022	103	

The result of the following query:

```
SELECT * FROM customer, invoice INTO DBF product1
```

would be Table 8-7.

Table 8-7. Cartesian product result.

PRODUCT1	CUST_NO	ADDRESS	PHONE	CUST_ID	INVOICE
	1022	123 Main	421-4523	1022	101
	1022	123 Main	421-4523	1023	102
	1022	123 Main	421-4523	1023	103
	1023	32 Second	424-4323	1022	101
	1023	32 Second	424-4323	1022	102
	1023	32 Second	424-4323	1022	103

The table resulting from a Cartesian product is of limited use except as a basis for further restrictions. It contains some random associations between attribute values and most often occurs when one forgets to include a join condition between the tables.

More on Joins

The feature that gives the relational model most of its character and a great deal of its power is the way relationships between tables are established. A logical interrelation between tables is expressed by the *join expression* in the SQL *SELECT* statement. Tables are linked dynamically by the comparing the values of columns in two tables. The joining columns are usually related somehow, as are the tuples in the two tables.

Consider the following *SELECT* with a join condition between the tables from Table 8-6:

```
SELECT * FROM customer, invoice ;
WHERE cust_no = cust_id INTO DBF result
```

The following RESULT table (Table 8-8) lists all the customers and their invoice numbers. This certainly represents more significant information than PRODUCT1 in Table 8-7. Because the join condition is on two columns that have the same meaning, a meaningful result is produced.

Table 8-8. RESULT from the SELECT with a join condition.

RESULT	CUST_NO	ADDRESS	PHONE	CUST_ID	INVOICE
	1022	123 Main	421-4543	1022	101
	1022	123 Main	421-4543	1022	103
	1023	32 Second	424-2343	1023	102

The format of the *SELECT* join expression is

```
TABLE1.ATTRIBUTE1 θ TABLE2.ATTRIBUTE2
```

where

- the symbol θ is the join operator, one of the comparison operators (=,==,<,<=,>,>=,<>)
- *TABLE1* is the name of one table
- *TABLE2* is the name of another table
- *ATTRIBUTE1* is an attribute from TABLE1
- *ATTRIBUTE2* is an attribute from TABLE2.

ATTRIBUTE1 and *ATTRIBUTE2* must have the same data types or be converted to similar types with a FoxPro function. In the following tables, INVOICE's customer ID is a character string. In the CUSTOMER table (Table 8-9), the customer number is a numeric value and so cannot be directly compared to the *CUST_ID* column.

Table 8-9. CUSTOMER and INVOICE.

CUSTOMER	CUST_NO	ADDRESS	PHONE
	1022	123 Main	421-4543
	1023	32 Second	424-2343
INVOICE	CUST_ID	INVOICE	
	'1022'	101	
	'1023'	102	
	'1022'	103	

A function such as *VAL()* is then required to convert *CUST_ID* to a numeric value for the join condition, as in the following:

```
SELECT * FROM customer, invoice ;
WHERE cust_no = VAL(cust_id)
```

If you want to join a table with itself, you'll need correlation names to clarify the occurrences of column references. For example, consider a table EMPLOYEE with the schema

```
EMPLOYEE(SSN, NAME, ADDRESS, ZIP, DEPT, SPOUSE)
```

where a column, *SPOUSE*, holds the spouse's social security number if he or she is employed by the same company. If you wanted a list of each employee whose spouse is employed by the same company, you could use the following query:

```
SELECT empl.name, emp2.name FROM employee empl, employee emp2 ;
WHERE empl.spouse = emp2.ssn
```

This query would list each pair of married employees twice. To avoid the duplicate listing, you could modify the query to:

```
SELECT empl.name, emp2.name FROM employee empl, employee emp2 ;
WHERE empl.spouse = emp2.ssn AND empl.ssn < empl.spouse
```

Subqueries

When queries are nested, those on the inside are called *subqueries*. A subquery can return only a one-column table and must be placed inside parentheses.

Suppose you wish to find information in the SALESREP table about the salesperson who generated invoice number 1022.

```
SELECT * FROM salesrep WHERE emp_no = ;
(SELECT emp_no FROM invoice WHERE invoice = 1022)
```

The subquery is executed first to find the *emp_no* for invoice 1022. The outer query then finds the *salesrep.emp_no* attribute value that matches that *invoice.emp_no*. When the outer query is joined to the inner query with a comparison operator, as in this example, the subquery must return at most one *emp_no*. If more than one value is returned, an error will occur.

Subqueries may return a set of values against which the outer query compares a value using the *IN* operator. For example, to list all the sales reps from the SALESREP table who have written invoices for customer 1022, you would use the following to produce the correct set of tuples:

```
SELECT * FROM salesrep WHERE emp_no IN ;
(SELECT emp_no FROM invoice WHERE cust_no = '1022')
```

The subquery is executed first to produce a set of *emp_no*s for any salesperson who has an invoice for customer 1022. The outer query then checks the *salesrep.emp_no* attribute values for membership in the set of *invoice.emp_no* resulting from the subquery.

Another way to get the same result without using a subquery is with the following:

```
SELECT salesrep.* DISTINCT FROM salesrep, invoice ;
WHERE salesrep.emp_no = invoice.emp_no ;
and cust_no = '1022'
```

To list the sales reps who have *not* written an order for customer 1022, use *NOT IN*:

```
SELECT * FROM salesrep WHERE emp_no NOT IN ;
(SELECT emp_no FROM invoice WHERE cust_no = '1022')
```

In this example, the subquery is executed to create a set of *invoice.emp_no*s for all the sales reps who have written an invoice order for customer number 1022. The outer query is executed, and the tuples for each sales rep whose *emp_no* is not found in the result of the subquery—in other words, the sales reps who have *not* written an invoice for customer 1022—are listed.

Correlated Subqueries

One of the least understood and most underused features of the *SELECT* statement is the correlated subquery. In the following query, notice which tables are being referenced in the *WHERE* clause of the subquery. Also note the tables listed in the subquery's *FROM* clause.

```
SELECT * FROM rep WHERE 2 <=;
( SELECT count(*) FROM invoice ;
WHERE invoice.emp = rep.emp)
```

The subquery in this example refers to a table not listed in its *FROM* clause; the REP table belongs to the outer query. This is known as a *correlated reference*, making this a *correlated subquery*. When the outer table is referenced from inside the query, the subquery should be executed for each outer tuple that meets any restrictions in the outer *WHERE* clause. The result of the subquery is then used to evaluate the expression that joins the inner query to the outer one (*2 <= count(*)*, in this case). If that expression evaluates to true, the outer tuple is projected into the result table.

Table 8-10. REP and INVOICE tables.

REP	EMP	LNAME	SALES
	123	Smith	104943.12
	155	Jones	231123.31
	451	Russell	324133.44

INVOICE	INVOICE	CUST	DATE	EMP	AMOUNT
	112233	1024	05/05/91	123	1345.50
	112234	4319	05/05/91	451	985.44
	112235	2055	05/07/91	155	243.75
	112236	4319	05/08/91	451	942.44
	112237	2055	05/09/91	155	2440.75

In the tables in Table 8-10, the subquery is executed for each sales rep. If a sales rep has two or more invoices in the INVOICE table, that rep will be in the resulting set of tuples:

```
SELECT * FROM rep WHERE 2 <=;
( SELECT count(*) FROM invoice ;
WHERE invoice.emp = rep.emp) ORDER BY emp
```

RESULT	EMP	LNAME	SALES
	155	Jones	231123.31
	451	Russell	324133.44

The next query further restricts the outer query by limiting the *emp* value to less than 300. This restriction prevents tuples in the REP table with a *rep.emp value* greater than or equal to 300 from being selected.

```
SELECT * FROM rep WHERE emp < 300 and 2 <=;
( SELECT count(*) FROM invoice ;
WHERE invoice.emp = rep.emp)
```

The result is shown in Table 8-11.

Table 8-11. RESULT table.

RESULT	EMPL	NAME	SALES
	155	JONES	231123.31

The *EXIST* operator is often used with correlated subqueries. It tells the subquery to return TRUE only if tuples are produced. The following query lists the sales reps who have created at least one invoice:

```
SELECT * FROM salesrep WHERE EXIST ;
(SELECT * FROM invoice WHERE salesrep.emp_no = invoice.emp_no)
```

The query steps through each SALESREP tuple, passes the value of *salesrep.emp_no* to the subquery, and executes the subquery. If the subquery returns TRUE (meaning at least one tuple was found in the INVOICE table), the tuple in the outer query is output. Note that in a correlated subquery using *EXIST* (or *NOT EXIST*), only a TRUE or FALSE value results from the subquery. Since no column of data is returned, you can use the *SELECT* * instead of listing a particular column. The following would produce the same result as the preceding query.

```
SELECT * FROM salesrep WHERE EXIST ;
(SELECT emp_no FROM invoice ;
WHERE salesrep.emp_no = invoice.emp_no)
```

A query to list all the sales reps who have never created an invoice would use *NOT EXIST*:

```
SELECT * FROM salesrep WHERE NOT EXIST ;
(SELECT * FROM invoice WHERE salesrep.emp_no = invoice.emp_no)
```

The subquery or outer query may also involve joins. To find the sales reps who have written invoices for more than the average dollar amount of all the invoices, you use the subquery to calculate the average amount of an invoice. The individual invoice amounts are then compared against that average in the outer query. If an invoice amount is greater than the average, the invoice tuple is joined to the SALESREP table to provide the sales-rep information. And since each sales rep may have produced more than one invoice that exceeds the average amount, you can use the *DISTINCT* function to eliminate any redundancy:

```
SELECT DISTINCT salesrep.* FROM salesrep, invoice ;
WHERE salesrep.emp_no = invoice.emp_no and invoice.amount >
(SELECT AVG(amount) FROM invoice)
```

The quantifiers *ANY*, *SOME*, and *ALL* are also useful with subqueries (*SOME* is a synonym for *ANY*). The quantifiers are used with the comparison operators whcn a subquery may return more than one value.

The following query lists all the invoices whose amount is greater than every amount found on an invoice written the rep with an *emp_no* of 101:

```
SELECT * FROM invoice WHERE amount > ALL ;
(SELECT amount FROM invoice WHERE emp_no = 101)
```

This is equivalent to

```
SELECT * FROM invoice WHERE amount > ;
(SELECT MAX(amount) FROM invoice WHERE emp_no = 101)
```

The next example uses the *ANY* quantifier:

```
SELECT * FROM invoice WHERE amount > ANY ;
(SELECT amount FROM invoice WHERE emp_no = 101)
```

This query lists all the invoices that have an amount greater than any amount found on an invoice written by *emp_no = 101*. This is equivalent to

```
SELECT * FROM invoice WHERE amount > ;
(SELECT MIN(amount) FROM invoice WHERE emp_no = 101)
```

The *GROUP BY* and *HAVING* Clauses

The output of the *SELECT* statement can be grouped into one or more columns.

The *GROUP BY* clause lets you output one tuple for each group and is normally used with some of the column functions to gather statistics on the groups. Consider the INVOICE table in Table 8-12.

Table 8-12. INVOICE table.

INVOICE	INVOICE	CUST	DATE	EMP	AMOUNT
	112233	1024	05/05/91	123	1345.50
	112234	4319	05/05/91	451	985.44
	112235	2055	05/05/91	155	243.75
	112236	4319	05/08/91	451	942.44
	112237	2055	05/09/91	155	2440.75

If we want to group by the rep's employee number (*EMP*) to compute the total invoice sales for each rep, the *SELECT* statement

```
SELECT emp, SUM(amount) AS total FROM invoice GROUP BY emp
```

produces the result in Table 8-13.

Table 8-13. RESULT table.

RESULT	EMP	TOTAL
	123	1345.50
	451	1927.88
	155	2684.50

In general, you'll want to project the columns by which you're grouping; otherwise, you can't see the groups that have partitioned the result. It usually only makes sense to include column functions in the *SELECT* list with the grouping columns. The exception is when a column has a one-to-one relationship with the grouping columns (such as *EMP#* and *SSN*).

The *HAVING* clause lets you define which groups are allowed in the output set of tuples. If we modify the previous query to

```
SELECT emp, SUM(amount) AS total FROM invoice ;
GROUP BY emp HAVING COUNT(*) > 1
```

we're specifying that only groups with more than one tuple are to be included in the output set. Since employee number 123 only occurs once in the INVOICE table, it won't be in the output set; the query will produce the result in Table 8-14.

Table 8-14. RESULT table.

RESULT	EMP	TOTAL
	451	1927.88
	155	2684.50

If we want to see only those reps who have produced $2,000.00 or more in sales and also see the number of invoices, the query would be:

```
SELECT emp, COUNT(*), SUM(amount) AS total FROM invoice ;
GROUP BY emp HAVING SUM(amount) > 2000.00
```

Table 8-15. RESULT table.

RESULT	EMP	COUNT	TOTAL
	155	2	2684.50

Earlier we saw the sample query

```
SELECT * FROM rep WHERE 2 <=;
( SELECT count(*) FROM invoice ;
WHERE invoice.emp = rep.emp) ORDER BY emp
```

An equivalent query using *GROUP BY* and *HAVING* is

```
SELECT rep.* FROM rep , invoice WHERE invoice.emp = rep.emp ;
GROUP BY rep.emp HAVING count(*) > 1
```

The *UNION* operation

The *UNION* operator combines the result of two or more queries into one set. The result of each query must have the same number of columns with exactly the same format. The query

```
SELECT emp_no FROM salesrep UNION SELECT emp_no FROM employee
```

produces a list of all employee numbers found in the SALESREP and EMPLOYEE tables. By default, duplicate employee numbers are eliminated; if you want to see duplicate numbers, insert *ALL* after the *UNION*:

```
SELECT emp_no FROM salesrep UNION ALL SELECT emp_no FROM employee
```

Using the *SQL-SELECT* in FoxPro 2

Combined with a report, the *SELECT* statement can quickly and easily produce attractive, informative reports. Even by itself, *SELECT* can provide a great deal of information. The next group of queries uses the *SELECT* statement alone and with FoxPro code to produce the desired output. The queries are based on the table schemas created in the chapters on relational database design for a sample parts business.

Listing 8-6 shows the structure of the tables involved in the queries.

Listing 8-6. Schemas for the *SQL-SELECT* examples.

```
TABLE customer (cust_no N(6, 0), ;
    company C(20), ;
    address C(20), ;
    zip C(10), ;
    phone C( 12))
```

```
TABLE invoice (inv_no N(6, 0), ;
    date D, ;
    cust_no N(6, 0), ;
    emp_no N(6, 0), ;        && who wrote the order?
    shipped L, ;             && has the order been shipped?
    total F(10, 2))

TABLE lineitem (inv_no N(6, 0), ;
    part_no N(6, 0), ;
    quantity N(6, 0), ;
    price_ea F(10,2), ;
    total F(10,2))

TABLE salesrep (emp_no N(6, 0), ytdsales N(10, 2))

TABLE employee (emp_no N(6, 0), ;
    name C(20), ;
    status C(1), ;       &&'A'=active'I'=inactive'S'=sick leave ;
    address C(20), ;
    zip C(10), ;
    hr_wage N(6,2))

TABLE zip (zip C(10), city C(20), state C(2))

TABLE check (emp_no N(6,0), ;
    date D, ;
    amount N(10,2), ;
    hours N(5,2))

TABLE timecard (emp_no N(6,0), ;
    week D, ;
    hours N(5,2))

TABLE part (part_no N(6,0), ;
    desc C(20), ;
    price N(10,2), ;
    count N(10), ;
    on_order N(10), ;
    restock N(10))              && reorder when count <= restock
```

```
TABLE supplier (supp_no N(6, 0), ;
    company C(20), ;
    street C(20), ;
    zip C(10), ;
    phone C( 12))

TABLE partsupp (supp_no N(6,0), ;
    part_no N(6,0), ;
    cost N(10,2))

TABLE order (supp_no N(6,0), ;
    part_no N(6,0), ;
    quantity N(6,0), ;
    cost N(10,2))
```

The following are ways you can use the SQL *SELECT* statement.

1. List all the active employees who did not submit timecards for the week of August 9, 1991, and who are not sales reps (reps work on commission).

   This query involves two *NOT IN* subqueries: You need to eliminate the sales reps and find those employees who are active but did not have a timecard dated 08/09/91.

   ```
   SELECT emp_no, name FROM employee WHERE status = 'A' ;
   AND emp_no NOT IN ;
   (SELECT emp_no FROM timecards WHERE week = {08/09/91}) ;
   AND emp_no NOT IN ;
   (SELECT emp_no from salesrep)
   ```

2. Create a file of the new checks to be issued for each employee with a timecard dated 08/09/91. Compute the gross amount as hourly wages times the number of hours worked.

   ```
   SELECT emp.emp_no, week, (hours*hr_wage) AS amount, hours ;
   FROM timecard, employee emp ;
   WHERE week = {08/09/91} ;
   AND emp.emp_no = timecard.emp_no INTO DBF newcheck
   ```

3. Do the same but add the new checks to the current check table. First we give an example that does not work in the current version of FoxPro 2:

```
SELECT emp.emp_no, week, (hours*hr_wage) AS amount, hours ;
FROM timecard, employee emp ;
WHERE week = {08/09/91} ;
AND emp.emp_no = timecard.emp_no INTO CURSOR newcheck
USE check IN SELECT(1)
APPEND FROM newcheck  && this does not work
```

This statement looks like it would work, but the *APPEND FROM* does not work correctly with cursors in FoxPro 2. We scan the temporary file and use the *SCATTER* and *APPEND FROM ARRAY* commands to append the records to the CHECK table. Since the TMPCHECK table is only temporary, we use a cursor that will be deleted when closed.

```
SELECT emp.emp_no, week, (hours*hr_wage) as amount, hours ;
FROM timecard, employee emp ;
WHERE week = {08/09/91} ;
AND emp.emp_no = timecard.emp_no INTO CURSOR tmpcheck
USE check IN SELECT(1)
SELECT tmpcheck
SCAN
SCATTER TO xx
SELECT check
APPEND FROM ARRAY xx
ENDSCAN
USE IN tmpcheck
```

4. Check the inventory and produce a report of all parts with a count less than or equal to the trigger amount, a condition that signals a restocking order:

```
SELECT * FROM part WHERE count <= restock
```

5. Check the inventory and produce a report of all parts that have a count of 0 or 1 and that have not been reordered.

```
SELECT * FROM part WHERE count <= 1 AND on_order = 0
```

6. Check the inventory and produce a report of all parts that have a count of 0 or 1 and that are not on order but that a customer has ordered in an unshipped invoice:

```
SELECT * FROM part WHERE count <= 1 AND on_order = 0 ;
AND part_no IN (SELECT part_no from lineitem, invoice;
WHERE invoice.inv_no = lineitem.inv_no;
AND invoice.shipped <> .T.)
```

7. Produce a list of each part that is low in stock (at or below the trigger level) and a list of the suppliers that can supply the part along with their phone numbers. For each part, list the supplier with the lowest cost first.

```
SELECT part.part_no, supplier.company, supplier.phone ;
FROM part, partsupp, supplier ;
WHERE count <= restock AND on_order = 0 ;
AND supplier.supp_no = partsupp.supp_no ;
AND partsupp.part_no = part.part_no ;
ORDER BY part.part_no, partsupp.cost
```

8. Do the same but produce a report listing each supplier and the parts it can supply that are at or below the trigger count. Order the output by supplier and then by part.

```
SELECT part.part_no, supplier.company, supplier.phone ;
FROM part, partsupp, supplier ;
WHERE count <= restock AND on_order = 0 ;
AND supplier.supp_no = partsupp.supp_no ;
AND partsupp.part_no = part.part_no ;
ORDER BY supplier.supp_no, part.part_no
```

9. Produce a list of all sales reps and the total sales for the week ending August 9, 1991.

```
SELECT emp_no, sum(total) as week_sum ;
FROM invoice WHERE date >= {08/03/91} AND date <= {08/09/91} ;
GROUP BY emp_no
```

10. Total the year-to-date sales for each sales rep and store the result for each in the *ytdsales* column of the SALESREP table.

```
SELECT emp_no, sum(total) as ytdtotal ;
FROM invoice WHERE date >= {01/01/91} ;
GROUP BY emp_no INTO CURSOR tmp
USE salesrep IN SELECT(1)
SELECT salesrep
REPLACE ytdsales WITH 0 FOR emp_no <> 0
SELECT tmp
SCAN
rep = emp_no
ytd = ytdtotal
SELECT salesrep
LOCATE FOR emp_no = rep
IF FOUND()
    ? "found"
    REPLACE ytdsales WITH ytd
    ELSE
    ? "not found"
ENDIF
ENDSCAN
USE IN tmp
```

11. Produce a list of all sales reps with the following year-to-date information: total sales, number of sales (invoices), largest sale, average sale, and number of customers to whom each has sold. Save that information in a .DBF named *report1* and update the SALESREP table with that *ytdsales*.

```
CLEAR ALL
SELECT emp_no, sum(total) as ytd, count(*), max(total), ;
    avg(total), ;
count (distinct cust_no) ;
FROM invoice WHERE date >= {01/01/91} ;
GROUP BY emp_no INTO DBF report1
USE salesrep IN SELECT(1)
SELECT salesrep
SCAN &&salesrep
mEmp_no = emp_no
SELECT report1
LOCATE FOR emp_no = mEmp_no
IF FOUND()
REPLACE salesrep.ytdsales WITH report1.ytd
ELSE
REPLACE salesrep.ytdsales WITH 0
ENDIF
ENDSCAN
```

12. List all the parts on order.

```
SELECT * FROM PART WHERE on_order > 0
```

13. List all the ordered parts that have not yet been shipped.

```
SELECT DISTINCT part_no FROM lineitem WHERE inv_no ;
IN (SELECT inv_no FROM invoice WHERE shipped <> .T.)
```

14. List all the parts that may be preventing each order from being shipped.

```
SELECT DISTINCT lineitem.part_no FROM lineitem, part ;
WHERE inv_no ;
IN (SELECT inv_no FROM invoice WHERE shipped <> .T.) ;
AND lineitem.part_no = part.part_no ;
AND part.count < lineitem.quantity
```

15. List the sales reps who wrote more than 10 invoices for the week ending August 9, 1991, and the number of sales for each.

```
SELECT emp_no, count(*) FROM invoice ;
WHERE date >= {08/03/91} AND date <= {08/09/91} ;
GROUP BY emp_no HAVING count(*) > 10
```

16. List each part along with the supplier that can provide it at the lowest cost.

```
SELECT supply.part_no, supplier.company, supplier.phone ;
FROM partsupp supply, supplier ;
WHERE supplier.supp_no = supply.supp_no ;
AND supply.cost IN (SELECT min(cost) FROM partsupp ;
WHERE part_no = supply.part_no)
```

17. Append to the ORDER table a set of new orders for all parts for which the sum of the current number in stock and the number on order puts that part at or below the trigger point. Order from the supplier that can provide the part at the lowest cost. If more than one supplier has the lowest price, pick any one of them. Order six of each part. (You'll need more than one *SELECT* statement.)

```
SELECT part_no, count, on_order, restock FROM part ;
WHERE count+on_order <= restock INTO CURSOR tmp
SELECT DISTINCT s.supp_no, p.part_no, 6, s.cost ;
FROM tmp p, partsupp s ;
WHERE s.cost = ;
(SELECT min(cost) from partsupp ;
WHERE part_no = p.part_no) ;
INTO CURSOR tmp2

USE IN tmp
USE order IN SELECT(1)
SCAN
SCATTER TO xx
SELECT order
APPEND FROM ARRAY xx
ENDSCAN
USE IN tmp2
```

18. Find the part numbers for which the two highest quantities were ordered this year; double the restock value in PART for both parts so we have more of these in stock.

```
SELECT part_no, sum(quantity) FROM lineitem, invoice ;
WHERE date >= {01/01/91} AND invoice.inv_no = lineitem. inv_no ;
GROUP BY part_no ORDER BY 2 DESC INTO CURSOR tmp

USE part IN SELECT(1)
FOR mcount = 1 TO 2
mPartNo = part_no
SELECT part
LOCATE FOR part_no = mPartNo
IF FOUND()
mRestock = restock*2
REPLACE restock WITH mRestock
ENDIF
SELECT tmp
SKIP
ENDFOR
```

19. Find the numbers for parts that have not been ordered this year. Increase their price by 10% if the restock value is less than four and by 20% if the value is greater than or equal to four.

```
CLEAR ALL
SELECT part_no FROM part WHERE part_no NOT IN ;
(SELECT part_no FROM invoice, lineitem ;
WHERE date >= {01/01/91} AND invoice.inv_no = lineitem.inv_no) ;
INTO CURSOR tmp
SCAN
mPartNo = part_no
SELECT part
LOCATE FOR part_no = mPartNo
IF FOUND()
mPrice = IIF(restock < 4, price * 1.1, price * 1.2)
REPLACE price WITH mPrice
ENDIF
ENDSCAN
```

20. When tables with a one-to-many relationship are joined, the result of column functions associated with grouping (*GROUP BY*) may be more difficult to predict. Consider the schemas for two tables that track patients by age and ID (*patient*). Each patient has one entry in the HOSPITAL table for each stay and an entry in the BILLITEM table for each charge during the stay.

```
HOSPITAL(Patient,Age,Days)
BILLITEM(Patient,Charge, Item)
```

For example, consider the Table 8-15.

Table 8-15. Hospital and Billitem.

HOSPITAL	PATIENT	AGE	DAYS
	1000	40	10
	1001	40	20
	1002	50	20
	1003	50	40

BILLITEM	PATIENT	CHARGE	ITEM
	1000	10.00	apple
	1000	20.00	blanket
	1001	10.00	cola
	1001	20.00	donut
	1002	10.00	eggs
	1002	20.00	food
	1002	30.00	grapes
	1003	10.00	honey
	1003	20.00	ice cream
	1003	30.00	jam
	1003	40.00	ketchup

Now suppose you want to generate a report showing the number of days each age group spent in the hospital and the total charges for each group. Will a join with a *GROUP BY age* work? Consider the following *SELECT* statement:

```
SELECT hospital.age, SUM(days), SUM(charge) ;
FROM hospital, billitem ;
WHERE hospital.patient = billitem.patient ;
GROUP BY hospital.age
```

This will produce an incorrect result. To see why, consider the result of the join between HOSPITAL and BILLITEM. If we create a *SELECT* statement just to do the join, it will look like this:

```
SELECT * FROM hospital, billitem ;
WHERE hospital.patient = billitem.patient INTO DBF HOSPBILL
```

The result of that *SELECT* would be in Table 8-16.

Table 8-16. Result of the SELECT.

HOSPBILL	PATIENT	AGE	DAYS	PATIENT	CHARGE	ITEM
	1000	40	10	1000	10.00	apple
	1000	40	10	1000	20.00	blanket
	1001	40	20	1001	10.00	cola
	1001	40	20	1001	20.00	donut
	1002	50	20	1002	10.00	eggs
	1002	50	20	1002	20.00	food
	1002	50	20	1002	30.00	grapes
	1003	50	40	1003	10.00	honey
	1003	50	40	1003	20.00	ice cream
	1003	50	40	1003	30.00	jam
	1003	50	40	1003	40.00	ketchup

Look closely at the resulting table (we added a blank tuple to separate the two age groups). What effect would the *GROUP BY age* have had on the *SUM(days), SUM(charge)* in the original query? Because each patient tuple joins to two or more item tuples, the patient information is repeated for each join. The *days* count is repeated, so the sum of that column would not produce the correct result for each patient.

Other DBMS products extend the ANSI SQL *SELECT* statement by adding a *COMPUTE* clause to handle different levels of grouping and produce reportlike results. We can get the correct answer into a table or report programmatically in several ways; here we'll use two steps, one to perform each part of the calculation:

```
SELECT patient,SUM(charge) AS total ;
    FROM billitem INTO CURSOR temp ;
    GROUP BY patient

SELECT hospital.age, SUM(days), SUM(total) ;
    FROM hospital,temp ;
    WHERE hospital.patient = temp.patient ;
    GROUP BY hospital.age
```

The first *SELECT* consolidates the multiple charge records into a single summary record for each patient. The join between HOSPITAL and TEMP is then a one-to-one relationship, and the summary will be correct.

Integrity Constraints

Integrity constraints are required by the relational model but unsupported by FoxPro 2.0; you can, however, add the mechanisms programmatically to enforce relational integrity. There are two kinds of relational integrity:

- *Entity integrity* means primary-key attribute values may not be null and the column values in the primary key must suffice to identify the subject to which the tuple refers.
- *Referential integrity* means every foreign key in a table must refer to an existing key in the related table or must be null (in other words, it doesn't refer to any key in any table).

Because FoxPro 2.0 doesn't support nulls, the following discussion assumes you chose some value (such as a blank entry) to represent a null.

You may want to support the declaration of primary keys and the enforcement of uniqueness for designated attributes in your application code (in other words, entity integrity). If a new tuple is added, its primary key should be checked for uniqueness and an error generated if it's not distinct or contains a null value. Any other attribute may be declared unique within a table, and that may also be managed by the application code.

You may also choose to support the referential-integrity rule, which requires that for each relationship you define the exact details of what is allowable and what effect operations will have. Look at the EMPLOYEE and DEPENDENT tables in Tables 8-17 and 8-18. The EMPLOYEE table has a primary key, *EMPLOYEE#*, and a relationship with the DEPENDENT table. For the programmatic mechanism to work, you must ensure that updates to either table are only done by the user through your program code. If users modify the tables directly, you can't prevent them from creating tables that don't follow the relational-integrity rules.

Table 8-17. EMPLOYEE*(EMPLOYEE#, L-NAME, F-NAME, DEPT#)*

EMPLOYEE	EMPLOYEE#	L-NAME	F-NAME	DEPT#
	1021	Smith	Dave	101
	1022	McKay	Kristen	103
	1023	Russell	Kyle	102

Table 8-18. DEPENDENT(*EMPLOYEE#, F-NAME, BIRTHDATE*)

DEPENDENT	EMPLOYEE#	F-NAME	BIRTHDATE
	1022	Keith	03-24-81
	1022	Shawn	11-29-89
	1023	Caitlin	10-29-88
	1021	Christine	05-14-80

If you add a new tuple to the EMPLOYEE table, you must make sure *EMPLOYEE#*, the primary key, isn't already entered in the table and isn't blank.

You can modify the nonprime attribute values easily, but if you change the primary key you must be sure the value you're entering for the primary key is unique and not blank, just as if you were adding a new employee tuple with that key.

If that employee tuple has a relationship with dependent tuples, you may prevent the parent key from being changed until the foreign-key value in the child tuples has been modified, or you can automatically update the foreign key to the new parent value. Either action requires that you know which tables depend on the parent table. You can handle these dependencies by hard-coding that information, or you may enter the relationships, key information, and constraints into a data dictionary. The latter approach is better and more flexible but is considerably more complicated.

To delete an employee tuple from EMPLOYEE, you must decide what will happen to the child tuples in DEPENDENT. There are several possibilities:

1. Delete the child tuples automatically when the parent tuple is deleted.
2. Insert a null value into the foreign key (*EMPLOYEE#*) of the child tuples.
3. Prevent the deletion of any parent tuple until all dependent tuples have been deleted.

To add a new tuple to the child table, check it against the parent table for integrity. The foreign key, *EMPLOYEE#*, must exist in the EMPLOYEE table or the addition must not be allowed. The primary key of DEPENDENT must also be unique within that table; the partial key *F-NAME+BIRTHDATE* must be sufficient to distinguish the children from each other. Is *F-NAME* alone enough to qualify the children of each EMPLOYEE?

Third-party developers will probably offer libraries that add relational features, such as integrity mechanisms, to FoxPro 2. Another option would be to use a database server, such as SQL Server, in systems that require a more complete RDBMS. Again, we expect to see third-party products that will allow connectivity between FoxPro 2 and other database servers in the near future.

PART IV

Database Design

Why Power Tools Won't Put Power Programmers Out of Business

A novice programmer looking at a demo of FoxPro 2 may conclude that he or she can use it to create a large application in a day or so. The ease with which one can create screens, reports, and menus is alluring. Will it make the programming jobs dry up, causing experienced database programmers to wonder if the money they used to make as a musician wasn't so bad after all? No. Database application programming is still not child's play. One area reveals this more than most: database design.

I started out as an end user, turning to programming rather than turning grey waiting for MIS to provide me with the tools I needed. With my analytical and mathematical background and my familiarity with the business I was modeling, I didn't feel I was missing anything that the unexplored realms of database design would reveal. We had no specifications, they were all in my head. When I picked up a copy of *DBMS* magazine, the articles on E-R diagramming, SQL, and client-server seemed impractical and irrelevant to me. (Fortunately, I saved those back issues.)

Looking back now, I see that even in that familiar business territory there were places where I didn't understand the situation completely. I really didn't start to notice my lack of training until I took my first consulting assignment: programming an order/inventory system for company in an entirely different business. I thought I was a hotshot programmer, familiar with all the commands and functions of FoxBASE+ and rapidly learning the new FoxPro 1. There was a stack of specification material: screen shots and database structures. Piece of cake.

About a month or two later, I started realizing how much I didn't know about this company's business. After demonstrating sections of the applications I had finished, I would find out that the company had something significantly different in mind. The specifications gave me a comfort level that wasn't warranted. If I had bothered to read some of those "useless" *DBMS* magazine articles or the chapters in this book,

I would have known what was missing. I wouldn't have had to restructure tables and rewrite whole sections of logic. In this situation, I couldn't rely on my intimate knowledge of the business to anticipate what the customer wanted, but hadn't yet articulated.

Database design helps you see how everything interrelates. It is also a communications tool to help both you and non-programmers clearly describe the information your company maintains and how it is used. There are just too many details to be kept in someone's head or loosely described in pounds of prose (two methods I'm familiar with). Graphical tools that represent logical relations can greatly simplify a complex process. By simplifying, errors and omissions show up more readily.

As you go through the process, your client or boss will begin to see the complexity of the task, and gain a greater appreciation for your needs. If nothing else does, this should prevent them from handing the job over to a $10/hour novice who can generate a hundred pretty screens in three days.

David McClanahan has been avoiding the pitfalls of ignoring database design for over a decade. After writing a database engine for a data-driven application generator, (before dBASE II even considered one) he and his firm used this tool in combination with the techniques of database design described in this section to provide complete database application solutions rapidly and efficiently. You can combine the information in these chapters with the tools of FoxPro 2 and enjoy the same benefits he did.

—Editor

CHAPTER 9

Conceptual Database Design

by David McClanahan

Database design of large systems is a complex task. With the increasing power of PC DBMSs and popularity of multiuser LAN systems, databases with millions of records and gigabytes of storage are becoming more common. As the size and complexity of databases increase, so does the importance of the design process.

Database design is essentially the identification of each data element and its function within the system. The goal of the design process is a database schema, which describes the structure of the data in a form that is stable, that accurately reflects the requirements of the system, and that allows for reasonable change and growth. Database design is very concerned with planning for the future.

Relational database design is the process of:

- Identifying the attributes (data elements) that represent the facts an enterprise is concerned with
- Discovering each attribute's meaning to the enterprise
- Finding the associations between the attributes
- Grouping those attributes into relations.

Entity-Relationship Modeling for Conceptual Design

Data modeling creates a representation of the data requirements and rules for an enterprise. Data modeling organizes the data into the optimal form for manipulation, flexibility, and stability. Flexibility means the data can be accessed in different contexts by multiple users. The data must be secure from unauthorized access, and access must be within the bounds of any integrity rules that have been defined.

Data modeling is data-driven as opposed to process-driven. It involves identifying the data entities the enterprise is concerned with, the relationships between those entities, and the attributes of the entities and their relationships; it's not concerned with the details of the processes that will access that data.

The data-processing model was once centered on the processes in a system. Data was considered to be input to a process, manipulated by the process, and output from that process. On mainframe systems, data was often read in sequentially and processed into another sequential file. Data is now seen as the center of the system, and processes create, update, retrieve, or delete data against that system.

Data is represented on three levels: conceptual, logical, and physical. The data-modeling approach presented here and in the next two chapters is to develop an abstract, overall view of the data; develop a logical view, where details of the data groups are developed; and design the physical level, where the details of the relational database are specified.

Requirements Analysis

Database design begins with research to determine the data requirements of the enterprise. We can do that by collecting and analyzing the requirements of the data system's users. This normally involves interviewing users, reviewing current reports and screens, and researching company procedures and documentation. It's important to recognize the data objects, the relationships between those objects, and the rules and constraints that will govern how information is created and manipulated. This process, called *requirements analysis* or *requirement specification*, results in documentation that summarizes the findings and is used as the basis of system design.

Conceptual Modeling

In the conceptual model, we develop the overall view of the database system by determining the major entities, relationships, and attributes the enterprise needs. At this level we're less concerned with details and more concerned with the larger picture of the data requirements that results in a conceptual schema.

This model will be a stable (or slowly changing) view of the enterprise's data requirements. It will provide a framework for building the logical model and physical system and is a good checkpoint for implementation details. Because of the abstraction involved in defining "real-world" objects and the lack of physical implementation detail, the conceptual model can serve as a basis for communication between different levels of employees. The conceptual model is the enterprise's view of the system.

The Logical Data Model

When translating the conceptual design into a relational schema, we must consider the different views users have of the data. We're more concerned with details, such as defining the data's attributes and the relations needed to express entities and relationships at the conceptual level. Normalization and other design rules are enforced, and the primary and foreign keys are determined.

The Physical Level

At the physical level, we're refining the details of the relations that will store the data groups identified at the logical data level. The physical level defines data types, file and record formats, indexes, and so on. It takes into consideration the access paths necessary through usage analysis to tune system performance.

Conceptual Design

A data model is a representation of data, relationships, operations, and rules (semantics). The highest level of abstraction is the conceptual one, where data is represented by entities, relationships, and attributes from the point of view of the enterprise. At this level, we're not worried about which DBMS will be used; we want to see the big picture without concern for the exact details of the implementation to follow. The goal is a conceptual database model, which is a description of the major elements, relationships, and constraints of the system, and which will serve as the basis for the completion of the database design.

The elements of the model are represented by diagrams that capture the logical meaning of the real-world items independent of access methods and physical storage requirements. The way these diagrams represent the data is similar to how the user views it. The system of creating diagrams and symbols that we use originated in an article by Peter Chen as part of the entity-relationship (E-R) data model, which he developed.[1] We'll be using a modified version of Chen's diagramming techniques to build a relational system. There are many variations on E-R symbols, but once you know one system you can easily understand the others.

Components of the Conceptual Model

The major components of the conceptual model are entities, relationships, and attributes. The key attributes are also noted, and many other details—such as integrity constraints and term definitions—are documented during the process of generating the conceptual design. The information developed is usually entered into a *data dictionary*, a repository for information about the data system.

Entity

An *entity* is an object about which information needs to be maintained. The object could be a person, place, thing, concept, or event. It's something that can be distinctly identified and is important enough to the enterprise to be entered into the database. An entity must have properties that can be described well enough to distinguish one entity from another.

For example, we can identify a number of customer entities for our company. These customers all have a similar meaning to our company and can be represented by one entity type, *CUSTOMER*. Entity types are represented by rectangular boxes with a label stating the type. The type should be represented by noun, preferably singular (*CUSTOMER* rather than *CUSTOMERS*), that's distinct from the labels of the other entity types in the database. Each occurrence of an entity type is called an *entity instance*, or just an entity. (See Figure 9-1).

Other entity types that would be common in a normal business are purchase order, meeting, employee, and project. The noun used for the entity should describe the meaning of the entity to the enterprise as well as possible. We chose *CUSTOMER* because it denotes the function of the entity in relation to our enterprise better than

[1] Chen, P.P., *The Entity Relationship Mode: Towards a Unified View of Data*, ACM TODS, 1:1, March 1976.

the more generic *COMPANY. COMPANY* could be a supplier, contractor, or shipping firm we do business with. Labeling the function is important so that when we return to this entity later, perhaps in from a different context, we'll know what it represents.

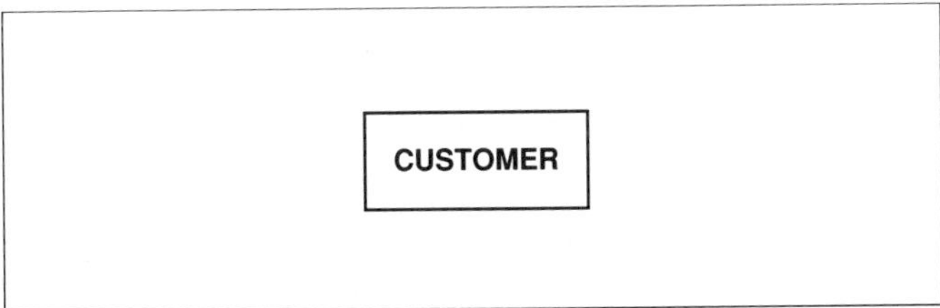

Figure 9-1. Sample entity CUSTOMER.

Attributes

Attributes are the significant properties or characteristics of an entity that help identify it and that carry the information necessary to interact with the entity. The actual content or quality of an attribute is an *attribute value*; for example, *SSN* is an attribute and *123-45-6789* is an attribute value. Each attribute in an entity has a range of possible values called the *domain* or *value set.*

An attribute with a basic data type is indivisible as far as the database is concerned and is called an *atomic value*. When an attribute consists of the concatenation of two or more basic attributes, it's called a *composite* attribute. *NAME* is a composite attribute if it contains both first and last name. An entity is actually only a collection of attribute values as far as the data system is concerned.

Attributes are noted in ellipses with a line connecting them to their entities. If an entity has many attributes, most likely more than one entity is involved. If so, they must be identified and separated. At the conceptual level, only the most important attributes are noted; we won't list every attribute in the system until we reach the logical level of design.

Each entity must have some unique attribute or set of attributes that allows it to be uniquely identified and clearly distinguished from the other entities of the same type. This attribute or set of attributes is called a *candidate key*. The most important candidate key becomes the primary key for the entity. If there are multiple candidate keys, choose the one that you consider to be most essential to the primary key. The attributes that make up a key are underlined in the attribute ellipse. The primary-key attributes are called *identifiers*, while the nonkey attributes are called *descriptors*.

Attributes that can be derived from other attributes are indicated by a ellipse consisting of a dotted line. An example of a derived attribute for an employee entity would be *AGE*, which is derived by subtracting the *BIRTHDATE* from the current date. The derived attribute may not need to be stored in the system.

Some attributes will appear to have multiple values for some entity instances. These appear within a double-line ellipse and are called *multivalued* attributes. We can have multivalued attributes on the first pass through the conceptual design; in fact, it often makes modeling easier. However, we almost always normalize the entity by removing repeating groups and placing them in their own entity or relationship type while still at the conceptual level.

The entity *EMPLOYEE* could have the attributes *LAST-NAME*, *MIDDLE-NAME*, *FIRST-NAME*, *SSN*, *BIRTHDATE*, *AGE*, and *PROJECTS*. The primary key could be *SSN* or a company-assigned employee number (*EMP#*). A name alone would not be a good choice because it may not be unique (see Figure 9-2).

The employee entity in the figure has an attribute *SSN*, which serves as the key attribute and is, therefore, underlined. The *NAME* attribute is a composite attribute made up of the first, middle, and last components of the employee's name. *PROJECTS* is inside a double-line ellipse because it's multivalued.

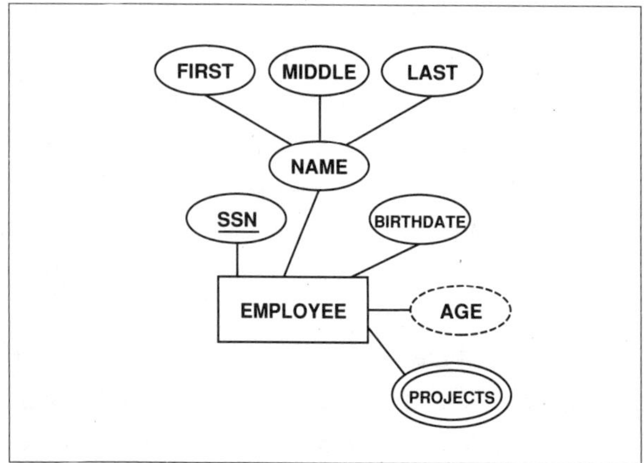

Figure 9-2. An entity with attributes.

Relationships

Associations that exist between entities are called *relationships*. Relationships may involve one or more entities and are classified into *relationship types*. These types are represented by a diamond shape and a label, normally a verb such as *teaches*, *manages*, or *works-for*. A line is drawn to each participating entity in the relationship. Relationships may or may not have attributes; some modeling systems don't allow relationships to have attributes, but in many cases it's logical and natural to associate an attribute directly to a relationship. An example is shown in Figure 9-3.

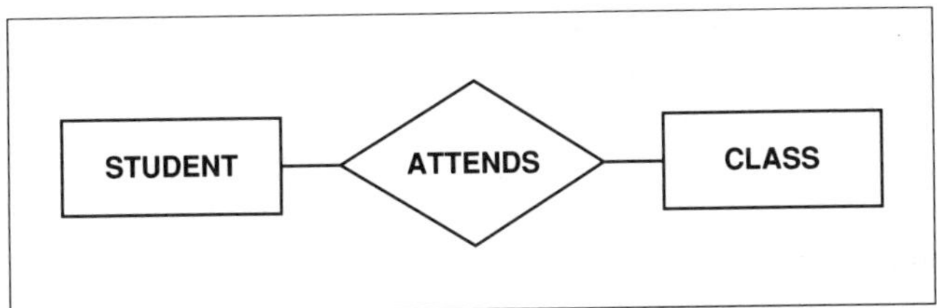

Figure 9-3. An example of the relationship (ATTENDS) between two entities.

Reading from left to right, it says "a student attends a class." From right to left, it would read "a class is attended by a student."

The number of entities that participate in a relationship is referred to as the *degree* of the relationship. Figure 9-3 is an example of a *binary* relationship, which has a degree of two and is the most common type. Relationships between more than two entity types are possible; a classic example of a *ternary* relationship (one with a degree of three) is the relationship between part, supplier, and project, where a certain part may be supplied by more than one supplier and used in many projects (see Figure 9-4). Naming is a often a little more difficult in the relationships with a degree greater than two but must show a relationship between each entity. Sometimes relationships are named after the entities that participate in them, such as *Supplier-Project-Part*, when it's difficult to find a verb or phrase that accurately describes the relationship. Some modeling systems don't allow relationships to have attributes and may allow only binary relationships, on the theory that this makes modeling easier.

Participation in a relationship may be mandatory or optional for the entities involved. The *conditionality* of a relationship is whether or not an entity instance is required to participate in a specific relationship. We note this optional participation by placing a zero through the line near the optional entity.

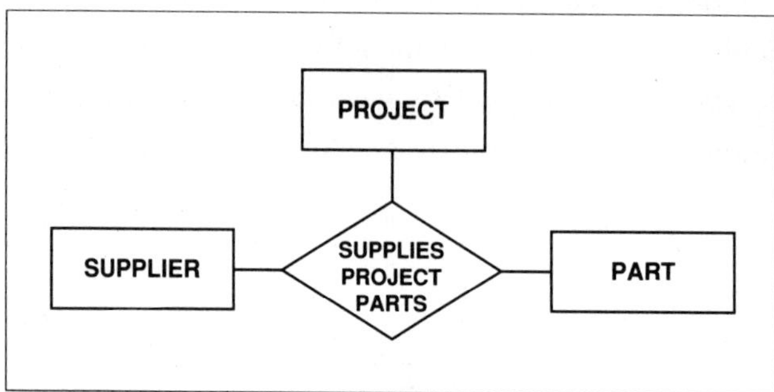

Figure 9-4. A ternary relationship.

The *connectivity* of a relationship shows the ratio of entities on one side of the relationship to the number of entities on the other. The connectivity can be *1*, *n*, or *m* and is labeled between the participating entity and relationship symbols. The following pairings of values are possible:

- 1:1 is a one-to-one relationship, where each entity can only be related to one other entity.
- 1:n is a one-to-many relationship, where each entity can be related to one or more entities.
- m:n is a many-to-many relationship, where both sides may contain multiple entities.

In Figure 9-5 a truck is assigned to one, and only one employee. Each employee can be assigned one truck, but the zero through the connectivity line means that the participation of the employee is optional in this relationship. This optional participation actually means that each employee may be assigned zero or one trucks.

A one-to-many relationship looks like a one-to-one relationship if viewed from the "many" side. In Figure 9-6, one employee can be assigned to only one project, but a project may have zero, one, or many employees assigned to it (zero because it has optional participation in the relationship). When the relationship is viewed from the employee side, each employee is assigned to one and only one project, which looks like a one-to-one relationship.

If each employee may be assigned to multiple projects, the relationship is many-to-many and would be noted as in Figure 9-7.

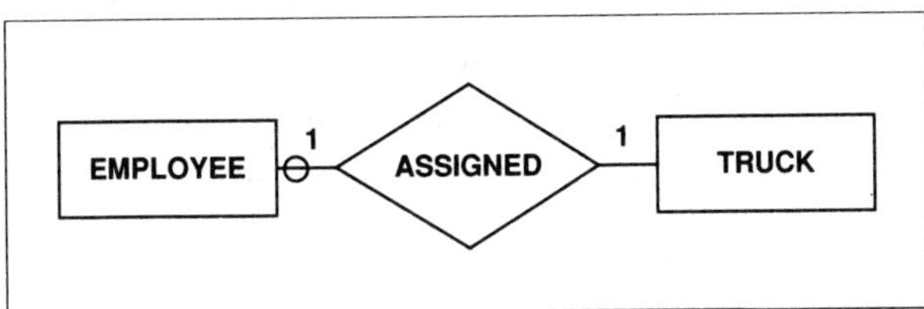

Figure 9-5. A one-to-one relationship.

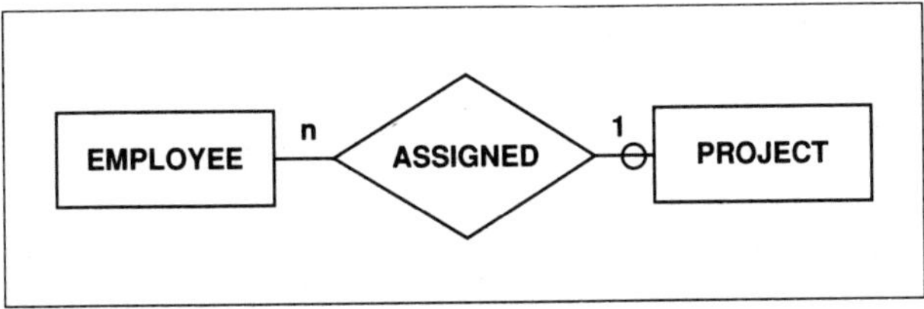

Figure 9-6. A one-to-many relationship.

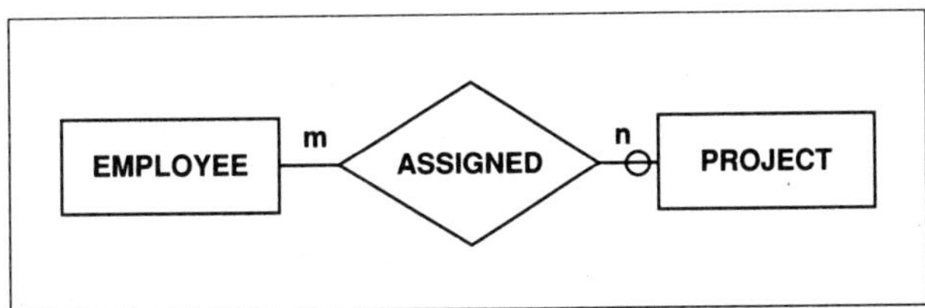

Figure 9-7. A many-to-many relationship.

Each employee must be assigned to one or more projects, while each project may have zero, one, or more employees assigned to it.

A many-to-many relationship is many-to-many in both directions and can't be directly implemented in relational systems. Instead, an *intersection* entity is added to represent the relationship in a later phase of the conceptual design. A many-to-many relationship is sometimes called a *complex* relationship, but because others use the same term to refer to relationships that involve the participation of three or more entities, we'll avoid using this term.

In ternary relationships, the connectivity is shown for each association between entities. A circle specifies the starting entity for each set of values.

Examine the connectivity values in Figure 9-8. To see the connectivity from the view of any participating entity, you must first find the starting point and then find the corresponding value in the set belonging to the other participating entities. The employee has a one-to-many relationship with the project entity and a one-to-one relationship with the manager entity.

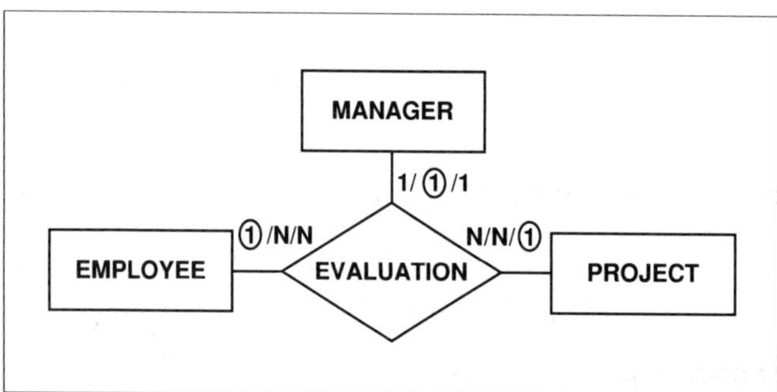

Figure 9-8. A ternary relationship with connectivity labels for each participant.

Look carefully at the example to find the circled *1* showing the connectivity as seen from the employee view. That corresponds to the first value in the *MANAGER* connectivity set, which is also a *1* (but uncircled) to represent the one-to-one relationship. The corresponding value for the *PROJECT* entity is *N* to represent the one-to-many relationship. *MANAGER* has a one-to-many relationship with both the *EMPLOYEE* and *PROJECT* entities. Finally, the *PROJECT* entity has a one-to-many relationship to *EMPLOYEE* but a one-to-one relationship to *MANAGER* because it can only be managed by one person.

It's often useful to label the connectivity with the ranges of possible values that are expected or required. This is called the *cardinality* of the relationship. The number of expected entities may also be recorded to provide information that will be useful during the physical design process.

It's important to understand all the details of each relationship and the cardinality and conditionality. Identifying relationships is generally more difficult than finding the entities. It often helps to examine the relationship from the view of each of the participating entities.

Figure 9-9 shows that the average number of employees working for each project is four and that the allowable range on any one project is from two to 10 employees. This notation will be used later to enforce this system constraint.

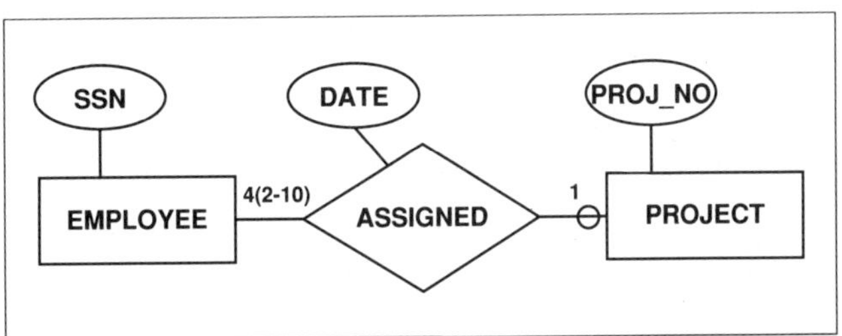

Figure 9-9. A relationship with an attribute and cardinality.

When an entity has a relationship with itself, this is called a *reflexive* relationship. The association between an employee and the manager of that employee could be expressed as a reflexive relationship.

Role names are additional labels that help clarify the role an entity plays in a relationship. This is especially important in the case of a reflexive relationship. In Figure 9-10, *manages* and *is managed by* are role names describing the function of an entity in the relationship. The labels for the role names are placed on the lines between the entity and the relationship to show the part the entity plays in that relationship and are separate from the relationship label.

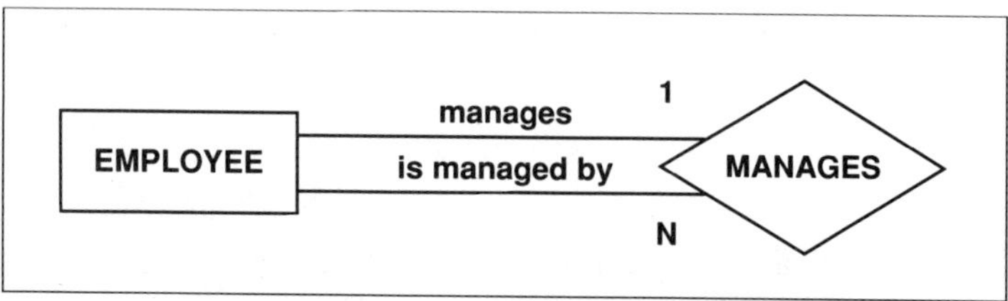

Figure 9-10. A reflexive relationship with role labels.

In Figure 9-10, note that the connectivity works as usual: Each manager manages one or more employees, while each employee is managed by one manager.

Weak Entities

Some entities that are identified owe their existence entirely to a relationship with another entity. If the entity on which they depend is removed, there's no basis for their continued existence and they must be removed. These are called *weak* or *dependent* entities. A weak entity must participate in a relationship with the *identifying owner*, which is the entity on which it depends. The relationship that connects the weak entity to its owner is called a *sustaining* or *identifying* relationship. Weak entities are indicated by a rectangular box with doubled lines. Similarly, the sustaining relationship's diamond box may use double lines to designate its classification.

A weak entity has no primary key that uniquely identifies it without a foreign key derived from the entity on which it depends. The part of the weak entity's primary key not derived from the parent entity is called a *partial key* and exists to distinguish the child entities of the same parent. One way to recognize weak entities is by a set of repeating attributes with a slight variation between them. Someone might have described *EMPLOYEE* as an entity with a repeating attribute dependent.

An example of a weak entity is *ORDER-LINE* in Figure 9-11. It depends on the *INVOICE* entity for part of its key value (*INVOICE#*) and is related through the sustaining relationship *CONTAINS*. It should be obvious that the *ORDER-LINE* entity wouldn't exist without the *INVOICE* entity. It also looks like a repeating attribute value (*INVOICE#*) may be repeated a number of times for each *ORDER-LINE* entity.

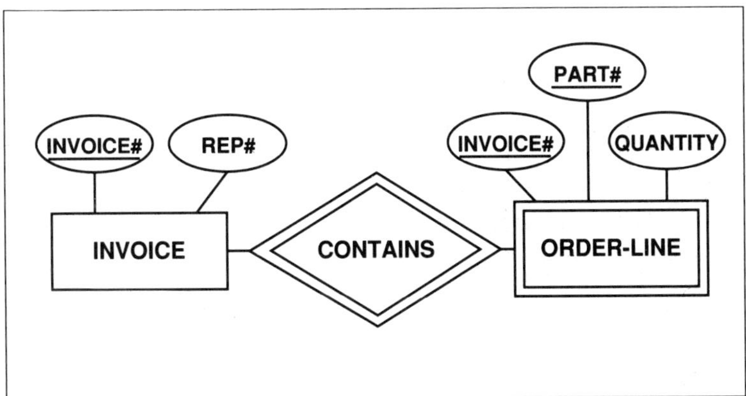

Figure 9-11. ORDER-LINE is a weak entity owned by INVOICE.

ORDER-LINE must add another attribute to participate in its primary key. This could be an attribute such as line number, but we have assumed that each part can only be entered on one line of an invoice and, therefore, have chosen *PART#* to complete the key. The weak entity type uses a double-lined box, and the relationship through which it associates with the owner entity is represented by a double-lined diamond. The weak entity has mandatory participation in the relationship.

You may also come across an *associative* entity, one that acts like a relationship. It may be an entity that consists of attributes that were originally associated with a relationship but were later separated and moved into an entity type. For example, suppose we have a relationship called *RENTS* between *COMPANY* and *EQUIPMENT*. If each occurrence of *RENTS* generates a set of attributes to track the rental, an associative entity called *RENTAL* can be created and attached to the relationship.

Generally, the label for an associative entity is similar to the label for the relationship with which it is associated. To indicate the associative entity, we'll use the regular entity rectangle but attach it to the relationship with an arrowhead as in Figure 9-12(a). You may see this diagrammed as a composite entity in modeling systems that don't allow relationships to have attributes. Figure 9-12(b) shows the symbol that is then used; it combines the symbols for a relationship and an entity using a diamond inside a rectangle.

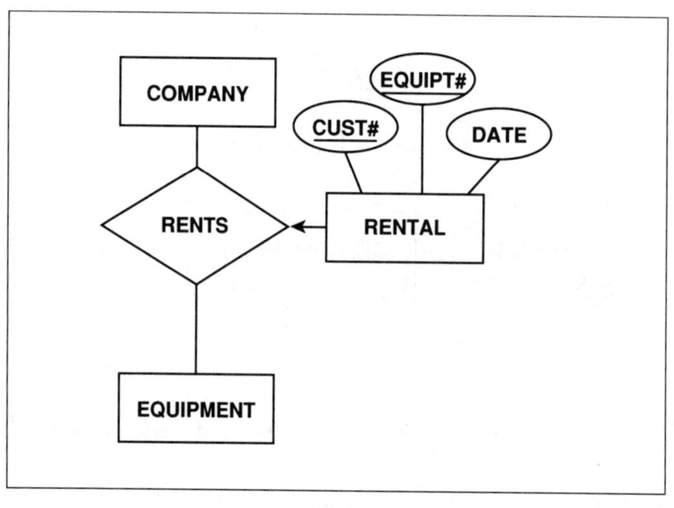

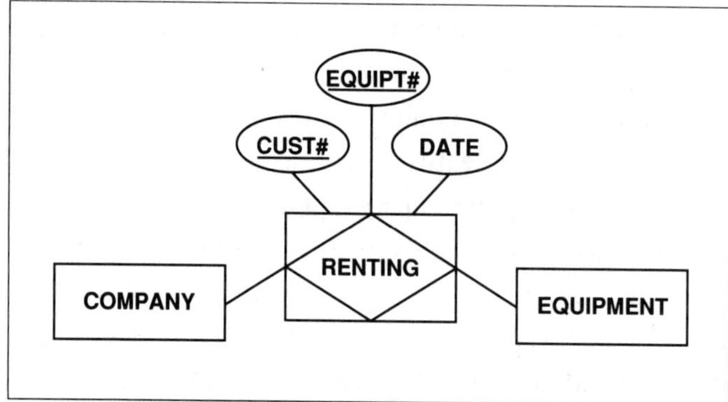

Figure 9-12. Two possible notations for an associative entity, RENTAL.

The associative entity could also be represented as attributes of the relationship. By moving the attributes from the *RENTAL* entity in Figure 9-12(a) to the *RENTS* relationship, we can remove the *RENTAL* entity entirely. Use whichever representation is more natural for you. You may even decide not to use associative entities at all; however, some analysts find they retain the expression of the original relationship better with an associative entity than with an intersection entity. They also find it quite natural to use an associative entity to represent an event associated with a relationship.

Sometimes two or more entities are found to have a number of attributes in common and similar meanings. We can generalize these entities into a *supertype* entity that contains all the attributes that they have in common. We can view the supertype entity as the source type from which the *subtype* entities are derived. For example, there are many types of employees in a company and several ways to represent them. One method is to create a supertype entity, *EMPLOYEE*, containing the attributes every employee has in common. This may include attributes such as *SSN*, *START-DATE*, and *DEPARTMENT*. Subtype entities are created for each variation of the *EMPLOYEE* type, such as *CLERK*, *SALES-REP*, and *SECRETARY*.

The supertype entity has a special relationship with its subtype entities. That relationship is labeled something like "IS ONE OF" or "ISA," to show that an employee can be classified as one and only one of the subtypes, or "MAY BE" to show that an employee may be classified as one or more of the subtypes (perhaps a *SALES-REP* can also be a *MANAGER*). A line intersects the connecting line between the supertype and the relationship symbol to mark this as the supertype entity in the relationship. (see Figure 9-13).

Each subtype contains the attributes unique to its subtype. The subtype entity is understood to contain all the attributes and relationships of the supertype entity from which it is derived. Each subtype entity has a foreign key that matches the primary key in the supertype entity. Subtype entities can also have their own relationships; for example, a *SALES-REP* entity has an association with the *INVOICE* entity for each sale the representative has made. The other employee subtypes don't participate in this relationship. Each of the subtype entities implicitly participates in any relationships the supertype participates in. Each of the subtype entities in Figure 9-13 has a manager through the supertype's participation in the *MANAGES* relationship.

Another way to show an employee's position is to add to the *EMPLOYEE* entity an attribute called *JOB DESCRIPTION* to show the role each employee has within the company (with values such as *clerk*, *manager*, and *sales*). Yet another method is to create a relationship to an new entity, *POSITION*, to hold the information. This is necessary if more than one attribute is needed to hold the information concerning each employee's position (see Figure 9-14).

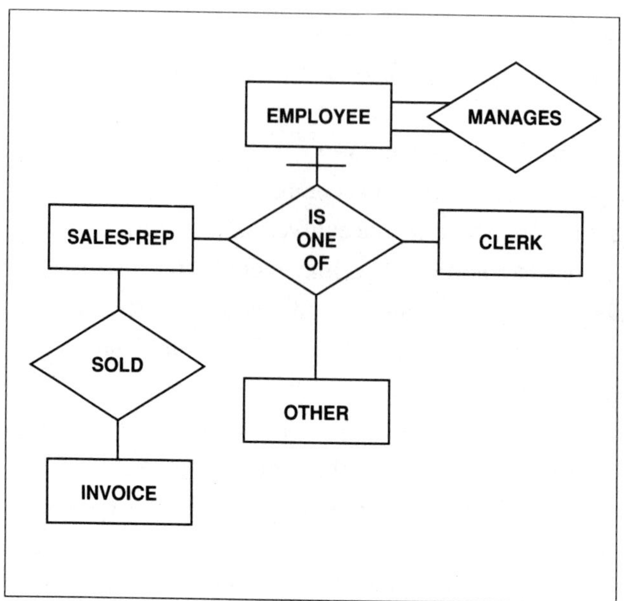

Figure 9-13. A supertype entity with its subtypes.

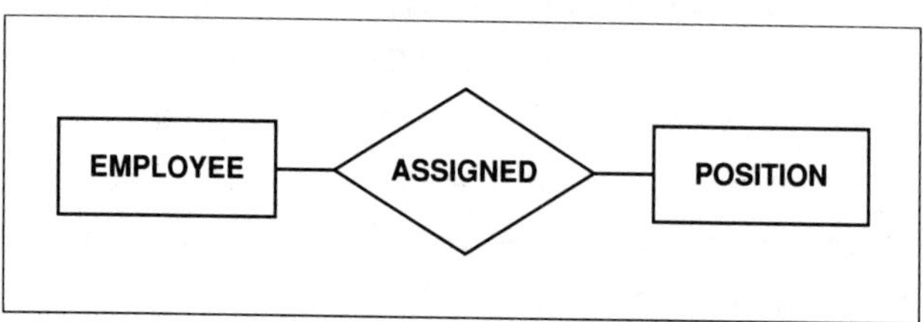

Figure 9-14. *POSITION* entity in relationship with *EMPLOYEE.*

As mentioned earlier, the relational model can't represent a many-to-many relationship directly. In this case, an intersection entity is added between the two source entities to allow a many-to-many link. To represent a many-to-many relationship between *EMPLOYEE* and *PROJECT* (from Figure 9-7), we add a new entity, *PROJECT ASSIGNMENT*, and give it the attributes necessary to hold information about the assignment. An employee may then be assigned to more than one project, and a project may have more than one employee assigned to it. This new entity captures the relationship by representing each occurrence of it. This includes the *EMPLOYEE* and *PROJECT* identifiers, which link the two entities. Each *PROJECT ASSIGNMENT* entity represents an instance of the *EMPLOYEE-PROJECT* many-to-many relationship (see Figure 9-15).

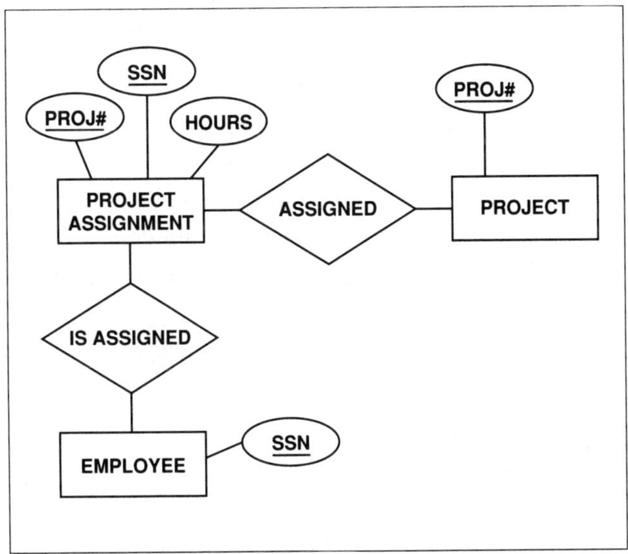

Figure 9-15. An intersection entity used to represent a many-to-many relationship.

The arrangement of the entities, relationships, and connecting lines on the page is flexible. Generally, the diagram is read from left to right and from top to bottom.

Associative entities are often just another way of expressing a many-to-many relationship. Consider changing the intersection entity we looked at in Figure 9-15 to an associative entity. To express it as an associative entity, we establish a relationship between *EMPLOYEE* and *PROJECT*. An associative entity named *PROJECT ASSIGNMENT* is then attached to the *ASSIGNED* relationship.

Other Details

Many other details should or must be recorded at this level of the database design. Integrity constraints that restrict the data values allowed, relationships, operations, and existence dependencies are noted on the requirements document.

Other semantics are also noted as necessary; perhaps the project leader must always be a department manager or may never be a department manager.

All the details concerning entities, attributes, and relationships are documented and usually placed in a data dictionary. This *metadata*, or information about data, is all we currently know about the enterprise's data and its structure in the database.

Developing a Conceptual Schema

The first step in developing a conceptual schema is to locate and identify the entity types about which the business will need to store information. We usually do this by interviewing people in the business who are aware of the details of the operation and know what data is required. Other sources of information are documents about the business, forms, and existing database objects.

Let's model a small business. A series of interviews with the business has turned up the following information:

- The business sells parts to customers. For each part we have a part number, a selling price, a description, and the count of that part currently in stock.
- Each sale is on an invoice to one customer. An invoice contains a line for each part ordered and a total amount due for that invoice.
- Each invoice is written by one sales representative, who is credited with the sale. Reps are paid 5% commission on total gross sales.
- Information must be kept on our own inventory of parts.
- There are multiple suppliers of parts; the price charged for a part by different suppliers may vary. This is called the *cost* of the part.
- An invoice to a customer contains customer information, a company name, an address, and a customer number.
- Employee information contains a name, social security number, employee number, address, and position.
- We must store the hourly wage each is paid (all employees except sales reps are hourly).

- One account is maintained for each customer to track charges, payments, and the current balance.
- The company needs to know if an invoice has shipped yet.
- Accounting must know which invoices have been paid.
- We must know total sales for a rep.
- We must know if an item is in stock at our company or on order from any company.
- Each hourly employee generates a timecard each week (Monday morning).
- Reps don't turn in timecards, just their total sales.
- All employees are paid weekly by check.
- We need to get a report each Monday telling us what each employee should be paid for the previous week.

The following entity types are evident:

Customer	Account
Invoice	Sales Rep
Employee	Parts
Inventory	Timecard
Supplier	Check

A partial schema for some of these entities might be:

CUSTOMER(Cust_id, Company, Address)

INVOICE(Invoice#, Parts, Total)

EMPLOYEE(Emp#, SSN, Name, Address, Wages)

SUPPLIER(Company, Address)

REP(Emp#, SSN, Address)

INVENTORY(Part#, Count)

This enterprise has a number of functional areas involved with this information including ordering, inventory, supplies, shipping, personnel, and payroll. We will be concerned mostly with the ordering and inventory areas for our examples.

The next step is to create symbols for these entity types and add the major attributes for each. When the entities have been identified, we look for relationships between them. We must search out the relationships and determine their details. We must also examine each entity and consider its function within the enterprise. That function will tell us something about the other entities with which it might be associated. For example, examine the *INVOICE* entity type and consider which entities are involved with an invoice. A *CUSTOMER* placed the order, and a sales *REP* wrote the order. How can this be represented?

Did you consider a ternary relationship between *REP*, *CUSTOMER*, and *INVOICE*? That was suggested as a possible relationship in Figure 9-16 because those three entities are required for an invoice to be written. There are several other ways to represent this; we'll see other possibilities as we continue to build our conceptual model.

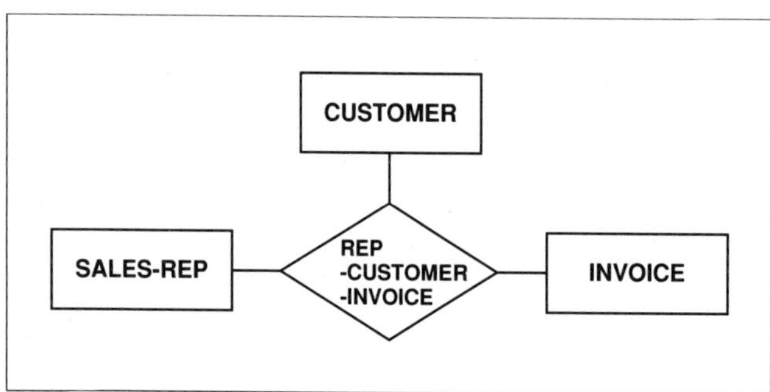

Figure 9-16. A ternary relationship.

More attributes are added to the entity types and perhaps also to the relationship types. In the process, other entity or relationship types may be discovered. For example, when adding attributes to the *INVOICE* entity we will have added *INVOICE#* and a repeating attribute, *PARTS*, to contain the items ordered on each invoice (see Figure 9-17).

CUSTOMER clearly has a relationship with *INVOICE*, so the relationship type <*ORDERS*> is discovered and connected to *CUSTOMER* and *INVOICE*. *REP* also has a relationship with *INVOICE*, so the relationship type <*WRITES*> is discovered and connected to *REP* and *INVOICE*.

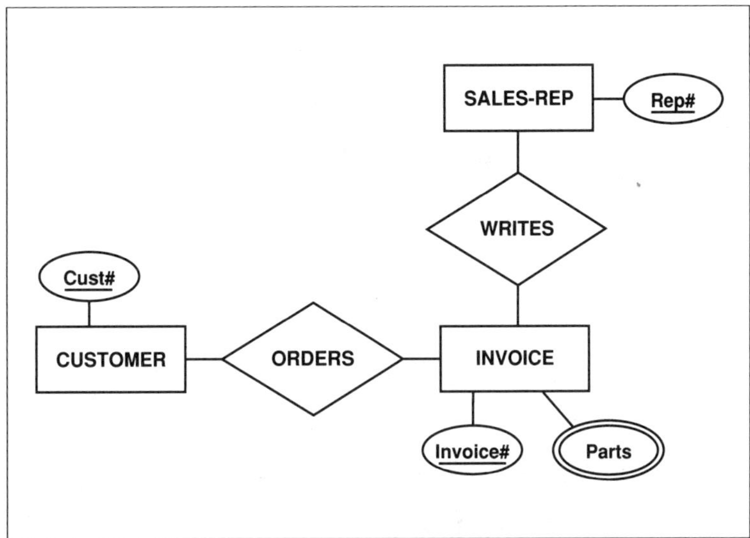

Figure 9-17. Un-normalized INVOICE entity.

In Figure 9-17, a repeating group holds the multiple occurrences of *PART#* on each line of the invoice. This isn't in first normal form, so the repeating group is moved to its own entity (but which one?).

The *LINE-ITEM* entity was introduced to remove the repeating group, *PART#*, from Figure 9-18. Each line in an invoice will be entered in this entity. A sustaining relationship, *CONTAINS*, was created and connected to *INVOICE* and *LINE-ITEM*. The new *LINE-ITEM* is a weak entity that depends on the *INVOICE* entity for part of its own key. The *CONTAINS* relationship will be the identifying relationship.

INVOICE# is required as a foreign key to identify the *LINE-ITEM* entities associated with a certain invoice. One or more attributes must be added to *INVOICE#* to create a primary key for the *LINE-ITEM* entity because *INVOICE#* won't be a unique qualifier if an invoice has more than one line. We could create the attribute *LINE-NUMBER* that, with *INVOICE#*, would ensure uniqueness. Because a certain *PART#* can only appear once in each invoice, that would also ensure uniqueness without requiring the creation of a new attribute. In this case, *INVOICE#+PART#* is the primary key. *PART#* is a partial key that distinguishes each child of a parent invoice from another.

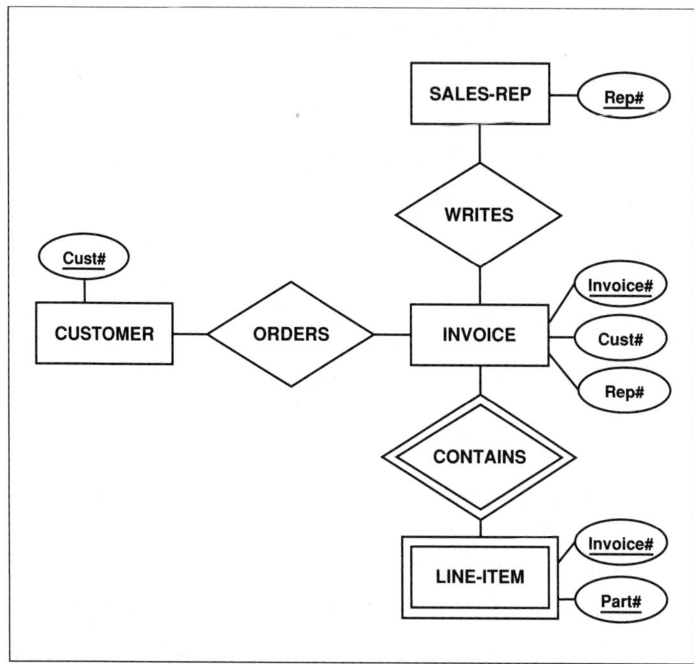

Figure 9-18. Normalized INVOICE entity.

Now consider the *PART* and *SUPPLIER* entities (Figure 9-19). This figure adds the *PART* entity and an *INCLUDES* relationship between it and *LINE-ITEM*. *PART* will also hold the inventory information if we add the *COUNT* attribute. The *PRICE* attribute is our selling price. Figure 9-19 also adds the *SUPPLIER* entity and its *SUPPLIES* relationship with *PART*. Is this correct?

A *SUPPLIER* entity exists and does supply parts to our business. But where is the cost of the part to be stored? Remember that the same part may have different costs depending on the supplier.

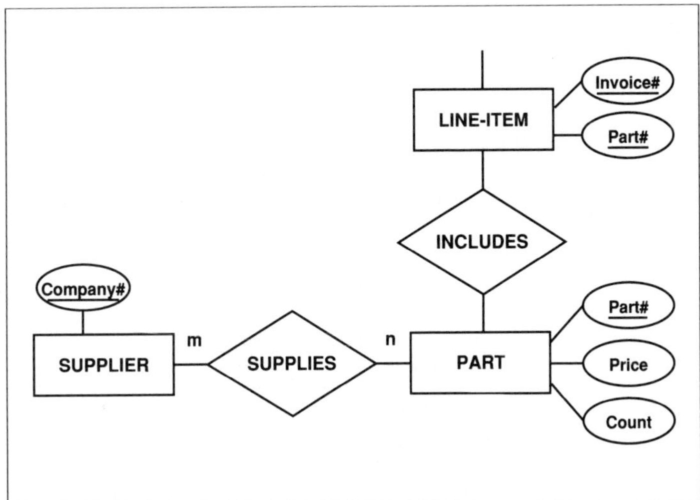

Figure 9-19. Where is cost of each part to be located?

Notice the other clue in the connectivity ratios for the *SUPPLIES* relationship: a many-to-many relationship between *SUPPLIER* and *PART*. This requires that an intersection entity be created. The primary keys from each entity are placed in the new entity to represent one part supplied by one supplier. This new entity, *SUPPLIED-PART*, also holds the cost attribute. Figure 9-20 shows this new entity.

Another way to represent this would be with an associative entity. The associative entity is then viewed as capturing each occurrence of the *SUPPLIES* relationship, as shown in Figures 9-21 and 9-22.

The attributes also could have been added to the *SUPPLIES* relationship (Figure 9-23). A list of the relationship types found would include:

ORDERS between customer and invoices

SUPPLIES between supplier and part

WRITES between rep and invoice

INCLUDES between invoice and line items

CONTAINS between line item and part#

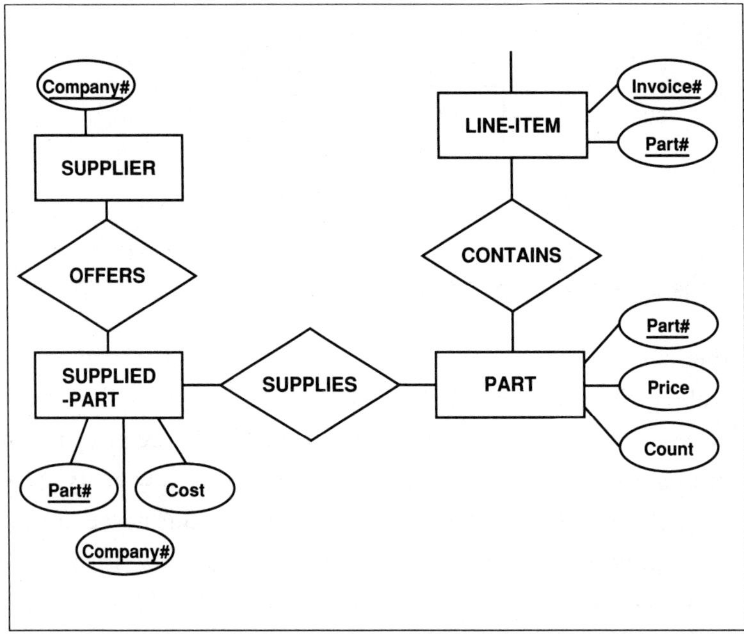

Figure 9-20. Adding SUPPLIED-PART.

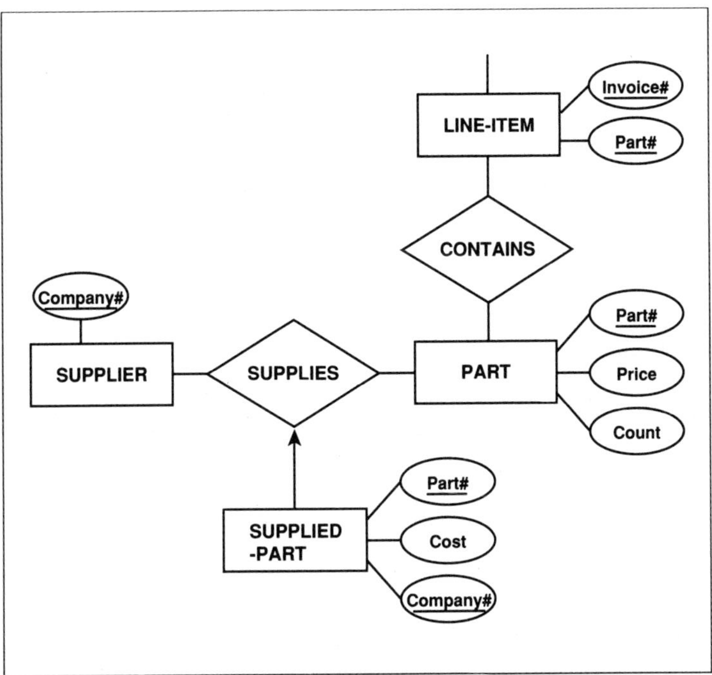

Figure 9-21. Adding SUPPLIED-PART attribute entity.

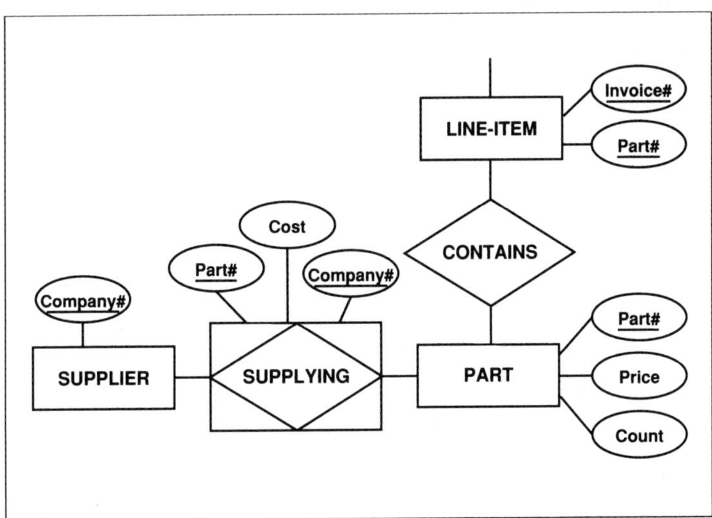

Figure 9-22. Adding SUPPLYING (alternative notation).

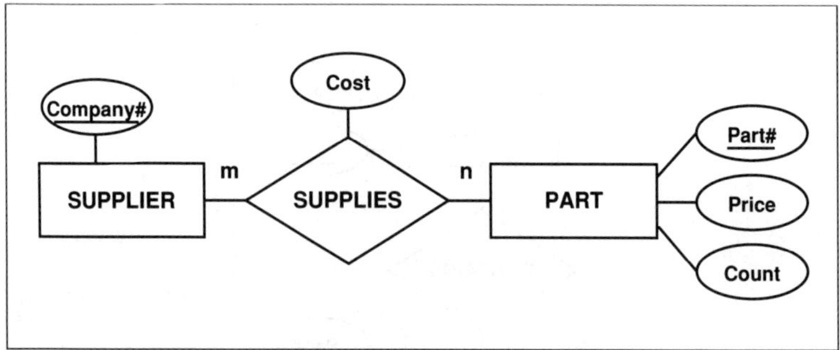

Figure 9-23. Adding attributes to the relationship.

This is as far as we'll take the example. If you wish to continue with this example, consider the following:

- Where do we keep track of the parts that we have on order with our suppliers?
- Notice the roles each entity plays. Are there any supertypes?
- Do you find any many-to-many relationships?
- What system constraints should be noted?
- Define the domains for each attribute.
- Find all candidate keys.
- Define the primary keys.

You may define foreign keys also, but that's actually an implementation detail of the relational model.

Figure 9-24 shows the E-R diagram for the conceptual data model as it stands. Not shown is all the documentation developed during this stage of the modeling process.

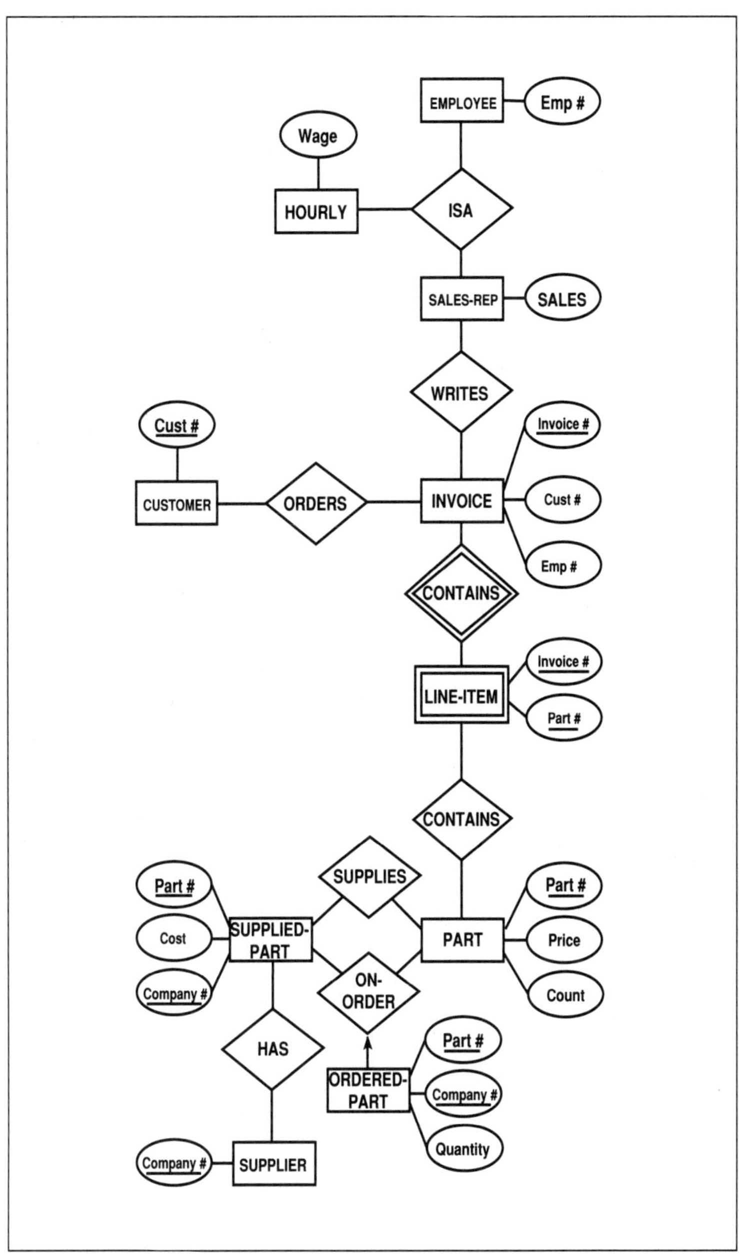

Figure 9-24. E-R model.

CHAPTER 10

Logical Database Design

by David McClanahan

Once the conceptual design of your database is completed (see Chapter 9, "Conceptual Database Design"), the next step in the design process is to translate the entity-relationship (E-R) model you've developed into a complete relational database schema consisting of all the individual relation schemas. The user views of all the data elements in the system are collected and analyzed. These views are merged, one at a time, to synthesize the logical data model. At the completion of this stage, the logical model will contain all the attributes in normalized relations, with primary and secondary keys defined, no many-to-many relationships left unresolved, and any necessary constraints documented. On the physical level, all the foreign keys will be determined, some denormalization may take place, and the schemas for each relation will be completed.

The conceptual model has defined the entities and relationships (with the major attributes) necessary for the enterprise database. Now we must determine the details concerning the exact views of that information required by users. By examining each user's perspective on the data elements in the system, we discover the remaining attributes and can then determine the correct location and associations for each. During this process, attributes are matched with the entities and relationships found in the conceptual design. At this stage, defects in the E-R model may be discovered and some adjustments to the conceptual level may be required. The process is an iterative one; that is, as new attributes and associations are found, entities and relationships may be created, modified, or deleted, perhaps uncovering new attributes that continue the process.

User Views

Each user's views of the data elements (which we'll call *user views*) must be documented and labeled. Generally, these user views are found through interviews, documentation, or existing reports or screens used to input or output data. For each user view, the containing E-R constructs must be found and the context verified. Each data element is examined in turn for functionality and association and is then documented in the data dictionary. The process of integrating each user's view into the logical model is a well-known technique developed by many authors. Basically, we're defining each attribute and its location (function) in the system. When all the data elements have been identified, the logical data model is complete.

We'll note this information using bubble-chart diagrams based on the system introduced by James Martin[1] for logical database design. I prefer this notation for a number of reasons. First, the bubbles look like the attribute symbols from the conceptual diagrams and have a similar meaning. Second, the functional dependencies and associations between each attribute are clearly and simply noted, and the final notation fits the relational view of normalized tables quite well.

Data Elements

Each data element at the logical level is drawn in an ellipse and is a node in the logical model. Data elements usually correspond to an attribute at the conceptual level and to a column label in a relational table, though a data element may be a combination of two or more attributes. Data elements that are key components are underlined the same way key attributes were on the conceptual design level; if the key contains more than one component, the elements are concatenated into one element with the components listed vertically and connected with a "+" sign. Figure 10-1 shows both types of data elements.

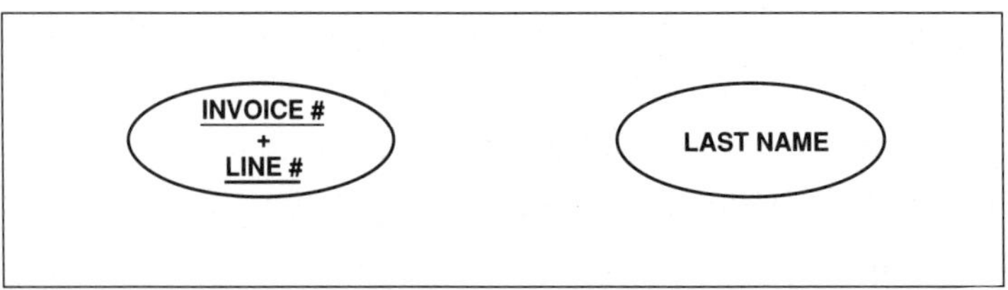

Figure 10-1. Two data items.

1 Martin, James. *Computer Data-Base Organization*, 2nd edition. Englewood Cliffs, N.J.: Prentice-Hall, 1977

Data Groups

The set of related data elements is called a *data group* and corresponds to a tuple in a relation. A data group will always consist of a key (the data elements that participate in the primary key) and attributes (nonkey data elements). Data elements of the same data group are listed horizontally; if more space is needed, indented rows of data elements are added. The data elements may be qualified individually with the entity (or relationship) name to which they belong as *invoice.number*, where *invoice* is the entity and *number* the attribute. Alternatively, the entity name can be placed outside the data elements as a label for the entire group; this is the notation we'll be using in this chapter. If no qualification is given, the first attribute will also serve as an informal label.

Arrows (curved lines with arrowheads on one or both sides) are used to connect each data element to the other data elements with which it is associated. The single and double arrowheads show the connectivity.

A single-headed arrow shows a one-to-one functional dependency and is called a *one-arrow*. Remember, *functional dependency* means one value exists for each dependent data element for each value of the data element on which it depends. If you know the value of the determinant data element, you can determine the value of the dependent element.

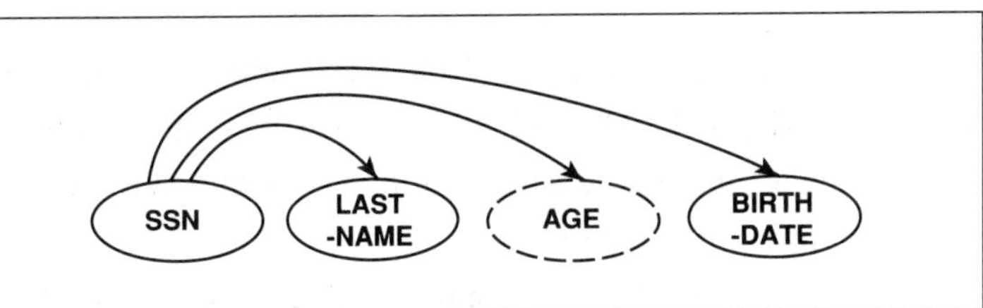

Figure 10-2. One-to-one associations.

A mandatory one-to-one association, as in Figure 10-2, shows a functional dependency of the data element pointed to on the data element from which the line originated. In this case, *LAST-NAME* is functionally dependent on *SSN*; in other words, if *SSN* is known, *LAST-NAME* can be determined and can have only one value. The

AGE attribute is also functionally dependent on *SSN*. It's an example of a derived attribute, which means its value could be determined by calculation and need not be stored; thus, its ellipse is drawn with a dotted line. The value could be determined by subtracting the birthdate from the current date. Are there other functional dependencies in Figure 10-2?

A double-headed arrow shows a one-to-many association and is called a *many-arrow*. Figure 10-3 has added the department attribute to the data group from Figure 10-2. The functional dependency between DEPARTMENT and SSN is signified by the one-arrow from SSN to DEPARTMENT. A one-to-many association also exists from the DEPARTMENT attribute back to the SSN. This means that for any one SSN there is only one possible value for a department assignment (and it's mandatory) but that for any DEPARTMENT value one or more SSNs are assigned to it.

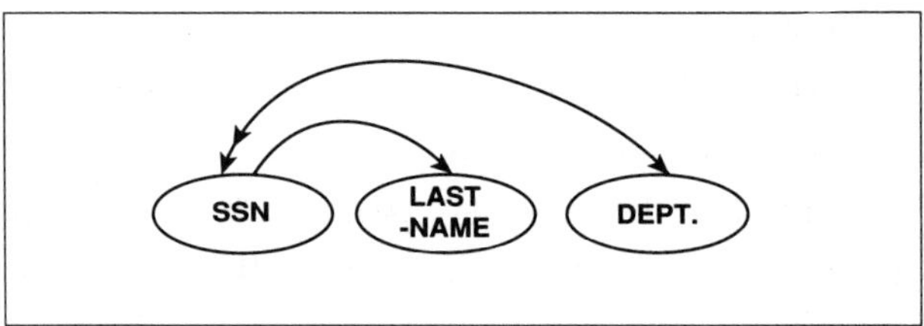

Figure 10-3. One-to-one association and one-to-many association.

Optional participation in an association is noted by adding a zero to the line near the arrowhead of the optional attribute. Combined with a one-arrow, this is called a *conditional dependency* and means there may be zero or one attribute. Without the zero, the participation is known to be mandatory.

For example, in Figure 10-4 PROJECT has a conditional dependency on SSN. An employee may be assigned to zero or one PROJECT (but not more than one). The zero at the end of the many-arrow means a PROJECT may be associated with zero, one, or many SSNs (one-to-zero/many), so it's possible that a PROJECT has no one assigned to it.

The identification and correct labeling of dependencies between data elements is critical for the development of a good, logical model. The designer must carefully analyze the associations because they're the basis of the normalization process. It is important to question the users of each view so that all uses of each data element are understood. The analyst is searching for the *semantics*, or meaning of the data to the user.

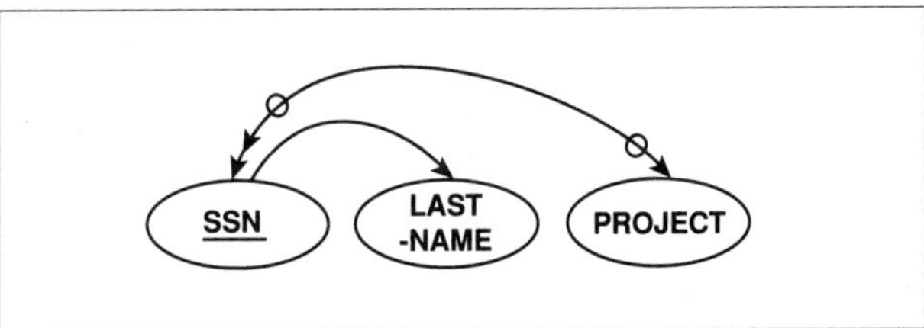

Figure 10-4. A conditional dependency and one-to-zero/many association.

Each data group must consist of a primary key, any nonkey attributes, and all the associations between elements noted in the bubble chart. The role of all data elements can be determined by the association arrows that connect them.

A prime data element is one that makes up a candidate key; the other data elements are nonprime or just attributes. A key has a line with a one-arrow leaving it. Nonprime data elements usually have no one-arrows leaving them.

A normalized data group has a primary-key data element, which has one or more one-arrows leaving it and often no one-arrows pointing to it (though in the case of a one-to-one association, as between SSN and EMP#, one will be chosen as the primary key and the two elements will still have a one-to-one association).

Optionally, a normalized data group contains nonkey attribute data elements, which have only one-arrows pointing at them and no arrows leaving them, and secondary key data elements, which have arrowheads leaving (usually many-arrows) and pointing to them.

Attributes (nonkey elements) may not have arrows between each other. If that occurs, it signals a transitive dependency and must be removed to ensure third normal form. Figure 10-5 shows a normalized data group.

The direction of the arrows shows associations, connectivity, and the direction of data access. In Figure 10-5, any data element must be accessed by reference to the invoice number. The invoice number is called an *entry point* because that's the value that must be known before any other can be determined (accessed). If you have the value of an entry-point element, you can determine the values of a data group. Entry points always have an arrow leaving their bubbles.

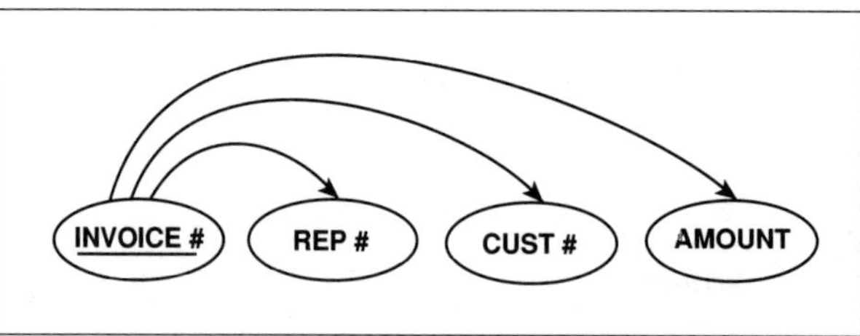

Figure 10-5. A normalized data group.

Look closely at the functional dependencies in Figure 10-5. You should see that each functionally dependent attribute can have only one value for each value of the *INVOICE#* element. Look for any possible dependencies between the attributes. Can *DATE* be functionally dependent on *CUST#* or *REP#*? Will *AMOUNT* always have a single value for each value of *CUST#* or *REP#*? No, because no other functional dependencies exist.

Figure 10-6 shows the same data group, but in this instance *REP#* is used to locate all the invoices for a certain sales representative. There may be one or more invoices for a *REP#*, so a many-arrow is drawn back to *INVOICE#*. This means *REP#* is a secondary key and an entry point since data elements can be located once a *REP#* value is known.

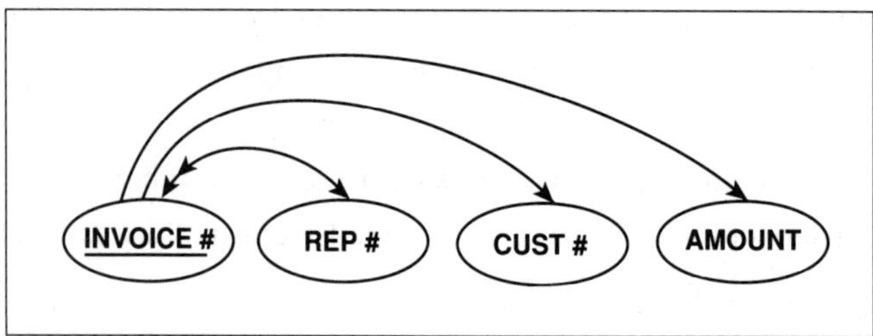

Figure 10-6. A data group.

Examine Figure 10-7 and consider the meaning of the associations.

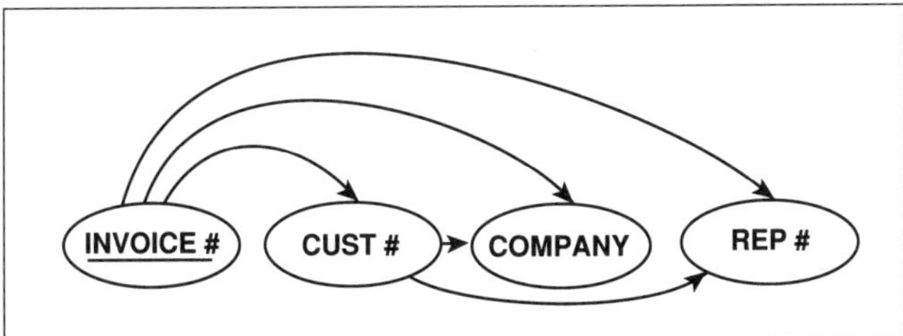

Figure 10-7. Is this fully normalized?

COMPANY is the name of the customer placing the order, so it's functionally dependent on *CUST#* and, therefore, is drawn with a one-arrow. *REP#* is also shown to have a functional dependency on *CUST#*, which would mean that one and only one sales rep could handle a particular company's invoice. That would be possible if each company were assigned one representative who was to handle all the orders placed by that customer. Consider whether this is fully normalized (in third normal form).

The first problem in Figure 10-7 is that the company attribute isn't functionally dependent on the key (the whole key and nothing but the key); it's dependent on another attribute and thus must be moved to its own data group (CUSTOMER). The same *REP#* must also be removed from this data group.

Relationships between data groups will also be noted with lines and arrowheads in a manner similar to that of the data element associations. For example, the normalized form of Figure 10-7 would be as shown in Figure 10-8.

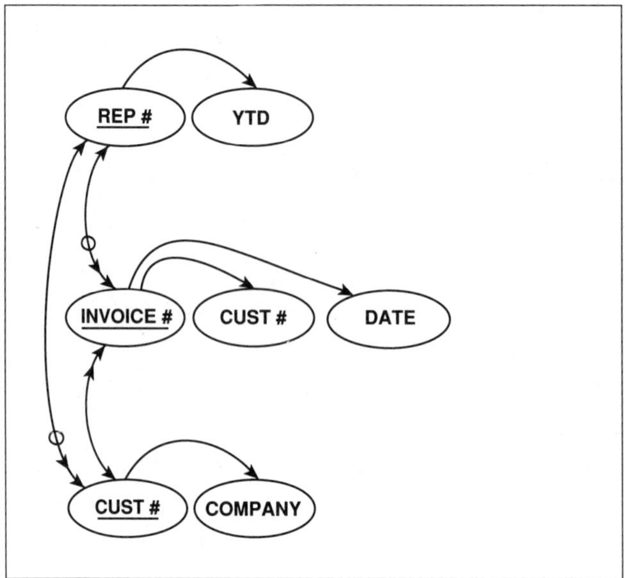

Figure 10-8. Associations between data groups

In this example, the INVOICE data group has a many-to-one association with the REP data group and with the CUSTOMER group. This means any invoice will belong to one rep and one customer.

Implementing Relationships

The following paragraphs discuss the implementation of relationships in the relational system and how the links between data groups will be created with foreign keys. These paragraphs show the goal toward which we are working (the creation of the relational schema).

In the relational database model, relationships between entities are implemented by comparing data values. Notice, however, the lack of a linking element between the REP data group and the INVOICE data group (how do we know which invoices belong to each rep?). When this happens, the primary key from the "one" side of the association is used as a foreign key in the "many" side. This is an implementation detail required by the relational data model. This section looks at how these associations would be created and shows the relationship between data groups and the relation schemas used to express these groups.

In Figure 10-9, the primary key element, *REP#*, from the REP data group (the "one" side) is added to the INVOICE data group (the "many" side). Now we can search the INVOICE group for a certain *REP#* to find all the invoices generated by each rep or search the REP data group with any value from the INVOICE.REP# group to find which rep generated a specific invoice.

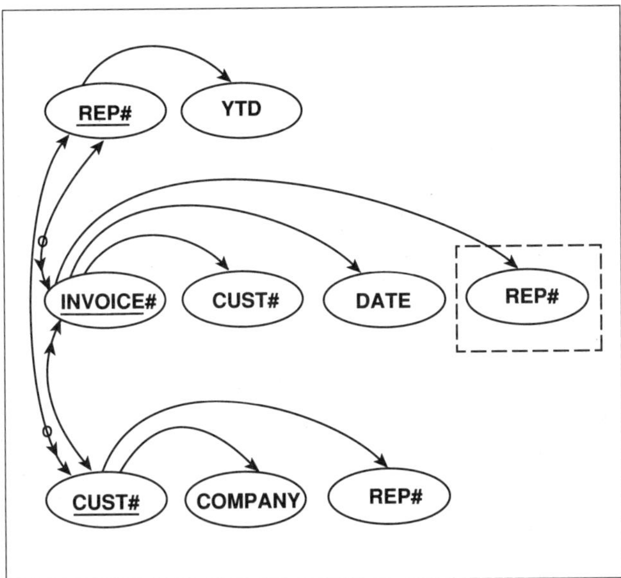

Figure 10-9. Foreign key.

However, this information is related to the physical implementation of the navigation between entities and we prefer not to include it in the logical model at this time (or just to separate it off to the side as a note for use later in the design process). The foreign keys will be assigned at the beginning of the next chapter ("Physical Database Design") in order to simplify and clarify the notation of the logical data elements. The foreign key element(s) may be placed in the logical diagram, if you prefer, after the associations between data groups have been determined.

When a many-to-many association is discovered between data groups, a new intersection data group must be created to express that relationship. The relational data model doesn't directly support many-to-many relationships, so the primary key from each data group is used as a component of the intersection data group's primary key. This may seem similar to the previous example, but the new data group is expressed at the logical level because no many-to-many associations between data groups may appear at the logical level. Figure 10-10 shows a many-to-many association between the EMPLOYEE and PROJECT data groups.

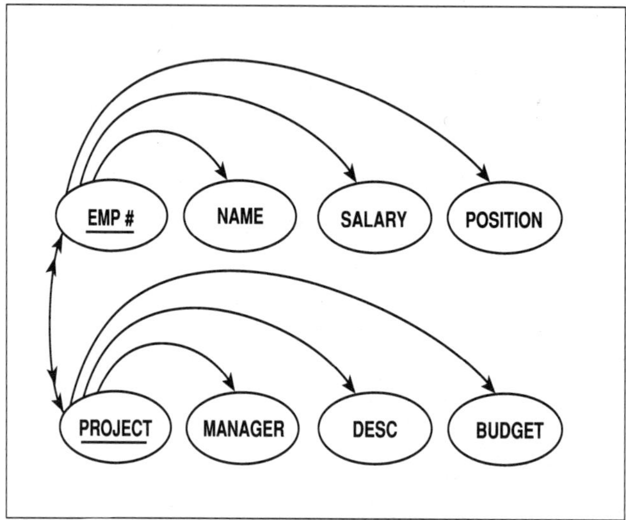

Figure 10-10. Many-to-many association.

To express the many-to-many association in this figure, we create a new data group, PROJECT-ASSIGNMENT, with *EMP# + PROJECT* serving as the primary key (see Figure 10-11).

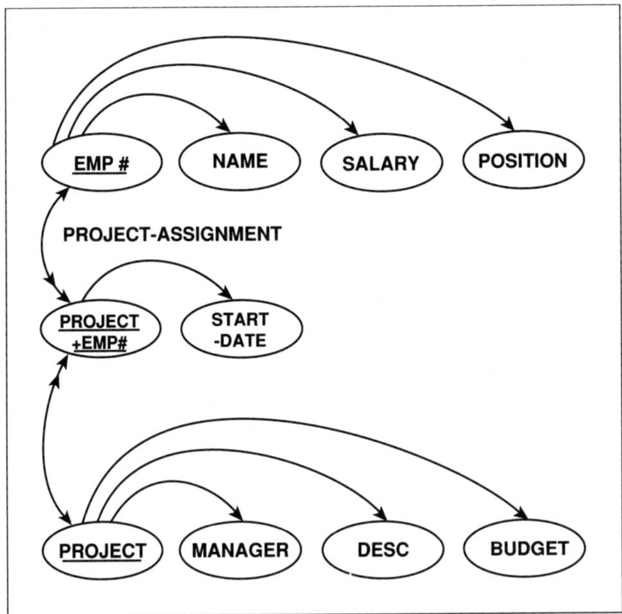

Figure 10-11. Intersection data group.

Each user's view involves at least one data group. As we add the information from each user view, we'll at times be adding to a data group created by a previous view; the data elements are combined and any redundancies removed. The resulting data group must have a unique name.

For example, Figure 10-12(a) shows the first user view developed for the EMPLOYEE data group. The second user view developed for this data group, Figure 10-12(b), shows another user's slightly different requirement for information about employees. Perhaps this view was from a user in the mailroom. Figure 10-12(c) shows the synthesis of the first two user views.

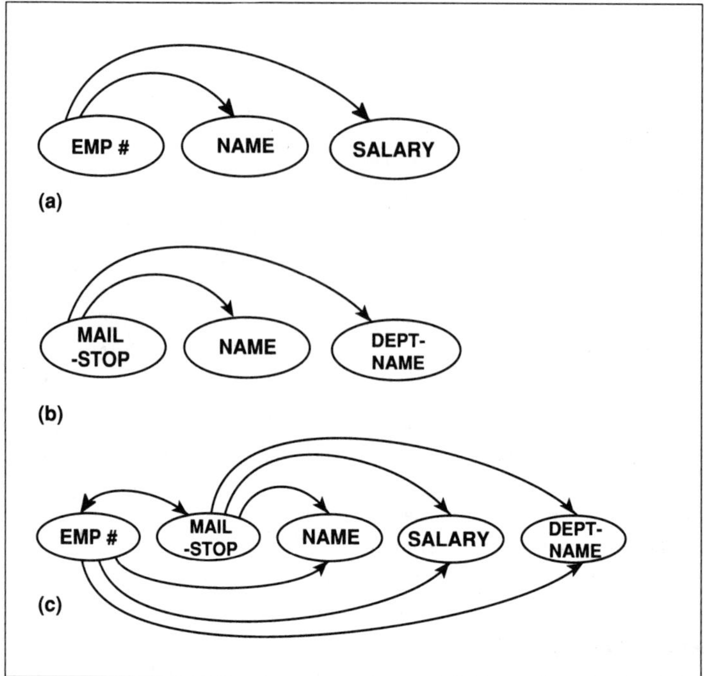

Figure 10-12. Merging two user views (first step).

In the first view, *EMP#* is the primary key with two dependent attributes. In the second view, someone saw *MAILSTOP* as the primary key with one attribute in common with the first view and a new unique attribute. The third view is a combination of the two. Notice that two data elements have one-arrows leaving them, which means they're key nodes. All nonkey nodes are functionally dependent on key nodes. This creates a redundancy in the synthesized data group, so one must be chosen as the primary key. In this case, *EMP#* may be the correct choice. The attributes that have more than one arrow pointing at them are *intersecting* attributes and are not allowed in the final bubble chart.

When the dependencies are revised, the result is as shown in Figure 10-13.

The *MAILSTOP* data element has been removed to its own data group. If it remains the only element in its data group, it may be added to the one or more groups with which it has a one-to-one relationships as a secondary key. Secondary keys generally have only many-arrows leaving them, but the association between *MAILSTOP* and *EMP#* is an unusual one-to-one association between secondary and primary keys.

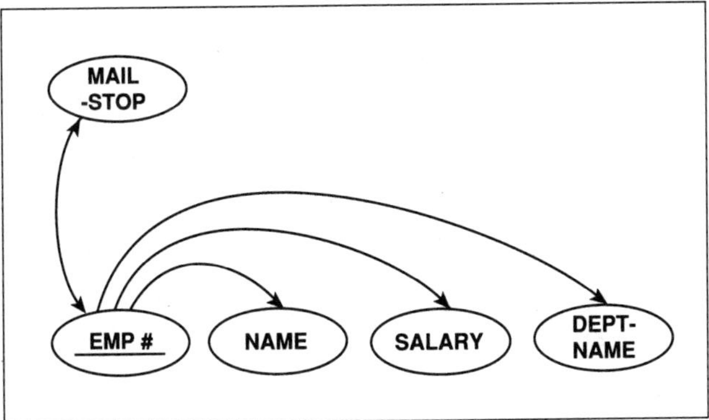

Figure 10-13. A synthesized user view.

In the next user view of the employee (Figure 10-14(a)), a user views the employee as having a position in the company and a project assignment that is multivalued (noted by the many-arrow). This is, of course, a violation of first-normal form (which allows no repeating groups), but we can normalize it by moving the project attribute out to its own data group. The association between the EMPLOYEE and PROJECT data groups is the many-to-many one shown in Figure 10-15(a).

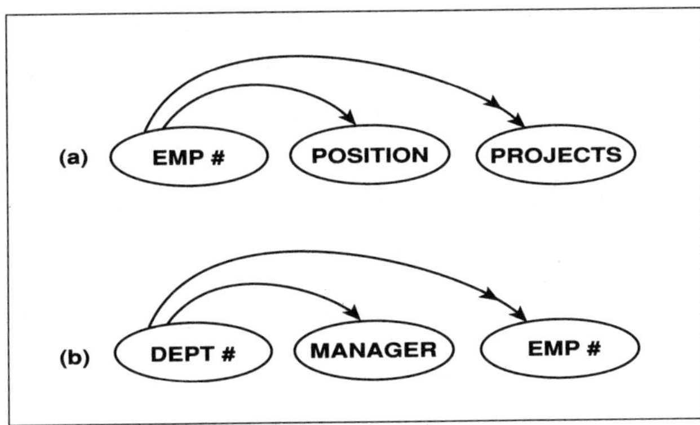

Figure 10-14. User views.

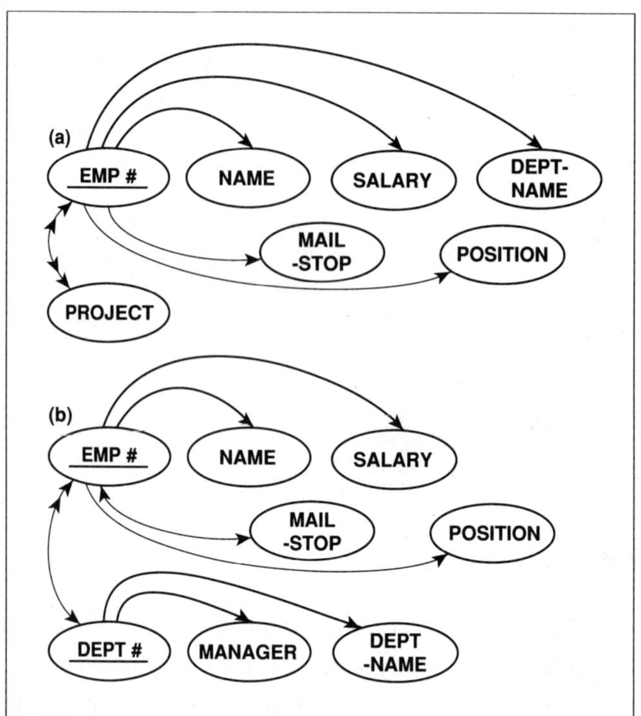

Figure 10-15. A synthesized user view: (a) is step one, (b) is step two.

In the next user view (Figure 10-14(b)), the DEPARTMENT data group is described as containing the data elements *DEPT#* and *MANAGER* plus a number of *EMP#*s. When *EMP#* is recognized as multivalued, it is removed to its own group. An existing EMPLOYEE data group already contains that element, so an association is created between those two groups to contain that information.

Also notice that in Figure 10-14(b) the association between *DEPT#* and *EMP#* in the DEPARTMENT group is one-to-many. The department name in Figure 10-15(a) is recognized as functionally dependent on *DEPT#* and is moved to that data group in Figure 10-15(b).

Building a Logical Model

The following are definitions of the user views from the case study described in Chapter 9 (see Figures 10-16 through 10-18):

(a) EMPLOYEE(EMP#, MAILSTOP, NAME, ADDRESS, HR-WAGE)

(b) REP(NAME, REP#, TOTAL-SALES, ADDRESS, MAILSTOP)

Payroll has the following view:

(c) INVOICE(EMP#, INVOICE#, AMOUNT)

Billing has the following view:

(d) INVOICE(CUST#, INVOICE#, AMOUNT)

Shipping has the following view:

(e) INVOICE(INVOICE#, PART#, COMPANY, ADDRESS, QUANTITY)

Inventory has the following view:

(f) PART(PART#, COUNT, PART-DESC)

(g) TIME-CARD(EMP#, HOURS, DATE)

(h) CHECK(EMP#, AMOUNT, CHECK, DATE)

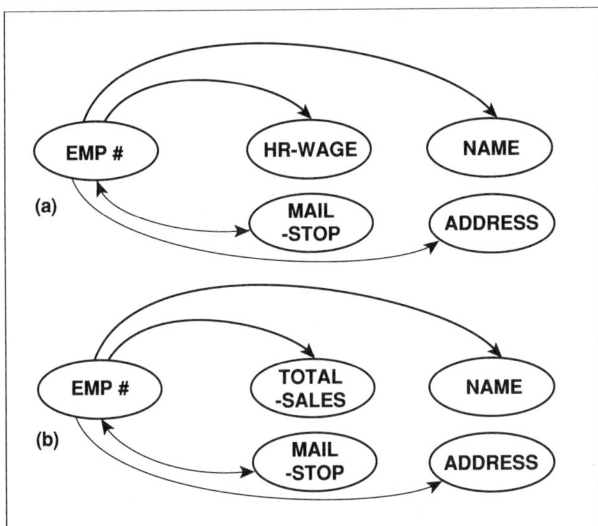

Figure 10-16. User views for (a) and (b).

Each user view is analyzed in turn and added to the logical data model diagram (a synthesized bubble chart). For each user view we must:

- Understand and document each data element.
- Determine what entity each element is concerned with.
- Order data elements into data groups.
- See whether the data element must be stored or can be derived.
- Relate the data groups to the E-R model.
- Uncover any other attributes.
- Look for synonyms, homonyms, and other relations with data elements that have already been entered into the bubble chart.
- Note the functional dependencies.
- Normalize the data groups.
- Synthesize each view into the logical data model diagram.

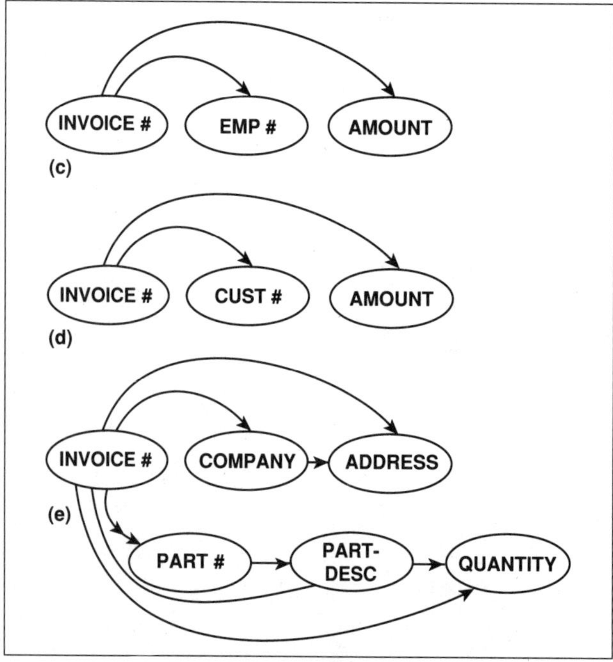

Figure 10-17. User views for (c), (d), and (e).

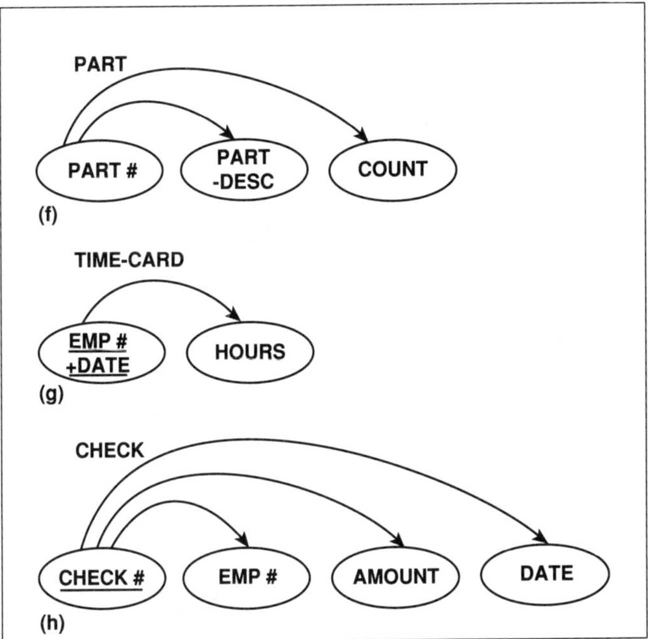

Figure 10-18. User views (f), (g), and (h).

The first user view, (a), is from an hourly employee. The only consideration is whether the *EMP#* or *MAILSTOP* should be the primary key; each is distinct, and the nonkey attributes are functionally dependent on either. The decision is made to use *EMP#* because it's a permanent, company-assigned value intended to be a unique identifier (though *MAILSTOP* could change if the employee moved to a new location).

The next user view (b) is that of a sales representative. It has almost the same data elements with the exception of the *TOTAL-SALES* attribute, which replaces the *HR-WAGE* amount from hourly employees. The fact that in this view all but one of the data elements are in common with the elements of (a) should cause us to consider whether these data groups are about the same entity or are subtypes of the same entity. The decision is made that they're subtypes of an *EMPLOYEE* entity. The data elements they have in common are placed in the supertype entity, and only the data elements unique to each are placed in the subtype entities. The synthesis of (a) and (b) is shown in Figure 10-19.

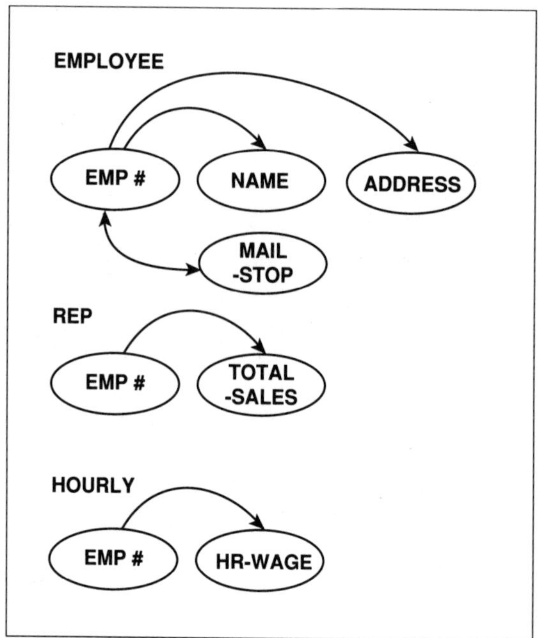

Figure 10-19. Synthesis of a supertype entity from (a) and (b).

Each subtype entity must then take the primary key from the EMPLOYEE data group to establish the *ISA* (is one of) relationship (see Chapter 9).

The next user view, (c), was submitted by the payroll department. That department needs to find each invoice generated, the amount of the invoice, and the *EMP#* of the sales representative who wrote it so the rep (who works on commission) will be credited with 5% of the sale. In this user view, the person who was interviewed mentioned the attribute *REP#*. On further research, we discovered that *REP#* was a synonym for *EMP#*, which we have already created; therefore, we merge the two and make a note of the synonym in case someone else uses it.

User view (d) is the view of an invoice entity from the billing department. You can see this department has a slightly different perspective. The data elements they mentioned include the *CUST#* to be billed for *AMOUNT*. This adds a new element to the INVOICE data group and results in the group shown in Figure 10-20.

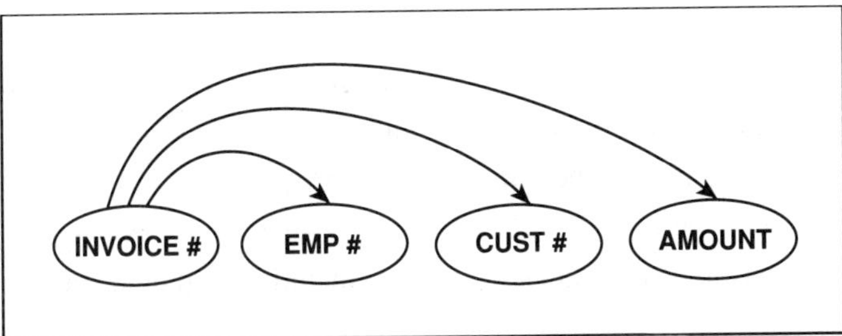

Figure 10-20. User view (d) from another department's perspective.

Notice that in user views (c) and (d) each department mentioned the data elements in the order they thought most important (*EMP#* for payroll, *CUST#* for billing). The analyst must objectively decide on the functional dependencies and key elements. In this case, *INVOICE#* is the element on which all the others are functionally dependent.

User view (e) is an interesting view from the shipping department. A shipping clerk gave us the data elements needed to be able to ship the parts for an invoice. They would like to have the company name, the address, and the list of parts and quantities so they can initiate a shipment. Notice the multivalued *PART#* element and two transitive dependencies on it. To normalize this situation, we move the part information out to its own data group. Also notice the transitive dependency between *ADDRESS* and *COMPANY*. When we move these elements into the E-R diagram, we find they're attributes of the *CUSTOMER* entity and place them there. We also replace *COMPANY* with the key of the *CUSTOMER* entity, *CUST#*. This step results in a much different bubble chart from the one we started with (Figure 10-21).

Inventory has its own user view, (f), of a PART data group. This group is found in the E-R model, so it presents no complications. We add it to the bubble chart along with an association between the LINE-ITEM and PART data groups.

A timecard has an association with HOURLY employees and not with REP employees and is added to the chart.

The CHECK data group, though, has an association with the EMPLOYEE data group. Both subtypes of the *EMPLOYEE* entity participate in the association through that entity.

Figure 10-22 shows these additions.

At the end of the logical design phase, the data groups are normalized and all the associations between data groups have been noted. The translation to the relational schema is easy because of the similarity between a data group and a table schema. The associations between data groups become relationships between tables; we express them by defining the foreign keys for navigating between tables. We're now very close to our goal: a relational schema. The actual translation to that schema is covered in the next chapter.

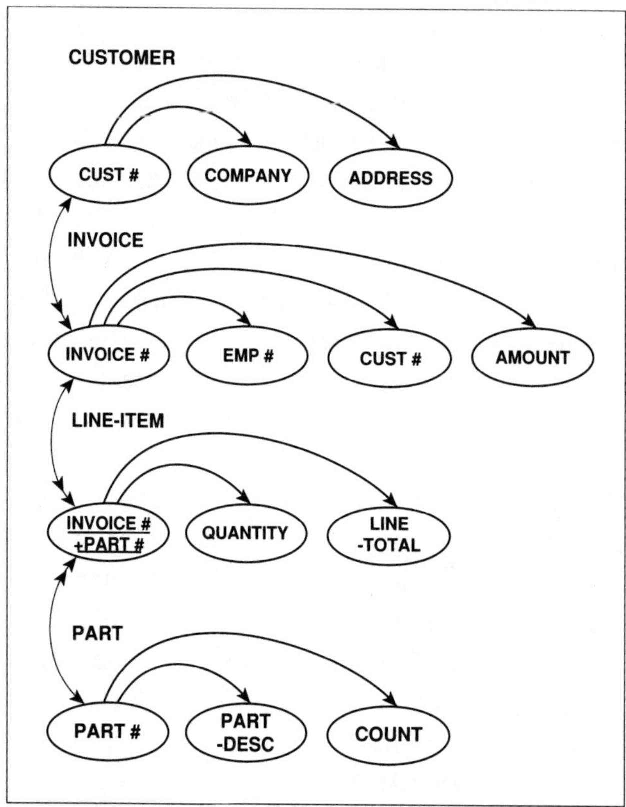

Figure 10-21. Incorporating user view (e).

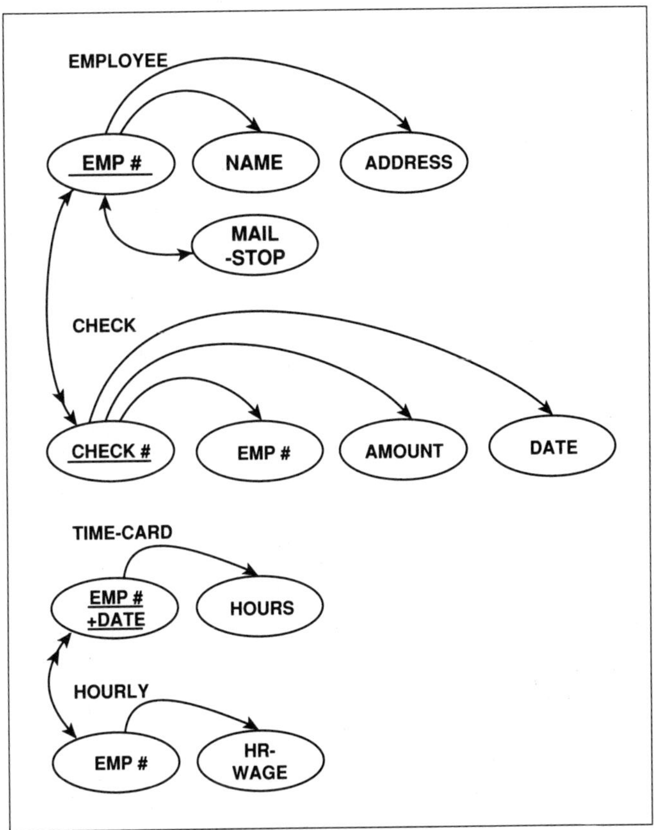

Figure 10-22. User views (e), (f), and (g).

CHAPTER 11

Physical Database Design

by David McClanahan

Defining the Relational Schema

At the end of the logical design phase, the analyst has produced the logical data model, which is a complete synthesis of all the user-views into a normalized bubble chart. The next step is to produce the FoxPro statements that will implement the relational database. The data definition language (DDL) in SQL is made up of the statements that are used to create and modify the structure of the relational database. These statements create objects, such as tables and indexes, and define the physical parameters of data storage in the database system. FoxPro does not support the ANSI standard for the DDL statements in SQL and has far fewer options. We will show examples of the data definition statements that FoxPro 2.0 offers in this chapter, after we complete the definition of the relational schema.

We ended the logical design phase in Chapter 10, just short of defining the final relational schema because the statements that create the database must reflect some of the physical considerations of the system. Since the logical design is normalized it can be converted into FoxPro statements to create the tables and indexes for the database system once the foreign keys have been determined and implemented. Tables are actually considered to be logical objects, and the DBF and FPT files are the physical mechanisms that implement them. Since the creation of the physical files is handled by FoxPro, we will cover the completion of the database schema and the creation of the data definition statements in the beginning of this chapter.

The logical model has determined the logical data elements, placed them into data groups, determined the primary key and perhaps secondary keys for each data group, noted the relationships between the groups, and detailed the system constraints. Each data group tentatively identifies a record type for a table in the database system. A great deal of the translation from the logical model to the FoxPro statements that will create the tables and indexes is a simple, mechanical process. This is one of the benefits of a good logical model that is fully normalized. The system constraints that have been documented in the design phases are not supported by the current version of the FoxPro DBMS, and must be handled programmatically.

Mapping the Logical Data Model to Tables

Each data element becomes a field in a .DBF file. We'll continue to refer to these files as tables to emphasize their relational basis. Each data group in the logical data model generally maps to a single table in the database system. There are exceptions, however, such as the combining of data-group elements when denormalization is desired. The primary key and all the attributes associated with it become the schema for a table and corresponds to a physical record type.

A unique name must be assigned to the table, generally the same name as, or at least similar to, that of the logical data group. A field name and a data type are determined for each data element in the data group. Some of the labels must be modified to meet the requirements of the DBMS being used for the implementation.

Foreign Keys

Foreign keys are used to implement relationships between data groups and can be determined by examining the logical data model. Each connectivity type has its own considerations for inserting foreign keys. Figure 11-1 shows a one-to-many relationship between two entities.

Each one-to-many association between data groups is expressed by inserting a foreign key, consisting of the primary key of the table on the "one" side, into the table on the "many" side. In Figure 11-1, EMPLOYEE is the "many" side and DEPARTMENT is the "one" side because one department may have many employees. The department ID (*DEPT#*) is placed in the EMPLOYEE record; therefore, if we want to know the *DEPARTMENT.description* for the department an employee is assigned to, we can look up the value of *DEPT#* in the corresponding EMPLOYEE record and use that value to look up a record in the DEPARTMENT table. This provides for the navigation from the EMPLOYEE table to the DEPARTMENT table, expressing the *ASSIGNED-TO* relationship.

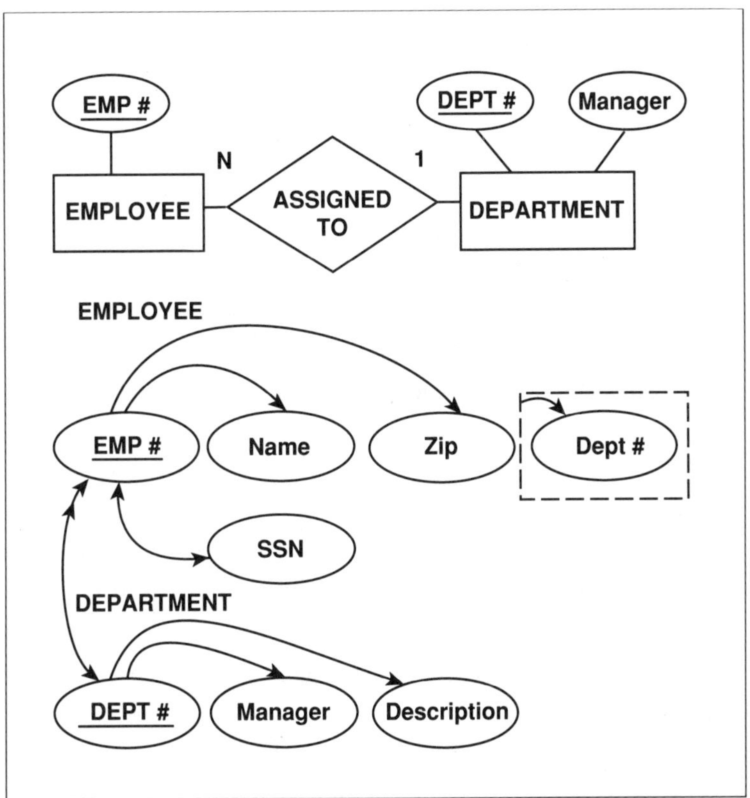

Figure 11-1. EMPLOYEE assigned to DEPARTMENT.

Instead of placing the "one" key into the "many" record, can we insert the key from the "many" side in the record on the "one" side? This is a trick question. We can't insert the "many" into the "one" because that would require a repeating set of fields to hold the unknown number of, but multiple values of, *EMP#* and would be a violation of first normal form.

Continuing with the employee and department example, can we navigate from the *DEPARTMENT.manager* field to the EMPLOYEE table? Suppose we want to get a list of all the employees working in the department managed by, say, Kristen McKay. Is it possible now? It would require that an entry point at the *DEPARTMENT.manager* data element be established so the *DEPARTMENT.dept#* for a certain manager could be located.

To do this, add a one-arrow in the DEPARTMENT data group from the *Manager* data element back to the *DEPT#* data element (this will be a secondary index later on). Now the employees working for Kristen McKay can be determined by finding that manager in the *DEPARTMENT.manager* field using the associated *DEPARTMENT.dept#* for that tuple (say it was 99), and then searching the employee table for the required value (99) in the *EMPLOYEE.department* field.

Notice also in Figure 11-1 that the city and state fields have been removed from the EMPLOYEE data group and placed in the ZIP data group (not shown). Since each zip code uniquely identifies a city and a state, this information need not be repeated in the EMPLOYEE data group. However, it does require an extra database access for each record accessed in the EMPLOYEE table to supply the city and state (from the ZIP table). If this turns out to slow the process noticeably, the city and state fields would be prime candidates for denormalization. The city and state fields would then be moved back into the EMPLOYEE table. The resulting table won't be fully normalized, but a trade-off has been made for better retrieval speed. This type of denormalization is fine for data relationships that don't often change. In this case, the city and state for a zip code would almost never be changed and would be an excellent choice for denormalization.

For a one-to-one relationship, one of the keys will be inserted into the other record or both keys may be exchanged. For example, Figure 11-2 shows a one-to-one relationship between EMPLOYEE and TRUCK. By inserting the foreign key *Truck#* into EMPLOYEE and the foreign key *Emp#* into TRUCK, we make the information available in each table.

Figure 11-3 shows another one-to-one example. A student will have one and only one thesis title, and each title must be unique. Would you place the student ID (*SSN*) in the THESIS table or the thesis title (*TITLE*) in the STUDENT table? How do you later need to navigate this relationship between STUDENT and THESIS? If you're looking at a THESIS record, can you determine which student is working on that particular thesis?

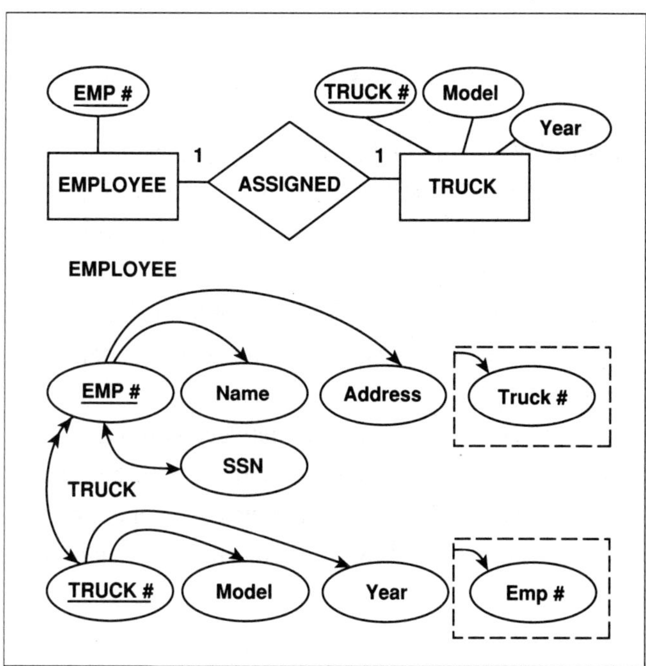

Figure 11-2. EMPLOYEE assigned TRUCK.

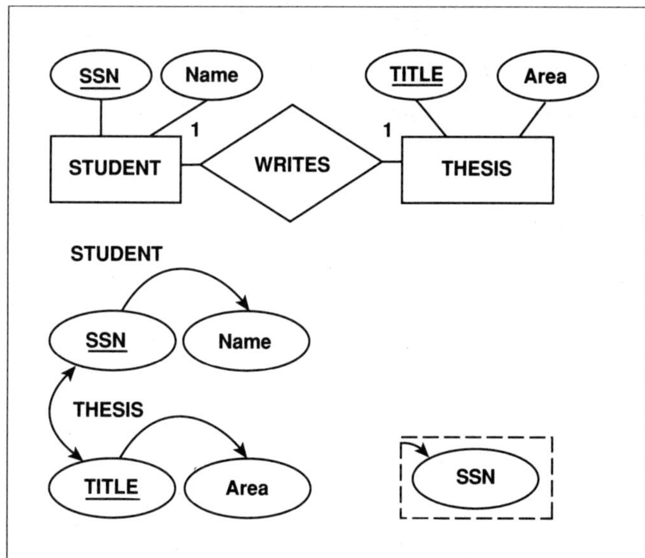

Figure 11-3. STUDENT writes THESIS.

If you use only one foreign key by inserting *TITLE* into STUDENT, you have introduced a field that may not apply to every student (some students don't have to write a thesis).

If you insert the STUDENT *SSN* into the THESIS record, can it be navigated in both directions? If you're looking at the STUDENT record, you can find the THESIS record (if there is one) using the *SSN* link. It also works in the other direction if you wish to find the name of the student writing a particular thesis.

Something else to consider is denormalizing the THESIS table and including all the information in the STUDENT table. Is this desirable? If not all the students have to write a thesis, the space is wasted.

For a table expressing a many-to-many relationship between two other tables, the key of both tables must be inserted into the intersection table. This is because the intersection record only exists in direct relation to both values and depends on the existence of two outer records. Figure 11-4 shows a many-to-many relationship between EMPLOYEE and PROJECT.

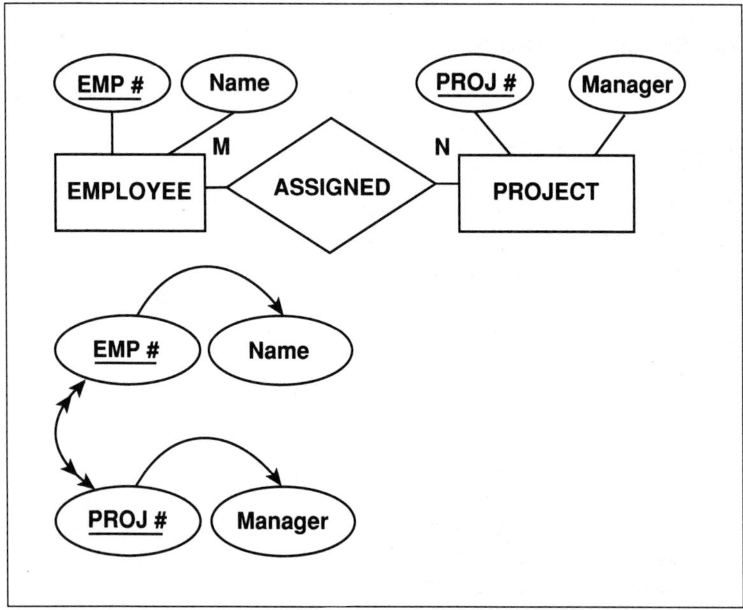

Figure 11-4. EMPLOYEE assigned PROJECT.

The new intersection entity *PROJECT-ASSIGNMENT* will capture the many-to-many relationship by including both *EMP#* and *PROJECT#* in one record. What navigation is possible in Figure 11-5? Can you determine all the *PROJECT-ASSIGNMENT*s for each employee and each project?

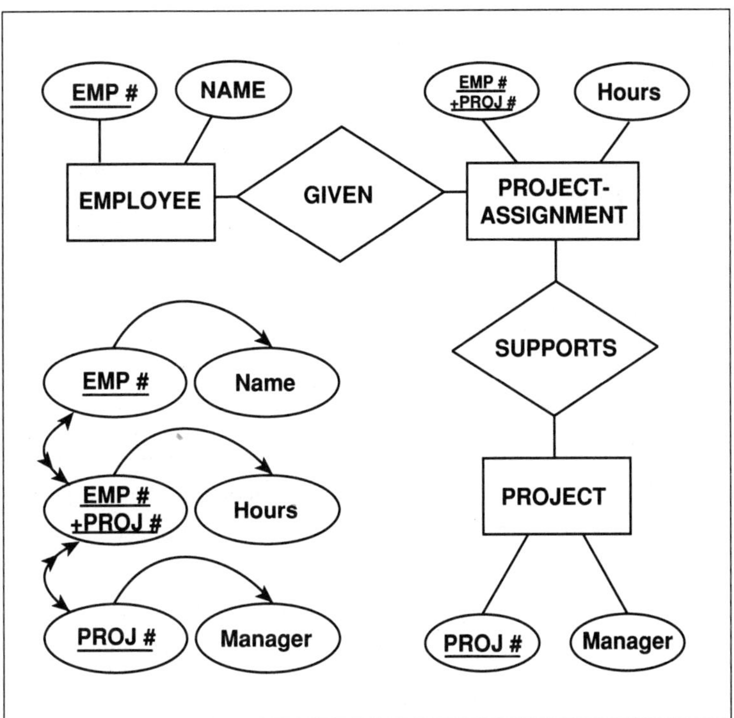

Figure 11-5. EMPLOYEE, PROJECT-ASSIGNMENT, and PROJECT.

An intersection table is needed to capture relationships with a degree greater than two. The primary key of each participating entity must be included as a foreign key in the new table. For example, the relationship in Figure 11-6 could be implemented as the following table schema:

```
PROJPART(SUPP#, PART#, PROJ#)
```

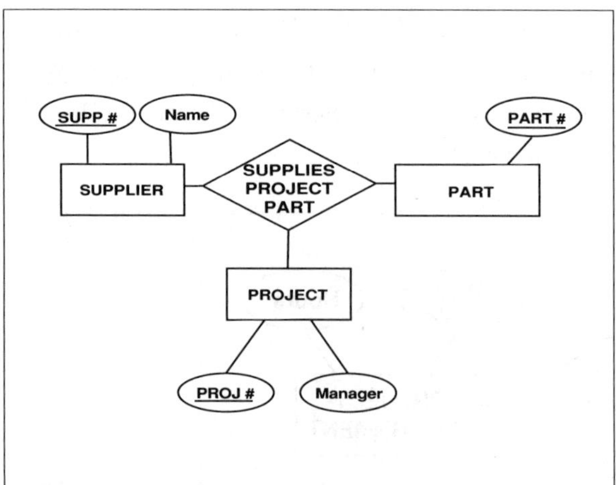

Figure 11-6. Ternary relationship

Here *SUPP#*, *PART#*, and *PROJ#* identify a unique occurrence of a specific part being supplied by a certain supplier for a particular project. The PROJPART table can be queried for all the parts for a particular PROJECT or from a particular SUPPLIER or for a certain PART. Any combination of the three can also be searched (to find the parts supplied by one supplier for one project, for example).

Identifying Indexes

Once the table schemas have been finalized, the next step is to implement the key-access methods. Primary and secondary keys are implemented as index tags in a FoxPro .CDX file.

Let's look at an example based on Figure 11-7 and 11-8, where the relational schema is implemented by creating the data-definition language statements for the system:

```
CUSTOMER(CUST#, COMPANY, STREET, ZIP, PHONE)

INVOICE(INVOICE#, CUST#, EMP#, TOTAL)
LINEITEM(INVOICE#, PART#, QUANTITY)
SALESREP(EMP#, SALE)
```

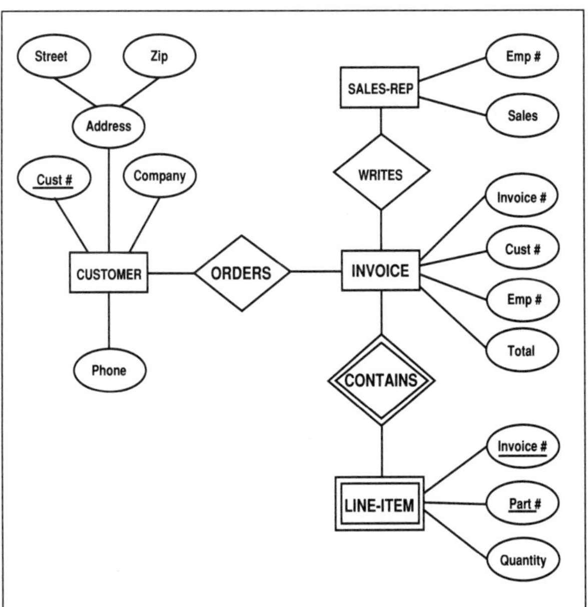

Figure 11-7. Expanded entity-relationship diagram.

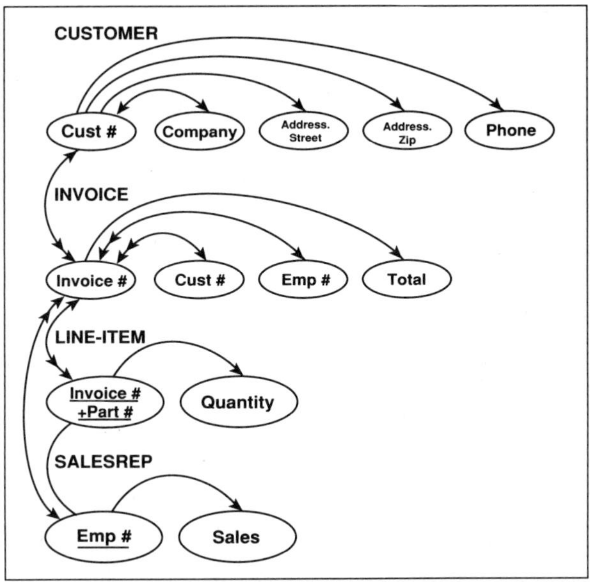

Figure 11-8. Logical model bubble chart.

Data Definition Statements

The statements in Listing 11-1 will create each table and implement the necessary indexes for both primary and secondary keys.

Listing 11-1. Data Definition Statements

```
CREATE TABLE customer (cust_no N(6, 0), ;
    company C(20), ;
    street C(20), ;
    zip C(10), ;
    phone C( 12))

INDEX ON cust_no TAG cust_no
INDEX ON company TAG company

CREATE TABLE invoice (inv_no N(6, 0), ;
    cust_no N(6, 0), ;
    emp_no N(6, 0), ;
    total F(10, 2))

INDEX ON inv_no TAG inv_no
INDEX ON cust_no TAG cust_no
INDEX ON emp_no TAG emp_no

CREATE TABLE lineitem (inv_no N(6, 0), ;
    part_no N(6, 0), ;
    quantity N(6, 0), ;
    price F(10,2))

INDEX ON PADL(inv_no,6,'0')+PADL(part_no,6,'0') TAG lineitem

CREATE TABLE salesrep (emp_no N(6, 0), sales N(10, 2))
INDEX ON emp_no TAG emp_no

CREATE TABLE zip (zip C(10), city C(20), state C(2))
INDEX ON zip TAG zip
```

Notice that the secondary indexes are created to allow rapid access to queries involving these fields. In the CUSTOMER table, the *Company* field is an entry point for locating the *Cust#* field and is indexed; otherwise, the entire file would need to be scanned for any query involving the *company* field. Also note that in general, many of the fields in this database that are numeric but not used for calculation (such as *inv_no* in the INVOICE table) would be better defined as character fields so they could be manipulated as such. We'll leave them numeric in this example for clarity.

The Physical Level

Physical database design transforms the logical data model into a physical representation of the data. The physical level defines table names, field labels, data types, file and record formats, and indexes. It also defines the views the user has of the data.

Physical design is concerned with refining the relations that will store the data groups and implementing the constraints identified at the logical data level. In addition, through usage analysis, it takes into consideration the access paths necessary to tune system performance.

At this point, the designer is concerned with the real-life issues of data systems, including maintenance, security, control, effectiveness for the users, and physical growth of the system. Performance is also considered when determining which indexes to create for critical operations, but much of the performance gains will take place later, when the system is tuned.

The physical design depends on usage analysis and on the data model of the DBMS being used. Usage analysis is most concerned with system performance and involves careful examination of how the data elements are used. It determines which indexes are created, which files should be sorted, and so on. The term *performance* is used here to represent both speed and the degree of accuracy in supporting the users' requirements.

The dBASE and FoxPro RDBMS's are much simpler than client-server systems and minicomputer or mainframe RDBMS's, where you have many options for storing the data. Larger systems may allow such techniques as clustering, hashing, and determining physical parameters where advantageous. Physical design for FoxPro is limited to determining table formats, choosing indexes, sorting files, documenting system constraints, and tuning the system's performance. Much of this tuning can be done by improving the code and by using the newer relational commands. Optimization is covered in Chapter 5, "Optimizing FoxPro 2.0."

At this point in the process, the preliminary physical model has been completed. The tables have been created, and index tags have been created for primary and secondary key fields. Test data can be entered and the program code tested against it.

Critical operations must be identified early on and resolved as soon as possible. A critical operation is one that will have an immediate, visible impact on the enterprise if not executed correctly and within a required time frame. For example, suppose our business sells items directly to the consumer on television (a shopping channel). What critical operations can you think of?

Data entry for the sales contact is one. When someone calls to place an order, the salesperson must be able to enter the information quickly or the order may be lost. Suppose that at peak moments multiuser access to the system is slower than acceptable. Perhaps the system has been tuned as well as possible and at times order volume still exceeds the capacity of the system. What can you do?

Some things to consider are:

- An upgrade to faster, more powerful hardware
- A change to a faster DBMS
- A software upgrade of the current system
- Review of the application and its methods.

The correct choice (or choices) depends on the hardware/software system in place. Changing to a different DBMS would be reasonable if all the application code didn't have to be ported. If everything that can be done has been done, it's time to consider the application design and the methodology it uses to create orders in the system. Perhaps the programmer can provide an alternative method, such as entering the data locally and dumping it into the system later, with a confirmation going to the customer at that time.

Even when you have identified critical operations, how do you know what the performance will be in the first implementation? You need experience to make a reasonable estimate, but even a well-educated estimate may not be enough. In the case of an operation critical to the business, a prototype must be set up and a test run on any issues that could seriously affect the enterprise.

Tuning the Physical Database

After the physical design is done and the preliminary version of the physical database is up and running, the design process continues with system tuning. This is another place usage analysis is useful: You can use it to spot bottlenecks in the system and add enhancements as users discover requirements not specified in the original system design.

The system undergoes continual change. As records are added and deleted, as tables are modified, as relationships change or are created, performance will change and adjustments will be necessary. Often new entry points are found in the system because a field has gained importance over time and is sometimes used to access data in the system. This field must be identified and, if usage analysis shows it's used often enough, indexed and added to the .CDX file.

Even the system software will undergo changes, including bug fixes and upgrades that may require a major revision for the database design. If the design was a good one, these changes will be limited to the physical level.

Consider for a moment the effect of FoxPro 2.0. The performance gain over FoxPro 1.0 is so great that it can have a dramatic effect on the way the system is used. Some queries are now orders of magnitude faster than before, encouraging the developer (and user) to incorporate more powerful transactions into the system. Queries that before were done as a report because of the execution time required may now be interactively executed in a reasonable time.

Another consideration is the entirely new index format introduced in FoxPro 2.0. The .CDX format has so many advantages over the .IDX format that it's desirable to convert to it, though doing so would require code changes and rebuilding existing indexes.

Once the system reaches an acceptable state, attention generally shifts to enhancement requests, bug fixes, and revisions. As the system grows and is modified, it's important to monitor its use and performance. At some point, you almost always need a visit to the E-R model to rethink those details as more major changes are added to the system. The same modeling techniques are again applied to ensure logical growth of the entire system.

PART V

Developing Multiuser Applications

At the Crossroads: From File Server to Client-Server

In the PC database marketplace, there exists a great confusion about the relative value of these two "competing" database architectures. Much of this confusion is due to ignorance about the salient features of actual implementations. In fact, we've heard the same complaint, that the "other" architecture suffers from poor performance, registered by loyalists of both camps. How can this be?

Anyone who reads the literature on client-server is impressed by the discussion of how a reduction of wire traffic increases performance for client-server DBMS's. At the same time, some client-server implementations, such as Oracle, are commonly ridiculed by file-server loyalists for their slowness. It is rare though, that those who are making the comments have considered the problem domains that each product answers best.

For example, FoxPro 2 is arguably the fastest database on any PC or mini platform when it comes to ad hoc single-user decision support systems. Yet, not many people actually use it for what it was designed. Typically, it is used for 5- to 30-user accounting or inventory applications where updating and data entry are the predominant activities.

SQL Server on OS/2 boasts the most PC front-end tools of any client-server DBMS. These tools are commonly used for user-friendly decision support. However, SQL Server's database engine performance is optimized for transaction processing. Like FoxPro, SQL Server is criticized for performance problems because it is used in problem domains outside those it was designed to solve.

Then there are performance issues that are ignored entirely by whoever is trying to defend his or her favorite system. FoxPro 2 offers no security features, so on a benchmark to test how well it reacts to security breaches, it will receive a score of zero. No matter how impressive Interbase is, it doesn't run on DOS; so shops that rely on DOS will give its performance a zero. If a FoxPro 2 application has to be written so as to pass the *ACID* test described in Chapter 14, the cost of adding custom code for features that are non-existent in the FoxPro database engine could make its price/performance ratio quite steep. The price/performance ratio also probably wouldn't look too good for an Oracle application you need to write in two days to do a simple three-user sales-lead tracking system with minimal support for data integrity.

The point is that each product is best at one particular domain. Some products are very good at handling two or three areas, but no product can do everything. This doesn't mean that you must spend your life learning different products so you always use the right tool for the right job. Compromises are always necessary.

This book looks at several multiuser databases and multiuser database issues. Naturally, the most in-depth discussion is about multiuser programming in FoxPro 2. Ham Ahlo discusses the problems and their solutions (including some compromises) in great detail in Chapter 12. Ham has spent many years wrestling with these issues in multiuser database applications in Fox and other database systems.

For a given set of circumstances, you may find the compromises unpalatable. I entreat you to read the chapters on client-server architecture and several implementations of it. The varied backgrounds of the authors gives a balanced perspective.

David McClanahan started using file-server databases on the mainframe before creating a client-server DBMS on a mini. Then he switched to FoxPro 2's file-server database. Currently, he is working on a distributed client-server engine. Jeff Jochum has worked intimately with PC database engines from several vendors to put them on speaking terms with each other. Peter Colclough connects PC databases to their counterparts on mainframes and minis. Initially disenchanted with my exposure to "big iron" databases in favor of the ease and speed of PC databases, I'm now drawn to them for exactly the same reasons, though for different problem sets.

Even if you feel satisfied and secure with the applications you're developing now, it will enlarge your effectiveness to understand the potential that lies on the other side of the fence.

—Editor

CHAPTER 12

FoxPro and Local Area Networks

by Hamilton M. Ahlo, Jr.

For the past five years, various industry publications have set aside space in their January issues to explain why that was to be "The Year of the Network." The irony that some journals did this for several years running seems to have escaped their editors. No single event could be heralded as the bellwether of network legitimacy; networks have been embraced gradually and cautiously over the past six or seven years.

Driving the growth of networks has been the need to share organizational data among multiple simultaneous users and the decreasing cost of doing so. The nature of this sharing was initially quite simple, limited as it was by both programming tools and network operating system hardware and software. As the capacity and speed of network hardware increased and network operating system software became more sophisticated and robust, organizations have come to demand more from their network data. In fact, they demand many of the features that were once available only on mainframe and minicomputer systems.

DBMS's designed for PC networks have attempted to meet these needs, with varying levels of success. In this chapter, we'll discuss the capabilities (and limitations) of FoxPro 2.0 and explore several issues facing FoxPro programmers attempting to implement multiuser systems.

FoxPro and Networks

The multiuser version of FoxPro 2.0 is designed for the file-server environment and inherits the advantages and disadvantages thereof. In the classic file-server/workstation model, a file server appears to the workstation as one or more remote disk drives, and the workstation uses the files on the server in much the same way as it uses files on its own local disk drive. Because the file server is communicating over a medium with a transmission bandwidth that is generally much slower than the data bus in the workstation itself, many workstations will experience a reduction in speed. Obviously, when more users are added to that file server and are using the same files, speed is degraded even further; the server has to struggle to keep up with demands for data, and the amount of traffic over the transmission medium increases. (Some workstations with very slow local drives experience an increase in speed; however, this is not typical.)

FoxPro doesn't take advantage of the vendor-specific features offered by major network operating systems. The multiuser features it does provide are primarily locking functions that were incorporated into MS/PC-DOS with version 3.0. The sole exception is its support of print queues in the Novell environment.

Because the single-user version of FoxPro 2.0 offers such outstanding speed on large databases, it was inevitable that many organizations would consider FoxPro for multiuser databases. FoxPro's Rushmore technology, which we'll get to momentarily, and the optimized SQL *SELECT* statement can speed many applications that query shared data files. While not as quick on a network as on a single-user machine, FoxPro 2.0 still outperforms much of the competition in the same environment (at least where queries are concerned). Still, FoxPro suffers from the bane of all database systems based on the file-server model: bandwidth.

When a workstation running FoxPro issues a query, it sends a request to read data from the file server. The file server then sends the requested data to the workstation, where it's processed. This means that if we wanted to locate a single record in an unordered, unindexed, million-record database, the server would have to send every record to the requesting workstation until either the search criteria were met or the data were exhausted. Imagine adding another 49 users issuing similar requests, and you get a feel for the volume of data that must be transferred over the network.

Eventually, even with multiple network interface cards in the server, multiple cable segments, and very fast servers and hard disks, network throughput will suffer. It will suffer not because the users issuing the query wanted to see a lot of data, but because their workstations had to process a lot of data to get the little bit they required. This throughput problem becomes significant on large networks, especially where ad hoc queries are being performed. To some degree, queries that are issued routinely can be optimized to minimize traffic over the network; however, the potential for that usually decreases as the number of simultaneous users increases.

To some degree, FoxPro 2.0's Rushmore technology reduces the volume of data flowing to the individual workstations. It allows FoxPro to scan indexes intelligently (typically resulting in significantly less data being passed over the wire than would have been possible with FoxPro 1.0x). Based on the results of this perusal, Rushmore permits FoxPro to forward to the workstation a much smaller data set than other DBMS's which are implemented on the file server model. As a result, in a system where data structures and indexes are designed to use Rushmore-optimizable expressions as much as possible, data traffic on the network can be reduced somewhat.

A more generic approach to the problem of wire traffic is rapidly gaining favor among vendors and users alike: the use of a client-server environment where the server functions not simply as a file server but as a database server. Simply stated, a database server is a computer running a program designed to fulfill users' requests for data. This computer would typically, though not necessarily, store the data on its local drive. This software serves as an intelligent back end for the program running on the users' workstations (the front end) and only supplies the data a user wants rather than all the data it needs to extract it. The determination of what data fulfills a user's request is made at the database server rather than at the workstation. The result is a significant reduction in network traffic and, ideally, an increase in the speed at which certain functions are performed.

Database servers can be simple or complex, but they share a common trait in that they generate much less wire traffic than does a typical file-server environment. This is especially important for large distributed networks, which commonly have one or more lower-speed links. Fox has promised a database-server product for the Novell environment sometime in the near future, but the current multiuser version of FoxPro 2.0 remains a file-server-based product.

Issues in Multiuser Programming

FoxPro is more a programming language than a DBMS in the spirit of most minicomputer and mainframe products. Many features of such DBMS's are absent or only partially implemented in FoxPro.

For example, FoxPro has literally no internal ability to enforce database integrity; the engine can implement neither the basic tenets of relational database design (such as entity and referential integrity) nor user-defined integrity rules ("no employee may work more than 40 hours a week"), placing a burden on the programmer to manage these issues internally. The absence of these features in a multiuser system makes the programmer's task even more difficult.

FoxPro differs from dBASE IV and Clipper 5.0 in certain aspects of its multiuser features, but fundamentally these products are all quite similar. FoxPro 2.0 implements nothing significantly new in terms of multiuser tools compared to FoxBASE+ or FoxPro 1.0x.

Some of the more common problems facing the FoxPro programmer—in particular, security, contention, and concurrency—are discussed in this chapter. The treatment is not exhaustive; rather, it is intended to alert the programmer to certain basic issues and potential ways to resolve them.

Security

Many organizations require that certain individuals or groups be accorded different levels of access to shared databases. This usually means that a set of rights is assigned to each individual or group regarding the data set and the manipulations that can be performed on it.

FoxPro presents special problems to those concerned with the security of shared databases on networks. Chief among these is that access to FoxPro databases isn't managed by a central database engine with definable data-authorization rules. Indeed, unlike Clipper, FoxPro provides a friendly, interactive environment that facilitates data manipulation.

FoxPro doesn't provide intrinsic functions for restricting access to data. Interactive FoxPro users typically have all rights to the data that the network operating system grants them (on a file-by-file, directory, or volume basis). That's because LANs on which FoxPro will run provide DOS file services; therefore, the standard suite of DOS commands is usually available on the file server.

This presents an immediate problem to the database administrator concerned with security: Users who have a right to access the data files in FoxPro also have a right to access those files at the DOS command line (provided they have access to the DOS command line). Depending on the network, you may not be able to restrict the user enough to prevent destructive access via the command line. On most networks, a user who can read or write to a file under program control is almost certain to have similar rights at the DOS prompt.

Can mission-critical FoxPro databases residing on a LAN ever be considered safe and secure? Probably not, though several potential solutions exist. The efficacy of these work-arounds will depend on the skill and determination of your users.

Restricting Access to Files

If your network permits, you can restrict user access rights within a subdirectory to read-only. Users can then open files to look at them, issue queries, and print reports, but they won't be allowed to update or delete data. FoxPro will issue the error message "Cannot write to a read-only file" if the user attempts to write to that file. In the browse or edit mode, no editing of information or appending blanks will be permitted.

Read-only access can be accomplished either by flagging the file as read-only or by restricting access rights on an individual user basis. FoxPro will recognize that the databases are read-only either way.

Another option for restricting access is to open all files via program control based on user-authorization rules defined by the system administrator. You could then install the report writer and FoxPro's RQBE facility in your menu system while at the same time disabling all functions that would allow the user to close a file, open a file, or modify a file in any way. In FoxPro 2.0, you can modify the system menus and easily restrict user access to any menu prompt. However, this may not be effective given the prevalence of file viewers (which allow you to browse the files in question), the availability of utilities that can modify the database itself, and FoxPro's interactive version.

Encryption

An obvious and widely applied solution to the problem of revealing sensitive data to users is encryption. FoxPro provides no native encryption functions, either via the engine (a la Paradox) or to the programmer. In fact, prior to version 2.0, it was virtually impossible to implement a robust encryption method in FoxPro because you couldn't create indexes based on user-defined functions.

Consider Table 12-1, a database of a single field and five records in plain-text and encrypted forms.

Table 12-1. Sample encryption algorithm.

PLAIN TEXT (ORDERED)	ENCRYPTED	ENCRYPTED (ORDERED)
ALDEBARAN	XLWOQOHXK	FSL
ALPHA CENTAURI	XLJRX POKGXZHU	JSLXHUF
BETELGEUSE	QOGOLIOZFO	QOGOLIOZFO
POLARIS	JSLXHUF	XLJRX POKGXUHU
SOL	FSL	XLWOQOHSK

Substitution KEY:

key= "XQPWOEIRUTYLAKSJDHFGZMCNVB"

alphabet="ABCDEFGHIJKLMNOPQRSTUVWXYZ"

Algorithm: black_text= chrtran(plain_text,alphabet,key)

In this very transparent character-substitution encryption algorithm (ignoring case), the letter *X* is substituted for every occurrence of the letter *A*. The result is data in the .DBF whose order bears no resemblance to the ASCII sort order of the plain-text examples. Encryption that retains the sort order of the original data is subject to very simple attacks and, except for deterring the casual browser, has no utility in applications that require real security. To order these encrypted strings for reports, queries, browses, and pop-ups, you must maintain an index of their unencrypted form. (FoxPro, by the way, doesn't let you sort on a user-defined function.)

Typical commands you might have to use when working on a database encrypted in this fashion include:

```
REPLACE charfield with chrtran(somestring,alphabet,key)

LIST all chrtran(charfield,key,alphabet)

INDEX ON chrtran(charfield,key,alphabet) ...

SELECT chrtran(charfield,key,alphabet), ;
    chrtran(anotherfield,key,alphabet) ;
    FROM somefile ;
    WHERE chrtran(charfield,key,alphabet)= "some string" ;
    GROUP BY 2 ;
    INTO CURSOR slowly
```

You can imagine the tedium of converting all your programs to encrypt and decrypt sensitive data fields using similar constructs.

In FoxPro 2.0, data encryption is feasible but remains impractical for any nontrivial encryption algorithm because of the extreme performance penalties of such indexes.

For example, a simple (unencrypted) index on 10,000 records on a 20-character field using the above algorithm took less than one third the time to create than did an encrypted index. (This test was run on an exclusively used .DBF on a NetWare 3.1 server executed from a 486/25 workstation with 16 megabytes of memory and running FoxProLX). Appending records while maintaining encrypted indexes causes similar performance problems. Bear in mind that this function is internal to FoxPro; a serious encryption algorithm that invokes a user-defined function will incur much more severe performance penalties.

In addition to the performance questions, the absence of encryption in the database engine itself requires that users know about the encryption functions if they are to use the RQBE feature. This is unlikely to excite most users and is likely to dismay most database managers. Yet the RQBE and its speed in executing free-form queries is one of the strengths of FoxPro 2.0 in both single-user and multiuser modes. However, the inability to provide data security severely hinders FoxPro's use in certain applications.

In summary, FoxPro has little to offer in the way of ensuring security. Virtually all security must come from your network operating system unless you can exclusively restrict users to program control. There is also no satisfactory way to provide encryption within FoxPro (though hardware options are reportedly available) and still give users easy access to the Report Writer and RQBE facility. While encryption of selected sensitive fields (such as user passwords and access levels) is feasible, such use should typically be kept to a minimum to ensure satisfactory performance.

Managing Contention

Contention occurs in multiuser situations because multiple workstations request the same resource at the same time. In FoxPro, contention can occur while opening files and locking records or files. The degree to which it becomes a problem in your application will depend on how the data and the application are structured with regard to the patterns of use experienced by the resources in question. If the data are contained in a very few large files, contention will be more of a problem than if they are distributed in a thoroughly normalized fashion. This is because requests for reads and writes against a normalized database will involve resources (i.e., files and records) which are more atomistic and more readily managed.

Opening Files

FoxPro provides no function for opening a file. Files are opened by commands, and a failed attempt must be handled by your own error routine or via FoxPro's error dialog. FoxPro's *REPROCESS* setting has no effect on file opens.

If a command to open a file occurred within a program and no error-handling routine is active, Fox will treat a file-open error as a bug, issue a "File in use by another; Cancel, Ignore, Suspend" message, and halt processing. If you have opened the file interactively from the command window without an active error handler, FoxPro will issue an alert saying "File is in use by another." The alert requires the user to press a key to proceed.

The typical way to handle file-open failures within a program requires an active error handler. A common way to detect open failures entails routing the error to your error handler and setting a flag that can be tested upon return to the calling routine. Alternatively, your error handler can pass control back to the calling routine, which then tests to see whether or not the file was opened successfully. A simple example of an *ON ERROR* trap to handle file-open errors is shown in Listing 12-1.

Listing 12-1. A file-open routine using a flag set in an error handler.

```
on error do bug_trap with error()
public OpenErr
use anyfile
if not OpenErr
*  work with the file
else
*  inform the user the file is not available
endif

procedure bug_trap
parameters TheBugNo
if TheBugNo = 108
   OpenErr= .f.
   return
else
*  handle other bugs
endif
```

Listing 12-2 illustrates one way code might be written if you didn't set a flag in the error handler. Note that while an error handler is activated, it really does nothing. The asterisk tricks the error handler into doing nothing because it indicates to FoxPro a comment line that won't be executed.

Listing 12-2. A code example that includes no error trapping.

```
on error *
use customer in select(1)
AllOpen= .f.
if used("customer")
   use inventry in select(1)
   if not used("inventry")
      use in customrs
   else
      AllOpen= .t.
   endif
endif
if AllOpen
*  do something with the files
else
*  inform the user
 endif
```

In some instances, it may be desirable to keep trying to open files for a given period of time or a certain number of attempts. Listing 12-3 shows an example that relies on the error trap shown above.

Listing 12-3. Trying to open a set of files for a given period of time.

```
on error *
FilesOpened= 0
FilesToOpen= 2
on error do bug_trap with error()
TimeOut= seconds() + 5  && when to stop trying
do while seconds() < TimeOut and FilesToOpen > FilesOpened
   if .not. used("file_1")
      use File_1 in select(1)
      FilesToOpen= FilesToOpen - iif(not OpenErr,1,0)
      OpenErr = .F.
   endif
   if not used("file_2")
      use File_2 in select(1)
      FilesToOpen= FilesToOpen - iif(not OpenErr,1,0)
      OpenErr = .F.
```

```
   endif
enddo
if FilesOpened= 2
*  do something useful
else
*  inform the user
endif
```

These examples always fail at some point; they don't keep attempting to open a file indefinitely. This avoids deadlocks, those situations where one workstation is waiting indefinitely for a file the other has open. The following is an example of a deadlock:

```
Workstation 1                       Workstation 2
on error *                          on error *
use file1 in select(1)              use file2 in select(1)
do while not used('file2')          do while not used('file1')
  use file2 in select(1)              use file1 in select(1)
enddo                               enddo
```

It's actually very easy to prevent deadlocks of this nature simply by ensuring that a *USE* attempt can fail. The command might be issued a number of times or for a specified period of time. After that, the user is notified and the routine is aborted.

It's probably easiest to use a function to open files. The following example describes such a function using an array passed (by value) to the open-file function. The passed array would contain several columns and as many rows as there were files to open. The contents of the array columns are:

- The name of the file to open (we're ignoring the capability to *USE...AGAIN* in FoxPro 2.0 here, but it could be accommodated with some additional effort).
- The order to set after opening or selecting the file.
- The alias to use in referencing the file; if this column is blank, the file name is assumed to be the alias.
- The mode in which the file is to be opened: 0 = shared, 1 = exclusive.

- How long (in seconds) to keep trying to open this file. My *openfiles* function actually accepts a second parameter that specifies the length of time (in seconds) to keep trying to open this *SET* of files. It's optional but, if passed, takes precedence over this array element.
- A flag, initialized to *.f.* but set by the function to indicate whether or not the file was previously open.
- If the file was in use, the order that was set.
- If the file was in use, the current record.

The open function returns true if all files were successfully opened and no errors occurred. The error handler may set flags for both network errors and other non-contention related errors resulting from attempts to open a file (for example, error 15, "Not a Database File"). The function is typically used as follows:

```
declare File_Ra_[FilesToOpen,8]

*  instantiate the array elements for as many files as
*  needed; this may also be done automatically via a
*  table kept for this purpose

File_Ra_[1,1]= "Filename"
File_Ra_[1,2]= "Tag_Name"
File_Ra_[1,3]= "AliasName"
File_Ra_[1,4]= 0
File_Ra_[1,5]= 3
File_Ra_[1,6]= .F.
File_Ra_[1,7]= ""
File_Ra_[1,8]= 0
if not openfiles(@File_Ra_)
*  tell the user and take appropriate action
endif
*  YOUR CODE GOES HERE
=shutfiles(File_Ra_)
```

The *shutfiles* function closes only those files that were opened in this module; it sets the order of the others that were previously opened and resets the record pointer in each. Because FoxPro 2.0 permits a form of modeless programming, recording the state of the system for later restoration becomes necessary in each module that changes these states. Using a function that handles all of this for you simplifies programming significantly.

Contending for Records

Once your files are opened and available, you'll no doubt want to use them. This brings up the second thing multiple users contend for—locks on both individual records and files. This typically occurs when two users simultaneously attempt to lock a file or a record in a shared file.

Record and file locks can be managed in two ways: explicitly and implicitly. Each has advantages and disadvantages, as you'll see.

Explicit locking of files and records is quite simple. You won't normally need an *ON ERROR* routine to manage file or record locks; both are called as simple functions. *RLOCK()* and its synonym, *LOCK()*, lock individual records, while *FLOCK()* locks the file. *FLOCK()* takes an optional parameter, the alias or work area of the file to lock (for example, *FLOCK('SOMEFILE')*). It provides read/write access to the lock holder and read/deny-write access to other users. *RLOCK()* takes an optional alias or work-area number and a comma-delimited list of record numbers to lock if the current setting for *MULTILOCKS* is on. It provides read/write access to the lock holder and read/deny-write access to others. These locking functions implement in FoxPro what DOS provides in version 3.0 and later.

If you don't use the locking functions and rely on FoxPro to do it for you, you're using implicit locking. Implicit locking is frequently implemented by soliciting data via direct reads to database fields rather than to memory variables that are later placed in the database. Any of the commands that permit a field to be changed, such as *REPLACE* and *BROWSE*, will attempt to secure a lock on either a record or the file depending on the command's scope of effect. If FoxPro can't lock the item in question, it may issue a message and retry the lock attempt depending on the setting of *SET REPROCESS*, *SET NOTIFY*, and *ON ERROR*. Implicit locks usually rely on FoxPro's *REPROCESS* setting to trigger a message indicating that FoxPro is attempting to secure a lock.

Both explicit and implicit locking strategies can use *REPROCESS* to control the number of locking attempts or their duration. *REPROCESS* can be set to indicate the maximum number of attempts to execute before the user is notified or the error is routed to an error handler (*SET REPROCESS TO 10*). It can also be set to retry the attempt for a specific number of seconds (*SET REPROCESS TO 10 SECONDS*). FoxPro will attempt to secure a lock approximately 20 times per second.

If you attempt to determine the current *REPROCESS* setting in FoxPro via the *SET("REPROCESS")* function, be aware that the return value, while correct, doesn't indicate whether or not it is expressed in retries or in seconds.

As with file-open strategies, manual coding is needed to prevent deadlocks in FoxPro. This is generally a minor problem and is easily addressed using the *SET REPROCESS* facility. Other strategies for preventing deadlocks are discussed in *Developing FoxPro Applications,* by P.L Olympia and K. Cea (Addison-Wesley, Reading, Mass.)

FoxPro has several peculiarities with regard to locking and unlocking records. The first is in the command *APPEND BLANK*. When a record is appended, FoxPro locks the database header where the counter containing the number of records is updated. The record that's actually appended isn't locked after the append, but the record pointer is positioned on the new, empty record. This can lead to a problem if several users are adding data at once and the system is designed to reuse empty records. The following example compares *SEEK*ing a blank record to *APPEND*ing a blank record.

```
User 1                 User 2
-----------------      ---------------
APPEND BLANK           IF SEEK(" ") && an empty key field
* some code here          IF RLOCK()
                             GATHER MEMVAR
                             UNLOCK
IF RLOCK()                ELSE
   GATHER MEMVAR          * tell the user
   UNLOCK                 ENDIF
ELSE                   ELSE
* tell the user           APPEND BLANK
ENDIF                     * etc.
                       ENDIF
```

The problem is that User 2 could find and lock the blank record that User 1 appended before User 1 obtained a lock on it. User 1 could then obtain the lock and update the record without knowing that User 2 used that record. User 2 in turn proceeds, not knowing that his or her work is now missing. You can minimize this contention substantially, but not prevent it, by placing the *RLOCK()* function immediately after the *APPEND BLANK* command. You can prevent contention by placing a lock on the blank record and testing to make sure it's still empty before using it. If it's not empty, your routine could either keep trying to get a blank record or, after some period, inform the user that the record can't be saved. Appending blanks also requires that aborted transactions clean up after themselves by deleting the unused blank records, yet another source of programming overhead.

A more general solution requires that all records to be added be stored in an array whose structure parallels that of the file into which they are added. It can handle those cases where multiple records have to be added to a file during a transaction (for example, a customer order containing 20 individual items).

The following code has the disadvantage of locking the entire file for brief periods of time:

```
select anyfile
if flock()           && keep trying for however long you want
   append from array some_ra
*  alternately, insert into anyfile from array some_ra
   unlock
endif
```

Nevertheless, locking the file and appending from an array may provide a higher aggregate throughput for all users given the overhead of finding and locking 20 blank records. It also increases the probability that the records will be added correctly. Whether or not this is appropriate depends on your application and how likely it is that contention for records will be heavy enough to make appending blanks a problem. The *APPEND FROM ARRAY* technique becomes more attractive as the number of additions to a table per transaction increases.

Another approach for adding multiple records is to let FoxPro handle locking automatically via the *SET REPROCESS TO 0* command. FoxPro can add records to a file very rapidly (the actual speed depends on your network, your workstation hardware, and the complexity of any indexes that must be maintained during an *APPEND*). In particular, the *APPEND FROM ARRAY* and *INSERT FROM ARRAY* commands are very fast, and you may find that FoxPro can handle locking well enough without program intervention. This may be adequate for your application, especially on systems with low transaction rates.

Two other items are worth noting. First, while FoxPro can lock multiple records in the same table, it cannot unlock them individually. Issuing the *UNLOCK* command unlocks all lock records in the current work area. Second, while multiple record and file locks are handy, you must ensure that your network operating system can accommodate as many locks as your system is likely to place at once. Depending on the system, this may entail modifying a configuration file for the workstation or invoking *SHARE* to specify a sufficient number of locks. Exceeding these limits can cause workstation crashes.

The strategies you use to lock files and records in your applications may vary widely in a single program to accommodate various needs. In general, while it's best to minimize the time any resource is locked and lock as few resources as possible for any given transaction, such an approach requires considerable overhead. You should consider the possibility that in some circumstances more encompassing locks (such as an *FLOCK()* followed by an *APPEND FROM ARRAY*) placed for shorter periods may yield better performance.

Measuring Contention

During the first month or two a multiuser application runs at the user site, I usually install an audit routine in my code to determine where locking delays and contention may be a problem. This routine consists of code similar to that in Listing 12-4.

Listing 12-4. An audit routine to find potential locking delays and contention.

```
* assume all data has been entered and validated

  m.aud_began= seconds()
  m.aud_stamp = dtoc(date()) + ' - ' + user_id
  m.aud_proces= program()
```

```
* attain all locks for all transactions here, then ensure
* that data on which the transaction is based hasn't changed

   m.aud_file= alias()  && the file contended for
   m.aud_ended= seconds()
   m.aud_code = C

* where C is a character coding for how we exited
* 0 = no errors, 1 = can't get locks, 2 = data changed
* if the lock attempt failed, the file that could not be
* locked is indicated in the m.aud_file variable

if monitor
*  monitor is a logical flag that allows me to turn off the
*  auditing system wide by resetting a memvar
   insert into audit memvar
endif
```

I usually place a similar routine in my file-open function and in all sections of code (usually just a few modules that are heavily used) that may encounter contention problems.

After the first month or so, you should have a good idea of where contention is a problem. You should also know whether data are being changed that require soliciting input from the user to check.

Concurrency

Many of the preceding examples skirted the issue of concurrency management to illustrate other aspects of FoxPro multiuser programming. However, concurrency is the reason we pay so much attention to file locks and record locks and is the only reason we use files in exclusive mode. In all programs, it's important to ensure that the data written to disk is in a consistent state. This can only be done if you're aware of the transactions in your system that have the potential for inconsistency.

Because FoxPro has no commit or rollback capability, be especially careful to secure all locks before you start updating records. The number of files and records involved in a lock should be kept to a minimum to ensure concurrency. Locks should also be released as soon as possible after the data is placed.

To illustrate several issues that must be addressed in multiuser programs, consider the following simple example, using data files with the structures in Table 12-2.

Table 12-2. Structure for tables used in example.

Table name	Fields
Customer	Customer number
Orders	Order number, customer number, order date
Lineitms	Order number, item number, quantity, unit cost
Inventory	Item number, description, cost, on-hand amount
Freight	Freight rates to destinations

The chain of events leading to the placement of this order is as follows (assuming the files are already open in shared mode):

1. The user enters a customer number.
2. The customer number and status are validated against the customer file (current balance, available credit, and credit status).
3. Order information is entered and validated, line items are validated against the inventory file (cost, stock on hand, back orders, and so forth), and freight is calculated.
4. A lock on the customer record is attempted. If it is successful, a free record is located in the orders file (we're ignoring the problem with *APPEND BLANK* for now) and the record is locked.
5. If step 4 is successful, as many free records as required are located and locked in the *lineitms* file to hold the order details.
6. Once the locks are placed, the program may put the data in the appropriate files.

There is still a problem, however. Between the time the data was validated and the time the program was ready to write that data to disk, some of the values may have changed. For example, let's say the freight rate is selected from a pop-up pick list. Once selected, if it's changed by another user after the lookup and before the data is written to disk, the freight rate for that order won't be current.

You can approach this problem in several ways. All involve trade-offs of some sort, and your solution will depend on the level of concurrency you're willing to sacrifice for performance.

The first and easiest solution is just to ignore the possibility that items in the lookup files may have changed. While this sounds drastic, it may be appropriate in certain instances. For example, if freight rates rarely change, and if those rare changes are usually very small, it may not matter whether a given order has a freight rate that's one second too old and $.02 per pound low. In this case, the effective time for the freight rate becomes the point at which all workstations have access to it.

The second and most restrictive alternative guarantees accurate information. In this case, locks are placed on all records that participate in any way in the transaction when those records become known. The record containing the freight rate for this order will be locked when the user picks the rate from the pop-up. This has the disadvantage (which may at times be severe) of locking other users out of that shared data. If several people are taking phone orders and want to use the same freight rate, and each order takes two minutes to enter and complete, the transaction throughput on this system will be abysmal.

Another alternative is to lock the records you want to update and, immediately before writing them to disk, make sure any data in the records that participated in the validation or lookup schemes hasn't changed. If only a few records are involved, this approach tends to be very fast and efficient. If there are numerous records in many files, it can be quite cumbersome. One way I've approached this problem is by including in each data file two character-type fields containing time-and-date stamps for the time the record was created and the time it was last updated. The stamps are generated by the following function:

```
function stamp
return str(86400*(date()-{5/01/1988}),9,0) + ;
   str(int(seconds()),5,0) + user_id
```

The date 5/01/1988 is an arbitrary one but should encompass the earliest transaction the system can expect. This function simply calculates the number of seconds between this instant and the arbitrary date, converts it to a string, and appends the ID code of the user who entered the record. The updated stamp is the same for all records in all tables that make up a single transaction. The advantage is that partial audits of transaction histories, particularly for debugging purposes, are allowed.

As a user enters data, the program reads the updated field for any record on which that entry relies and stores it. In the preceding example, the updated field for the customer record and the freight rate are stored in variables when the records are read. When the program has locked the appropriate records and is ready to write the data to disk, it rechecks to see that the values in memory are the same as those on disk. If they have changed, the user is notified and returned to the input screen to try again. This function is similar to the dBASE IV *CHANGE()* function but is implemented programmatically in FoxPro. More sophisticated systems can be used to determine if portions of the record relevant to the transaction have been updated.

You must consider the users in this scenario. If they have just entered several screens of data, you don't want to punish them by restoring all the default values for the screens if you must return them to the entry screen because the data in some validation file has changed. In this case, you should consider selectively informing them of the problem areas, perhaps by using colors to highlight the *GET*s that may require reconsideration.

A third approach to this problem is to restrict access to all files that serve primarily as lookup tables. This requires exclusive use of those tables for any modifications. This is a very simple and, on smaller installations, workable approach. In larger setups, however, where transactions involving lookups occur throughout the day, it may not be feasible to require exclusive use of these files at any time.

Other approaches include:

- Using the transaction-tracking features of the network operating system. (This is possible with NetWare but unlikely with other systems; implementation on NetWare with FoxPro requires third-party utilities and incurs a significant performance penalty.)

- Write your own transaction system in FoxPro. (This option is slow and still subject to contention and concurrency issues.)
- Use a record status table that programs can check to see if a record was part of an ongoing transaction before modifying the record (again, performance may be affected, and any use of a table requires consideration of contention issues).

Transaction Ordering

Certain kinds of transactions require that their elements occur in a specific order, both internally to that transaction and externally in terms of processes executing concurrently on other workstations.

Consider the simple example in Figure 12-1, in which Transaction 1 transfers an amount from one account to another and Transaction 2 transfers a percentage of the current balance from one account to another. The commands have been fleshed out to indicate what's happening. While in a real program they may or may not be phrased this way, the point is that each transaction comprises four elements: a read and write of account A and a read and write of account B. Let the balance in accounts A and B be $100.00 each before the transactions take place.

TRANSACTION 1	TRANSACTION 2
(Account A) m.balance= cust.balance m.balance= m.balance - 50.00 replace cust.balance with m.balance	(Account A) m.balance= cust.balance discount= .25 * m.balance m.balance= m.balance - discount replace cust.balance with m.balance
(Account B) m.balance= cust.balance m.balance= m.balance + 50.00 replace cust.balance with m.balance	(Account B) m.balance= cust.balance m.balance= m.balance + discount replace cust.balance with m.balance

Figure 12-1. Sample transaction demonstrating serializing problems.

The resulting balances will depend on the order in which these commands are executed. If they're executed in the order they're listed here, the balance in Account A will be $75.00 and the balance of Account B will be $150.00. If Transaction 1 is executed before Transaction 2, the balances in the accounts will be $37.50 and $162.50. If Transaction 2 is executed before Transaction 1, the account balances will be $50.00 in A and $150.00 in B.

These transactions demonstrate the problem of serializability. FoxPro programs must specifically address serializability issues.

The way you handle serializability will depend on your application, of course, but it does require a thorough understanding of the nature of the transactions, the possible consequences of concurrent transactions against the same data, and the mechanisms to preclude these problems.

There are several approaches to serializability. The first and easiest to implement is simply to lock all records involved in the transaction before allowing it to proceed. In the preceding example, accounts A and B would be locked until Transaction 1 completed; only then could Transaction 2 proceed. You would then perform Transaction 2 knowing that the amounts in accounts A and B were correct and current. The operator could then be certain that the information on which the transaction was based was current and valid. If other users are unlikely to be inconvenienced significantly, this scheme works well. If, however, the transaction involves many files and records, the files may be locked for a relatively long time as the operator enters the requisite data, inconveniencing other users.

The technique of time-stamping all record updates is also possible in this situation.

Modeless Programming

FoxPro 2.0 introduces many new features that allow the development of modeless applications. In other words, you can develop software in which the user may (usually via a mouse) select numerous actions from a menu concurrently. The user isn't locked into completing the task most recently selected from a hierarchical menu system before selecting another task. This feature means significant flexibility for the user, a programming challenge for single-user programmers, and a headache for multiuser programmers.

In modeless programming, the user dictates the order in which many tasks are executed, and certain tasks may be interrupted to begin another. For example, let's say an order-entry clerk receives a phone order from Jane Doe. The clerk may opt to add Jane to the database because her reply to the question "Have you ever ordered from us before?" was "Gee, I don't remember." However, to be safe, he or she first queries the database to see if any customers with the same phone number are on file and then checks to see if any with the same last name and zip code are on file. It turns out that Jane Doe, having moved since her last order, is on file with an old address and phone number. Additionally, she has an unpaid balance due on a prior order. The clerk is prohibited from placing a new order until the old one is cleared, but Jane is willing to make good on the old debt using a credit card. The clerk must now suspend the query and begin a new task (entering a receipt).

During the course of this transaction, the clerk has suspended the order-add, customer-add, and query tasks. In each task, different files may be in use or, more likely, some of the files used in one task may also be used in another. A problem in accommodating this type of interaction in FoxPro arises when the file-open mode and locks required in one module differ from those in another.

As discussed earlier, FoxPro has only two explicit record-lock states—locked and unlocked—and (functionally, though not technically) three file-open modes—read/write/deny none, read/write/deny writes, read/write/deny reads and writes. Successful migration between these states can't be assured within FoxPro. Bear in mind that the two record-lock states exist only in the read/write/deny-none open mode.

Table 12-3 illustrates when the migration of a lock from one mode to another will fail safely—in other words, either guarantee the transition to a new state or guarantee that the current state is maintained if the transition can't be completed.

Table 12-3. Lock persistence during migration between locking modes.

Current Mode	Desired Mode: No locks	Record lock	File lock	Exclusive use
No locks	N/A	Y	Y	N
Record lock	Y	N/A	N	N
File lock	Y	Y	N/A	N
Exclusive use	N	N	N	N/A

In a truly modeless program, a user should be able to select almost any task at any time. The programmer must ensure that the files needed for a task are opened and closed as required and that locks are applied and released as required.

When designing such applications, however, you must consider the inability to migrate from a certain lock mode to another with either a guarantee of success or a guarantee that the current lock status can be maintained. If the user is in a task that requires a record lock (which he has) and switches to a task with a normal open mode but that requires a file lock, what is the appropriate course of action? An unsuccessful attempt to gain the file lock will release the previously placed record lock. Should the file lock be released and a record lock applied (the transition isn't guaranteed), or should the file lock be retained since it can achieve the same end? These are difficult questions, and the interaction becomes even more complex in large systems.

The simplest solution is to minimize all file locks and exclusive locks and require the routines that use them to be modal. All other routines that participate in the modeless paradigm could be written to use record locks exclusively, but this brings up another problem in that FoxPro can't unlock single records in a set. All locked records in a file must be unlocked at once.

Consider a user who is executing a task (Task 1) that locks a record in a file. Prior to completing Task 1, the user switches to another task (Task 2) that requires a lock on another record in the same file. The user then completes Task 2, which dutifully cleans up after itself by unlocking the updated record. Unfortunately, this also unlocks the record held by Task 1, which has no way to make sure it can regain a lock on that record (in the short time between tasks, another user may have locked it).

These problems have solutions, but those solutions are certain to entail both programming overhead and performance degradation as well as a loss of flexibility in implementing modeless environments within FoxPro. One such solution is to implement a control database where records are "checked out" rather than locked; another is to design your application so that switching from module 1 to module 2 is prohibited if module 1 has placed any locks.

Both solutions have obvious drawbacks. The nascent state of FoxPro among the suite of tools used to implement modeless applications is apparent in the immaturity of its multiuser locking mechanisms. Let's hope this changes in future versions.

FoxPro and Direct Reads

As users have become enamored with network environments, software vendors have offered products that purport to manage the multiuser issues of concurrency and contention without user intervention. FoxPro has been among those touting such features.

In a multiuser environment, FoxPro attempts to secure locks automatically for many of the commands that modify a database. These include the traditional *APPEND BLANK* and *REPLACE* statements as well as the newer SQL *INSERT* command. Most of the multiuser programs I've seen that rely almost entirely on FoxPro for locking use the technique of direct reads (in other words, a *GET/READ* statement with a field object rather than the more traditional variable object). The programmer or user appends a blank record to the file and issues a series of *GET*s using the field names in the file. Valid clauses attached to each field may provide validation of user input. Direct reads into temporary or scratch tables that are subsequently appended to the actual working tables aren't discussed here because they differ little from reads to memvars.

FoxPro provides automatic locks in multiuser mode when it determines that someone has modified the contents of a field. It will then attempt to lock the entire record. If the record isn't available, FoxPro will warn the user appropriately depending on several factors—for example, the retry timeout (*SET REPROCESS TO nn SECONDS*) or retry count (*SET REPROCESS TO nn*) allotted in the system setup. Further customized processing is possible via an *ON ERROR* routine that can handle reprocess attempts and notify the user.

Direct reads are also frequently implemented via the *BROWSE* construct, though ensuring data integrity this way is a little more difficult. In a browse screen, if any attempt is made to change data in a record, FoxPro will lock that record and records in associated files that are displayed on the same line in the browse. If the browse contains the *SET SKIP TO* clause, all subsidiary records of the database from which the relation is set will be locked.

One way to append records in a browse is to press Ctrl+N. This appends a record and positions the record pointer to it but doesn't lock that record until the user types something in it. If enough time elapses between when the record is appended and when the first entry is typed in, someone else can obtain a file lock. The original user is then unable to add records or back out the appended record, leaving the database in an inconsistent state.

While direct reads are indeed convenient for many simple applications, especially those involving a single file, for nontrivial applications the concept of implicit locking and direct reads leaves much to be desired. Consider the following, fairly straightforward transaction involving a customer order of several items. The transaction involves only two files:

Orders:	order_no, customer, orderdate
Lineitms:	order_no, part_no, quantity

This is a simplified example; in a real system, many other files would be involved in the transaction (payments, customers, back orders, and shipping addresses, for example).

Recall the concept of a transaction as a logical set of updates to one or more tables. Transactions should be an either/or proposition: Either they should all be completed or none of the transaction elements should be applied. It's difficult to implement robust direct reads when one-to-many relationships exist. The preceding example may require appending numerous line-item records and waiting for user input into those records. As each record is added, the user enters data into the fields for that record, moves on to add another, and so forth. As a user moves off each record that was added, that record becomes visible to other users and is unlocked. If on the tenth record the user decides to abandon the entry, he or she must locate the other nine records, obtain locks on them, and delete them or blank them out. If this person fails to obtain those locks, what should the next action be?

Such a strategy is difficult to implement in a direct-read scenario without exposing the database to potential corruption, either by hardware failure at the workstation or server or by loss of access to the file on the workstation. When many records representing partial, uncommitted transactions are present, the database in which they reside becomes invalid until the transaction is completed or removed. Compounding the problem is that blank records are visible to other users as soon as they're appended; data entered into them becomes visible to other users as soon as the data-entry person moves to a new record. This presents problems for users who are querying the database. Those query processes must be able to determine which records are in the process of being entered, which have been abandoned, and which are valid.

It is possible to implement transaction entry systems for one-to-many relationships via direct reads and implicit locking schemes. It is also not wise. The main argument against such programming techniques is that the duration of exposure of uncommitted data is too great in systems where active queries and significant amounts of other transactions are being made against the same data. Faults caused by the server or workstation hardware and communications problems on the network media have a much higher probability of corrupting data files that contain incomplete transactions.

While direct reads may be adequate for very simple systems (particularly flat-file systems), think carefully about their long-term impact in terms of client satisfaction and premature aging.

Optimizing FoxPro LAN

The general goal in optimizing hardware and programs for performance in the FoxPro 2.0 network environment is to minimize use of the server. Using the server increases wire traffic, slows other processes on that server, and brings up the issue of contention for files and resources.

The following are some general guidelines for enhancing performance. They're for average installations (a mix of transaction entry, querying, and reporting) on Novell networks but should apply equally well to networks with five or more users.

If you have fewer users, you may not be as affected by network limitations as by workstation limitations and may want to review the chapter on hardware optimization.

Reduce Server Use

Overlays: FOXPROL.OVL

Standard FoxPro carries about a large body of code, much more than can reside in conventional (sub-640K) memory. It swaps code segments in and out of memory as required from its overlay file. When the overlay is on a server drive, you'll experience significant delays as the overlay segments are read from a busy server.

The best solution is to use the extended version of FoxPro with machines that have 4 MB or more of RAM. This precludes any code swapping since FoxPro can load itself entirely into system RAM. With less memory this becomes problematic, but you should benefit more from loading the extended version in tighter memory situations than you would in a single-user situation when the overlays would have been located on a file server.

Alternatively, you can place the overlay on a RAM disk if you can't run the extended version but still have lots of RAM.

Program Cache

FoxPro also does a lot of disk I/O to a file (or files) which Fox refers to as the *program cache*. This is a temporary file, and Fox suggests that it not exceed 400 KB. One file per user is created at run time. While Fox's manuals contradict themselves on this issue, it's probably the second item to try to place on a local drive (either RAM disk or fixed disk). These files are given unique names at run time.

The location of this file is governed by the *PROGWORK* setting in the CONFIG.FP file.

Resource File

The resource file is a .DBF in which FoxPro stores data like color sets, window sizes and positions, browse configurations, and so forth. The default name is FOXUSER.DBF, but it can be named otherwise. This file is normally opened on entry and held open during the course of a FoxPro session. A great deal of read and write activity occurs to this file over the course of several sessions; as a result, it can become quite large, particularly if you use FoxPro interactively. This file should also be placed on a local drive unless it's not required or space constraints dictate otherwise.

Because this file stores defaults for a particular user or workstation, it can't be shared on a LAN if users must write to it. However, it can be flagged as read-only at the operating-system level and then shared. Users won't be able to save any preferences in it, but flagging it as read-only will allow many users to read from it without the overhead of their writing to it constantly during work sessions. If certain users must write to it, they can be given their own copies of the file in private subdirectories.

Temporary Files

Over the course of a session, FoxPro may create many temporary files. For example, the *SORT* command will create an intermediate file that is erased when the sort is completed. Certain SQL *SELECT* statements will also create one or more temporary files; these files are never shared and should, if possible, be directed to a local storage device. If you're working with large databases, however, they can become quite large, so make sure the temporary files don't exceed the capacity of your local storage media.

The location of these files can be set by the *SORTWORK* and *EDITWORK* lines in your CONFIG.FP file.

Adding RAM to Workstations

If you're doing queries using Rushmore or are doing a lot of SQL *SELECT* queries, consider adding RAM to your workstation. While FoxPro won't cache shared data files to the same extent as when they're used exclusively, it will benefit from extra RAM to cache indexes in these situations.

Reduce Network Traffic

Every time a program requests data, the server sends it as much as (and almost always more than) it asked for, leaving the program to sort the wheat from the chaff. As mentioned earlier, on a heavily used network this can result in slowdowns due to bandwidth limitations of the communications medium as well as increased use of the server. The following steps can be taken to offload a busy network:

Create a FoxPro Print-Job Server or Print to Local Printers

Printing to a network queue always results in more network traffic than would be generated if the report were printed to a local queue. This is because the network sends the workstation more than just the data that must be printed (including, for example, indexes that are being scanned). The workstation then selects the data it wants from that set, formats it, and routes it to a print server or the file server. If routed to the file server, it then impacts file-server use in addition to increasing network traffic.

If many people routinely print long and complex reports over the course of a normal day on a busy network, much LAN traffic will be created and user time and workstations will be tied up. One solution is to use a FoxPro print station. Typically, one or more workstations are set up with fast local printers attached to them. These workstations don't participate in the normal digital intercourse of the other workstations on that network; they run a special program that does nothing but check a shared file for records that specify which reports to print. One possible structure for such a file is shown in Figure 12-2.

The program running on the FoxPro print server monitors this database for new records. When it finds one or more that need to be printed, it prints the one with the highest priority. The various options for the report can be stored in an array, which is saved in the options memo field.

User requests for print jobs that aren't needed immediately can be printed remotely and the workstation returned to productive use. The user can always pick a different destination for the printer at run time if the queued job list is too long.

Structure for database: C:\FOXQUEUE.DBF

Number of data records: 0

Date of last update: 08/27/91

Memo file block size: 64

Field	Field Name	Type	Width	
1	REPORT_NO	Character	5	
2	OPTIONS	Memo	10	
3	PRIORITY	Character	1	
4	STATUS	Character	1	(printing?)
5	REQUESTOR	Character	10	(user name)
6	SUBMITTED	Character	17	(date & time)
7	COMPLETED	Character	17	(date & time)
		** Total **	62	

Figure 12-2. Structure for a table to queue print requests.

Consider Special-Purpose Workstations

In situations where FoxPro is used to generate ad hoc queries and reports against large, shared databases that are being actively updated, consider specialized query workstations. These workstations are set up to hold a complete (but not current) set of the data that resides on the shared workstations. Generally, many of the what-if, historical, and ad hoc management information queries don't need to include data current to the last transaction. Sometimes data that's current through the end of the previous day, week, or even month will suffice. These machines can be updated with current data periodically as needed.

Given the relatively low cost of drives and workstations, a machine with 16 MB of RAM, a 33-MHz 80386 processor, and one gigabyte of storage can be had for about $5,000. The cost of such a machine may be justified if it can offload enough processing from the network to increase the workers' productivity.

Know your Network Operating System's Hardware Requirements

I don't want to instigate yet another network hardware debate here, but I do want to point out that FoxPro demands much more of a network server than does WordPerfect or Lotus or daVinci Email. Whether you're using a low-end, DOS-based network like InvisibleNet or a more robust, high-performance network like Novell's Netware 3.11, the factors governing server performance are the same.

In a busy, transaction-based environment, disk read and write speed is critical to good performance on any server. Additionally, fast network interface cards and lots of RAM are a must if you want maximum performance. If your network supports multiple network interface cards or duplexed drives, consider those alternatives. In many instances, it's cheaper to upgrade a server's hardware than to pay a programmer to wring more performance from FoxPro.

Meeting the Multiuser Challenge

In the DOS file-server environment, FoxPro provides a great deal of programming flexibility, an interactive environment that can be both boon and bane to users and database administrators, and excellent performance relative to its major competitors. Compared to its relatives in the dBASE family tree, it's an excellent product. With its SQL *SELECT* optimization and Rushmore technology, it has redefined the standard of performance that other DOS-based database programs must meet.

The world is changing, however. As more and more critical organization data is ported to PCs, database administrators, programmers, and users are demanding more robust DBMS's that implement security features, concurrency-management mechanisms, data-integrity constraints, and internal query optimization. Additionally, as networks become more complex and dispersed over greater distances, the volume of traffic generated by the traditional file-server model becomes untenable.

Fox's announced solution to these problems is a database server implemented as a NetWare-loadable module for NetWare 386. This server should offer even greater speed and more fully implement the relational model. Until that time, the challenge of designing multiuser applications should keep you busy. I hope some of the issues discussed here will help you confront that challenge.

CHAPTER 13

The Client-Server Architecture

by David McClanahan

The client-server architecture is becoming increasingly popular for multiuser database systems with shared resources. It separates a system's database functions from its application functions and moves them to a separate program (or process) called the *server*. The server generally runs on a dedicated hardware unit and provides a set of database services to client programs (or processes) that run at other stations on the network.

In the PC world, this architecture is set up in a local area network such as a token-ring or Ethernet system. Figure 13-1 shows a typical setup with one server and three client stations on the network.

The client and server communicate over the network via messages. Messages from the client to the server carry the request, and messages from the server to the client contain the results of that request. In the example in Figure 13-1, a client application made a request for the name of the company with an ID of "1," and the server responded with "ACME." The server could be based on any data model, but for the purposes of this discussion we will assume the server is based on the relational database model.

Figure 13-1 looks similar to the configuration for a file-server system, but communication for the client-server system is at the database level rather than the file level. (Note: FoxPro programmers often refer to a table as a database; we will use the term *database* to refer to a collection of tables.)

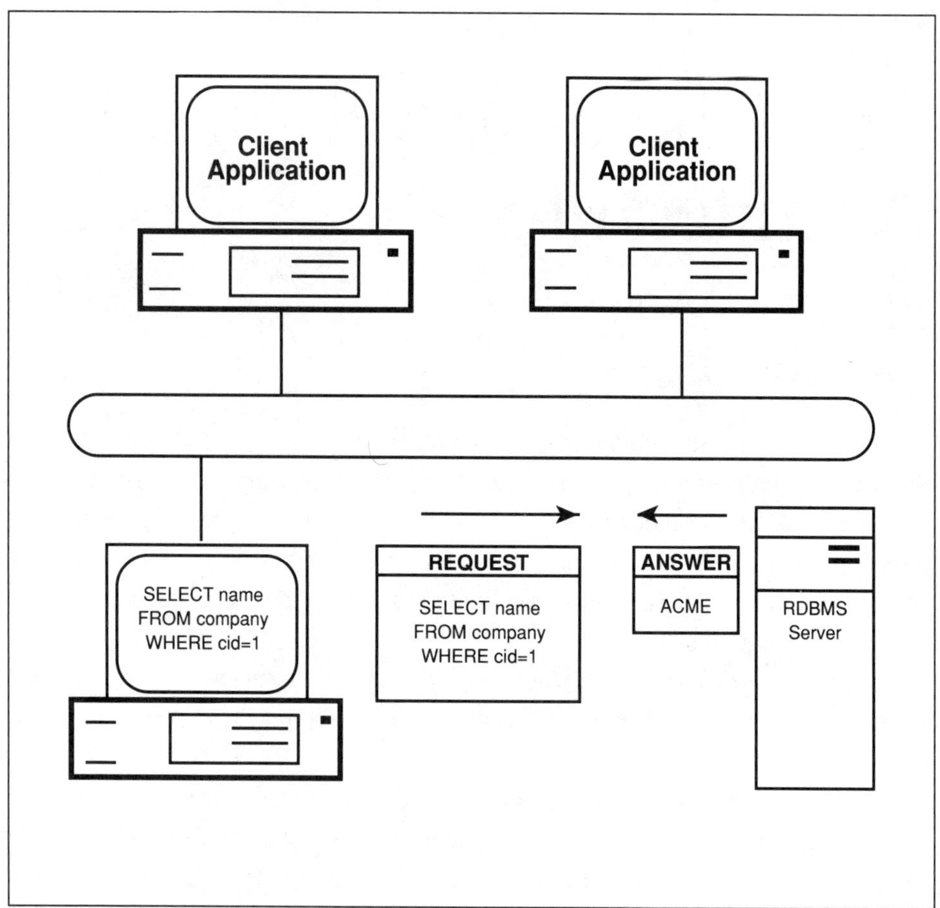

Figure 13-1. The client-server system.

The Client

The client stations run what is referred to as the *front-end* component of the system. This is an application program providing all the processing that is localized on the client station. Because the client need not provide database services, it can be fully dedicated to other functions (such as providing the user interface and graphics). Whether the front-end application is a spreadsheet, a communications program, or any other sizable program, at some point it will have data that needs to be managed.

The client process sends the application's request for a database transaction over the network to the server element, referred to as the *back end*. The requests are in the form of messages with a format defined by the server and generally in a high-level language like SQL. The database transaction request is placed into a network packet or multiple packets on the client station by the network system software, addressed to the server, marked with the return address of the client making the request, and shipped over the network to the server. The server completes the request and returns the results to the client process.

An important feature of the client-server model is the protocol that allows this communication between client and server. This protocol is usually published so other companies can develop front-end software to communicate with the server. The client can run on a variety of hardware platforms—including IBM PCs, Macintosh computers, and Sun workstations—as long as the platform can send and receive messages in the specified format. This generally requires a version of the database library for each platform or adding other functions to supply the communication.

With IBM's Systems Applications Architecture (SAA), PCs can even access a remote mainframe running IBM's DB2 DBMS as if it were located on the network. The library functions that provide the Applications Programming Interface (API) handle the details by communicating with the network operating system functions.

The Server

The server implements the features of the relational database model, as discussed in Chapter 7, and provides much or all of the functionality usually associated with a mainframe DBMS. For a relational database server, this functionality is expressed as a high-level database operation such as a transaction-based manipulation of a set of tuples. It is set-oriented because the relational model and relational languages deal with sets of tuples.

Besides translating the application's logical view of the database into the actual physical implementation, the server provides data definition, data manipulation, data integrity, and system administration.

The server receives messages through the network system software. The network software on the server "listens" for packets addressed to it, takes them off the network, and assembles them into the original transaction requests. The server parses each statement to determine the nature of the request and whether or not it is legal and may then translate it into some internal form. If the requested statement is valid, the optimizer determines how best to execute it and generates an internal representation of the execution plan.

The transaction is executed statement by statement. If any statement fails, the transaction is aborted; the server determines a return code and leaves the database in its original state (as it was just before the transaction began execution). The server returns the resulting set of data or just a return code, depending on the request, to the requesting client station. It does this by packing the result into packets, addressing them to the requesting client, and shipping them over the network.

The server component could be one of multiple processes (perhaps including a client process) running on a unit but is often the sole task. Generally, the server runs on a multitasking operating system.

The Pros and Cons

The disadvantages of the client-server architecture are the initial cost of the hardware and software required to set up the system and the complexity of the architecture.

Some of the advantages of the client-server architecture are:

- The server is highly specialized and offers much greater functionality than does a file server.
- Servers provide *transaction processing*; in other words, individual requests are grouped together and executed as a unit. Either all the requests succeed or none are applied against the database, allowing the state of the database system to be determined after each transaction. Because the server deals with multiple users making concurrent requests against the database, one user's request to update the database must not interfere with related operations of another user.
- The server provides for the integrity, control, and security of the data

elements in the database. The integrity of the database must be ensured even with concurrent transactions taking place. Processes can be triggered to enforce integrity constraints, such as entity integrity, relational integrity, and any rules that can be expressed and stored in the system (ranges of legal values, for instance). Data security is best controlled by the server, with different users having different levels of access to the data in the system.

- The data may reside on a single unit or may be distributed over several units. The location of the data is transparent to the client process, which refers to the logical database system through a high-level language without the details of the data's physical representation.
- The loading of data into the database, backup of the database system, and recovery from system failures can also be controlled by the server. The server can often back up the database in the background; clients will be unaware of the backup as they continue to access the data.

  The server may also keep a transaction log. Any transactions occurring since the last backup can then be applied against the backup to make it current.
- Stored procedures—precompiled SQL statements that can be invoked by the client by name—offer improved performance for important transactions.
- Because the server has its own hardware unit, it can use the optimum hardware—such as large, fast hard drives, more powerful CPUs, and RAM—to ensure the best possible performance. The system hardware can be distributed to maximize performance for a certain hardware collection. Client stations don't need the high-performance I/O components and can have less powerful CPUs (though the power might be redirected toward higher resolution, faster graphics, sound, or other services not required by the server).
- Network traffic is much lighter for a client-server system than for a file server. A file server ships all the requested records, which may include both data and index records, over the network to the client. Compare that to a

client-server system, where the client sends a request describing the work to be done and the server does that work off the network. Only the data requested by the client is returned over the network.

Consider a situation in which a nonindexed field value is the only search criterion for the client request. Further assume that the restriction value is found in only three records out of a table of a million records. A file server would ship every record in the database over the network to the client application, where the comparisons for the field value would take place. In a client-server system, the search would take place at the server's location and only three records would be sent over the network.

- Servers can choose the file structure, data compression, and indexing scheme that's best for a particular situation. For example, .DBF files have a rather inefficient format; a server system can use the best internal formats and then translate the data to .DBF format for the client.

A client-server system can bring mainframe database power to microcomputer LANs at a fraction of the cost. In many cases, downsizing a gigabyte mainframe system to a LAN system will pay for its cost within the first two years. New applications will perform data analysis and reporting in a fraction of the time currently taken on mainframe systems. The performance of the system should exceed that of any multiuser product once the number of client stations increases to the point where the amount of traffic on the network caused by the file accesses becomes a factor.

Programming for Client-Server Systems

SQL is a sublanguage; in other words, it is not a complete programming language in itself but is designed to handle a subset of functions (in this case, database functions). The SQL statements are generally combined with a host language such as C or COBOL. The host language is a complete programming language but, although it normally has some file-handling abilities, has no higher-level database functionality.

The SQL statements can be executed through an API, which provides a library of function calls (and macros) that can be made from the host language. The parameters of the function calls define the particulars of the SQL request being formulated. The library, which is linked in as the executable module is compiled and generated, must be made available to the linker as any other run-time library would be, and the header files containing the information necessary to use the function calls must be accessible to the compiler. In some systems, the library may be dynamically linked at run time rather than at compile time.

Alternatively, the SQL statements can be embedded in the host language with some type of surrounding control statements. These control statements set up the SQL statements and provide an interface between the database operations and the host language. The embedded SQL statements are then precompiled by a program that makes a pass through the source code and outputs another source-code file. The precompiler may translate the embedded code into calls to the API library.

Listing 13-1 is an example of C code with embedded SQL. (This is general code not tailored to a specific system and is therefore not functional.)

Listing 13-1. C with embedded SQL.

```
#include <stdio.h>
#include <sqlheader.h>/* the include file for the server library */

main()
{
EXEC SQL INCLUDE SQLCA;

EXEC SQL BEGIN DECLARE SECTION;
    int cust_no;
    char company[30];
    char city[20];
EXEC SQL END DECLARE SECTION;

EXEC SQL
DECLARE REQUEST CURSOR FOR
    SELECT COMPANY, CITY FROM CUSTOMER
    WHERE CUSTNO = :cust_no;
```

```
GetCustomerNumber(&cust_no);
EXEC SQL
OPEN CURSOR REQUEST;

EXEC SQL
FETCH REQUEST INTO :company, :city;

printf("the company name is %s in the city of %s\n", company,city);

EXEC SQL CLOSE REQUEST;
}
```

An example of a section of C code with API calls to the database library for SQL Server is given in Listing 13-2. Again this is generalized example and therefore is not a functional section of code.

Listing 13-2. API calls to the database.

```
#include <stdio.h>
#include <apiheader.h>  /
* the include file for the server library */

#define COMPANYLEN 30
#define CITYLEN 20

main()
{

LOGINREC *logindata;
DBPROCESS *dbproc;
int cust_no;
char company[COMPANYLEN];
char city[CITYLEN];
int rc;        /*return code*/

logindata = dblogin();
DBSETLUSER(logindata,"dave");
DBSETLPWD(logindata, "hello");
dbproc = dbopen(logindata, "");
```

```
GetCustomerNumber(&cust_no);
dbcmd(dbproc, "select company, city from customer where custno= ");
dbcmd(dbproc, cust_no);
 dbsqlexec(dbproc);
if (dbsqlexec(dbproc) != FAIL)
{
   rc = dbresults(dbproc);
   if (rc == SUCCEED)
   {
      dbbind(dbproc, 1, STRINGBIND, COMPANYLEN, company);
      dbbind(dbproc, 2, STRINGBIND, CITYLEN, city);
      printf("the company name is %s in the city of %s\n",
                                                 company, city);

   }
}
dbexit();
}
```

The client opens a server connection, makes a transaction, and closes the connection.

Client-Server and the Dbase World

A number of servers are available for PC-LAN systems, but the most important—both in quality and features and in the number of front-end products for it—is probably SQL Server. Ashton-Tate's dBASE Server Edition allows dbase clients to communicate with SQL Server, and third-party developers will likely offer add-on products for FoxPro 2.0 (through the API) that will allow communication with SQL Server.

In the future, servers may be developed specifically for dbase clients. Certainly SQL will be the major language for communication between such clients and the server, even for dbase applications. The language used to send requests must be a high-level relational one; the client will not be selecting work areas, record numbers, and so forth on the server. If the client asks for data, it will be able to do anything on any level the dbase language allows. The server, on the other hand, will be better able to make the decisions about query optimization, transaction processing, and data integrity and control than the client because it has all the information about the system.

Some major obstacles will need to be smoothed out between the dbase and SQL systems; dbase is a record-oriented, slightly relational language, while SQL is a set-oriented, fully relational language. SQL will continue to be integrated into the dbase dialects and the relationality expanded.

In the long run, as developers implement increasingly complex systems and require more of the features of the relational model, they will most likely switch to systems such as Paradox, SQL Server with front-end applications, and OS/2 Extended Edition. Many developers now feel that dbase is bloated and see new projects as a chance to make a new start with a system that begins with a next-generation implementation of the relational model.

CHAPTER 14

Approaching Client-Server: Emerald Bay, Oracle, SQL Server, and Interbase

Jeff Winchell, Peter Colclough, and Jeff Jochum

The previous chapter introduced the concepts of client-server architecture. This chapter looks at four client-server DBMS's (Emerald Bay, Oracle, SQL Server, and Interbase), to see how they implement these features. We have chosen these four because it is probable that there will be links to most of them from FoxPro 2 by the time you read this.

This is not an outright recommendation for any of these products. Currently, the field of client-server DBMS's is wide open. If you are in a quandary as to which way to move in the client-server market, please sample all of the offerings on the market, and draw your own conclusions about which product is best for you and your applications.

The Contenders

Oracle was the first commercial relational database management system. It was born out of the IBM's System/R prototype. Oracle's best known feature is its portability. It is currently available on 102 different platforms. While not originally a client-server database, it has moved into this area, bringing with it the dominant DBMS marketshare in this arena.

The next three DBMS's were launched about a decade after Oracle, which allowed them to learn from the trials of the first generation. Sybase SQL Server originated on OS/2 as a UNIX-based RDBMS, marketed by Microsoft. It is well known for providing high-performance on-line transaction processing, in addition to advanced features such as procedural SQL, stored procedures, and triggers.

Interbase was founded as a distributed RDBMS by Jim Starkey after he left Digital. This pedigree explains its strong connectivity to the Digital DBMS's Rdb and RMS. Interbase runs on a variety of UNIX platforms as well. Jim Starky coined the term BLOB (Basic Large Object) and implemented them in Interbase, as well as BLOB filters and multi-dimensional array BLOBs. Interbase is also noted for its high performance in complex transaction processing, advanced handling of triggers, event alerters, and bitmap query optimization. This feature set is likely to grow as its new owner, Borland International, is basing much of its growth on the success of Interbase.

While these first three high-end DBMS's were born in the big iron shops, Emerald Bay has more humble roots. Its founder, Wayne Ratliff, was also the creator of dBASE. Emerald Bay is a client-server for the common man. You don't need eight megabytes of RAM, a high-end, multi-user operating system, or a six-figure budget to implement it. Like its predecessor, dBASE, it also isn't relational. However, its main front-end, Vulcan (which is also the name of the product that was renamed dBASE II), takes the best of dBASE and throws the rest away, making the transition to a client-server DBMS easier for the millions of dbase programmers.

While many have touted, and rightfully so, the performance advantages of client-server, there are many other features in these products that are potentially of even greater value to FoxPro developers. They fall under the general categories of concurrency and transaction processing, data integrity, and portability and security. We will cover them first, and then return to performance issues.

Concurrency and Transaction Processing

When it comes to transaction processing, the fundamental question is: How well does the DBMS manage the problems caused by users simultaneously attempting to write data to shared files? In Chapter 12, the limitations of FoxPro's multiuser approach are enumerated in great detail. To pass the *ACID* test requires a great deal of programming with a concomitant decrease in performance. In case you're not familiar with this test of the Transaction Processing Council, ACID stands for atomicity, consistency, isolation, and durability.

Atomicity

Atomicity ensures that a logical group of operations (a transaction) are completed in an "all-or-none" fashion. In the client-server DBMS's discussed here, this requirement is met by using a few simple commands for things like *BEGIN TRANSACTION*, *COMMIT*, and *ABORT*.

Consistency

Consistency requires that any transaction take the database from one consistent state to another. This is like the natural law for the conservation of mass and energy (in a closed system, the sum of mass and energy remains constant). Consistency guarantees that transactions won't result, for example, in a bank customer gaining money when he or she transfers funds from a savings account to a checking account. You can achieve this easily in FoxPro by locking everyone out of all affected tables, but the performance penalty to other users is rather steep. (Chapter 12 describes some better programming solutions.) For more transparent solutions, with higher performance, you can turn to a client-server DBMS that has locking controls built in.

Isolating

Transactions that are isolated so that each is completed before the next begins are known as serial transactions. Processing parallel (concurrent) transactions should produce results that are identical to when transactions are performed serially. This property is called *serializability*. Serial transactions yield consistent answers by forcing others to wait. Serializable transactions increase concurrency and performance. Manually programming serializable transactions in FoxPro is no small task. Fortunately, most of these client-server DBMS engines handle this for you, with varying degrees of improved performance.

The notable exception is SQL Server. In default mode, when a page is touched by a transaction, a shared lock is placed on it. Pages are blocks of data, generally containing more than one record. When the page is no longer accessed in that transaction, the lock is released. This invites the following scenario:

User A:

```
BEGIN TRANSACTION
SELECT SUM(Income) FROM Master WHERE State = 'CA'
SELECT SUM(Income) FROM Master WHERE State = 'WA'
```

User B:

```
UPDATE SET State = 'WA' FROM Master WHERE
State = 'CA' AND ; Age = 34
```

In User A's query, the database engine might place a shared lock on a page while it reads a particular record that says the state is California. When it reads a record that's not in that page, the previous page's shared lock is released. It continues reading other pages for some time before getting to the second SQL *SELECT* where the state is Washington. But before it executes this second query, User B's *UPDATE* changes the record User A had read so that the state is Washington. User A will see that record when it looks for the Washington state records and the record will be counted twice.

This is not a serializable transaction. In a banking application, it isn't acceptable. For a mailing list, it might be. It depends on the value of your data. SQL Server does give you a manual method to guarantee serializability. You can place a *HOLD* lock on the data. Once a page is touched by a transaction, the lock stays until the entire transaction is committed or aborted. By relaxing the serializable constraint, performance is increased because User B can write his or her data sooner, rather than waiting for User A's entire transaction to complete. SQL Server gives you both options.

Durability

Durability pertains to the ability of the DBMS to handle system failures. The amount of manual programming that's required, along with the procedures for manual recovery, varies. FoxPro requires a great deal, while Interbase requires none.

Emerald Bay's Locking Controls

In Emerald Bay, an application may lock any number of records or tables at a time. Emerald Bay offers both implicit and explicit locks. Records changed during a transaction are automatically locked. As you move to a record, it is automatically given a *READ_LOCK* that blocks anyone from modifying the record. If the record is then written to, the lock would be upgraded to a *WRITE_LOCK*, preventing anyone from even reading the record. This lock, if successful, will be held until the transaction is finished.

However, if the attempt to lock a record isn't successful, a check must be made. This is done with a call to the *CONFLICT()* function. The lock attempt is made only once. There is no environment setting to retry when a lock fails like the SET REPROCESS statement in FoxPro. These retry attempts must be programmed manually. This results in pseudocode as in Listing 14-1.

Listing 14-1. Transaction processing in Emerald Bay.

```
BEGIN TRANSACTION
go to some record
read a value into memory
IF CONFLICT()
    routines to decide whether to retry or TRANSACTION ABORT
ELSE
    user edits the memory variable
    write the data back to the table
    IF CONFLICT()
        more routines to handle failure
    ELSE
        TRANSACTION COMMIT
    ENDIF
ENDIF
```

As with FoxPro, in Emerald Bay you can program procedures to help prevent deadlock, or too many transaction aborts leading to cascading rollbacks. Some of those procedures could use the explicit locking feature in Emerald Bay.

One significant difference from FoxPro is that you don't have to program the steps to abort a transaction. These are handled for you. Emerald Bay keeps a log of changes to allow you to restore data using a *ROLLBACK*.

The *READ_LOCK* feature is also a nice addition. In FoxPro, the only way to prevent someone from writing to a record is a lock that also prevents that person from reading it.

*READ*s of uncommitted transactions are a problem in FoxPro. Emerald Bay doesn't write changes to the tables until the *TRANSACTION COMMIT* statement. If you don't mind the risk involved, you can do a *dirty read*, reading data from a record that is *WRITE_LOCK*ed. Lastly, Emerald BAY has a Browse mode that will implicitly lock the entire table for exclusive access. If that lock fails, it will transparently degrade to a read-only status, preventing the user from doing too much damage to the data.

Concurrency Management in Oracle, SQL Server, and Interbase

The next step up, and a necessary one for high-performance, robust transaction systems, is for the database engine to manage transaction concurrency, rather than the programmer. Oracle, SQL Server, and Interbase take this approach as part of their SQL transaction support.

These SQL transactions are attempted *multiple* times, in contrast to Emerald Bay. Also, because SQL is set based, a single SQL statement will often replace many statements in a record-based engine such as Emerald Bay. You will still need to check a function after each SQL statement to see if deadlock occurred and you need to abort the transaction, but this still requires less programming.

To manage the complexities of concurrent transaction processing, Oracle and SQL Server make use of table-level and page-level (or record-level, in Oracle's case) locking in shared (read access to any) and exclusive (read/write access to one) modes. This locking covers the index pages as well as the table pages.

There are many sophisticated algorithms used in these engines to manage deadlock and keep contention to a minimum that are beyond the scope of this chapter. As an example, SQL Server for OS/2 can suspend a transaction if it can't get access to some data. The engine will wait for a message saying that data is available and then activate the transaction. In the UNIX version, as a transaction takes more CPU time to complete, its priority may be lowered.

SQL Server takes the approach of optimizing its transaction mechanisms rather than letting the programmer manage them. It does have one additional manual control: *SAVE TRANSACTION <savepoint name>*. This saves the state of the database at this point in a complex transaction. A subsequent *ROLLBACK <savepoint>* will back out changes since the named savepoint.

Oracle takes the middle ground. For example, a programmer can manually escalate locks. If the time required to obtain multiple record locks is believed to be too great, a programmer can lock the entire table instead, much more quickly. This speedup can result in MORE concurrency in some cases. The database administrator has several global controls to reduce contention for rollback statements. He or she can set lock sizes (table-level or row-level), the number of locks a transaction can have, lock escalation (the rules for replacing many record-level locks with a single table-level lock), and timeout limit.

Interbase has a more advanced feature to increase performance in complex transaction processing beyond SQL Server and Oracle's capabilities. Interbase uses a *multi-generational* architecture. This addresses the problem of one transaction attempting to read a data item while another is attempting to write to that same data item. SQL Server and Oracle use lock management techniques that preclude simultaneous read and write access to a data item (with one exception for Oracle described below). For a long read transaction typical in decision support systems, all other transactions attempting to write that data must wait until the read operation is finished. Interbase maintains multiple versions of the same record, allowing writes to operate concurrently with reads to the same record. In Figure 14-1, the second transaction updates the Customer record for Susan Vining in between two read statements in a transaction that will use her record.

Order of Events
User 1 (Transaction ID 1)
1 SELECT SUM(Sales) FROM Customer WHERE State = 'CA'
3 SELECT SUM(Sales) FROM Customer WHERE State = 'CA' AND ;
City = 'San Mateo'
User 2 (Transaction ID 2)
2 UPDATE Sales SET State = 'WA' and City = 'Seattle' ;
WHERE Custid = '915'

Figure 14-1. Interbase's multi-generational records manage transaction contention.

Here's the initial state of the customer record before the first transaction (TX ID = 0):

Record	TX ID	CID	City	State	Sales	Name
415	0	915	San Mateo	CA	1000	Susan Vining

and the state of the customer record after User 1's first *SELECT*:

Record	TX ID	CID	City	State	Sales	Name
415	0	915	San Mateo	CA	1000	Susan Vining

Here's the state of the customer record after User 2's *UPDATE*:

Record	TX ID	CID	City	State	Sales	Name
415	2	915	Seattle	WA	1000	Susan Vining

At this point, a difference record is created with the pre-*UPDATE* changes:

Record	TX ID	City	State
415	0	San Mateo	CA

When User 1's second *SELECT* is executed, Interbase recreates the original record using the difference record to give the same consistent read throughout the transaction. User 1 can't see the change made by User 2 because User 2's transaction started after User 1.

To keep these difference records from piling up needlessly, Interbase transactions cooperate in *garbage collecting* as they access records in the database. Difference records are subject to deletion when there are no longer any active transactions that started before the difference record was created.

Oracle has a more limited approach to maintaining read consistency. Oracle allows transaction-level read consistency to be explicitly set with the *SET TRANSACTION READ ONLY* statement. After a transaction has been set to read-only, all subsequent queries in that transaction will only see changes committed before the transaction began. Without this explicit declaration, read consistency is only maintained within single SQL query statements for the duration of that statement.

Recovery From System Failures

Maintaining high performance during transactions gets a high profile in client-server discussions, but for some organizations, how the server responds to system failures is more critical. A single workstation's failure can cause databases and indexes in FoxPro LAN to become corrupt. The effects of this may not be apparent immediately, especially with index files, where index pointers can point to the wrong record. When the failure is noted, manual intervention is required to repair the situation. If the application programmer has written a transaction logging procedure, it will be possible, after some downtime, to restore the databases. If the databases are very large, the necessary index rebuilds could take additional time. And if no transaction logging program was written, restoration from a backup will be necessary.

Much of this work is eliminated with Emerald Bay's recovery mechanisms. Transaction logging is a feature of the database engine. If individual workstations using transaction processing fail, they won't corrupt the database. If the server fails, the recovery routine will be aware of any indexes that were open at the time of failure. This could reduce the number of indexes that will have to be rebuilt. The databases themselves are rebuilt using the transaction log (unless the programmer took the risk of turning that feature off).

Oracle and SQL Server take recovery one step further by including index recovery information in their transaction log. When the database is restarted, the index pages are rolled back, so that rebuilding an index from scratch isn't necessary. No manual intervention is required to activate this feature.

These steps make recovery relatively smooth and fast compared to FoxPro, but when instant transparent recovery is required, consider Interbase. For example, one credit card transaction business determined that every minute the server is down costs the company $10 million in revenue. Because Interbase is able to completely restore a database in *one second*, it was the only choice for this business.

Interbase is able to do this because it doesn't use transaction logging in the traditional sense. With SQL Server, every time a transaction statement is executed, a before and after copy of the data is entered into a separate transaction log. When the database is recovered, the entire log must be replayed to rebuild the database.

Interbase instead uses difference records and monitors the status of records involved in a transaction in the transaction information page (TIP). This page stores only two bits for each record denoting, four possible states of a record: active, deleted, committed, and limbo (for distributed transactions). When the database is restarted after a failure, the TIP is scanned and all bits noting active status are changed to delete status, thereby rolling the transaction back. That's it.

Data Integrity

Backups, recovery, and consistent transaction processing are only the first step in maintaining data integrity. They don't prevent users and programmers from entering the wrong information. FoxPro handles this with thousands of tedious validation statements usually coded as user-defined functions called by *GET*s and *BROWSE*s. The relational model prescribes a simpler declarative method.

The concepts of *entity integrity*, *referential integrity*, and *domain integrity* are covered in Chapter 7. Briefly, entity integrity ensures that there is only one key value to access a particular record. Nonunique primary keys and null values violate this principle. Referential integrity is used to prevent an invoice record from including a customer number that no longer exists in the separate customer file. The domain of a field describes the complete set of possible values. If these three rules are stored with the database, the server engine can enforce them without the need for redundant and perhaps incorrect coding for each application that accesses the database. It sounds like a nice idea, but in practice, the vendor's implementation of these rules varies greatly. Since FoxPro has no data dictionary, all of these rules must be enforced at the application level.

To enforce entity integrity, Emerald Bay uses its data dictionary to flag the *Required Field*, signifying that nulls aren't allowed. You also need to create a unique index on that field. All indexes in Emerald Bay are maintained automatically, the same as FoxPro 2's structural compound indexes. If someone tries to enter a null or a non-unique value into a field set up this way, an error is triggered. Oracle, SQL Server, and Interbase use similar methods.

Emerald Bay has one other method to automatically enforce entity integrity: the record number field. Emerald Bay automatically stores the record number in a field. While this violates relational tenants, it does provide a convenient primary key field. However, this presents special problems if you delete a record. All record numbers have to be renumbered and any other tables that use that column as a foreign key will need to be updated. This makes deleting records very problematical.

Referential integrity at the server level is supported by SQL Server and Interbase. (The others require application-level coding.) SQL Server and Interbase achieve this by using *triggers*. Procedures coded into the data dictionary can be executed whenever a *DELETE*, *UPDATE*, or *INSERT* is encountered. These triggers are part of transaction processing, so transaction rollbacks will undo their actions as well.

SQL Server allows one trigger for each of the three basic operations (*DELETE*, *UPDATE*, and *INSERT*) for each table. This can make coding, testing, and maintenance of large triggers difficult. Interbase has no limit on the number of triggers per table. Interbase's modular triggers allow one trigger to call another, even allowing a trigger to call itself recursively. Interbase also has pre- and post-triggers, which are analogous to a FoxPro *WHEN* and *VALID* clauses. Within those two categories you can sequence the firing of multiple triggers by simply numbering the triggers.

SQL Server and Interbase also provide some support for domains. In SQL Server a domain rule is stored as a procedure in the data dictionary attached to each field. Interbase enforces domain integrity through validation criteria. The validation procedures are attached to a global field name. Any field in the database can reference a global field and automatically bring in the validation criteria.

Emerald Bay has a weak form of domain integrity. The data dictionary can store the valid range of values for a field. This means a salary field could be constrained to range from 10,000 to 50,000. More complex definitions are not possible (for example discrete lists like 10,000, 20,000, 30,000 or several ranges.)

Default values aren't part of domain integrity, but are useful nonetheless. The default value of a field can be stored in Emerald Bay's data dictionary. SQL Server goes one better by providing for a procedure to determine the default value. Another useful feature is providing a display format. Emerald Bay, SQL Server, and Interbase all have this capability.

Portability and Connectivity

Most large organizations have common data stored in numerous databases around the organization. One solution is to move this data onto one RDBMS, and make the RDBMS available to any program that needs it. A client (such as FoxPro) could access any information held on any server, provided adequate network support is given. This means that any application can use source data, as opposed to copies, for validating data entry, generating reports, and a host of other activities.

There are two major portability advantages of a client-server environment:

- **No code changes are required between platforms**. Because all data is held in one medium, the code for accessing it does not need to change, regardless of where the data actually resides. Whether you are accessing a database on OS/2 or on a Sun system, the method of access from the PC does not change.

- **You can move data storage without changing the application**. Here we have the concept that really benefits the developer of client applications. Let us assume that you have a system that took three months to write, with further enhancements over a period of six to nine months. The application currently runs fine. Initially, this system was set up in pure FoxPro, using .DBFs. However, a year from now the data set will have grown so large that you'll need to start looking at other methods of storing it. This could well mean a total rewrite of the application, because your new data storage device does not allow access from FoxPro, or there are no add-ons to provide that access. What you are looking at is a waste of development resources. You can avoid, or at least put off, this problem by planning for access to data on a server from the start.

Now, let's backtrack to the design of the system. You designed it to run against a client-server system on an OS/2 server. It worked and all was well. You'll still hit the situation a year from now, when the data becomes too much for the server, but this doesn't matter now; you'll be able to solve it easily. You'll recommend moving to a Sun, or Digital, or IBM, or the latest gigabyte-driven system. All will be required is to move the data and to add the relevant network support. Not a single line of code will need to be changed.

This is one advantage of portability: In time, it will save on development costs, and people resources.

So we are able to move the data source? Yes, to any supplied platform. The error-prone, antiquated methods in the non-connected dbase world (rekeying data and file upload/downloads) are no longer necessary. This also means that we can develop an application against a single-user version of the DBMS on a PC, and run it against a mini/mainframe. This has the further advantage of freeing up expensive CPU time, from the development cycle.

In the fictional ideal world, users would extend this so that applications could mix any hardware vendor and any client software vendor with any database vendor. With the plethora of vendors and the large investment in existing software and hardware and data, these concerns are not fictional. For vendors it is a catch-22. To justify the costs of supporting many platforms, they need to sell software. To sell more software, they need to support more platforms.

The company that has come the closest to this ideal is Oracle. Oracle is able to function in many different ways, on many different platforms. At last count, Oracle could be installed on about 102 different platforms. By using network and communications support programs, the Oracle tools (and any package that uses the Oracle tools) can access any of these platforms from any other platform. Also, given Oracle's dominant market share, it is much easier to find front-end tools on multiple platforms that support Oracle. Naturally, there are constraints to this access, but this is Oracle's goal.

With Microsoft's marketing muscle, SQL Server has the largest number of PC-based front-ends supporting its OS/2 version. In the UNIX world, SQL Server is present on all major minicomputer and workstation platforms. However, it doesn't run on mainframes or super computers. And unlike Oracle, there is no DOS version.

Emerald Bay, on the other hand, is supported on DOS. In fact, this is the only platform Emerald Bay runs on. Its tools are similarly restricted. There are C and Pascal APIs, as well as a dbase dialect, Vulcan. SuccessWare also sells an API, CLIP2EB, that links Clipper applications to Emerald Bay. Given the predominant market share of the dbase language, Emerald Bay is an attractive dbase-like alternative for client-server.

This should change soon with the emergence of Interbase. Interbase now is owned by Borland International, who also owns Ashton-Tate's dBASE. A direct link from dBASE and Paradox to Interbase should be available sometime in 1992. Borland's purchase of Interbase should increase the number of PC tools dramatically (at the time of this writing, Interbase had very limited front-end tools). Interbase is currently based entirely in the UNIX world. There are no mainframe, supercomputer, DOS, or OS/2 versions. But there is a UNIX version running on PCs, and we would expect an OS/2 version very soon, given Borland's commitments to IBM and OS/2. When you talk about Interbase's portability, the discussion naturally leads to distributed processing.

Of all the client-servers available, Interbase is arguably the most distributed. However, just as no database is fully relational according to Codd's rules, no database is fully distributed according to Date's rules. In fact, vendor conformance to the distributed rules is even less than for the relational rules. Bearing that in mind, what do these platforms offer as distributed DBMS's?

Oracle's most noteworthy distributed feature is the ability to maintain location transparency. This is achieved through the use of *synonyms* that are held in the data dictionary. You can set up a synonym for a given table or view, which includes the owner name, the database on which it is stored, and the network node for that database. This means that if you decide to move the table name, owner, database, or network node, all you need do is modify the synonym to reflect these changes, and the system will be up and running again. However, if this results in distributed data, only queries are allowed, no updates. Oracle does not yet support distributed updating.

SQL Server can perform distributed updates, but the *two-phase commit* (2PC) requires significant programming at the application level. Interbase, in contrast, handles the 2PC automatically. Queries in Interbase can also access multiple databases, but, as in Oracle's case, there is no distributed query optimizer. (We'll be talking more about query optimization shortly.)

Security

Due to the built-in security of Oracle and many other DBMS's, it is possible to dispose of a lot of code that manages user access. For example, if you have a system where some users are allowed to update information, and some are only allowed to read this information, you will ordinarily need two separate programs, that will process both kinds of information appropriately.

Handling both kinds of access is cumbersome to code and maintain in a normal environment. Oracle's security system has three main levels of access to a database: Connect, Resource, and DBA.

Connect rights allows a user to look at information in tables where he or she has been granted query access and write to tables where he or she has been granted manipulation access. The user can also create views and synonyms on tables where he or she has been granted user access.

The next highest access level, resource, allows a user to grant and revoke access to any table created by this user. Within this table, a user can grant rights in two dimensions. One dimension refers to table-level, field-level, or record-level access. The other refers to the actual operations performed. *UPDATE, INSERT, SELECT, INDEX, DELETE, ALTER* (modify table structure), and *ALL* are the defined operations.

DBA (Database Administrator) is the all-powerful access reserved for system managers. This type of user can create users, tables, views, or anything else they desire.

What this means to the developer is that only one program need be written, and Oracle will take care of the access based on the user's rights. If a user attempts to amend data, and that user does not have the rights, the database will bar access.

Emerald Bay also has a security system at the table and field level. In addition, you can use the limited encryption facility by setting a flag on the field in the data dictionary. This may stop the casual browser, but it isn't heavy duty protection. For Emerald Bay in a network environment, there is built-in protection because the database need not be directly accessible to random users. Database access is through the Emerald Bay engine. In any case, except for strings, the file format is sufficiently convoluted that only very dedicated individuals would be able to crack it.

SQL Server and Interbase extend security management with groups or classes of users. SQL Server has a Group ID extension field accessible to its SQL. Interbase handles it through its proprietary 4GL. In either case, the levels of security are similar to the ANSI SQL standards of *SELECT, INSERT, DELETE*, and *UPDATE* to tables and views.

Performance Issues: Wire Traffic, Query Optimization, and Physical Design

Wire Traffic: The Raison D'Etre of Client-Server

As we stated earlier, the performance advantages of the client-server architecture are often touted as *the* reason to switch from the file server architectures as used by FoxPro, Clipper, Paradox, and others. The chief reason for this is wire traffic.

Most database products use index files based on B-tree technology. When B-tree index files are shared on a file server, there are serious performance reductions compared to using the same data and index in a single-user mode.

Each time the database processor repositions the record pointer, it must first traverse the B-tree for the controlling index. This ensures that it knows about any changes that have been introduced by other network programs sharing the database and indexes. The program must perform additional disk seeks for each layer of the B-tree and move this index node information over the network to the workstation. This amount of index node information can be several times the amount of data to be moved.

In a more modern approach, the database server opens the files and indexes to be shared by the network workstations. The server is the sole owner of these disk files, and the workstations send requests to tell it to open certain files. Subsequent commands are sent to the server to store and retrieve data.

In a client-server architecture, the index information never moves on the network. This results in a massive reduction in network traffic. Also, since the database server can make use of cached information regarding index node content, server technology can reduce the number of disk seeks involved in the transaction. It must be said however, that FoxPro 2 is capable of caching shared indexes. FoxPro 2 can sense whether an index has changed since the information was first cached and reread the index if it detects such a change.

Query Optimization

By placing most of the database load on the server, rather than at the workstation, client-server applications may stress the ability of the server's horsepower to fulfill every query in a timely fashion. To ameliorate this condition, query optimizers are used to find the quickest path to an answer. To their chagrin, most client-server DBMS's don't handle query optimization nearly as well as FoxPro 2. Emerald Bay has no query optimizer at all, and Oracle's is suspect. To Interbase's credit, bitmapped index optimization was built into its product some time before FoxPro 2's similar Rushmore Technology.

Briefly, bitmap index optimization creates a tiny representation of each portion of an expression that matches an existing index. These bitmap representations can then be ANDed and ORed together to build a result containing the record numbers of the result set. For example,

```
SELECT * FROM Customer WHERE State = 'CA' AND Sales > 10000
```

If there is an index on the state and sales fields, each index is scanned to create a list of 0's and 1's in bits, one bit per record. If the tenth record has the value "CA" in the state field, the tenth bit in the state bitmap is a 1. These bitmaps can be created and evaluated extremely rapidly. The records are then retrieved sequentially, based on that list.

This contrasts with the traditional optimization technique for such a query. The query optimizer would guess (perhaps based on stored statistics, as in SQL Server's case) which condition, *State = 'CA'*, or *Sales > 10000*, will result in the fewer records, use the index to retrieve those records (in indexed order), and then cull through the found records to throw out those that don't satisfy the *Sales > 10000* criteria. Since Oracle doesn't store statistics, it can't do cost-based optimization and performs even worse. Oracle takes tables as they are ordered in the *WHERE* clause. The individual who's writing the SQL statement is responsible for its optimization.

Interbase also dynamically adjusts the memory buffer size when a query needs more memory. If you feel you can do better than the optimizer, you can also specify the order of joins.

Another facet of query optimization is the time taken to parse the query and form an execution plan. For commonly executed queries, this could be done ahead of time by pre-compiling and storing the binary representation with the database. This *stored procedure* will take less time to execute. SQL Server alone provides this feature.

Physical Design

The improper design of a database can impact performance perhaps more than any single factor. The more options a programmer has to tune a database, the better the performance.

Emerald Bay stores all of the tables in a database in a single file. All indexes are stored in a separate file. When indexes are used to find records in an indexed order, information from the table will usually be scattered randomly throughout the file. Information in the index will be largely sequential. If the index and table are stored on the same physical device, disk drive head movement will schizophrenically bounce from sequential to random access. Emerald Bay allows you to store the index and table files on separate drives while still keeping the automatic index maintenance capability.

The positive side to keeping all tables in a single file is that you circumvent DOS file handle limits. The other side is that the database must now control fragmentation. Emerald Bay uses variable-length records. Initially, this results in *much* smaller disk space requirements than typical FoxPro applications. However, as records are updated, and deleted, the Emerald Bay database becomes fragmented. To combat this, Emerald Bay has 30 to 40 different record-size blocks. When a record is added, Emerald Bay fits the record into one of these blocks. Records that grow are moved to another location with a larger block. Still, after a while the empty space will grow to a point where the DBA will want to *PACK* the database, thereby defragmenting and shrinking it.

In addition to variable-length records, Emerald Bay has single-dimension arrays. These can be processed more efficiently than if the data were contained in normalized database records. Emerald Bay also supports a large variable-length binary field analogous to a BLOB. Like FoxPro's memo field, this field can contain up to 2 GB of data (subject to the DOS 4 and DOS 5 restraints of 2 GB for the entire Emerald Bay database file).

SQL Server can use *clustering*. This is similar to using a sorted database. Records with similar key values are stored together in blocks. This makes scanning a section of the database on that cluster key field very fast. One downside is the time required to load a clustered table. It is much slower due to the implied indexing.

Interbase optionally allows you to load tables without any associated indexes. This results in a much faster load time if you decide you don't want to cluster. Interbase stores its data internally in a compressed format. Data compression can also be achieved by using array fields of up to 16 dimensions. BLOBs have types and subtypes and can be as large as the operating system permits.

Oracle provides an array of physical tuning parameters. You can adjust the size of various data structures, including the buffer cache, context areas (cursors), and the data dictionary cache. Like Emerald Bay, you can store tables and indexes on separate disk drives. Oracle also has clustering, but in a different fashion from SQL Server. In Oracle, you can interleave tables so that the detail records are located physically near the master records. This helps joins between two tables and hurts sequential scans of one table. Oracle doesn't support BLOBs.

Conclusion

This is not the "Year of Client-Server," and all our problems have not gone away. The front-end tools provided by the client-server vendors are not as full featured as FoxPro 2. However, the products mentioned here, as well as other client-servers that we haven't mentioned, provide possibilities to make database programming easier. By combining the strengths of FoxPro 2 with the strengths of a good client-server database, we can tackle problems we wouldn't consider before.

PART VI

Using the Application Program Interface

Application Program Interfaces (APIs): Tools for an Imperfect World

In some ideal world, one product addresses all your needs, but in the real world, you'll need help. You want to choose the best collection of tools for your job, and hope that they will communicate with each other as though they were one. There is no perfect solution to this problem, so we will take a look at many approaches to an API in this section of the book, to help you find the one that meets your needs.

APIs may not provide a seamless integration of products, but they can allow two products to talk to each other so that at least the major features of each can be accessed by the other. Of the approaches we discuss, FoxPro 2's API comes closest to this goal, as long as you limit which products are doing the talking.

In the first two chapters of this section, Peter Colclough and Ted Means explain how to use the two officially supported languages that communicate with FoxPro 2's API: Watcom C and Assembler. Peter's and Ted's efforts to create links to Oracle and Btrieve with FoxPro 2's API have given them plenty of insights on taking advantage of the potential of this API.

You'll note I said these are the only two *officially* supported languages. The requirement to use only these two products is a severe one in some cases. While one can recompile Microsoft C source code into Watcom C, you won't always have that source code available. You will find it difficult to obtain the source code for large and valuable products such as SQL Server and Oracle. Unofficially, there are some potential solutions. For example, Phil Smith of Black & White has developed a product using FoxPro 2's API in conjunction with Microsoft C and Borland's Turbo

C. As this book was going to press, Ted Means also verified this method. There are still many difficulties with implementing it, but this is an important first step.

If you need a database that talks to Microsoft C more easily than FoxPro 2, you might be tempted to try Clipper. Jeff Jochum uses many APIs to deal with the various problems of each. In chapter 18, he discusses these API options, including Clipper. All APIs are lacking some aspect of seamless integration; Clipper's limitation is its "one-way street" approach. With Clipper, as with Arago, you can access other languages from within a database application. However, these databases do not make it easy for other languages to access their database features. Clipper has an undocumented API that handles this, and some vendors (including Jeff Jochum's company) have bravely ventured into this territory.

It would seem that the only solution is to buy a different database/language/API combo for each application. That grim answer isn't the only solution, but if you are faced with that prospect, perhaps an operating system-level API would simplify your purchase orders. Randy Brown discusses the Macintosh API that Fox's Macintosh product uses. Currently, this API is more like the one-way street approach, but we've got big hopes for a change in this direction soon. This chapter may also give you a glimpse of some of the issues that will arise in FoxPro/Windows when it integrates an operating system-level API (the Windows API) with its own API.

As you can see, there are many ways to implement an API, depending on what the goals are. Some APIs are designed primarily to access external data files (Paradox Engine and Babelfish), some (Clipper, Arago, Fox's Macintosh API) are designed to extend a product's language to include other languages, such as C. Yet another (FoxPro 2's API) is designed to extend itself to other languages as well as to allow those languages to access its internal data files.

All these approaches have limitations: The goal of this section is to address them and to look at the possibilities they provide for bringing new features to your database applications. With FoxPro 2, C programmers may even choose to write C applications that take advantage of FoxPro's database and event-driven features. Fox has finally opened up its architecture. Now it's time to use it to your advantage.

—Editor

CHAPTER 15

FoxPro's API

by Peter Colclough

What is an API?

In case you're not up to date with the TLA jargonizers,[1] an API is an *Application Program Interface*. APIs are the means to add sections of re-usable code to your application. Some developers like to call them the "back door" to a package. Some like to ignore them completely. But the reality is that the API is the way to accomplish tasks that the package does not include. Personally, I like to think of them as the developer's answer to the age old question: "If only...."

APIs were invented to fill the need of users to perform specific tasks that were not a part of a general purpose package. The easiest way for developers to accomplish this was to provide "hooks" in their packages that users could tap into. Nowadays, APIs have expanded into complete subsystems that augment a standard package to provide more flexibility and functionality to programmers and end users.

The Evolution of API Methods

Perhaps the first applications of an API-type strategy was the simple transfer of data from a stand-alone application, such as Lotus 1-2-3, to another application. ASCII-formatted Lotus data could be read into the application's data files.

Then came the concept of running external code from within the package. These bits of code were usually in the form of .BIN (binary) files. A .BIN is a piece of code that performs a specific function, for example converting a number to a character string. It can be called from within an application, and values or parameters can be passed to it. The .BIN can change these values, if necessary.

[1] And in case you're *really* not up to date, TLA stands for three-letter abbreviation.

This methodology is much more flexible than pulling data in from ASCII format, as the .BIN is actually tied into the application program, and can be used from different areas of that program. dBASE II and its derivatives applied the .BIN approach in later years. The drawback to this approach is that each .BIN is a separate piece of code the application needs in order to run. Systems that need 30 or more .BIN files will be difficult to maintain.

Another methodology, similar using .BIN files, was to build in a "hook" to a named program. For example, the Omicron accounting package allowed developers to build a compiled BASIC program called NUSERRTN.EXE. If NUSERRTN.EXE was present when the Omicron General Ledger was run, it would appear as an option on the Main Menu. Extra functions could thus be written outside of the main package, but use data generated by the package. This also provided a seamless (to the user) link.

With the advent of compilers, it was possible to maintain libraries of code. This code would be linked into the final executable (.EXE), and could be distributed in its entirety. Clipper was the first to allow this for dbase compilers. Code written in C (initially Lattice C, and then Microsoft C, starting with Clipper S87) and assembler could be used in a seamless manner. A large group of add-on vendors soon appeared, writing libraries of functions to perform dedicated tasks.

As API technology develops, hooks into other parts of the system are made available—such is the case with Fox 2.0.

The general strategy of dbase APIs is for the application to build a *stack*, or queue, of parameters, and to pass the address, in memory, of where this stack starts to the API function. This address is called a pointer. In lay terms, a pointer is simply a "Mailbox" that tells the software where to look, in memory, for the information. Generally, the stack will consist of the following:

- The number of parameters
- A place for the return value
- A pointer (Mailbox) for each parameter on the stack

The API can use the stack construct to tell how many parameters have been passed up, their data types, lengths, and other useful information. Without this information, the API routine may try to do something silly, such as adding a number to a character string.

To be effective, an API needs a minimum of three things:

1. A calling program with the ability to pass values up to it.
2. The ability to return a value to the calling program.
3. The ability to change a value that is passed up to the API routine. This ability has become necessary in recent years due to the increased flexibility required by API programmers.

How the FoxPro API Works

The FoxPro 2.0 API is different from a compiled-language API in that it needs to be able to function with FoxPro in interactive mode. To do this you build the API using a compiler and linker, producing a specially constructed .EXE. This special .EXE file will from now on be called a .PLB, the special name for a FoxPro 2.0 library. It is run by FoxPro if it is needed. To run the file, FoxPro needs some specific information about the functions it contains, and it also needs to know where to start looking for this information. With compiled APIs, the compiled routine is brought into the .EXE at link time.

The Libhdr Module

For FoxPro to find your function, you will need to give it the following information:

- The name of the function as it appears in your .PRG, or in the Command Window.
- The "Name" of your function.
- The number and types of the parameters to be passed up to the function.

For this to occur, FoxPro requires you to build a specific module into your .PLB. This module is called the Libhdr module. Listing 15-1 is an example of such a module.

Listing 15-1. Libhdr module.

```
Libhdr.c
--------

#include "..\pro_ext.h"

extern far myfunc();

FoxInfo FoxPara[] = {
{"MY_FUNC",                   /* Program Call     */
   myfunc,                    /* 'C' function     */
   2,                         /* number of Paras */
   ".C,.?"}                   /* Data Types       */
};

FoxTable _FoxTable =
{
   (FoxTable FAR *)0,
   sizeof (FoxPara) / sizeof (FoxInfo),
   FoxPara
};
```

Listing 15-1 starts with the inclusion of the relevant C header files, which are needed for the Watcom C compiler to understand the information in the C program.

Then the external declaration of the function is called; in this case it is *myfunc()*. This enables the linker to bring in the function at link time. Without the '*...extern far myfunc...*,' the linker would ignore the function, and you would not be able to call it from FoxPro. (Not very useful!)

There are two tables of information that FoxPro uses to access your function: the Foxinfo table and Foxtable table.

Foxinfo Table

This table holds the relevant details FoxPro needs to know about your function. Each function you write will have an entry in this table, composed of the four items shown in the example for myfunc().

The first item is the name that will be used by your .PRG, or typed in at the Command Window. Unlike other commands and functions, you must use the whole name. You can't, for example, use "*MY_FU('Z',2),*" you have to use "*MY_FUNC('Z',2).*" This limitation is mainly to reduce the chance for name conflicts. Also, the function name has its own code segment in the EXE. If you used only four characters, FoxPro would not be able to find the code and data segments.

The second item is the C function name that FoxPro will call when it encounters *MY_FUNC()*.

The third item is the maximum number of parameters that will be passed up to the function from FoxPro. You need not pass this many parameters each time, but cannot pass more than this number, or FoxPro will give an error. The number of parameters is necessary for FoxPro to build the Parameter Block that is passed to your function.

You can also substitute some FoxPro-specific macros for the number of parameters, for example:

#define INTERNAL	-1	Not called by FoxPro
#define CALLONLOAD	-2	Called when Library opened
#define CALLONUNLOAD	-3	Called when Library closed

Finally, the fourth item is information on the type of parameters that will be passed. Parameters fall into the following categories:

C	Character
I	Number (Integer)
N	Number (any other type)
D	Date
L	Logical
?	Free format, any data type

Unless you are 100% sure of the data type required by your routine, always use the "?" so your function can use any data type that's passed up. All syntax checking should be done within your C program.

Any combination of parameter types can be passed. In Listing 15-1, the first parameter must be a character type, and the second any type of parameter.

These parameters are used by FoxPro for creating the Parameter Block that is passed to the library, and also for a Level 1 syntax check. This means that FoxPro can check the parameters in your call prior to the call being made, which is very useful.

Foxtable Table

This table is for FoxPro's internal use.

When you issue the command *SET LIBRARY TO Lib_name (Additive)*, it is possible to have more than one library active at a time. FoxPro looks for the named .PLB file, then searches for the relevant tables mentioned above. The names and function name pointers are loaded into FoxPro's internal symbol table. You can display the names of the functions in the library by typing at the Command window:

```
Set Library to My_lib
Disp Status
```

At the end of the status listing will be a list of the functions in the function library.

To recap, you should now know the rough outline of how FoxPro 2.0 uses an API library, and how to set up the routines in the library for FoxPro to be able to access them. What I have not done is actually build a function. So...on to the next section.

Building Blocks (Functions)

To build a function correctly, you need to know two things. First, how to read the parameters (if any) passed up by FoxPro to your function. Second, how to return a value, if necessary, to FoxPro. Without these you would be able to process only a C program that worked internally, but did not use anything from FoxPro or pass anything back for FoxPro to use later. This would be an inherent waste of time!

Always write your functions in two parts: a FoxPro part and a C part. One part will deal with reading parameters from FoxPro and writing to those parameters, or passing values back. The other part will contain the actual function code. The function should be written like normal C code. Then, if the calling convention changes, you need only change that part of the code, and not the entire function library. (This also lets you move towards object-oriented and event-driven programming. By splitting the parameter unloading and loading, you are already thinking in terms of events and objects. It's more a state of mind than a methodology.)

Reading Parameters

Parameters are read from FoxPro by means of the Parameter Block (ParamBlk), which is constructed internally by FoxPro, and a pointer to it that's passed to your function by FoxPro. All FoxPro functions are declared in C with one parameter, and with a pointer to the Parameter Block. For example:

```
My_func(ParamBlk FAR *paramblk)
{
}
```

The parameter block is a union of two structures. It lets you find the following information:

- The number of parameters passed up
- The data types of the parameters
- The values of the parameters
- If the parameters were passed by reference or by value. (If passed by reference, you can write values back to these parameters.)

For each parameter passed up, there will be a value structure, which holds information on the datatype and the value of the parameter, and a locator structure, which holds information on the status of the parameter.

The Value Structure

The value structure tells you the datatype, C, N, I, D or L; the width (for a number); the length (or number of decimal places for a number); and the value.

ev_type	This tells the data type (C,N,I,D,L)
ev_width	Numeric display width
ev_length	String length for character variables, logical value, or number of decimal places for numeric
ev_long	Value for integer
ev_real	Value for number and date
ev_handle	Memory handle for character type

Memory handles are the way that FoxPro handles memory. All character parameters are accessed via a memory handle. The parameter's value is found by using the FoxPro API function *HandToPtr()*, which converts a memory handle to an actual character pointer that can be read from.

The Locator Structure

The locator structure tells if the parameter was passed by value or by reference, and if it is a memory variable or a field. If a field, it gives the number of the database containing this field, and the field number in the structure. If it's a memory variable, it will indicate if it is an array, and if so, whether it is a 1- or 2-dimensional array.

l_type	*R*, if passed by reference
l_where	Number of database, or –1 if a memory variable
l_NTI	The position of the parameter in the internal FoxPro symbol table
l_offset	If a field, the field number in the database
l_subs	If a memory variable, the number of subscripts:

0: memory variable

1: 1-dimensional array

2: 2-dimensional array

l_sub1: 1st dimension setting

l_sub2: 2nd dimension setting

The use of the *l_sub* elements are as follows. *l_sub* tells the type of variable. If it's an array, it will be set to greater than 0. To read the first element, set *l_sub1* to 1, and read the associated value structure. To read element 1,2 (second subscript, element 1), set *l_sub1* to 1 and *l_sub2* to 2, and read the associated value structure. To determine the number of array elements passed, FoxPro has supplied the *_Alen()* function.

The C program "Foxpara.c," which is included on the disk that accompanies this book, shows the use of these structures. This program is a higher-level set of C calls that determine the type and size of the parameters passed up from FoxPro.

Returning Values

The FoxPro API has a complete set of methods for returning values to FoxPro. They are:

_RetChar()	Returns a character string.
_RetInt()	Returns a integer value.
_RetFloat()	Returns a double precision number.
_RetDateStr()	Returns a character as a date in the format 'mm/dd/yyyy.'
_RetLogical()	Returns a logical value: 0 for false, 1 for true.
_RetVal()	Returns a Value structure.

Except for *_RetVal()*, these routines are self explanatory. They are obviously easier for the simple function call, for example, returning the fourth character in a given string. If you are writing a series of functions geared towards a given subject, say for a communications library, it is best to have one return function that all your routines can use. In this situation, use the *_RetVal()* function.

The most important function is *_RetVal()*. It enables you to pass back any data type in your own value structure. Although more cumbersome at first, it is by far the most flexible.

_RetVal() allows your API routine to return a whole value structure. It is your responsibility to fill the value structure correctly before calling the function. The advantage is that you can return any FoxPro data type (except memo) through one function call.

For example, to return an integer value, such as the position of a character in a string, see Listing 15-2 (Pseudo-ish Code).

Listing 15-2. Returning a value structure.

```
Fox_at(ParamBlk FAR *parm)
{
Value FAR *val; /* Pointer for Structure */
int count=0;
find the position of the string, place in count;

/***********************
Build a Value Structure
***********************/
val = _Alloca(sizeof(Value)); /* Declare the structure */
val->ev type = 'I';           /* Integer               */
val->ev_long = (long)count;   /* value for count       */
_retVal(val);                 /* Give it to Fox        */
return;
}
```

To return a character string, you must use the FoxPro memory functions to allocate a memory handle, copy the string to the memory pointed to by that handle, and place the handle in the value structure. If you want to pass back a character string with embedded nulls, you must use *_RetVal()*, because the *_RetChar()* function assumes a null terminated string.

The final thing you need to know about parameters is how many were passed up. This is achieved very simply by the pCount element of the ParamBlk structure. For example:

```
void FAR my_func(ParamBlk *parm)
{
int para_count;
para_count = parm->pcount;  /* Number of Parameters */
return;
}
```

You should now know how to pass parameters to FoxPro; how to discover information on these parameters, such as datatypes, lengths, and values; and how to return information from your routine back to FoxPro. But there's one more thing you need to know about before you can do anything really useful: memory allocation.

Memory Allocation

Most APIs handle memory allocation so as to use the application's own memory, rather than using direct calls to the operating system. If you were to allocate memory outside the main application, you could well cause conflicts that lead to system crashes and worse.

So how do you allocate memory? FoxPro has two methods. The first is for temporary storage, and the second for more permanent storage.

_Alloca()

The *_Alloca()* function allocates memory from FoxPro's internal stack. The allocation will exist until your routine returns to FoxPro. At that point all memory allocated via this function is released. This is useful for creating a string to be passed back to FoxPro, or for temporary "buffer" space. *_Alloca()* should *never* be used to allocate memory that will be used by your routine after returning to FoxPro (say on a secondary call to your library).

The syntax for *_Alloca()* is as follows:

```
_Alloca(unsigned int size)
```

If you wanted to return a library version, the code might look like Listing 15-3.

Listing 15-3. Use of _Alloca()

```
void FAR Lib_ver(ParamBlk FAR *parm)
{
   char FAR *libver;
   if ((libver = _Alloca(12)) == 0) /* Failed */
      _RetLogical(FALSE);
   else
      {
```

```
            _StrCpy(libver, (char FAR *)"Version 1.0");
            _RetChar(libver);
        }
    return;
}
```

Here we've allocated enough memory to hold the required string, and tested for the successful execution of the function. If FoxPro is unable to allocate this much memory, it will return a *(char FAR *)0*. In this example, this would give me great cause for concern! As you can see, we do not free this memory; it is automatically freed when we return to FoxPro.

Coupled with *_Alloca()* is an inquiry function, *_StackAvail()*, which allows you to find out how much memory is available.

_StackAvail()

_StackAvail() returns the total amount of memory available to be allocated by an external routine. Taking the above example, we could have written Listing 15-4.

Listing 15-4. Use of _StackAvail()

```
void  FAR   Lib_ver(ParamBlk  FAR*parm)
{
    unsigned int memreq = 12 + 1024;    /* Required Stack Space*/
    char FAR *libver;
    if (_StackAvail() < memreq)         /* Not enough memory */
        _RetLogical(FALSE);
    else
        {
            libver = _Alloca(memreq -1024);  /* This will work */
            _StrCpy(libver, (char FAR *)"Version 1.0");
            _RetChar(libver);
        }
    return;
}
```

You will notice that we have added 1K to the required amount. This is to guard against losing the stack if we perform a *Call Back* routine, such as *_Execute*. If you perform a FoxPro *Call Back*, FoxPro needs to hold onto its stack information, and this requires 1K. When allocating from the stack space, always add 1K to your requirement, before checking with _StackAvail().

The second method for allocating memory is for memory that will be needed when you move between FoxPro and our library. There are times when you may need to allocate a large chunk of memory, and hold onto it between function calls. For example, a *Linked* list holds a pointer to the start of the list, or the current position in the list. In this case, you want FoxPro to keep the memory in "real" memory. To do this, you lock the handle (in the same way you lock a file), so FoxPro can't reorganize this memory. When you are locking memory, observe these rules:

1. Make sure the memory is not locked for longer than necessary
2. Lock only the smallest possible amount of memory

This way, the application is not being greedy with memory space.

How do you accomplish this with FoxPro? Fox Software has gone to a great deal of trouble to give developers a good use of memory management. The functions provided are as follows:

_AllocHand()	Allocate a handle
_FreeHand()	Free a handle
_HandToPtr()	Convert a handle to a pointer (activate memory)
_GetHandSize()	Find the size of a memory handle
_SetHandSize()	Resize a memory handle
_HLock()	Lock a handle
_HUnLock()	Unlock a memory handle

_AllocHand()

The syntax is as follows:

```
_AllocHand(unsigned int hsize)
```

where *hsize* is the size of the memory you want.

_AllocHand() is used in the same way as *_Alloca()*. If it is not possible to allocate the memory, *_AllocHand()* returns a *null* (defined as *(Long)0)*. If it is successful, it returns a new *MHANDLE* (the FoxPro definition for a memory handle) to identify that memory. However, this memory is not yet available for use. Here's an example:

```
{
MHANDLE m_hand;
unsigned int m_size = 20000;  /* 20,000 bytes */

if ((m_hand = _AllocHand(m_size)) == NULL) /* Failed */
   _RetLogical(FALSE);
}
```

_FreeHand()

_FreeHand() is the opposite of *_AllocHand()*. It is used to free a handle no longer required by our library.

_HandToPtr()

This converts a memory handle to some usable memory. *_HandToPtr* returns a pointer to real memory. Let's assume that you have passed up a character string from FoxPro, and want to find the *nth* byte in that string. See Listing 15-5. The byte you want is passed up as the second parameter.

Listing 15-5. Use of _HandToPtr()

```
void FAR find_byte(ParamBlk FAR *parm)
{
char FAR *string, result[2];
int m_byte;
MHANDLE handle, mHand;
unsigned int m_len;

m_len = parm->p[0].val.ev_length;       /* Length of string  */
handle = parm->p[0].val.ev_handle;      /* Get the Handle    */
m_byte = parm->p[1].val.ev_long;        /* Find which Byte   */
mHand = _AllocHand(m_len);
string = (char FAR *) _HandToPtr(mHand);
```

```
_MemMove(string, _HandToPtr(handle),m_len); /* Copy the string */
result[0] = getbyte(string, m_byte);    /* Call a 'C' function */
result[1] = '\0';     /* Return value must be null terminated.*/

_RetChar(result);                        /* Pass back to Fox    */
_FreeHand(mHand);
return;
}

char FAR *getbyte(char FAR *str, int byte)
{
   str+= byte -1;                 /* move str up byte bytes*/
   return(*str);
}
```

_GetHandSize()

This function allows us to find the size of memory being held by a given handle. In the example above, we found the size of the character variable passed up from C by the line:

```
m_len = parm->p[0].val.ev_length;
```

This could also have been achieved by a call to *_GetHandSize()*:

```
m_len = _GetHandSize(handle);
```

This function is most useful when you need to add to a memory block, say in building up a string *READ* from a comm port. In this situation you wouldn't necessarily know the total size required. So you could allocate a handle of a given size, say 2K, and check the size before writing to it. If the size is smaller than the total required, add a further 2K to it with *_SetHandSize()*.

_SetHandSize()

_SetHandSize() lets you change the size of the handle, if required. The syntax is as follows:

```
_SetHandSize(MHANDLE handle, unsigned int size)
```

The only constraint is that if the handle is locked, you must first unlock the handle, resize it, and lock again. This is similar to using files in a network environment, but in reverse. If *_SetHandSize()* is unable to resize to the requested level, it returns a *null*.

_HLock(), and _HUnlock()

These last two functions deal with locking and unlocking handles in memory. When a handle is created, or passed up from FoxPro, it defaults to being unlocked, so it can participate in memory re-organization. If you need to hold onto this memory, lock it using the *_HLock(handle)* call.

This is fairly straightforward. However, unless care is taken, it's possible to lock a chunk of memory and then remove the library from FoxPro's library list. This memory would remain locked throughout the application, until FoxPro itself was exited. There would be no way to release it. So *always* unlock all memory locked by your API.

It is advisable to have a linked list of handles, and a routine that is called when the library is unloaded that moves down the list, freeing all memory that has been allocated.

It should be noted that although the Memory routines "look" like a Virtual Memory Management system, at the moment they are not. All memory is allocated from Real Mode, and is not swapped to Extended/Expanded or disk.

FoxPro has supplied a series of memory movement routines to enable easy copying and moving of data. These are provided as alternatives to the Watcom C routines, and enable easy porting to other environments supported by FoxPro. The danger in using a compiler's internal functions is that they may use a different memory allocation method. (A classic example, printf(), uses *malloc()*, which is the biggest "no-no" in the book). By using the FoxPro routines, the API will port quicker to UNIX or Macintosh systems than if you use a specific compilers library functions. If Fox chooses a different compiler, they will still maintain these routines. Also, the Fox routines take the FAR keyword, which allows use of a "flat 32-bit" pointer (in extended memory) under Watcom 386, when FoxPro lets us run Libs in extended memory.

Where possible, you should use FoxPro's routines rather than the Watcom standard routines. For reference purposes, they are as follows:

_StrCpy()	Copy one string to another (NULL terminated)
_StrLen()	Find the length of a NULL terminated string
_StrCmp()	Compare two NULL terminated strings
_MemMove()	Copy *x* bytes from one pointer to another
_MemCmp()	Compare *x* bytes in two pointers
_MemFill()	Fill an area of *x* bytes with a character

This section has covered the basic building blocks of the FoxPro API. The documentation provided by Fox is worth reading to get a more in-depth grasp of the functions mentioned here. The header file supplied with the FoxPro API is also worth a look: It contains many hidden secrets.

The next section will discuss some of the more advanced features available to the API developer.

Objects and Events

Those who come this far in the FoxPro documentation may have discovered the warning that "...to make full use of the API you must have a full understanding of Event Driven Programming...."

Our intention is to remove some of this mystique, and introduce some of the functionality that is given to you, the API programmer. We'll start with some background on dbase languages' (including FoxPro) symbol tables and linked lists.

Symbol Tables

Symbol tables consist of names and pointers to values associated with them. Names can be memory variables or field names. They can also be databases, indexes, and other "objects" required to run the system. When you issue the command *"Use Invoices.Dbf,"* the name *Invoices* is added to a table of DBFs, and the fields are added to the table of names. Although there are variations on this theme, this is the underlying principle.

Linked Lists

A linked list is a chain of a specific type of information. It's usually held internally as a structure, a part of which will be a pointer to the next item in the list. There could also be a pointer to the previous item in the list. This is the way FoxPro handles arrays. For example, if you issue the command:

```
Declare My_array[10]
```

the internal language sets up a list of 10 structures, which could look like this:

```
{
char *value;          /* Pointer to value */
int datatype;         /* Data type of element */
long width;           /* Width of element */
int item;             /* Element number */
char *nextitem;       /* Next element or null if last */
char *previtem;       /* Previous element or null if first*/
}
```

The symbol table will have the name *My_arr* added to it, with a pointer to the first item in the list.

This is a fairly simple concept. It is also the way the dbase language can change the datatypes of elements of an array. In C a true array can't do this without some *very* intricate programming.

Event/Idle Drivers

With the concepts of symbol tables and linked lists in mind, if you look at event drivers, the event-driven approach falls into place.

FoxPro has two other symbol tables. First, a list of functions to perform if an event occurs, and second, a list of functions for when "nothing is going on." This second list is the "Idle Routines" list.

Events

An event is defined as a keystroke, a mouse movement, or a button press. When one of these events occurs, FoxPro looks to see where the cursor or mouse is on-screen, and goes to the top of the event list. Each item in the list is passed a pointer to an event record, as seen in Listing 15-6.

Listing 15-6. The FoxPro 2 event record.

```
typedef struct
{ unsigned short what;      /* Event code                  */
Ticks           when;       /* Ticks since startup         */
Point           where;      /* Mouse location              */
unsigned long   message;    /* Key/window                  */
unsigned long   misc;       /* Event dependant misc info   */
unsigned long   misc2;      /* Event dependant misc info   */
unsigned char   mbState;    /* Mouse buttons state         */
unsigned char   mcState;    /* Mouse cond activate state   */
unsigned short  modifiers;
} EventRec;
```

It is the responsibility of each "driver" in the list to determine if the event is related to it. If the driver says "Yes, I want that," which is usually determined by the Window handle (*WHANDLE*) of the window in which the event occurred, the driver will process the event and return a TRUE. If it does not require the event, it will return a FALSE. This tells the event-driving process whether to look for another event (TRUE), or to pass the event down the list.

You, as an API programmer, can create your own functions to use this concept. It is most useful for the user-interface aspect of an application, for your own windows. To use it effectively, create your function as follows:

```
FPFI my_event(WHANDLE whand, EventRec evrec)
```

This function will receive a *WHANDLE* of the Window in which the event occurred, and an event record. To add it to the list of event drivers you need to execute the function:

```
_ActivateHandler().
```

This function returns an "unsigned int," which is the identifier of the handler. This value is required to remove it from the list, so you should store it as a *GLOBAL*, or in your own linked list of handlers. I would suggest the linked list, as you could then have a routine that is called when the library is dropped from FoxPro that moves down this list, removing the handlers from the event list.

Add the handler to the linked list with the following:

```
unsigned int my_handler = _ActivateHandler((FPFI)my_event);
```

To remove it from the list, use the opposite function:

```
_DeActivateHandler(unsigned int my_hand)
```

(Strange, isn't it?). Once activated, the handler will receive messages from the internal FoxPro event process, and will be required to process them accordingly.

Idle Routines

Idle routines work in a similar way as event handlers. Each "tick" of the MS-DOS timer causes FoxPro to look and see if something occurred (an event). If nothing happens, FoxPro passes down a table of "idle" routines. These routines can be very useful.

One example would be if you had your own memory management, and it needed to perform "garbage collection" (the process of de-fragmenting memory). This is normally done when memory is freed. An idle routine could handle it when the system is doing nothing, which is more time efficient.

Another example is a communications interface. A byte coming down the comm port is not defined as an event, and this type of interface takes care of reading the comm port. When FoxPro hits a period of no activity, your routine could go and read the comm port, and process anything that occurs. (So yes, you can have E-mail coming in over a normal FoxPro application!)

The routines required for adding and removing an idle driver to the idle list are, surprisingly, as follows:

```
unsigned int _ActivateIdle(FPFI handler)
                                           /*handler is the function*/
void _DeActivateIdle(unsigned int)
```

So you activate with:

```
unsigned int m_idle;
m_idle = _ActivateIdle(FPFI my_idler);
```

and de-activate with:

```
_DeActivate((unsigned int)m_idle);
```

There's one other function I haven't mentioned yet. This is *_GetNextEvent()*. This function can be called from your API routine, to read the next event. However, great care must be taken, as this "branches" from the internal FoxPro controller.

Never call *_GetNextEvent()* from an idle routine. This would remove control from the internal FoxPro driver, and pass it to your routine. Control can't be passed back, so your library would stop working as designed.

Objects

Objects are defined as:

- Windows
- Menus
- Memory variables
- Databases

Be careful not to get confused with the OOP paradigm here. An *object*, as far as this section goes, is a *thing*. As an API programmer you have complete access to FoxPro objects. You can create and move windows; create menus and add them to the current menus, or have them as separate entities; create and resize memory variables; and perform all the functions on database files that you can perform from within FoxPro. You also have access to FoxPro's low-level file access routines.

For the purpose of this section, we'll look at the concepts behind handling Windows and Menus only.

Windows

Windows are some of the more versatile "hooks" into the API. As an API programmer you are given full control over the windowing aspect of FoxPro. It is strongly advised that you manage your windows via an event handler, as this fully integrates your routine into the FoxPro environment.

Here are the available window functions:

_WOpen()	Opens a window
_WFindWindow()	Finds a window for a given point on screen
_WOnTop()	Which window is on top?
_GlobalToLocal()	Translates a screen point to a window point
_WClose()	Closes a window
_WHide()	Hides a window
_WShow()	Shows a hidden window
_WZoom()	Zooms a given window
_WSelect()	Brings a window to the front
_WSendBehind()	Places a window to the rearmost position
_Wtitle()	Get the title of a given window
_WSetTitle()	Set the title of a given window
_WGetPort()	Which window currently allows user output?
_WSetPort()	Change the user-output window

There is a series of functions that cover the actions that can be taken on a given window. These will be covered later.

The *_WOpen()* function allows you to create a window. The parameters it requires are:

int top	Top row of window
int left	Left column of window
int bottom	Bottom row of window
int right	Right column of window
int Flag	Status flags of the window–see table below
int scheme_num	Color scheme number
Scheme FAR *scheme	Color scheme
char FAR *bord	Border type (see pro_ext.h)

FLAG Values are any combination of the following (these definitions are in pro_ext.h):

WCURSOR	The cursor is displayable in this window
ZOOM	The window can be zoomed
ADJ	The window can be re-sized
CLOSE	The user may close the window
MOVE	The user can move the window
AUTOSCROLL	Output to the window is scrollable
WEVENT	The window receives and activates Events
SHADOW	The window casts a shadow
WMODAL	The window can't be sent to the back
WMINIMIZE	The window can be minimized

The function returns the *WHANDLE* for this new window. This *WHANDLE* should be placed in a linked list, so you can check on its situation with the event handler, and also remove it when you unload the library. The power of the flag values mean that you can allow FoxPro to perform all the activations, without requiring routines of your own to handle each type of event. You can, however, write these routines yourself. For the purpose of this exercise we will allow FoxPro to handle the Events.

We will call our window "Display_window." In C we would issue the commands as in Listing 15-7.

Listing 15-7 Open a FoxPro window.

```
WHANDLE wind_hand;
wind_hand = _WOpen(02, 02, 10,15,              /* Co-ordinates    */
   WCURSOR|ZOOM|CLOSE|MOVE|WEVENT|             /* Flag Values     */
   |SHADOW|WMINIMISE,2,                        /* Color Scheme    */
   (char FAR *)0,                              /* No name needed  */
   WO_PANELBORDER)                             /* Standard border */
```

Listing 15-7 will create a window, and allow FoxPro to handle all the movements within it for us. As with the parameter passing mentioned earlier, FoxPro can perform a great deal of work for the API programmer, prior to making a call to the API routine.

Now set a title for the Window, using the *_WSetTitle()* function. See Listing 15- 8.

Listing 15-8. Adding a title to a window.

```
char FAR *title;                          /* Declarator          */
title = _Alloca(15);                      /* Give it some memory */
_StrCpy(title, (char FAR *)"Display Window", 13); /* Copy title */
_WSetTitle(wind_hand, title);             /* Set the title       */
```

We now have a window that has been fully activated, titled, and added to the list of windows that FoxPro needs to maintain. It is that simple.

By adding the handle to an internal linked list, when our event handler is called, it can scan down that list until it finds the relevant handle, and pass this on to the required function. If the handle that is passed to the event handler does not exist in our list, the event handler can reject the event.

To close the window, call *_WClose()*, passing the *WHANDLE* that you want to close. In this case that would be:

```
_WClose(wind_hand);
```

If you had placed this in a linked list, you will need to remove it from the list.

There is a full set of commands to navigate, process information within the window (scrolling, clearing lines, and so on), and to output data to a window. Data can be output with the *_WPutChr*, (meaning "write one character"), or *_WPutStr* ("write a NULL-terminated string"). Unfortunately, this is a subject worth two chapters on its own.

Note: When your window is called, if it is not set at the current User Output Window, determined by the *_WGetPort()* function, you will need to reset the User Output Window with *_WSetPort()* before returning to FoxPro. For example, see Listing 15-9.

Listing 15-9. Swapping output windows.

```
void FAR window_proc(WHANDLE wh)  /* Called from Event Handler */
   {
   WHANDLE save_hand;             /* Save Window Handle   */
   if (_WGetPort() != wh)         /* Not Current Output   */
      {
      save_hand = _WGetPort();    /* Save Current Output */
      _WSetPort(wh);              /* Make ours the Output */
      }

      Do some processing;

      _WSetPort(save_hand);       /* Reset Output Window */
      return;
   }
```

Menus

FoxPro menus are handled in much the same way as the rest of the API. Hooks are available to create, activate, de-activate, and "tag" into system menus. Any standard FoxPro menu can be created: PAD, BAR, or POPUP, through the API. As with windows, the menus are identified by a *MENUID* (*WHANDLE* with Windows). This is a "typecast" that exists in pro_ext.h.

Perhaps the most interesting aspect behind the menus section of the API is the ability to add a menu to the FoxPro System menu. In this way your API routine can be made to look like a part of the FoxPro package.

Let's take a look at some of the basic menu functions:

_GetNewMenuid()	Returns a new menuid
_GetNewItemId()	Returns an itemid for a menu item
_NewMenu()	Creates a menu
_DisposeMenu()	Removes a menu
_MenuId()	Returns menuid of a system menu
_NewItem()	Creates a new item for the menu
_DisposeItem()	Removes an item from the menu
_SetMenuPoint()	Override position of menu
_SetItemText()	Sets the text for an item
_GetItemText()	Gets the text for an item
_OnSelection()	Function to execute when item selected
_ActivateMenu()	Activate a menu
_MenuInteract()	Work menu

As you can see, this is a fairly rich set of functions. Let's see how you can use them. As an example (a simple one), we will create a pulldown menu (BAR menu) that is called "Maintain." (See Listing 15-11.) It will have three options—Add, Change, Delete—and will be added to the system menu. As with windows, you will need to hold on to the menu and item IDs. This is best done in a linked list, under normal circumstances. Each structure in the list could look like in Listing 15-10.

Listing 15-10. Example menu structure.

```
struct {
   MENUID menu_id;
   ITEMID item_id;
   FPFI funct;               /* Function for this menu */
   struct FAR *next_item;    /* Points to next item */
   struct FAR *next_menu;    /* Points to next menu */
   }MY_MENUS;
```

To keep the code clear, we will not use this structure, but for normal API work, information on your menus should be held in a list of structures, to enable the easy removal of menus options from the system menu bar.

The *_ActivateMenu()* function displays the menu. Control is returned immediately to the calling program. *_MenuInteract* is the function that operates the menu. The *save_item* value is set to the initial selection, and the selected item is returned into *found_item.*

Although Listing 15-11 is a simple example of a menu, it should give you a good starting point to creating your own menus, from within the API. By careful use of the API routines, and the event drivers, you can build complex menu systems that will effectively call your API library routines.

The *_ActivateMenu()* function displays the menu. Control is returned immediately to the calling program. *_MenuInteract* is the function that operates the menu. The *save_item* value is set to the initial selection, and the selected item is returned into *found_item.*

Although Listing 15-11 is a simple example of a menu, it should give you a good starting point to creating your own menus, from within the API. By careful use of the API routines, and the event drivers, you can build complex menu systems that will effectively call your API library routines.

Listing 15-11. Basic menu creation.

```
#include "pro_ext.h"
void FAR *my_menu()             /* Creative naming conventions */
   {
```

```
MenuId system_id;              /* System Menu id */
MenuId menu_id;                /* Menu id */
ItemId item[3];                /* Item ids for each item */
int found_item;                /* Selected Item or Error */
int save_item;                 /* Default Selection */
system_id = _Menuid(_SYSMENU);/* System Menu ID */
menu_id  = _GetNewMenu();      /* Our Menu ID */

if ((_NewMenu(MPOPUP, menu_id)) != 0) /* Create new menu */
_Error(Menu_error)

/* Now create the Items */
for (i = 1; i<=3 ; i++)
{
item[i] = _GetNewItemId(menu_id);
_NewItem(menu_id, item[i]
{
   case 1:
      ret_val=_NewItem(menu_id,item[i],(char FAR*)"Add");
      _SetItemCmdKey(menu_id, item[i], 23,(char FAR *)"");
      save_item = item[i];  /* Need this for default */
   break;
   case 2:
      ret_val=_NewItem(menu_id,item[i],(char FAR*)
                                              "Change");
      _SetItemCmdKey(menu_id, item[i], 24,(char FAR *)"");
   break;
   case 3:
      ret_val = _NewItem(menu_id, item[i],-2, (char FAR *)
                                              "Delete");
      _SetItemCmdKey(menu_id, item[i], 25,(char FAR *)"");
   break;
   case 4:
      ret_val = _NewItem(menu_id, item[i],-2, (char FAR *)
                                                "Quit");
      _SetItemCmdKey(menu_id, item[i], 26,(char FAR *)"");
   break;
   default:
      ret_val = _NewItem(menu_id, item[i],-2, (char FAR *)
                                             "Default");
```

```
        _SetItemCmdKey(menu_id, item[i], 27,(char FAR *)"");

      break;
      }

   _SetItemSubMenu(sys_id, item[i], menu_id); /* Set up option */

   }

/*-----------------------------------------------------------
   Activate Menu
   save_item holds new value of selected item
   found_item holds return value
-------------------------------------------------------------*/
   _ActivateMenu(menu_id);               /* Sets the menu up */
   found_item=_MenuInteract(&menu_id, &save_item);
                                      /* FoxPro takes control */
   if (save_item < 0)
      _Error(save_item);
    }
   }
 }
```

Converting Clipper API to Fox API

The major difference between the Clipper and FoxPro 2 APIs is in the added functionality of the Fox API. Clipper allows you to read and return parameters, store values to a parameter passed up by reference, and allocate memory from Clipper internal pool. Outside this, the C programmer is left to his or her own devices. Fox allows the same flexibility, as well as providing hooks to the other sections of the package: windows, menus, databases, and so on. For the purpose of this short section, we will look at the functions you will need to change to make your C code work with Fox.

Declarations

Clipper functions are declared as type *CLIPPER*, and preprocessed to the native *void PASCAL*. Fox functions are of type *void far*. An easy transformation would be to include the following in your header file:

```
#ifdef CLIPPER
   #undef CLIPPER
   #define CLIPPER (void far)
#endif
#define x() x(ParamBlk FAR * parm) /* Careful though! */
```

This will allow the preprocessor to set the function declaration correctly, without changing the actual code.

Parameters

The Fox parameter access method is a level below that of Clippers's *_parxx()*, *_retxx()*, and *_storxx()* functions. The program FEXTOR.C, which is provided on the source code disk available with the book, mimics the Clipper function calls.

Returning Values

You can use straight one-for-one substitutions for returning values, as shown below. Or your can "roll your own," using the *_RetVal()* function to reduce code size.

```
Clipper          FoxPro 2

_ret()         Nothing needed
_retc()           _RetChar()
_retni()          _RetInt()
_retnl()          _RetInt()
_retl()           _RetLogical ()
_retclen()        _RetVal() - using a Char type.
```

The Clipper Extor functions are replaced by the Fox *_Store()* function, which also requires a Value structure and the correct setting of a locator. You can replicate the Clipper *_parxx()* functions for reading parameters by using the Value structure passed up in the Param Block.

Memory Management

FoxPro handles memory management differently than Clipper does. The Fox API uses a VM-type system, whereas Clipper currently uses a memory-pool system. You will probably need to change your memory access modules to deal with this. With Fox, you can allocate temporary stack storage by using the *_Alloca()* function. This memory is only active while the function is being performed, and it is released automatically on exit. There is no equivalent in Clipper.

Parameter–Type Macros

Clipper's *_parinfo/_parinfa* functions can all be substituted by using the *ev_type* and length members of the Value structure. The *_Parinfo(0)* function, which returns the total number of parameters passed, is substituted by *parm->pcount*.

The major drawback of the Fox API is that it can't pass up a variable number of parameters. With the Fox API, you must declare the parameter types and numbers in the Foxinfo structure. To pass up a variable number of parameters, it is best to use a two-dimensional array.

In Summary

In this chapter, you have seen how to build a base API routine, how to pass parameters to and from FoxPro, and have had a brief look at memory handling, event/idle drivers, and windows and menus.

Aside from these it is also possible to create and size memory variables, directly access fields in databases, access points on the screen where the mouse is, and use low-level file access. These topics would cover a book on their own, so my best advise to you is..."Crack open the API, play with the simple ideas first, then look into the header file, and read the documentation."

With a bit of imagination, and some application, you should soon be making FoxPro do things that you never dreamt possible. And one last point: Never ask "Why can't I do...?," because the answer is "You can!"

CHAPTER 16

The FoxPro API and Assembler

by Ted Means

FoxPro is more than a database system; it also includes a rich set of low-level functions that you can access programmatically from your own applications. The mechanism for accessing these functions is the API, or Applications Programming Interface. There are many ways to access an API; the most common approach is to write C code that calls API functions. However, assembly language is more efficient in some situations. In this chapter we'll look at how you can use assembly language to interact with the FoxPro 2.0 external routine API. We won't cover the use of C or the individual routines that make up the API; both topics are discussed elsewhere in this book. A working knowledge of both assembly language and FoxPro is assumed.

The examples in this chapter were written for version 2.0 of Borland's Turbo Assembler. Because code can be ported from one assembler to another with very little difficulty, however, you can use any commercial assembler (such as Microsoft Assembler or SLR Systems' OPTASM). An excellent shareware assembler called A86 can also be used to write API routines.

Why Assembler?

FoxPro is written in C, and the API is designed to use C calling conventions and data types. So why would you use assembly language instead of C?

The most obvious reason, of course, is performance. C programmers are fond of calling C a "high-level assembler" and question the sanity and motives of anyone who actually uses assembler. C is versatile and widely used, but it is definitely *not* a high-level assembler. If you've ever examined the code generated by a C compiler, you know it tends to be larger and slower than that produced by a good assembler programmer. C has its place, but a RAM-hungry product like FoxPro will benefit from small, efficient routines that make few demands on system resources.

Another reason for using assembly language is its low-level nature. The API opens the door to a wide array of tasks that otherwise would be difficult or impossible to accomplish with FoxPro. Some of these tasks, however, require low-level access to the hardware or operating system that C is ill-equipped to provide. Interrupt handlers, serial communications, access to I/O ports, and various hardware interfaces are all best handled with assembly language. Assembler's low-level nature also offers tremendous flexibility. C's portability is largely a myth—one need only look at the FoxPro API for proof. The only C compiler that can be used to write API routines for FoxPro is Watcom's; FoxPro was written in Watcom C, and other C compilers produce incompatible code (although you can make the API work with other compilers with some additional programming). Turbo C and Microsoft C, for example, use a stack-based calling convention (all parameters are passed on the stack). Watcom C uses a "hybrid" calling convention—parameters are passed in CPU registers whenever possible and on the stack only when absolutely necessary. Assembly language doesn't suffer from this lack of compiler compatibility. Since the programmer is in complete control, routines can be tailored to comply with any calling convention.

API Overview

The FoxPro 2.0 API is a huge improvement over .BIN files. Whereas .BIN files have been retained solely for the dubious sake of dBASE compatibility, the API is a complete set of tools that enriches FoxPro tremendously. The very nature of .BIN files imposes all sorts of limitations, while the API is almost completely open and allows unprecedented access to FoxPro's services.

With the API you can call external routines as though they're internal to FoxPro, pass arguments and receive return values, access FoxPro's memory-management subsystem, use FoxPro's file and record I/O routines, create and access memory variables and arrays, use FoxPro's rich set of user-interface tools, execute FoxPro commands, evaluate FoxPro expressions, install event handlers, and much more. All these tasks are performed via the many routines and data structures that make up the API.

Using these tools does take some work, however. Calling an external routine from FoxPro isn't simply a matter of writing the routine and then linking it into your application, as with other languages. FoxPro is a complex product in which applications may be run in a variety of interpretive and compiled environments. The API must be able to accommodate these different and sometimes conflicting platforms. For example, an external routine that uses the API properly will run under both standard and extended FoxPro and will work the same whether the application is interpreted, a compact .EXE file, or a stand-alone .EXE file. A little extra programming effort is a small price to pay for such tremendous flexibility.

Once an external routine has been developed, it must be included in a library before FoxPro can use it. A library in FoxPro 2.0 is somewhat different from a library in another language. In most languages, a library is simply a convenient medium for storing one or more object files, which are combined with other object and library files at link time to produce an executable file. A FoxPro library, on the other hand, contains no object files. It has the same structure and form as a normal .EXE file but is usually given the extension .PLB. The different extension points out that this file is of little use as a stand-alone executable (if you're curious, rename a .PLB file with the extension .EXE and try to execute it from the DOS command line). The .PLB file is then loaded dynamically at run time (or from the command window) using the *SET LIBRARY TO* command.

Why did Fox choose the .PLB format instead of using more conventional .LIB files? This information has not been made public, so one can only speculate. One possible answer might be the problem of unresolved symbols. As you may know, a .LIB file is simply a group of .OBJ files that have been grouped together for easy access. Since .OBJ files may contain references to public symbols that may be located in other .LIB or .OBJ files, the possibility exists that those files would not be available when FoxPro tried to load a library. By using .PLB files instead (which are merely renamed .EXE files) FoxPro is guaranteed that all external references have been resolved.

Perhaps another reason for choosing .PLB files is that if .LIB files were used, FoxPro would have to perform a link each and every time a library was loaded. As you know, .LIB and .OBJ files can contain many other things besides executable code–data, constants, comments, information for the linker, and so on. The job of a linker is to sort through all the items in a .LIB or .OBJ and hold onto only those that are needed to produce an executable. If FoxPro were to try to dynamically load a .LIB file, it would have to perform a link in order to generate executable code. This would undoubtedly have a detrimental effect on FoxPro's performance. Since a .PLB file is already in executable form, this problem is avoided.

Once the library has been loaded, the functions it contains may be called as if they were native FoxPro functions. FoxPro goes so far as to verify the data types of any arguments and will generate a run-time error if an invalid argument is passed. Once the function has completed its task, it typically returns a value of some sort, much like user-defined functions written in FoxPro.

Developing an External-Routine Library

The cornerstone of any external-routine library is a data structure called __FoxTable (Figure 16-1). This structure, which must be declared as a public symbol, contains the information FoxPro needs to make the functions in the library available. Included in __FoxTable are such things as the number of functions in the library and a pointer to a table that contains their names, their addresses, and the number and data types of any arguments they expect. When an attempt is made to invoke a function in the library, FoxPro uses the information in __FoxTable to verify arguments and locate the function in memory.

```
Struc     FoxTable
NextLib      DD ?
FuncCount    DW ?
InfoPtr      DD ?

Ends FoxTable
```

Figure 16-1. The __FoxTable structure.

The *NextLib* field is for FoxPro's internal use. If more than one library is in use at a time, FoxPro maintains a linked list to keep track of them using this field. *NextLib* should be initialized to zero and then left alone. The *FuncCount* field informs FoxPro of the number of functions in the library, and *InfoPtr* is a far pointer to a table containing data about each function.

The table to which *InfoPtr* points is made up of one or more FoxInfo structures (Figure 16-2), one for each function in the library. Each structure contains information on the function and the arguments it expects to receive.

```
Struc     FoxInfo
FuncName     DD ?
FuncPtr      DD ?
PCount    DW ?
PTypes    DD ?

Ends FoxInfo
```

Figure 16-2. FoxInfo structure.

The purpose of the *FuncName* field should be fairly obvious: It contains a far pointer to the name that will be used in FoxPro to invoke the function. The name must be uppercase, may not be longer than 10 characters, and must be null-terminated. The *FuncPtr* field is a far pointer to the actual function. *PCount* identifies the number of parameters the function expects to receive. Finally, the *PTypes* field contains a far pointer to a null-terminated string that describes the data types of the parameters.

Both __FoxTable and the table of FoxInfo structures must be stored in a data segment, which must be included in DGROUP. The data segment may also contain any data items needed by the functions in the library. For example, your functions may need to use other data structures provided by the API. These structures may be stored in the same data segment as __FoxTable and the table of FoxInfo structures.

If all this sounds a bit confusing, perhaps an example will help clarify the issue. Say you want to create a library consisting of two functions, *ThisFunc()* and *ThatFunc()*. *ThisFunc()* accepts two parameters, a string and an integer. *ThatFunc()* expects to receive three parameters: a numeric, a date, and a logical. The data segment for this library might look like Figure 16-3.

```
Struc       FoxInfo
FuncName    DD   ?
FuncPtr     DD   ?
PCount      DW   ?
PTypes      DD   ?
Ends FoxInfo

Struc       FoxTable
NextLib     DD   ?
FuncCnt     DW   ?
InfoPtr     DD   ?
EndsFoxTable

Public      __FoxTable          ; Must be public

Group       DGROUP   _Sample

Segment     _Sample   Word   Public    "DATA"

PList01     DB   "C,I",0        ; Param list for ThisFunc()
PList02     DB   "N,D,L",0"     ; Param list for ThatFunc()
Name01      DB   "THISFUNC",0  ; FoxPro name for ThisFunc()
Name02      DB   "THATFUNC",0  ; FoxPro name for ThatFunc()

FuncList FoxInfo <far ptr Name01, ThisFunc, 2, far ptr PList01>

FoxInfo <far ptr Name02, ThatFunc, 3, far ptr PList02>

__FoxTable      FoxTable <0, 2, far ptr FuncList>

EndsSample
```

Figure 16-3. FoxPro data segment for a library.

Note that if *ThisFunc()* and *ThatFunc()* aren't in the same source file as the data segment, the *EXTRN* pseudo-operation will need to declare them (this also means *ThisFunc()* and *ThatFunc()* must be public symbols). Since modularity isn't an issue with FoxPro libraries—once a *SET LIBRARY TO* command is issued, all functions in the library are available—all functions should be placed in the same source file as the data segment. This eliminates the need for *EXTRN* and reduces the number of public symbols. If you prefer separate source files because they make modifications easier, consider using the *INCLUDE* pseudo-op to combine the files at the time of assembly. You'll get the best of both worlds—the source files are still separate, but *INCLUDE* obviates the need for *EXTRN* and public symbols.

Also note that the FoxInfo and _FoxTable structures were defined in the source code. This is not strictly necessary since the Library Construction Kit contains *INCLUDE* files that declare these structures for you. The *INCLUDE* files were designed for Microsoft Assembler, so if another assembler is used the *INCLUDE* files will have to be modified.

As you can see, building the data segment is a simple, straightforward process. However, it must be done carefully and accurately. FoxPro uses the information in __FoxTable to locate the functions in the library; any error in the setup of __FoxTable or the table of FoxInfo structures is likely to result in a library that doesn't function properly.

Setting up the data segment correctly is important, but equally important is writing the functions that make up the library. Here the rules are simpler. Each function must be declared as a *FAR* procedure (in other words, it must return via an *RETF* instruction) and must restore any registers it alters. If callbacks—documented FoxPro services defined as part of the API—are used, the SS and DS registers must be restored before the callback is invoked. Callback routines preserve all registers except AX and ES. If these registers contain needed values, be sure to preserve them before invoking callbacks.

Several aspects of library development deserve further attention: FoxPro memory management, passing parameters from FoxPro, invoking callbacks, and returning results to FoxPro.

FoxPro Memory Management

FoxPro's sophisticated memory manager does everything it can to optimize the use of available memory. Unlike traditional memory managers, FoxPro can reorganize memory whenever necessary. For example, suppose you start out with 40 KB of available memory and allocate three 10-KB strings. FoxPro will probably allocate three contiguous chunks of memory to hold the strings. Suppose the second string is deallocated. Now 20 KB of memory is available, but it's not contiguous; if you try to store a 15-KB string, the allocation will fail. FoxPro's memory manager avoids this problem by reorganizing memory so that as much of it as possible is contiguous.

As you might imagine, this scheme makes traditional pointer-based memory-management techniques useless. With other memory managers, dynamic memory allocation is simply a matter of allocating the RAM and keeping a record of its location. With FoxPro, this isn't feasible. Because memory may be reorganized at any time, FoxPro will likely relocate the allocated RAM and thus invalidate the pointer. Obviously, we need another way to control the use of allocated memory.

FoxPro's designers supplied just such a method. When a chunk of memory is allocated, FoxPro gives it a numeric identifier known as a *handle*. Any time that memory needs to be used, deallocated, or otherwise accessed, you reference the handle instead of a pointer. The memory manager examines the handle to find out where the memory it references is located, allowing FoxPro to reorganize memory as necessary and maintain the actual addresses internally.

The implications for the API are important but not very difficult to grasp. Simply remember that you must use a handle instead of a pointer. The only exception is when you need to write to or read from the memory referenced by a handle. In this case, the memory manager provides the necessary services (a function called *_HandToPtr_*) to translate the handle into an actual memory address.

Extreme care is needed to avoid memory corruption. For example, say you translate a handle to a pointer, execute a callback, and then attempt to write to the pointer previously obtained. With very few exceptions, FoxPro reserves the right to reorganize memory whenever it has control, and it may have done so during the callback. The pointer in this case has become invalid, and writing to that address will probably corrupt memory.

You can avoid this problem by locking the memory handle. FoxPro doesn't allow locked handles to participate in memory reorganization, so any pointers associated with locked handles will remain valid. Because locked handles reduce the amount of RAM available to FoxPro, this technique should be used only when necessary and only for as long as necessary.

The FoxPro API provides a full set of tools for allocating, sizing, locking, unlocking, and deallocating memory handles. Consult your FoxPro documentation for further details.

Passing Parameters from FoxPro

One of the more powerful features of the API is that it lets you write functions that accept passed parameters. This is a far cry from the days of .BIN files, which were extremely limited in this respect. With the API you can pass any number of parameters of any data type. FoxPro automatically enforces parameter checking, and the wrong number of parameters or those of the wrong data type will generate a run-time error.

FoxPro can do this because the __FoxTable structure contains the number of parameters the function expects to receive. FoxPro simply compares this number with the number of parameters that were actually passed. In addition, the FoxInfo structure contains a list of valid data types; FoxPro uses this list to determine whether or not any invalid parameters have been passed. The valid data types are:

C Character string

N Floating-point numeric

I Integer

D Date

L Logical

R Passed by reference

? Any of the above

Any of these types may be preceded by a period to indicate that the parameter is optional.

Parameters are easy to access from your assembler routines. When FoxPro passes control to an assembler function, DX:AX contains a pointer to a 16-bit integer representing the number of parameters passed (analogous to the *Parameters()* function in FoxPro). This value is only useful if your function allows optional parameters; otherwise, FoxPro will transfer control to the assembler function only when the correct number of parameters have been passed. If your function doesn't allow optional parameters, you may safely ignore the parameter-count value.

Immediately following the parameter count is an array of parameter blocks, one for each passed parameter. If the parameter was passed by value, the parameter block will contain a Value structure (see Figure 16-4); if it was passed by reference, the block will contain a Locator structure (Figure 16-5).

```
Struc      Value
DataType   DB   ?
Filler     DB   ?
Width      DW   ?
Length     DW   ?
LongInt    DD   ?
Double     DQ   ?
Handle     DW   ?

EndsValue
```

Figure 16-4. Value structure.

```
Struc      Locator
DataType   DB   ?
Where      DW   ?
NTI        DW   ?
LOffset    DW   ?
Subs       DW   ?
Sub1       DW   ?
Sub2       DW   ?
Filler     DB   7 dup (?)

EndsLocator
```

Figure 16-5. Locator structure.

In the Value structure, the *DataType* field indicates the data type of the parameter and will be either C, I, N, D, or L. The *Filler* field is unused. The *Width* field is used for integer and numeric types and indicates the display width of the value. The *Length* field is used by three data types: C, N, and L. For the C data type, it indicates the length of the string. For N, it gives the number of significant decimal places. For L, it indicates *.T.* or *.F.* (0 for *.F.*; anything else indicates *.T.*). The *LongInt* field, used only for the I data type, indicates the value of the integer. The *Double* field is used for the N and D data types and in both cases is an IEEE 64-bit floating-point real number. Finally, the *Handle* field is used by the C data type and contains the memory handle for the string.

Note that many of the fields depend on the data type. You must examine the *DataType* field to see which of the other fields are valid.

In the Locator structure, the *DataType* field will always contain an R; this is the best way to see if a Value or Locator structure is in use. The *Where* field contains either a -1 for a memory variable or the work area of the database if the parameter is a database field. *NTI*, the Name Table Index, is for FoxPro's internal use only. *L_Offset* is also for internal use only and contains the field number within the database. The *Subs* field is for memory variables only and contains the number of subscripts (0 if the parameter isn't an array, 1 if it's a one-dimensional array, or 2 if it's a two-dimensional array). The *Sub1* field contains the first subscript if the *Subs* field isn't 0. The *Sub2* field contains the second subscript if the *Subs* field is 2. The *Filler* field is unused and is present only to ensure that the Locator and Value structures are the same size.

Note that in both structures the first byte contains the data type. It might seem reasonable to assume, then, that your API routines should make sure each parameter is of the correct data type. In practice, this is unnecessary and generally a bad idea. Constantly validating parameters will make your API routines larger and slower than they need to be, especially when you consider that FoxPro will verify the data types for you and generate a run-time error if an invalid parameter is found. (The error can then be custom-handled by your *ON ERROR* procedure.)

The only time your API routines need to be concerned with data-type validation is when the data type may vary. In this case, you can specify a value of "?" in the

FoxInfo structure's parameter list (indicating that the parameter's data type should not be enforced by FoxPro) and perform data-type validation in your API routine.

Because the Value and Locator structures are both 20 bytes long, parameter blocks are easy to locate. Remembering that DX:AX will point to the parameter count and that the parameter blocks immediately follow, you can see that the first parameter block will be at DX:AX+2, the second at DX:AX+22, the third at DX:AX+42, and so on.

The Locator structure doesn't contain the parameter's value. To get it, you have to rely on a translator routine provided by the API. This routine, called *_Load_*, accepts two parameters: a pointer to the Locator structure and a pointer to the Value structure. It uses the information in the Locator structure to look up the parameter's value, which is then stored in the Value structure.

Implicit in the idea of passing parameters by reference is the ability to change the value of the passed parameter. Another API routine, *_Store_*, is used to change values. Like *_Load_*, it accepts a pointer to a Locator structure and a pointer to a Value structure. In this case, however, it takes the value defined in the Value structure and stores it in the memory variable identified by the Locator structure. Naturally, your assembler routine must not modify the contents of the Locator structure passed from FoxPro, and the address of the structure must be preserved so that it may be passed to *_Store_*.

Using Callbacks

The true power of the API comes from FoxPro's rich set of services. Using callback routines, you can manipulate menus, databases, memory, strings, and files, install event handlers, access FoxPro's user-interface tools, and much more. No other database product currently offers such complete access to internal routines and services.

All the callback routines are fundamentally alike. Parameters are passed via the AX, BX, CX, and DX registers, and in some cases the stack is used as well. The callback routine uses the passed parameters to determine its course of action. Any return value is typically returned in either the AX register, the DX:AX register pair, or AX:BX:CX:DX for floating-point values. Consult your FoxPro documentation for information about specific routines and the registers they use.

When using callbacks, be careful to preserve the FoxPro environment. FoxPro is a complex product, and a stray pointer or invalid memory reference could easily cause a system crash. Be sure to lock any memory handles that will be used later and check return results for error codes.

Returning Results to FoxPro

The final task of most external routines is returning a value to FoxPro. As you might expect, the API provides the services to do this easily and efficiently. The most basic routine for returning a value, and the most flexible, is *_RetVal_*. You must build a complete Value structure and pass its address to *_RetVal_*. Because a Value structure is used, *_RetVal_* can return a value of any data type.

To build the Value structure *_RetVal_* uses, you must somehow provide 20 bytes of memory. There are several ways to do this; perhaps the easiest is simply to declare a static Value structure in the library's data segment. This method has one drawback: The memory taken by the Value structure cannot be deallocated until the library is unloaded. Another method is to use FoxPro's memory manager to allocate a handle. This allows you to deallocate the memory when you're finished but introduces unnecessary code overhead to manage the memory handle. Still another method is to allocate the necessary memory on the stack by subtracting 20 from the SP register. This adds very little overhead but lets you deallocate the memory simply by restoring the SP register to its original state.

For the sake of convenience, the API offers several routines that don't require a Value structure. These routines allow you to pass only the return value and do most of the dirty work for you. For example, the *_RetChar_* function returns a character string to FoxPro and requires only the address of the string to be returned. The string must be null-terminated, however, so *_RetChar_* may not be used to return strings that contain embedded nulls (for this you must use *_RetVal_*).

Each data type has a convenient return-value function. In general, these functions are preferable to *_RetVal_* because they're easier to use. They aren't required, however, and *_RetVal_* may always be used instead.

Assembling and Linking

After developing an external-routine library, you need to assemble the source code and link it into a .PLB file. The first step is to assemble the source file (MYLIB.ASM, in this example):

```
TASM /mx MYLIB
```

(If you don't use Turbo Assembler, consult your assembler's documentation for instructions.) If your source file assembles without errors, you're ready for the link step. The linker combines the source file with objects and libraries in the Library Construction Kit to produce the external-routine library. Nearly any linker can be used; the example here uses Microsoft LINK version 3.65.

```
LINK /noe API_L+MYLIB,MYLIB.PLB,,PROAPI_L
```

This tells the linker to link the FoxPro-supplied file called API_L.OBJ with MYLIB.OBJ to produce MYLIB.PLB. PROAPI_L.LIB, another FoxPro-supplied file, completes the library link. The */noe* switch tells the linker not to use the extended dictionary contained in the .LIB file and is needed to prevent unresolved symbols.

Once the library has been linked, the resulting .PLB file will contain the external-routine library. It may be loaded into FoxPro with the *SET LIBRARY TO* command and will remain in memory until removed, either by another *SET LIBRARY TO* or by a *QUIT* command.

These examples are extremely simple. If you use multiple source files or other library files, your assembling and linking methods will probably be different.

Using a Debugger

The debugger used in the examples in this chapter is Borland's Turbo Debugger, but the same concepts—if not the actual mechanics—can be applied to CodeView, Periscope, or any debugger you choose.

The first step in using a debugger is to make sure it can intercept calls to your library routines. As you may know, the most common way to do this is via the *INT 3* instruction, otherwise known as the breakpoint interrupt. Write an API routine called *BreakPoint* that contains nothing more than an *INT 3* instruction followed by an *RETF* instruction. When you declare this routine in the table of FoxInfo structures, use a value of -2 for the parameter count:

```
FoxInfo  <far ptr Name, BreakPoint, -2, far ptr Null>
```

Obviously, you can't pass -2 parameters, so this number must have some special meaning. The -2 tells FoxPro to call this routine immediately when the library is loaded rather than waiting for an explicit invocation. This is perfect for debugging—once the routine is called, the debugger will halt execution when it encounters an *INT 3* instruction. You'll see why this is important in just a moment.

Once the source file has been assembled, ask your linker to produce a .MAP file (consult your linker's documentation for instructions). You'll then convert the .MAP file to a Turbo Debugger symbol table using the Borland utility TDMAP:

```
TDMAP MYLIB MYLIB.TDS
```

Your library is now ready for debugging. Examine the .MAP file to find the segment address where the *BreakPoint* routine is located; the address will be used later.

Load FoxPro into Turbo Debugger and press the F9 key. This causes the program to execute until the next breakpoint is reached. Because we asked FoxPro to execute the *BreakPoint* routine as soon as the library was loaded, the debugger should halt execution there. Now go to the debugger's File menu and load the symbol table created earlier. Return to the File menu and choose *Table Relocate*; you'll be prompted for a segment address at which to load the symbol table. Subtract the value you obtained from the .MAP file from the current contents of the CS register. Enter the resulting value at the prompt. The symbol table is now loaded, and you may set a breakpoint at any routine you wish to debug.

If using symbol tables for debugging sounds like too much trouble, consider this simpler, cruder method: Include an *INT 3* instruction in any routine you wish to debug. Load FoxPro into the debugger, press F9 to begin execution, and run your application or invoke the desired function from the command window. When the debugger encounters the *INT 3*, it will halt execution. You may begin debugging the routine at that point.

A Sample Library

The following sample library contains several useful functions and is a good example of how an external-routine library can be constructed using assembly language.

Listing 16-1 Sample.asm.

```
;;;;;;;;;;;;;;;;;;;;;;;;;;;;;;;;;;;;;;;;;;;;;;;;;;;;;;;;;;;;;;;;;;
; This sample library is very small and is not intended to be ;
; a complete, commercial-quality function library. Instead, it ;
; merely illustrates the techniques involved in creating an    ;
; External Routine Library with the use of assembly language. ;
; The five functions in the library are useful and you are     ;
; welcome to use them in your applications. The functions are:;
;                                                               ;
;   BenchMark()-Short example that demonstrates speed of API. ;
;   SetMPos()  -Set the position of the mouse cursor.          ;
;   ChDir()    -Change the current directory.                  ;
;   MathChip() -Check for the existence of a math coprocessor.;
;   WorkDays() -Calculate number of days between two dates.   ;
;                                                               ;
; See the various .ASM files for details about syntax and      ;
;                                              return values.  ;

; To assemble:TASM /JIDEAL /MX /M3 SAMPLE                      ;
;                                                               ;
; To link:TLINK /X /C /N API_L+SAMPLE,SAMPLE.PLB,,PROAPI_L+    ;
;                                                   FOXCLIBM   ;
;;;;;;;;;;;;;;;;;;;;;;;;;;;;;;;;;;;;;;;;;;;;;;;;;;;;;;;;;;;;;;;;;;

Public  __FoxTable

Include "API.INC"               ; Contains various structures

Extrn   _HandToPtr_:Far         ; Declare API routines used by
Extrn   _RetInt_:Far            ; this library
Extrn   _RetLogical_:Far
Extrn   _RetVal_:Far
Extrn   __FDU4:Far
```

```
Group    DGROUP    _SampleData ; Put data segment with DGROUP

Segment  _SampleData      Word      Public    "DATA"

PType01   DB     "?",0          ; Param type list for BenchMark()
PType02   DB     "I,I",0        ; Param type list for SetMPos()
PType03   DB     "C",0          ; Param type list for ChDir()
PType04   DB     0              ; Param type list for MathChip()
PType05   DB     "D,D",0        ; Param type list for WorkDays()

BenchMark DB    "BENCHMARK",0 ; Names of functions as called
SetMPos   DB    "SETMPOS",0   ; from FoxPro
ChDir     DB    "CHDIR",0
MathChip  DB    "MATHCHIP",0
WorkDays  DB    "WORKDAYS",0

; This is the table of FoxInfo structures.

FuncList
FoxInfo <far ptr BenchMark, _BenchMark, 1, far ptr PType01>
FoxInfo <far ptr SetMPos, _SetMPos,  2, far ptr PType02>
FoxInfo <far ptr ChDir,   _ChDir,    1, far ptr PType03>
FoxInfo <far ptr MathChip,_MathChip, 0, far ptr PType04>
FoxInfo <far ptr WorkDays,_WorkDays, 2, far ptr PType05>

; And finally, the declaration of __FoxTable, the cornerstone
; of any library.

__FoxTable     FoxTable <0, 5, far ptr FuncList>

Ends     _SampleData

Segment  _Sample    Word     Public    "CODE"
         Assume     CS:_Sample,DS:DGROUP

Include  "BENCHMRK.ASM"
Include  "SETMPOS.ASM"
Include  "CHDIR.ASM"
Include  "MATHCHIP.ASM"
Include  "WORKDAYS.ASM"

Ends     _Sample
End
```

Listing 16-2 Accompanying files for Sample.asm: Benchmark.asm, Api.inc, Setmpos.asm, Chrdir.asm, Mathchip.asm, Workdays.asm.

```
;;;;;;;;;;;;;;;;;;;;;;;;;;;;;;;;;;;;;;;;;;;;;;;;;;;;;;;;;;;;;;;;;
;                          api.inc                              ;
;;;;;;;;;;;;;;;;;;;;;;;;;;;;;;;;;;;;;;;;;;;;;;;;;;;;;;;;;;;;;;;;;

PBSize   EQU     20
InVal    EQU     (Value Ptr ES:BX)

Struc    FoxInfo
FuncName DD       ?              ; Pointer to function name
FuncPtr  DD       ?              ; Pointer to its address
PCount   DW       ?              ; Number of parameters
PTypes   DD       ?              ; Pointer to param description
Ends     FoxInfo

Struc    FoxTable
NextLib  DD       ?              ; Points to another foxtable
FuncCnt  DW       ?              ; Number of functions
InfoPtr  DD       ?              ; Points to foxinfo structure
Ends     FoxTable

Struc    LongInt
LowWord  DW       ?
HighWord DW       ?
Ends     LongInt

Struc    Value
DataType DB       ?
Filler   DB       ?
Width    DW       ?
Length   DW       ?
Long     LongInt ?
Double   DQ       ?
Handle   DW       ?
```

```
Ends      Value

;;;;;;;;;;;;;;;;;;;;;;;;;;;;;;;;;;;;;;;;;;;;;;;;;;;;;;;;;;;;;;;;;;;;;;;
; Function: BenchMark()                                               ;
;                                                                     ;
; Purpose:  Return the same value that was passed from FoxPro.;
;           Use to demonstrates overhead involved in calling          ;
;           API routines by comparing with equivalent FoxPro          ;
;           routine. The results may surprise you!                    ;
;                                                                     ;
; Syntax:   BenchMark( <exp> )                                        ;
;                                                                     ;
; Parameters:<exp> is a value of any data type.                       ;
;                                                                     ;
; Returns:  The same value that was passed to the function.           ;
;;;;;;;;;;;;;;;;;;;;;;;;;;;;;;;;;;;;;;;;;;;;;;;;;;;;;;;;;;;;;;;;;;;;;;;

Proc      _BenchMark       Far

      Inc      AX          ; Skip past param count
      Inc      AX
      Call  _RetVal_       ; Return value passed from FoxPro
      Ret

Endp      _BenchMark

;;;;;;;;;;;;;;;;;;;;;;;;;;;;;;;;;;;;;;;;;;;;;;;;;;;;;;;;;;;;;;;;;;;;;;;
; Function:    SetMPos()                                              ;
;                                                                     ;
; Purpose:     Move the mouse cursor to the desired coordinates;
;                                                                     ;
; Syntax:      SetMPos( <expN1>, <expN2> )                            ;
;                                                                     ;
; Parameters: <expN1> is the desired screen row.                      ;
;              <expN2> is the desired screen column.                  ;
;                                                                     ;
; Returns:     Nothing                                                ;
;;;;;;;;;;;;;;;;;;;;;;;;;;;;;;;;;;;;;;;;;;;;;;;;;;;;;;;;;;;;;;;;;;;;;;;

Proc  _SetMPos Far

      Push     ES                        ; Save modified registers
      Push     BX
      Push     CX
```

```
        Mov     ES,DX                  ; Load ES:BX with pointer
        Mov     BX,AX                  ; to parameter info

        Inc     BX                     ; Skip past param count
        Inc     BX

        Mov     CL,3                   ; Set shift value

        Mov     AX,[InVal.Long.LowWord]; Get desired row
        SHL     AX,CL                  ; Multiply by eight
        Push    AX                     ; Save for later
        Add     BX,PBSize              ; Point to next param block

        Mov     AX,[InVal.Long.LowWord] ; Get desired column
        SHL     AX,CL                  ; Multiply by eight
        Mov     CX,AX                  ; Put horizontal in CX
        Pop     DX                     ;Retrieve vertical from stack
        Mov     AX,4                   ; Mouse service--move cursor
        Int     33h                    ; Call mouse driver

        Pop     CX                     ; Restore registers
        Pop     BX
        Pop     ES
        Ret
Endp  _SetMPos

;;;;;;;;;;;;;;;;;;;;;;;;;;;;;;;;;;;;;;;;;;;;;;;;;;;;;;;;;;;;;;;;
; Function:   ChDir ()                                          ;
;                                                               ;
; Purpose:    Change the current directory                      ;
;                                                               ;
; Syntax:     ChDir( <expC> )                                   ;
;                                                               ;
; Parameters: <expC> is the desired path specification.         ;
;                                                               ;
; Returns:    The error code as returned by DOS. Generally,     ;
;             this should be:                                   ;
;                                                               ;
;             0 if successful                                   ;
;             3 if path not found                               ;
;;;;;;;;;;;;;;;;;;;;;;;;;;;;;;;;;;;;;;;;;;;;;;;;;;;;;;;;;;;;;;;;
```

```
Proc _ChDir  Far

     Push    ES                    ; Save modified registers
     Push    BX
     Push    SI
     Push    DI
     PushF

     Mov     ES,DX                 ; Load ES:BX with pointer to
     Mov     BX,AX                 ; parameter info

     Inc     BX                    ; Skip past param count
     Inc     BX

     Push    [InVal.Length]        ; Save string length for later
     Mov     AX,[InVal.Handle]     ; Get handle
     Call    _HandToPtr_           ; Convert to pointer
     Pop     CX                    ; Get string length from stack

     Push    DS                    ; Save FoxPro's data segment
     Push    BP                    ; Save BP
     Mov     BP,SP                 ; Set up stack reference
     Sub     SP,CX                 ; Allocate room for string
     Dec     SP                    ; Make room for null terminator

     Mov     DS,DX                 ; Put segment in DS
     Mov     SI,AX                 ; Put offset in SI
     Push    SS                    ; Move SS . . .
     Pop     ES                    ; . . . to ES
     Mov     DI,SP                 ; Load DI with offset
     CLD                           ; Make sure direction flag clear
     Rep     Movsb                 ; Copy string to local buffer
     Mov     [Byte Ptr BP - 1],0   ; Include null terminator

     Mov     DX,SP                 ; Get offset of string
     Push    SS                    ; Move SS . . .
     Pop     DS                    ; . . . to DS
     Mov     AH,3Bh                ; DOS service -- change directory
     Int     21h                   ; Call DOS
     Mov     SP,BP                 ; Deallocate local buffer
```

```
     Pop      BP                    ; Restore BP
     Pop      DS                    ; Restore FoxPro's data segment
     JC       @@Report              ; If error, report it . . .
     Xor      AX,AX                 ; . . . otherwise set to zero

@@Report:Xor DX,DX                  ; Clear high word
     Mov      BX,1                  ; Set display width
     Call     _RetInt_              ; Return integer

     PopF                           ; Restore registers
     Pop      DI
     Pop      SI
     Pop      BX
     Pop      ES
     Ret
Endp _ChDir

;;;;;;;;;;;;;;;;;;;;;;;;;;;;;;;;;;;;;;;;;;;;;;;;;;;;;;;;;;;;;;
; Function:   MathChip()                                       ;
;                                                              ;
; Purpose:    Check for the presence of a math coprocessor     ;
;                                                              ;
; Syntax:     MathChip()                                       ;
;                                                              ;
; Parameters: None                                             ;
;                                                              ;
; Returns:    .T. if math coprocessor found, .F. if not found  ;
;;;;;;;;;;;;;;;;;;;;;;;;;;;;;;;;;;;;;;;;;;;;;;;;;;;;;;;;;;;;;;

Proc   _MathChip Far

     Push  BP                       ; Save BP
     Mov   BP,SP                    ; Set up stack reference
     Sub   SP,2                     ; Allocate temporary RAM

     Mov   [Word Ptr BP - 2],0 ; Initialize local
     FLDPI                          ; Try to load PI via coprocessor
     FISTP [Word Ptr BP - 2]        ; Try to store PI into local
     FWait                          ; Wait for coprocessor to finish
     Cmp   [Word Ptr BP - 2],3 ; Local == 3?
     JE    @@True
     Xor   AX,AX                    ; Set return value to .F.
     Jmp   @@Done                   ; Finished
```

```
@@True:Mov AX,1                ; Set return value to .T.

@@Done:Call _RetLogical_       ; Return value to FoxPro
      Mov  SP,BP               ; Deallocate local
      Pop  BP                  ; Restore BP
      Ret
Endp  _MathChip

;;;;;;;;;;;;;;;;;;;;;;;;;;;;;;;;;;;;;;;;;;;;;;;;;;;;;;;;;;;;;;;;
; Function:  WorkDays()                                        ;
;                                                              ;
; Purpose:   Calculate number of working days between two dates;
;                                                              ;
; Syntax:    WorkDays( <expD1>, <expD2> )                      ;
;                                                              ;
; Parameters:<expD1> is the beginning date.                    ;
;            <expD2> is the ending date.                       ;
;                                                              ;
; Returns:   A numeric value.                                  ;
;;;;;;;;;;;;;;;;;;;;;;;;;;;;;;;;;;;;;;;;;;;;;;;;;;;;;;;;;;;;;;;;

Proc     _WorkDays Far

         Push    ES             ; Save modified registers
         Push    BX
         Push    CX
         Push    BP
         Mov     BP,SP
         Sub     SP,8

         Mov     ES,DX          ; Load pointer to
                                ; param block
         Mov     BX,AX

@@Date1: Inc     BX             ; Skip past param
                                ; count
         Inc     BX
         Push    ES             ; Save pointer for
                                ; later
         Push    BX
```

```
          Mov     DX,[Word Ptr ES:BX + 10] ; Load double value
                                           ; for date
          Mov     AX,[Word Ptr ES:BX + 16]
          Mov     CX,[Word Ptr ES:BX + 12]
          Mov     BX,[Word Ptr ES:BX + 14]
          Call    __FDU4                   ; Convert to integer
          Pop     BX                       ; Restore param block
                                           ; pointer
          Pop     ES
          Mov     [Word Ptr BP - 2],DX     ; Save integer
                                           ; version of date
          Mov     [Word Ptr BP - 4],AX

@@Date2:  Add     BX,PBSize                ; Point to next
                                           ; param block
          Mov     DX,[Word Ptr ES:BX + 10] ; Load double value
                                           ; for date
          Mov     AX,[Word Ptr ES:BX + 16]
          Mov     CX,[Word Ptr ES:BX + 12]
          Mov     BX,[Word Ptr ES:BX + 14]
          Call    __FDU4                   ; Convert to integer
          Mov     [Word Ptr BP - 6],DX     ; Save integer
                                           ; version of date
          Mov     [Word Ptr BP - 8],AX

          Sub     AX,[Word Ptr BP - 4]     ; Subtract ending date
          SBB     DX,[Word Ptr BP - 2]     ; from beginning date to
          Test    DH,80h                   ; verify that it's
                                             larger
          JNZ     @@Swap                   ; Smaller, so need to
                                           ; swap dates

          Or      AX,DX                    ; Are the dates equal?
          JNZ     @@Adjust                 ; No, so continue
          Mov     AX,1                     ; Default to one day
          Jmp     @@Done                   ; Dates are equal,
                                           ; so quit

@@Swap:   Mov     AX,[Word Ptr BP - 8]     ; Get low word of
                                           ; ending date
          Mov     DX,[Word Ptr BP - 6]     ; Get high word of
```

```
                                               ; ending date
        XChg    AX,[Word Ptr BP - 4]           ; Exchange low words
        XChg    DX,[Word Ptr BP - 2]           ; Exchange high words
        Mov     [Word Ptr BP - 8],AX           ; Store new ending
                                               ; date low word
        Mov     [Word Ptr BP - 6],DX           ; Store new ending
                                               ; date high word

@@Adjust:Sub    [Word Ptr BP - 4],1            ; Subtract 1 from
                                               ; beginning date
        SBB     [Word Ptr BP - 2],0            ; so beginning day
                                               ; is included

@@Calc: Mov     AX,[Word Ptr BP - 8]           ; Get ending date low
                                               ; word
        Mov     DX,[Word Ptr BP - 6]           ; Get ending date
                                               ; high word
        Sub     AX,[Word Ptr BP - 4]           ; Subtract beginning
                                               ; date
        SBB     DX,[Word Ptr BP - 2]
        Call    Day2Week                       ; Convert day count
                                               ; to week count
        Push    CX                             ; Save remainder
        Mov     BX,5                           ; Set multiplicand
        Mov     CX,DX                          ; Save DX for later
        Mul     BX                             ; Multiply low word by 5
        Push    AX                             ; Save low word of result
        Mov     AX,CX                          ; Get high word
        Mov     CX,DX                          ; Save high word of result
        Mul     BX                             ; Multiply high word by 5
        Add     DX,CX                          ; Add previous carry
        Pop     AX                             ; Restore low word
        Pop     CX                             ; Get remainder back
        JCXZ    @@Done                         ; If remainder zero,
                                               ; we're done

        Push    DX                             ; Save value for later
        Push    AX
        Xor     BX,BX                          ; Clear counter
```

```
@@Top:    Push    CX                      ; Save loop counter
          Mov     DX,[Word Ptr BP - 8]    ; Load ending date
          Mov     AX,[Word Ptr BP - 10]
          Inc     AX                      ; Go back CX - 1 days
          Sub     AX,CX
          SBB     DX,0
          Call    Day2Week                ; Get day of week
          Cmp     CX,5                    ; Saturday or Sunday?
          JNB     @@Bottom                ; No,so don't include day
          Inc     BX                      ; Increment counter

@@Bottom:Pop      CX
          Loop    @@Top
          Pop     AX                      ; Recover value from
                                          ; stack
          Pop     DX
          Add     AX,BX                   ; Add day count to total
          ADC     DX,0

@@Done:   Mov     BX,10                   ; Set display width
          Call    _RetInt_                ; Return value to FoxPro
          Mov     SP,BP                   ; Restore stack and
                                          ; registers
          Pop     BP
          Pop     CX
          Pop     BX
          Pop     ES
          Ret
Endp      _WorkDays
```

```
;;;;;;;;;;;;;;;;;;;;;;;;;;;;;;;;;;;;;;;;;;;;;;;;;;;;;;;;;;;;;;;;;;;;;;;;;
; Local procedure: Day2Week                                              ;
;                                                                        ;
; Purpose:          Convert a day count to # of weeks                    ;
;                                                                        ;
; Call with:        Long integer in DX:AX                                ;
;                                                                        ;
; Returns:          # of weeks in DX:AX                                  ;
;                   Remaining days in CX                                 ;
;                                                                        ;
;;;;;;;;;;;;;;;;;;;;;;;;;;;;;;;;;;;;;;;;;;;;;;;;;;;;;;;;;;;;;;;;;;;;;;;;;

Proc     Day2Week  Near

         Push      BX             ; Save BX
         Mov       BX,7           ; # of days in a week
         Xor       CX,CX          ; Clear remainder
         XChg      AX,CX          ; Swap remainder with low word
         XChg      AX,DX          ; Swap remainder with high word
         Div       BX             ; Divide by seven
         XChg      AX,CX          ; Swap remainder with low word
         Div       BX             ; Divide by seven
         XChg      CX,DX          ; Swap remainder with high word
         Pop       BX             ; Restore BX
         Ret
Endp     Day2Week
```

Porting Routines from Other Products to the FoxPro 2 API

Many products allow programmers to pull in routines written in other languages. For example, with Clipper it is possible to mix routines written in C, assembly language, Pascal, or a combination of these. A typical task for programmers who use both FoxPro and Clipper is to port their Clipper routines to the FoxPro API. This is much easier said than done, however.

Much of the code involved in using Clipper's Extend System or FoxPro's API is simply the overhead required to meet the needs of the host language. Each product has certain requirements for receiving parameters and returning values that must be followed for the function to work properly . Unfortunately, Clipper's Extend System and the FoxPro API are so different in this regard that very little code survives the transition. Only the "core" of the function (the part that actually does the work) will remain scrapped and rewritten. Porting functions from Clipper to FoxPro can be done, but it is not a trivial task.

Using "Unauthorized" Languages with the API

One of the more unfortunate aspects of the FoxPro API is Fox Software's insistence that WatCom C and assembly language are the only two officially supported languages. This is not good news for the legions of developers who own C compilers from other vendors, or who wish to use other languages such as FORTRAN or Pascal.

All is not lost, however. With a little clever hacking, you can alter the API to meet the needs of the compiler of your choice. FoxPro was written in WatCom C and its register usage is incompatible with other C compilers. Fortunately for us, this is not an insurmountable problem. The API routines are very small and do nothing more than set up CPU registers with the appropriate values before calling FoxPro internal services. As shipped, these routines accommodate the WatCom C calling convention. If you need to use another calling convention, you can simply rewrite the API routine that sets up the CPU registers; the call to FoxPro's internal services remains unchanged. Using this method, it should be possible to make any language work with the API, whether it's another C compiler or a language like Pascal or FORTRAN. However, you can't use code with floating point variables; that brings in the WatCom startup code.

This is not an easy task, but with persistence and the use of a good debugger, it can be done. I have successfully used the API with Microsoft C, and other users report success with Turbo C and other products. In addition, WatCom has the reputation of producing products with a high degree of interoperability. It may be possible to use WatCom Pascal or WatCom FORTRAN without altering the API at all.

CHAPTER 17

Fox's Macintosh API

by Randy Brown

The external command, or *XCMD*, has its origins in the Macintosh software product HyperCard. Apple developed HyperCard so that users could plug in their own external commands and functions for features nonexistent in the base product. Fox has duplicated the functionality of the HyperCard 1.x XCMD in FoxBASE+/Mac, with a few additional features specific to FoxBASE+/Mac. As a result, developers can often use existing HyperCard XCMDs within FoxBASE+/Mac.

In programming terms, an XCMD is known as a *code resource*: a segment of code that can't run on its own but must be called by the currently running application. You may be familiar with other types of code segments; *init*s and *cdev*s, for example, are loaded into the system at start-up and control system environmental states such as sound and screen attributes (screen savers, virus checkers, password schemes, and sound enhancements are examples). *cdev*s are similar to *init*s, but they allow the user to access and adjust these attributes through the control panel (*cdev* is short for *control panel device*). These segments are usually written in C or Pascal but can also be in BASIC or assembler.

XCMDs can be found in a variety of places. The most common are on-line computer bulletin boards, such as CompuServe and GEnie. The FoxForum BBS on CompuServe contains many FoxBASE+/Mac-specific XCMDs, including the FoxTools XCMD Library, a collection of more than 30 useful public-domain externals. In addition, you can find many HyperCard XCMDs on the Macintosh forums. A number of HyperCard XCMD libraries that may or may not work with FoxBASE+/Mac are also available commercially.

In this chapter, we'll focus more on features in the FoxBASE+/Mac XCMD interface than on using XCMDs in FoxBASE applications; that topic is covered quite well in the Fox manuals. Since the release of FoxBASE+/Mac, HyperCard (now under the control of Claris Corp.) has been updated, with several new features added to the XCMD interface. We'll touch on some of those features and the direction FoxPro/Mac is likely to take in expanding its own Application Programming Interface, or API.

Because XCMDs are written in lower-level languages, this chapter contains a good deal of Pascal code and several programming constructs. You should also be familiar with common Macintosh ToolBox routines and features such as QuickDraw, and pointer and handle datatypes.

DOS API vs. Macintosh API

FoxBASE+/Mac and Fox Software's other Macintosh program, FoxPro/Mac, don't approach the API the same way as the DOS product, FoxPro 2.0. An important distinction exists between the DOS and Macintosh APIs as implemented in Fox's database products. The DOS API under FoxPro 2.0 is an interface to Fox's own internal architecture; the user can access database structures as well as Fox's main event loop. The Macintosh XCMD allows direct access not to Fox's internals, but rather to the much broader set of routines in the Macintosh ToolBox ROM. In other words, the Macintosh API provides direct access to the operating system, while the DOS product doesn't.

If you're thinking that the Macintosh XCMD has more power, you're only partially right. For example, if you define an external window from an XCMD, FoxBASE+/Mac won't recognize that window except within the XCMD itself; Fox's own event loop doesn't know another window is on the desktop. With the DOS API, you can define an external window (such as a simple word processor) and include it directly in your FoxPro code because Fox's internal event loop will recognize the existence of that externally created window.

The XCMD Structure

This section covers the basics of writing an XCMD, with coding examples in THINK Pascal. The elements of the XCMD interface are in separate files and are linked and compiled. This process of linking and compiling is similar to that used by the project manager in FoxPro 2.0. The result of compilation is the XCMD code resource, which is then stored in a resource file that will be called later within a FoxBASE+/Mac routine.

An XCMD has three basic components: a parameter block, glue routines, and the XCMD code.

XCmdBlock Record

The XCmdBlock (Listing 17-1) provides the actual interface of external code to FoxBASE+/Mac and the Macintosh ROM. The XCMD passes its parameters back and forth to Fox using this interface.

Listing 17-1. Internal XCMD data structure.

```
XCmdPtr = ^XCmdBlock;
XCmdBlock = record
   paramCount: INTEGER;
   params: array[1..16] of Handle;
   returnValue: Handle;
   passFlag: BOOLEAN;

   entryPoint: ProcPtr;
   request: INTEGER;
   result: INTEGER;
   inArgs: array[1..8] of LongInt;
   outArgs: array[1..4] of LongInt;

   {FoxBASE+/Mac Unique Fields}

   version: INTEGER;
   options: INTEGER;
   onscreen: WindowPtr;
```

```
offscreen: Grafptr;
printRec: THPrint;
printPort : TPPrPort;
foxuser: INTEGER;
setresource: INTEGER;
utillong1: LongInt;
utillong2: LongInt;
utillong3: LongInt;
utillong4: LongInt;
utilhandle1: Handle;
utilhandle2: Handle;
utilhandle3: Handle;
utilhandle4: Handle;
publong: LongInt;
pubhandle: Handle;
reserved1: LongInt;
reserved2: LongInt;
END;
```

The field definitions are discussed in the FoxBASE+/Mac manuals, but we'll touch on a few of the more common ones. The first three mentioned are used in almost all XCMDs for error checking and parameter passing; code examples show how these fields are typically incorporated.

paramCount—This field is read-only and contains the number of parameters passed with the XCMD during the Fox *CALL* command.

```
IF paramPtr^.paramCount <> 1 THEN
WrongFormat;
```

params— This field is a 16-element array of handles to each of the parameters passed. Since Fox passes and receives variables as null-terminated strings, you'll need to convert them to the proper data type.

```
ZeroToPas(paramPtr, paramPtr^.params[1]^, ParamStr);
```

returnValue —This field returns a variable to Fox (write-only). If nothing is passed, this field is empty.

```
paramPtr^.returnValue := PasToZero(paramPtr, errStr);
```

options—This multipurpose integer field can be set to 1 (bit 0 set on) to cause a screen refresh from the current offscreen grafport (i.e., bitmap). If the value is set to 3 (bit 1 set on), the *returnValue* field is evaluated as a picture field. When you manipulate picture fields with glue routines that access such fields as *GetFieldByName*, be sure to set *options* to 3.

onscreen—This is a windowptr (a pointer to a window) to the current onscreen bitmap. FoxBASE+/Mac updates its active screen from an offscreen bitmap. You can control this update using the *options* field. If you plan to use QuickDraw routines, always write to the offscreen bitmap; Fox will overwrite the onscreen bitmap during normal execution.

offscreen—This field is a grafptr (pointer to a grafport) to the current offscreen bitmap. You can use standard typecasting (such as *WindowPtr(paramPtr^.offscreen)*) to change the pointer type. Always write to this field if you want the image to stay on the screen.

utillong—The *utillong* read-write fields are used to store long integers for use by the currently loaded XCMD. Therefore, you can call that XCMD any number of times without releasing it and still have access to these global variables, which are initially set to zero. The following example shows how to store the address of a pointer to a window created in an XCMD (a) and later call that window via the XCMD (b).

```
a) paramPtr^.utillong1:=Ord4(FoxWindowPtr);
b) FoxWindowPtr:= WindowPtr(paramPtr^.utillong1);
```

utilhandle—The *utilhandle* fields are similar to the *utillong* fields except that they store handles instead of integers.

publong—This storage area is similar to the *utillong* fields except that all XCMDs, including those subsequently loaded, have access to it.

pubhandle—This field is similar to *publong* except that it stores a handle instead of an integer.

XCMD Glue Routines

The glue routines are used to manipulate data within an XCMD. Most XCMDs use several of them. We'll discuss a few of the more common routines.

PasToZero—Converts a Pascal string to a zero-terminated one.

```
function PasToZero (paramPtr: XCmdPtr; str: Str255): Handle;
```

ZeroToPas—Converts a zero-terminated string to a Pascal string.

```
procedure ZeroToPas (paramPtr: XCmdPtr; zeroStr: Ptr; var
pasStr: Str255);
```

StrToLong—Converts a Pascal string of type *Str31* to an unsigned long integer.

```
function StrToLong (paramPtr: XCmdPtr; str: Str31): LongInt;
```

EvalExpr—Evaluates a FoxBASE+/Mac expression within the XCMD. The result field in the XCmdBlock can be used to check for call success.

```
function EvalExpr (paramPtr: XCmdPtr; expr: Str255): Handle;
```

SendCardMessage—Similar to *EvalExpr* except that it's a procedure.

```
procedure SendCardMessage (paramPtr: XCmdPtr; msg: Str255);
```

GetFieldByName—Returns a handle to the contents of a FoxBASE+/Mac database field specified by the field name. All field types can be accessed, including memo and picture fields. The *options* field in the XCmdBlock must be set properly when you're working with picture fields.

```
function GetFieldByName (paramPtr: XCmdPtr; cardFieldFlag:
BOOLEAN; fieldName: Str255): Handle;
```

SetFieldByName—Similar to *GetFieldByName* except that it writes the contents of the handle to the specified field.

```
procedure SetFieldByName (paramPtr: XCmdPtr; cardFieldFlag:
BOOLEAN; fieldName: Str255; fieldVal: Handle);
```

GetGlobal—Returns a handle to the contents of a memory variable.

```
function GetGlobal (paramPtr: XCmdPtr; globName: Str255): Handle;
```

SetGlobal—Sets the value of a memory variable to the contents of the handle.

```
procedure SetGlobal (paramPtr: XCmdPtr; globName: Str255;
                                    globValue: Handle);
```

XCMD Code

The source code for an XCMD is in a separate file from the XCmdBlock and glue-routine files. The latter two can be used universally between XCMDs without modification. The following source code is actually only a generic template with simple error handling, such as parameter count checks. Most of the code will reside in the section of Listing 17-2 indicated by "***ENTER CODE HERE***." This standard template will be used later to build the sample XCMD in Listing 17-3.

Listing 17-2. Generic XCMD Template.

```
UNIT MyXCMD;
{XCMD Template Code}
{File name:Generic_XCMD.Pas }
{History: 01/90 Original by Randy Brown. }
INTERFACE
   USES
      XCmdIntf, XCmdUtils;
   PROCEDURE Main (paramPtr: XCmdPtr);

IMPLEMENTATION
```

```
  PROCEDURE TheXCMD (paramPtr: XCmdPtr);
     VAR
        message, ParamStr: str255;
        ParamNum: integer;
     PROCEDURE FAIL (errStr: Str255);
     BEGIN
        paramPtr^.returnValue := PasToZero(paramPtr,errStr);
        EXIT(TheXCMD)
     END;

     PROCEDURE WrongFormat;
     VAR
        return, str, str2, str3, str4: str255;
        txthndl: handle;
     BEGIN
        return := chr(13);
        str2 := 'XCMD <expN1> <expN2>';
        str3 := ' <expN1>: param 1';
        str4 := ' <expN2>: param 2';
        str := Concat(str2,return,return,str3,return,str4);
        txthndl := PasToZero(paramPtr, str);
        SetGlobal(paramPtr, 'ALERTMESS', txthndl);
        SendCardMessage(paramPtr, 'Alert Note 7 ALERTMESS');
        DisposHandle(txthndl);
        Fail('Error: Incorrect XCMD format.');
     END;

     BEGIN
        IF paramPtr^.paramCount <> 0 THEN
           WrongFormat;

           {***ENTER CODE HERE***}

     END;

     PROCEDURE Main;
     BEGIN
        TheXCMD(paramPtr);
     END;
END.                               {End of unit}
```

Programming XCMDs for FoxBASE+/Mac

Code resources are a bit peculiar when it comes to using many of the routines in the Macintosh ToolBox ROM. A number of calls and variables should never be used in an XCMD because they'll interfere with the operating system and/or the application itself (in other words, FoxBASE+/Mac). The most important are the initialization routines associated with the various ROM managers. These routines commonly include *InitWindows*, *InitMenus*, *InitDialogs*, *InitFonts*, and *InitGraf*. You can, however, use the *InitCursor* routine, which simply changes the cursor to an arrow.

System global variables can't be included in an XCMD or any other code resource because they aren't true applications. This includes *ScreenBits*, a commonly used global that gives the address (coordinates) of the screen. One solution is to use the *GetGrayRgn* function, which returns a handle to the desktop region (and takes into consideration multiple monitors):

```
deskRgn := GetGrayRgn;

myevent,where,h := ((deskRgn^^.rgnBBox.Right -
deskRgn^^.rgnBBox.Left) div 2) - (304 div 2);
```

First-time XCMD authors commonly forget to dispose of handles. The data structure of type *handle* is simply a pointer to a master pointer. It tracks addresses while allowing the Memory Manager to move blocks of memory when compacting the heap. If you don't dispose of your handles before exiting the XCMD, a system bomb may occur. The one situation in which this rule doesn't apply is at the end of the XCMD routine, where a value is returned.

```
paramPtr^.returnValue := theHandle;
DisposHandle(theHandle); {this will cause a system error}
```

Error checking is probably the most important consideration in writing XCMDs. Memory Manager errors can often be checked by calling *OsErr*, which returns critical operating system errors. Many ToolBox routines, such as those associated with the File Manager, perform a function and then return an error code.

```
err := FSOpen(filename, VrefNum, XrefNum)
IF err <> noErr THEN
   ERRORCHECK;
```

Hardware and software versions are another important factor. Depending on the nature of the XCMD and the ROM routines it uses, both hardware and system software should be checked. If the XCMD works with color only, for example, make sure the processor chip is a 68020 or higher. This will become more important as people develop 32-bit clean code for System 7 software. While Apple has made a concerted effort to maintain backward compatibility, a variety of system versions are still out there, and some of the older ones may wreak havoc with your XCMDs. Try to limit XCMDs to machines running on at least System 5 or higher (preferably 6 or 7).

FoxBASE+/Mac refreshes screens from an offscreen bitmap, a process that can be controlled through the *options* field. When the XCMD exits, the screen automatically refreshes. (A refresh is necessary if you're manipulating windows or using QuickDraw routines.) Another way to force a screen refresh without XCMDs is by using a *KEYBOARD CHR(13)* followed by a *READ* command. The *options* field causes the offscreen bitmap to write to the onscreen bitmap (this is how Fox itself updates screens). If you write directly to the onscreen bitmap (*paramPtr^.onscreen*), eventually Fox will overwrite it with the offscreen one. This is useful for XCMDs that perform visual effects on the screen.

Here are some additional programming tips:

- Always save and restore FoxBASE+/Mac environmental states. For example, if the record pointer in a database is moved by the XCMD, it should be returned to its original position.
- Use constants instead of numbers in the code to make it more readable.
- Test your XCMDs extensively. Always run the XCMD in a large loop that calls it many times. You can check to see if memory is being depleted, such

as when a handle is left undisposed.

- Provide *complete* error checking. In addition to parameter counts, test the types of parameters as well as their contents.
- Coordinate commonly used code (such as fail and error checking) into functions or procedures.
- Provide feedback to the user. All XCMDs should be documented. A nice touch is to provide a routine similar to *WrongFormat* in the sample XCMD at the end of this chapter (Listing 17-3) that puts up a dialog box containing the correct XCMD syntax.
- Use the *utillong* and *publong* fields to save information between XCMD calls.
- You can return more than one value to Fox. You can approach this task in several ways; the easiest is simply to return comma-separated values. The Fox program can then extract those values. Another approach is to assign return values to various memory variables using the *SetGlobal* glue routine.
- FoxBASE+/Mac commands and functions can be used inside XCMDs using the *EvalExpr* and *SendCardMessage* glue routines, often saving many lines of code. (For example, the *ALERT NOTE 1* command is a simple way to put up a dialog box without having to write the code you would need if you were using the native XCMD language.) These routines access the Fox language without noticeable loss of performance.

Incorporating XCMDs in FoxBASE+/Mac Applications

Since XCMDs are code resources, not files, they must be stored in resource files. A resource file is any file Fox designates as such by the following command:

```
SET RESOURCE TO <resource file>
```

The default is the FoxUSER file, which contains other resources such as alerts (dialog boxes), picts (*PICT* files), and icons. You can easily copy XCMDs into this file or any other resource file using a resource mover like ResEdit.

After setting your resource file, you simply load the name of the XCMD:

```
LOAD <XCMD> |FUNCTION|
```

If the code resource is of type *XFCN* (external function), you must use the *FUNCTION* parameter. XCMDs and XFCNs are processed identically by Fox. Once the XCMD is loaded, it can be called a number of times before being released (with *RELEASE MODULE <XCMD>*). With FoxBASE+/Mac, you can load a maximum of 16 XCMDs at a time.

When you want to call an XCMD in your Fox program, use the following command:

```
CALL <XCMD> WITH <parameter list> TO <memvar>
```

The parameter list is the set of parameters passed to the XCMD (up to 16). The memory variable is the value returned by the XCMD. The value returned is of type *character*, so any numbers passed back must be converted using the *VAL()* function.

XCMDs are a great way to enhance an application and give added functionality not available in Fox's language. Before using them, however, you should be aware of the following considerations:

- Always test the XCMD on sample data first. Many XCMDs, especially those distributed in the public domain, are not properly tested and debugged. When your program is running inside the XCMD, the XCMD's direct interface to the Macintosh ROM increases the likelihood of a major operating system crash. It's a good idea to test the XCMD by calling it with a variety of parameter combinations.

- The process of calling an XCMD within an application is relatively slow. If you need to call an XCMD repeatedly in a loop, such as when skipping through a large database, try running the routine during hours when database activity is light.

- Be aware of memory constraints. If the DBMS is on a machine with limited

RAM, loading too many XCMDs at a time will add so much overhead to the system that Fox could crash.

- Be careful when using HyperCard XCMDs. As mentioned before, several glue routines take a native application command as a parameter. For instance, if an *EvalExpr* function were used in a HyperCard XCMD to return the contents of a field on some card, Fox would have a hard time interpreting the expression.

The Future of FoxBase/Mac

In concluding, I'd like to share a few comments on the future direction of Fox's Macintosh API. As of this writing, FoxPro/Mac is in the development phase and many of the new XCMD features are not yet available. A few new features have already been worked into the program; for example, XCMDs in FoxPro/Mac can be called in a manner similar to UDFs. You'll no longer need to *LOAD* and *CALL* the XCMD.

You'll also be able to lock the XCMD in the heap. FoxBASE+/Mac has had several memory-addressing problems related to heap fragmentation (a loaded XCMD may be moved unexpectedly). The ability to lock the XCMD should alleviate many of these problems. In addition, performance times for loading XCMDs will be comparable to native FoxBASE+/Mac commands and functions. FoxPro's handling of picture and character data passed back and forth from XCMDs will also be improved.

When HyperCard 2.0 was released, several new features were added to the XCMD interface; these features may or may not be included in FoxPro/Mac. The most notable enhancement is the external window. As described at the beginning of this chapter, the XCMD interface doesn't give the user sufficient access to Fox's internal architecture. The external window, if implemented, will give the user access to Fox's event loop. For example, you could write an XCMD to put up an external window that provides a graphic drawing environment in which picture fields can be edited directly. You can do this now, but FoxBASE+/Mac doesn't recognize the existence of the external window except within the XCMD itself.

A Sample XCMD

The sample XCMD in Listing 17-3, XMEMOTXT, puts a text file into a memo field. Three parameters can be passed. The first one, which is required, is the name of the memo field. The second is a code *(0/1)* telling the XCMD to append or overwrite the contents of the memo field. The third parameter, which is optional, is the name of the text file. If no name is given, an Open File dialog box is presented.

Listing 17-3. A Sample of a Complete XCMD.

```
UNIT XMEMOTXT;

{File name:XMEMOTXT.Pas }
{Function: }
{History: 04/90 Original by Randy Brown. }
{Format: XMEMOTXT <memofield> <appendcode> |<textfile>| }

INTERFACE
   USES
      XCmdIntf, XCmdUtils;

   PROCEDURE MAIN (paramPtr: XCmdPtr);

IMPLEMENTATION

   PROCEDURE XMEMOTXT (paramPtr: XCmdPtr);
      CONST
         RootDir = 2;
      VAR
         str, str1, str2, str3, str4, str5, return: Str255;
         fieldname, section, filename: str255;
         err, err2, vRefNum, zeroByte, XrefNum, numparams:
                                                   Integer;
         writecode, logEOF, newlen: LongInt;
         txthndl, myBuffrHndl, zeroHndl, fieldhandle: handle;
         mCARDFLD: Boolean;

      PROCEDURE WrongFormat;
      VAR
```

```
    str, str1, str2, str3, str4, str5, return: Str255;
    txthndl: handle;
BEGIN
    return := chr(13);
    str1 := 'XCMD Format:';
    str2 := 'Xmemotxt <expC1>,<expN>,|<expC2>|';
    str3 := '<expC1>: memo field name';
    str4 := '<expN>: 0-overwrite,1-append';
    str5 := '<expC2>: text file (w/fullpath)';
    str := Concat(str2,return,return,str3,return,str4,
                                        return,str5);
    txthndl := PasToZero(paramPtr, str);
    SetGlobal(paramPtr, 'ALERTMESS', txthndl);
    SendCardMessage(paramPtr, 'Alert Note 7 ALERTMESS');
    DisposHandle(txthndl);
    Fail('Error: Incorrect XCMD format.');
    END;

PROCEDURE FAIL (errStr: Str255);
BEGIN
    paramPtr^.returnValue := PasToZero(paramPtr, errStr);
    EXIT(MEMOTXT)
END;

PROCEDURE ERRORCHECK;
BEGIN
    CASE err OF
        bdNamErr:
            str := 'Bad File Name';
        extFSErr:
            str := 'External File System';
        fnfErr:
            str := 'File not found';
        ioErr:
            str := 'I/O Error';
        nsDrvErr:
            str := 'No Such Drive';
        nsvErr:
            str := 'No Such Volume';
        paramErr:
```

```
            str := 'No Default Volume';
         opWrErr:
            str := 'File Already Open';
         tmfoErr:
            str := 'Too many files open';
         OTHERWISE
            str := Concat('Unknown Error:', NumToStr
                                           (paramPtr, Err));
      END;
      txthndl := PasToZero(paramPtr, str);
      SetGlobal(paramPtr, 'ALERTMESS', txthndl);
      SendCardMessage(paramPtr,'Alert Note 1 "System
                                 Error: "+ALERTMESS');
      DisposHandle(txthndl);
      Fail(str);
   END;

   FUNCTION GETFILE: Str255;
   BEGIN
      filename := '';
      txthndl := PasToZero(paramPtr, filename);
      SetGlobal(paramPtr, 'mFILE', txthndl);
      SendCardMessage(paramPtr, 'Store GETFILE("TEXT") TO
                                                   mFILE');
      SendCardMessage(paramPtr, 'Store SYS(1033,&mFILE)
                                                TO mFILE');
      txthndl := GetGlobal(paramPtr, 'mFILE');
      ZeroToPas(paramPtr, txthndl^, filename);
      DisposHandle(txthndl);
      IF filename = '' THEN
         Fail('XCMD Cancelled');
      GETFILE := filename;
   END;

BEGIN                        {main program}
   {Parameter Checks}
   numparams := paramPtr^.paramCount;
   IF (numparams <> 2) AND (numparams <> 3) THEN
      WrongFormat;
   ZeroToPas(paramPtr, paramPtr^.params[2]^, section);
   writecode := StrToLong(paramPtr, section); {0 - Overwrite,
                                               1 - Append}
```

```
IF (writecode <> 0) AND (writecode <> 1) THEN
   BEGIN
      SendCardMessage(paramPtr, 'Alert Note 1 "Param
                                  eter must equal 0 or 1"');
      Fail('Error2. WriteCode param must equal 0 or 1');
   END;

{Start Program}
ZeroToPas(paramPtr, paramPtr^.params[1]^, fieldname);
VrefNum := 0;
mCARDFLD := true;
IF numparams = 2 THEN
   filename := GETFILE
ELSE
   ZeroToPas(paramPtr, paramPtr^.params[3]^, filename);

err := FSOpen(filename, VrefNum, XrefNum);
IF err <> noErr THEN
   ERRORCHECK;
err := GetEof(XrefNum, logEOF);
IF err <> noErr THEN
   BEGIN
      err2 := FSClose(XrefNum);
      ERRORCHECK;
   END;
myBuffrHndl := NewHandle(logEOF);
err := MemError;
IF ((err <> noErr) OR (myBuffrHndl = NIL)) THEN
   BEGIN
      err2 := FSClose(XrefNum);
      ERRORCHECK;
   END;
MoveHHi(myBuffrHndl);
HLock(myBuffrHndl);
err := FSRead(XrefNum, logEOF, myBuffrHndl^);
Hunlock(myBuffrHndl);
IF err <> noErr THEN
   BEGIN
      DisposHandle(myBuffrHndl);
      err2 := FSClose(XrefNum);
      ERRORCHECK;
```

```
            END;
         zeroHndl := NewHandle(1);
         zerobyte := 0;
         zeroHndl^^ := zerobyte;
         Hlock(zeroHndl);
         err := HandAndHand(zeroHndl, myBuffrHndl);
         HUnlock(zeroHndl);
         DisposHandle(zeroHndl);
         IF err <> noErr THEN
            BEGIN
               DisposHandle(myBuffrHndl);
               err2 := FSClose(XrefNum);
               ERRORCHECK;
            END;
         HLock(myBuffrHndl);
         IF writecode = 0 THEN         {overwrite code}
            SetFieldByName(paramPtr, mCARDFLD, fieldname,
                                                   myBuffrHndl)
         ELSE
            BEGIN                      {append code}
               fieldhandle := GetFieldByName(paramPtr,
                                          mCARDFLD, fieldname);
               SetHandleSize(fieldhandle, GetHandleSize
                                             (fieldhandle) - 1);
               err := HandAndHand(myBuffrHndl, fieldhandle);
               newlen := GetHandleSize(fieldhandle);
               SetFieldByName(paramPtr, mCARDFLD, fieldname,
                                                   fieldhandle);
               DisposHandle(fieldhandle);
            END;
         HUnlock(myBuffrHndl);
         DisposHandle(myBuffrHndl);
         err := FSClose(XrefNum);
         paramPtr^.returnValue := PasToZero(paramPtr, filename);
      END;                             {End of procedure}

      PROCEDURE MAIN;
      BEGIN
         MEMOTXT(paramPtr);
      END;
   END.                             {End of unit}
```

CHAPTER 18

Extending the DBMS Languages: The APIs of Clipper, Arago, Paradox, and Babelfish Data Drivers

by Jeff Jochum

C, with its open architecture and ability to give low-level control over hardware, is arguably the most powerful programming language on the market today. It's no wonder programmers turn to it when they need to go beyond the capabilities of their language or when performance is below the level of acceptance or expectation.

However, C lacks the high-level control functions to perform database tasks, while the advantage of using a database compiler is that it provides a set of commands and functions for handling those same tasks. For example, if you wanted to open a text file, read its contents, and return it to the state in which you found it, C can do the job faster, more cleanly, and more efficiently. If, on the other hand, you're working with a structured data file rather than a text file, a database language is undeniably better suited to your needs because you won't need to describe the characteristics of the file's structure before accessing it.

This chapter describes the methods many database language compilers use to allow extensibility using C. We'll discuss the extend system as implemented by

Nantucket's Clipper and Wordtech's Arago; Borland's C Tools product, the Paradox Engine, used to extend the Paradox DBMS; and SuccessWare's Babelfish Paradox data drivers, which allow access to Paradox data files from Clipper/FoxPro and Arago applications. Clipper, Arago, and the Paradox Engine use the Microsoft C compiler, version 5.x; the Paradox Engine supports Borland's C and C++ compilers as well. The Babelfish drivers were developed in Microsoft C but have been modified to support the DBMS languages mentioned.

Clipper's Extend System

Since Clipper already uses the concept of user-defined functions (UDFs) and is compatible with Microsoft C, you might think that to access a C function you simply need to create it, compile it to an object file, and link it to your Clipper application at run time. You would be wrong.

In essence, Clipper can call any C function without making a special arrangement between the calling program and that function. Unfortunately, you generally don't just want to *call* the C function; you want to pass it some data or even get the function to return data to Clipper. Since C and Clipper store their data in different ways (and in different places), we need an intermediary to allow the two systems to exchange data. This is the basis for the extend model.

In spite of the uncanny similarity between C code and Clipper code (particularly Clipper 5.0), the two are not naturally compatible. Some of the issues we'll discuss are:

- Calling conventions
- Function-naming conventions
- Parameter-passing and -receiving functions
- Memory models and allocation
- Floating-point considerations.

Calling Conventions

C functions can be called from Clipper in two ways. First, you can use the *CALL* command and pass parameters as arguments:

```
CALL <c function> WITH <parm1>, <parm2>, ...
```

The second, and preferred, option is to use UDFs seamlessly as part of the code:

```
RetVal := C_FUNC(parm1, parm2, ...)
```

Not only is this method more elegant, it lets you return a value to the calling program. Oddly enough, the design of the C function being called is the same regardless of the calling method you select. For the sake of consistency (and common sense), you should use only the UDF calling syntax.

Function-Naming Conventions

Because Clipper and C functions must coexist in your compiled application, you should adhere to certain naming conventions.

The first rule is that Clipper UDFs must begin with a letter or an underscore and contain only letters, numbers, or underscores. This restriction doesn't normally cause a problem, except when you want to prefix all your assembler functions with a numeric identifier. Since Clipper only allows numerics *within* the UDF name, this problem is best resolved by either adding an underscore to the beginning of the name or converting the numeric identifiers to their alphabetical equivalents.

Rule number two limits the length of the UDF name to 10 characters. The restriction isn't immediately apparent because Clipper will compile and link UDFs with names that exceed 10 characters; unfortunately, it also does you the "favor" of truncating any characters beyond the tenth. If you haven't taken care to ensure the first 10 characters of every UDF form a unique name, you'll have a hard time debugging the application.

Rule three is less a rule than an exception. It stipulates that even though you can use upper- and lowercase letters in UDF names, Clipper converts them to uppercase during compilation. Like the second rule, this could cause you some consternation if you were expecting your Clipper functions to be as case-sensitive as your C functions.

Finally, rule four states that while many C compilers form the name of a public symbol by placing an underscore before the function name, Clipper-callable functions should not have an underscore.

Parameter Passing

The traditional C parameter-passing convention isn't used when values are passed from Clipper to C. In C functions, you prototype parameters by putting them in parentheses following the function name:

```
void C_func(float parm1, char *parm2)
```

Since Clipper maintains its own internal data stack and can't pass parameters on the C stack, you need other tools to pass data from Clipper to a C function. A series of functions from the Clipper library have been supplied for just this purpose.

```
_parc()  // converts Clipper character to C type char*
_parni() // converts Clipper numeric to C type int
_parnl() // converts Clipper numeric to C type long
_parnd() // converts Clipper numeric to C type double
_parl()  // converts Clipper logical to C type int
_pards() // converts Clipper date to C type char*
```

With these functions, you can retrieve the value of the Clipper data element and convert it to a C data type in one call. The actual function you use to "catch" this Clipper data depends on the type of data it should be.

Prototyping each function in C is simply good common sense because the return type and parameter types are specified. The compiler can then do some of your debugging for you by checking the types at compile time, even if the called function is defined externally. The prototypes for the extend functions are in the file EXTEND.H, which should be included in any C program that connects to Clipper. Taken directly from the header itself, the following are the prototypes for Clipper's parameter-passing functions:

```
typedef double XDOUBLE;

/* parameter values */

extern char *_parc(int, ...);
```

```
extern int _parni(int, ...);
extern long _parnl(int, ...);
extern XDOUBLE _parnd(int, ...);
extern int _parl(int, ...);
extern char *_pards(int, ...);
```

Notice that the first parameter for each function is prototyped as an integer. That's because the first parameter itself indicates the location of the parameter to be processed on the list of parameters passed to the C function.

For example, if four parameters were passed to the C function—the first two being numbers, the third a date, and the fourth a character string—you might retrieve the data in those parameters as follows:

```
CLIPPER Cfunc()
{
   int parm1    ;
   long parm2   ;
   char *parm3 ;
   char *parm4 ;
   parm1 = _parni(1) ;
   parm2 = _parnl(2) ;
   parm3 = _pards(3) ;
   parm4 = _parc(4)  ;
   .
   .
   .
}
```

The parameters passed to the *_par()* functions identify the parameter to convert to a C data type as passed to the C function from Clipper.

If the Clipper parameter is a single array of data, the second *_par()* parameter identifies the element in the array. Multidimensional arrays are handled in similarly, using the third, fourth, fifth, and successive parameters in the *_par()* functions.

A final note on parameter passing between Clipper and C: If you want to pass the actual data element from Clipper to C (not just the *value* of that element, as we've been discussing), you can use another set of functions that works identically to the *_par()* system but passes the data by reference instead. These functions are prefixed with *_stor* and are commonly referred to as the *EXTOR system.*

Returning Values from C to Clipper

We've examined two ways to send data from Clipper to C, but what happens when you want to move data in the opposite direction? The same logic that limits our direct access of Clipper data from C and forces us to perform a set of transition functions also prevents data from being passed directly from C to Clipper.

Since Clipper uses an internal data structure to catch the values returned from C functions (this structure also contains information on the type of data being returned), we must once again pass the data through a system of functions to make it acceptable to Clipper. This is known as *posting a return value* and can be performed by the *_ret()* functions. Like the other C-callable Clipper functions, these functions not only place the data where Clipper can use it but also convert the data from a C data type to a Clipper data type. The following is a list of these functions and their return value types.

```
_retc()  // converts C type char* to Clipper character
_retni() // converts C type int to Clipper numeric
_retnl() // converts C type long to Clipper numeric
_retnd() // converts C type double to Clipper numeric
_retl()  // converts C type int to Clipper logical
_retds() // converts C type char* to Clipper date
_ret()// returns nothing if no value is required
```

The value is the result of the Clipper UDF and is returned to the application program the same way as any other UDF.

Memory Models and Allocation

Clipper applications are known as *large-model* programs and the addresses used within them as *far* addresses. To understand this, let's take a brief look at the Intel 80x86 memory-model scheme.

Programs are organized into individual memory segments, each up to 64 KB long. Each segment is identified by its memory address, which consists of a segment number and an offset. Whenever an application program needs to access a memory location, it loads the appropriate segment number into the segment register. The offset is then used to determine the data to be accessed in that segment.

By identifying Clipper programs as "large model," we're indicating that more than one of the memory segments is needed to house and maintain the Clipper code. In small-model programs, the code must fit entirely into one memory segment.

Now that we have the basics, we can look at some of the ways Clipper uses them. If you're a C programmer, you know that you must be constantly aware of memory use (and abuse). It's up to you to allocate and release certain memory areas for your own use.

Normally, the C functions *malloc()* and *free()* are used to claim and release certain blocks of memory, respectively. Alas, Clipper doesn't allow even the C programer such freedom. Instead, it provides replacement functions that dynamically allocate and release memory: *_xalloc()* and *_xgrab()* replace *malloc()*, and *_xfree()* replaces *free()*. The only difference between *_xgrab()* and *_xalloc()* is the way they handle errors. *_xalloc()* returns NULL if it fails to allocate memory, while *_xgrab()* generates a run-time error.

Under no circumstances should you call Microsoft's *malloc()* or *free()* from a C function that will be linked to a Clipper program.

Floating-Point Potholes

In spite of the fact that Nantucket has a license from Microsoft, the floating-point arithmetic functions supplied as part of the Clipper library aren't the same as those provided with Microsoft C. Instead, they're a subset of Microsoft C functions and are identified as an "alternate" floating-point system.

The reason for using an alternate system, apparently, is to provide maximum execution speed on computers that lack a math coprocessor. If your C functions use floating-point calculations, you must compile them using Microsoft C 5.0 or higher and using the */FPa* flag. This tells the compiler to use the alternate floating-point system.

If you fail to use the */FPa* flag at compile time, the presence of floating-point functions will cause the resulting object file to link references to the standard floating-point package, which is incompatible with Clipper, and the program will crash.

Some Guidelines

When building C routines to be called from Clipper, remember the following:

- Use the large-model calling convention for your library functions.
- Never dynamically allocate memory using the default Microsoft functions *malloc()* and *free()*.
- If you use floating-point operations, always compile your C object using the */FPa* flag.
- Beware of graphics-oriented functions libraries; many use *malloc()* to allocate memory.
- The C string-handling functions in Clipper's library are identical to the functions found in Microsoft's C library.

Arago's Extend System

Arago comes in two flavors: compiler (Quicksilver) and interpreter (dBXL). While the compiler is quite different from Clipper, it handles C routines the same way. dBXL, on the other hand, has added an interesting twist to the concept of add-in C libraries. From the interpreted environment of dBXL, you can actually tell the system to look into a C function library for command-line callable functions.

To use this new feature, you must first prepare your C code with some extra bits of information for dBXL to identify. The key data supplier, referred to as the AragoLibraryTable structure, lists the functions in the library so the Arago program knows what is available to it.

For example, if your library contains C functions called *Aone* and *Atwo*, one of your C programs must include:

```
ARAGO Aone( void )   ;
ARAGO Atwo( void )   ;

UDF_HEADER AragoLibraryTable[] =
{
```

```
    { "Aone", Aone      },
    { "Atwo", Atwo      },
    { "", 0L      }  /* end-of-array marker */
};
```

That's it! Now you need only compile your C code into an object (which would include an Arago-specific object for the interface between Arago and your code) and issue the *SET LIBRARY TO <yourlib>* command at the dBXL prompt.

Like magic, all the functions defined in the function table are available to the Arago program. You can load more than one library at a time by using the optional parameter *ADDITIONAL* in the *SET LIBRARY* command. Listing 18-1 shows an example of this process.

Listing 18-1. Sample C Program for Arago.

```
/* Aragotest.c                                            */
/* Note that all constants are defined in header files */
/* not identified in this example.                        */

ARAGO Aone( void );
ARAGO Atwo( void );

UDF_HEADER AragoLibraryTable[] =
{
    { "Aone", Aone },
    { "Atwo", Atwo },
    { "", 0L     }                    /* end-of-array marker */
};

ARAGO Aone()
{
    int x,y           ;
    x = _parni(1)     ;
    y = _parni(2)     ;
    _retni(x*y)       ;               /* Returns integer value */
}

ARAGO Atwo()
{
    printf("\n You are nor in function Atwo");
    _ret()    ;                       /* Returns nothing */
}
```

```
/* End of Program */
```

Now, compile this code with the Microsoft C compiler using the flags */AL* (for large model), */GS* (disables stack checking), and */C* (suppress linking).

You then link the resulting object code with the proper start-up object for Arago and create an executable:

```
C:> Link Aragotest.obj + AragoLib.obj, Atest.exe
```

Load dBXL and issue the command

```
XL > SET LIBRARY TO Atest.exe
```

From now on, you can call any of the functions identified in the AragoFunctionTable structure from dBXL as you would any standard UDF or internal function:

```
XL > ? Aone(5,10)
   50        <<< Returns 50
```

It doesn't get much easier than that!

Borland's Paradox Engine

The Paradox Engine represents an interesting approach to integrating C programs into an existing DBMS programming environment. Unlike the compiler languages we've just explored, Paradox uses an interpreted, script-based language called Paradox Application Language.

PAL is difficult to define in simple terms. Outwardly, its structure resembles a common procedural language. Upon closer examination, however, you'll notice that it also incorporates nonprocedural menu macros as well as a declarative querying capability. PAL's tight integration with Paradox's user-interface menus necessitates a nonstandard approach to learning the language and a strong grasp of menu operations.

The way PAL allows C programs to coexist is even more unusual. In fact, PAL doesn't allow for any specific method of extending to the engine's C API. This will become evident as we explore the process of creating a Paradox Engine application.

Unlike other methods of linking C to the host language, Paradox/PAL doesn't require that the C program allocate memory through predefined C functions or work in conjunction with the base application when passing values to the stack. It couldn't care less how or why you process data in your C program because it isn't directly dependent on or related to that data.

To create a PAL extension, you simply write the C application as if you were building it as a stand-alone program. You then compile and link it to an .EXE condition.

Now you're ready to integrate the application into Paradox/PAL. From within the PAL script, call the C program using the following syntax:

```
RUN [BIG] myCprog.exe
```

The *RUN* command suspends Paradox and executes your C program. The current state of the Paradox environment is saved; when the C program is done, Paradox restores the environment and resumes with the next command line in the script.

RUN makes about 200 KB available to your program on a 640-KB system in DOS 4.x. Adding the keyword *BIG* will cause Paradox to write itself to disk, making upwards of 500 KB available to you. The disadvantages of using *BIG* are the time it takes to write the environment to disk and the requirement that you have sufficient disk space for it. This can be a problem on a diskless workstation with no write access to the server's drives.

How do you pass values between your C program and Paradox/PAL? Without an internal structure for such a mechanism, your only option is to use the data tables themselves or text files that PAL reads back into memory after the C program has been processed.

This may seem like a less-than-perfect way to integrate external programming into an application. But if you're like me and are less concerned with the method than with the result, you may find that this kind of integration is all you need in certain cases.

Babelfish Paradox Data Drivers

If you need access to Paradox data tables to be integrated more tightly into your application, the Babelfish Paradox data driver (BabelPDX) library may be for you. Like Borland's Paradox Engine, BabelPDX is an API library. Unlike the Paradox Engine, it has been modified to work directly with the host DBMS language so that no C coding is necessary. This also makes the transition from the .DBF data file to the Paradox table structure much easier.

The key difference between using the Paradox/PAL interface as the core programming environment for an application and creating standalone executable (.EXE) applications using FoxPro/Clipper/Arago with the BabelPDX lib should be self-evident: The PAL method requires a "runtime" environment to interpret the program while the executable has integrated the add-in library functions seamlessly.

A Foot in the Door

Please note that when I speak of integration here I mean *database* and not *language* merging. PAL syntax is considerably different from dBASE, and I have found that due to its high dependency on the Paradox User-Interface for many of its high-level commands, any consideration of easily moving program code from one environment to another should not be approached lightly.

As you can see, BabelPDX's and the Paradox Engine's approach to the API is quite different from Clipper's and Arago's. The basic premise for the extend systems of Clipper and Arago is to gain connectivity with other languages, while the Paradox engine and BabelPDX use another programming language to gain access to different database management systems. The key advantage to all of this is the increased ease with which you can move your application programs between historically incompatible development environments.

References

Apple Computer, *Apple Human Interface Guidelines.* Reading, MA: Addison-Wesley, 1991.

Beizer, B., *Software Testing Techniques*, 2nd edition, New York, NY: Van Nostrand Reinhold, 1990.

Chen, P. P., "The Entity Relationship Mode: Towards a Unified View of Data," *ACM TODS,* 1:1, March 1976.

Codd, E.F., "A Relational Model of Data for Large Shared Data Bands," *Communications of the ACM*. 13:6, June 1970.

Codd, E.F., *The Relational Model for Database Management: Version 2*. Reading, MA: Addison-Wesley, 1990.

Date, C. J., *A Guide to the SQL Standard*, 2nd edition. Reading, MA: Addison-Wesley, 1989.

Grey, J. et al., *The Benchmark Handbook*. San Mateo, CA: Morgan Kaufmann, 1991.

Groff, J. R. and Weinberg, P. N., *Using SQL*. Berkely, CA: Osborne McGraw-Hill, 1990.

Korth, H. F. and Silberschatz, A., *Database System Concepts*, 2nd edition. New York, NY: McGraw-Hill, 1991.

Martin, J., *Computer Data-Base Organization*, 2nd edition. Englewood Cliffs, NJ: Prentice-Hall, 1977.

Myers, G. J., *The Art of Software Testing*. New York, NY: John Wiley and Sons, 1979.

Norman, D. A., *The Design of Everyday Things.* New York, NY: Doubleday/Currency, 1990.

Pascal, F., *SQL and Relational Basics.* Redwood City, CA: M&T Books, 1990.

Sanchez, Julio, and Maria P. Canton. *IBM Microcomputers: A Programmer's Handbook.* New York, NY: McGraw-Hill, 1990.

Systems Application Architecture, Common User Access: Advanced Interface Design Guide (SC26-4582-0). IBM, 1989.

Winchell, Jeff. "FoxPro 2's Rushmore." *DBMS*. 4(10):54 (Sept. 1991).

Winchell, Jeff. "Memory Hog." *Data Based Advisor*. 9(4): 106 (April 1991).

Third Party Products Using the FoxPro 2 API

These products were shipping or due to ship by the second quarter of 1992.

Graphics

dGT (shipping)
Blackhawk Data Corporation
(312) 236-8473

SilverPaint (shipping)
SilverWare
(214) 247-0131

dGE (Q1)
Pinnacle Publishing
(206) 941-2300

Espia (Q2)
Devices Inc.
(805) 565-3838

Communications

SilverFox SPCS (shipping)
SilverWare
(214) 247-0131

Comm Tools (Q1)
Pinnacle Publishing
(206) 941-2300

Comet (Q2)
Compusolve
(800) UDF CMET

Database Connectivity Links

DBFTrieve (Novell Btrieve) (shipping)
SofTech
(316) 729-9315

RaSQL/B (Novell Btrieve) (Q1)
Pinnacle Publishing
(206) 941-2300

RaSQL/X (Novell SQL) (Q1)
Pinnacle Publishing
(206) 941-2300

Babelfish Data Driver (Paradox) (Q2)
SuccessWare 90
(714) 699-9657

Biton (Oracle) (Q2)
Biton
011-44-727-50658
Compuserve 100012,600

dbSQL (SQL Server) (Q2)
DataWiz International
(415) 571-1300

Other

ASE 2.0 (shipping)
Black & White International
(212) 666-4030

The Compressor (shipping)
Tech III
(800) 543-9941

FpNet (shipping)
Platinum Software
(301) 330 5118

Network System Calls for FoxPro (shipping)
Benning Computer Systems
(818) 347-0208

PhDBase (shipping)
Korenthall Associates
(212) 242-1790

Netlib (Q1)
Pinnacle Publishing
(206) 941-2300

Pkware Data Compression Library (Q1)
Pkware
(414) 352-3670

About the Authors

Hamilton M. Ahlo, Jr. has spent the last 10 years attempting to nurture a consulting and programming firm that specializes in computer-friendly users. Over the years, Ham has programmed in a variety of languages and has written applications ranging from sewage flow modeling to communications. His firm, Applied Logic, currently focuses on multiuser database applications in the Novell environment.

He is aided in this endeavor by the patience of his wife Janet, three children, and too many pets. He lives and works in Kealakekua, Hawaii, in an environment of sun and sea that warms the soul but provides more than its share of serious distractions to both author and programmer.

Randy Brown is a senior consultant with Ernst & Young in the National Energy group. He has worked extensively with Fox and dbase dialects since the early '80s. In addition to his experience on the DOS platform, Randy has also developed numerous Macintosh applications using Fox Software's FoxBASE+/Mac. His FoxTools XCMD Library has become well known with developers as a primary source of XCMDs for use with FoxBASE+/Mac. Randy has written a number of database articles for computer journals and is a regular speaker at the Fox Software Developers Conference.

Peter Colclough is a capitalist hippie throwback from the '70s. He was born in Montreal, Canada, in 1957, and attended private schools in the UK and Belgium. A brief excursion into the music industry in the mid-'70s proceeded his training as an accountant, where he "fell into" microcomputers in 1980. Peter has provided consulting services to clients worldwide since 1985. His systems have been geared for the leading edge of the technology, predominantly for the banking and oil industries.

More recently, Peter has been developing links from popular PC packages to mainframe and minicomputer RDBMS's. He can often be seen at or near the development center in Whitby, N. Yorks (UK), rescuing his cats from the attentions of herring gulls.

Jeff Jochum has been developing dbase language software since 1982. He is president of SuccessWare 90, Inc., and creator of the Babelfish Database Drivers, a series of API libraries that allow Fox, Clipper, and dBASE programmers to access Paradox, Emerald Bay, and Lotus 1-2-3 database systems. Jeff is also the co-developer of CALC(db), the full-featured Clipper spreadsheet library currently published by Pinnacle.

Jeff lives in Temecula, Calif., with his wife Lori and "two of the greatest children ever born to humans," Corey and Holly.

David R. McClanahan is database specialist and senior software engineer at SDRC. He worked on the SQL implementation and query optimization for FoxPro 2.0. He has over 10 years experience with database technology as a systems programmer and as consultant for database design. As principal systems engineer for Bell and Howell's Publication Services Division, he developed the DBMS for the IDB-2000 Technical Reference System, a state-of-the-art network image database, and worked on the file server for that system. He also has taught classes on database theory, and has nearly completed a Ph.D. in music.

Ted Means is the author of DBFTrieve, a link from FoxPro and Clipper to Novell's Btrieve Record Manager. Ted Means is the president of SofTech Microsystems, a software consulting and development firm. Ted has been a professional programmer for several years, and is fluent in several computer languages, although assembly language is his hands-down favorite. He writes a monthly column on assembly language for *The Aquarium*, a Clipper newsletter.

Ted and his wife live in Wichita, Kansas. Their first child was born in December of 1991.

Alan Schwartz is a principal of MicroMega Systems, a San Francisco consulting, software development, and training company that specializes in Fox Software databases. At MicroMega, Alan wears several hats: chief scientist, vice president of software development (with several custom applications and three products), and curriculum co-designer for MicroMega's Fox classes and courseware. Alan has 10 years' background in all aspects of PC application development and is a regular speaker at the Fox Software Developers Conference.

Prior to his work with computers, Alan was president of a restaurant and entertainment company; the benefits of his practical business experience provide a foundation for his technical expertise. Outside work, Alan is married, with one child. His hobbies include juggling all the above while occasionally eating and sleeping.

Ron Talmage is a software developer for Infosystems International in Seattle. He is responsible for the design and coding of their TRAK-A-DIAL Telecommunications Facilities Management product, a large vertical-market application written in FoxPro and FoxBase Unix.

Ron has been a college teacher and administrator in Montana, a COBOL programmer in Seattle, a Boeing 747 factory worker, a newspaper sports copy boy, and studied philosophy and physics in college.

Jeff Winchell seems predisposed towards asking irritating questions. Upon graduating from college, he found someone to pay him to do this, as an actuary. This quality was enhanced while he was a developer on a healthcare data analysis system, CHAMP, at William M. Mercer. Convinced that "there was gold in them thar hills," he moved west to Seattle to start his own firm, Practical Healthcare Innovations. Now he is busy creating a data analysis tool to make annoying questions easier to *answer*.

Jeff takes time off to sample the scenery and fine foods of Seattle with his wife Susan as his guide. He can be found on CompuServe's DBMS Forum, where he is a confirmed Tap-aholic. He also enjoys writing irritating articles about FoxPro for *DBMS* and *Data Based Advisor*.

Index

M&T BOOKS

A Library of Technical References from M&T Books

Clipper 5: A Developer's Guide
by Joseph D. Booth, Greg Lief, and Craig Yellick

An invaluable guide for all database programmers developing applications for Clipper® 5. Provides a quick introduction to Clipper 5 basics and discusses common programming needs such as designing data files, user interfaces, reports, and more. Advanced topics include networking, debugging, and pop-up programming. Code examples are used throughout the text, providing useful functions that can be applied immediately. All source code is available on disk in MS/PC-DOS format. 1300 pp. approx.

Book & Disk (MS-DOS)	**Item #242-X**	**$44.95**
Book only	**Item #240-3**	**$34.95**

DOS 5 User's Guide
A Comprehensive Guide for Every PC User
by Dan Gookin

Take control of the MS-DOS® operating system with this complete guide to using the world's most popular operating system. *DOS 5 User's Guide* contains clear, concise explanations of every feature, function, and command of DOS 5.0. Novice PC users will gain a quick start on using DOS, while advanced users will learn savvy tricks and techniques to maneuver their way quickly and easily through the system. Practical discussions and helpful examples teach readers how to edit text files, use directories, create batch files, and much more. Advanced topics include using EDLIN, the DOS text editor; configuring the system; and using the DOS shell. 771 pp.

Book only	**Item #188-1**	**$24.95**

Available at bookstores everywhere or call 1-800-533-4372 (in CA 1-800-356-2002)

A Library of Technical References from M&T Books

Delivering cc:Mail
Installing, Maintaining, and Troubleshooting a cc:Mail System
by Eric Arnum

Delivering cc:Mail teaches administrators how to install, troubleshoot, and maintain cc:Mail, one of the most popular E-mail applications for the PC. In-depth discussions and practical examples show administrators how to establish and maintain the program and database files; how to create and modify the bulletin boards, mail directory, and public mailing lists; and how to diagnose and repair potential problems. Information on using the management tools included with the package plus tips and techniques for creating efficient batch files are also included. All source code is available on disk in MS/PC-DOS format. 450 pp.

Book & Disk	**Item #187-3**	**$39.95**
Book only	**Item #185-7**	**$29.95**

The Complete Memory Manager
Every PC User's Guide to Faster, More Efficient Computing
by Phillip Robinson

Readers will learn why memory is important, how and when to install more, and how to wring the most out of their memory. Clear, concise instructions teach users how to manage their computer's memory to multiply its speed and ability to run programs simultaneously. Tips and techniques also show users how to conserve memory when working with popular software programs. 437 pp.

Book	**Item #102-4**	**$24.95**

Available at bookstores everywhere or call 1-800-533-4372 (in CA 1-800-356-2002)

M&T BOOKS

ORDER FORM

To Order:

Return this form with your payment to M&T Books, 411 Borel Avenue, San Mateo, CA 94402-3522 or **call toll-free 1-800-533-4372 (in California, call 1-800-356-2002).**

ITEM #	DESCRIPTION	DISK	PRICE
		Subtotal	
		CA residents add sales tax ___%	
		Add $4.50 per item for shipping and handling	
		TOTAL	

Charge my:

- ❑ **Visa**
- ❑ **MasterCard**
- ❑ **AmExpress**

❑ **Check enclosed, payable to M&T Books.**

CARD NO. ______________________________

SIGNATURE ______________________ EXP. DATE __________

NAME ______________________________

ADDRESS ______________________________

CITY ______________________________

STATE ______________________ ZIP __________

M&T GUARANTEE: If your are not satisfied with your order for any reason, return it to us within 30 days of receipt for a full refund. Note: Refunds on disks apply only when returned with book within guarantee period. Disks damaged in transit or defective will be promptly replaced, but cannot be exchanged for a disk from a different title.

8050